There must be more̶
—MAURICE SENDAK

TRAVEL

I never travel without my diary. One should always have something sensational to read in the train.—OSCAR WILDE

DREAMS

If one is lucky, a solitary fantasy can totally transform one million realities.—MAYA ANGELOU

TAXES

Only little people pay taxes.—LEONA HELMSLEY

FEMINISM

I am glad to see that men are getting their rights, but I want women to get theirs, and while the water is stirring I will step into the pool.—SOJOURNER TRUTH

SPEAKING

Talk low, talk slow, and don't say too much.—JOHN WAYNE

You have in your hands a truly distinguished dictionary of quotations that includes centuries of wit and wisdom as well as today's most entertaining, pertinent, and thought-provoking aphorisms, maxims, and bon mots. Designed to boost your power in communicating and to provide fast access to the information you need, the *21st Century Dictionary of Quotations* is innovative in design, remarkably easy to use, and fully comprehensive. It is an indispensable reference that will never leave you without the right words.

21ST CENTURY DICTIONARY OF QUOTATIONS

EDITED BY

THE PRINCETON LANGUAGE INSTITUTE

Produced by The Philip Lief Group, Inc.

A LAUREL BOOK

Published by
Dell Publishing
a division of
Bantam Doubleday Dell Publishing Group, Inc.
1540 Broadway
New York, New York 10036

Published by arrangement with The Philip Lief Group, Inc.
6 West 20 Street
New York, New York 10011
Copyright © 1993 by The Philip Lief Group, Inc.

ISBN: 0-440-21447-5

Printed in the United States of America

Published simultaneously in Canada

June 1993

10   9   8   7   6   5   4   3

CONTENTS

INTRODUCTION

QUOTATIONS FOR THE 21ST CENTURY

Readers, writers, and public speakers have long found quotation references to be a great source of inspiration and an important tool for reinforcing and enhancing expression. The words of others, aptly employed, move us to new understandings, shared realizations about our world and experience. Indeed, it is common for speech-makers, journalists, and report writers to consult quotation collections frequently for pithy observations that will add insight or polish to their talk, article, or paper, and help them to drive their point home.

The consistent drawback when attempting to use traditional books of quotations effectively—for student, professional, and at-home users—has always been in knowing exactly what words or quotable personage to look *for*, and in knowing just *where* to find that perfect thought or personality within their dense pages. Most standard quotation books consist of an exhaustive listing of archaic and timeworn old chestnuts referenced to a predictable assortment of subject categories. Users make their way through pages and pages of inappropriate, outdated material before perhaps stumbling upon a quotation that may work to suit the purpose or occasion.

By contrast, the *21st Century Dictionary of Quotations* features subject categories that focus on cutting-edge topics, issues, and interests, such as **AIDS**, **Ecology**, **Multiculturalism**, and **Space**—and reinterprets ageless general subjects, such as **Duty**, **Freedom**, **Knowledge**, and **Power**, to include citations in contexts relevant to the modern sensibilities of today's Information Age readers. Thousands of carefully chosen classic and contemporary quotations are assembled within hundreds of subject areas, alphabetically arranged. Sources quoted are as startlingly diverse as the **Bible** and filmmaker **Spike Lee**, presenting a compelling mix of timeless wisdom and timely intelligence, on matters of both far-reaching and immediate significance.

Above all, the *21st Century Dictionary of Quotations* is convenient, the most user-friendly resource of its kind. All of its subject category headings are referenced to three different indices—Subject, Concept, and Author— created to facilitate the search for the right quotation. No more afternoons at the library poring through the old obsolete standards, playing a frustrating game of hit or miss. Savvy quote seekers will recognize in the *21st Century Dictionary of Quotations* a state-of-the-art format and an all-new, comprehensive quote selection designed to supply users with perfect sound bytes to add richness to any spoken or written expression.

SPECIAL FEATURES OF THE
21ST CENTURY DICTIONARY OF QUOTATIONS

Dictionary Format

Easy access is provided in the arrangement of seven thousand quotations within eight hundred alphabetically organized subject categories. Sources ranging from **Shakespeare** to **Bette Midler** and **Voltaire** to **Ross Perot**, speak out— sharing their opinions on subjects as controversial as **Con-**

traception, amaranthine as **Courage**, and funky as **Rock 'n' Roll**. The *21st Century Dictionary of Quotations* brings together centuries of wit and wisdom and the most current of voices and topics to inform, educate, and expand the 21st century user's vocabulary of ideas.

Indices

- **Subject Index**

  This easy-reference index of content is an alphabetical listing of each subject category that appears in the dictionary, followed by the page number on which it can be located.

- **Concept Index**

  This invaluable compendium of 21st century quotation resources breaks new ground by offering an interactive Concept Index that allows users to hone their search for the perfect quotation. If an initial survey of a subject category doesn't turn up the right words, the Concept Index automatically provides alternatives. The Concept Index enriches every subject category by highlighting related concepts, activating thought in a way that mirrors the cognitive process of the human brain. By considering a subject category and its related concepts, one notion naturally leads to another until the user makes a logical path to a suitable quote of choice. This innovative and accessible cross-reference source broadens exploration intelligently, encourages browsing, or allows users to zero in on specific target subjects—whichever pathway she/he prefers. Whether making a quick search through concepts referenced to an individual subject category, or simply entering the index itself with just a vague idea in mind, the *21st Century Dictionary of Quotations'* Concept Index is a fast and reliable research tool.

- **Author Index**

  The full name of every person to whom a quotation has been attributed will be listed alphabetically in the Author Index, along with the subject categories to which each of the source's quotations are referenced.

  A quick scan of the Author Index can guide users to consider sources that may not appear to be likely candidates at first glance. Or, if a user is searching for a quote by a particular person, the Author Index gives an immediate selection of wide-ranging possibilities.

  Brief biographies are also provided in the Author Index for each individual quoted, including years of birth and death, nationality, and occupation. This feature is especially useful for quote seekers who may have found the perfect words in the dictionary but don't easily recognize the personage who said them.

HOW TO USE
THE REVOLUTIONARY CONCEPT INDEX

The Concept Index found in the *21st Century Dictionary of Quotations* works as your own personal reference librarian. Each of the alphabetically arranged subject headings throughout the dictionary is followed by a number (or numbers) that refer users to conceptual categories—there are 880 to explore. Once in the Concept Index, quote seekers find an array of subject headings related to the one with which the search was begun. From here, any or all of the suggested pathways are waiting to be investigated. For example:

A quotation is needed to anchor a student's report on capitalism. After looking up **Capitalism** in the Subject

Index to determine the right page number, she/he looks in the dictionary to find this quotation selection:

CAPITALISM
(also see concepts 231, 628)

Freedom in economic arrangements is itself a component of freedom broadly understood, so economic freedom is an end in itself . . . Economic freedom is also an indispensable means toward the achievement of political freedom.—MILTON FRIEDMAN

Under capitalism we have a state in the proper sense of the word, that is, a special machine for the suppression of one class by another.—V.I. LENIN

You show me a capitalist, I'll show you a bloodsucker.
—MALCOLM X

Man is the only creature that consumes without producing.—GEORGE ORWELL

Every man, as long as he does not violate the laws of justice, is left perfectly free to pursue his own interest his own way, and to bring both his industry and capital into competition with those of any other man or order of men.
—ADAM SMITH

The trouble with the profit system has always been that it was highly profitable to most people.—E.B. WHITE

To get to an even broader selection, the student then refers to the concept categories, #231 and #628, in the Concept Index to find a variety of subject headings that list quotes on topics related to **Capitalism**:

231. ECONOMICS business, capitalism, communism, inflation, money, recession, socialism

232. PROPERTY capitalism, economics, home, houses, investment, possession, wealth, wills and inheritance

For still more alternatives, she/he looks to **Capitalism** as a concept in its own right within the Concept Index. Listed as concept #88, the student sees these subject headings linked to the idea of capitalism:

88. CAPITALISM   banks and banking, buying and selling, economics, ideology, property

If the student decided to further explore the concepts linked to each of the subjects referenced to **Capitalism**, the possibilities are multiplied. If the student doesn't find the right quotation, it will be because no one has said it yet!

Here's another scenario:

A speaker is preparing to give a lecture on the complex relationships between men and women. Scanning through the Concept Index, the speaker finds:

494. MEN AND WOMEN   compliments, love, opposition, relationships, sex, weddings

After reading the quotations featured under most of these subject categories, the speaker finds some interesting prospects but hasn't yet hit upon a quotation that seems to stick vaguely in the memory,—one by **Baudelaire**. Under **Baudelaire** in the Author Index, the speaker sees:

BAUDELAIRE, CHARLES (1821–1867). French poet. *Debauchery*, *Poets and Poetry*, *Sex*.

There, under the subject heading of **Sex**, are the desired words from famous French writer: "Sexuality is the lyricism of the masses."

With its comprehensive system of indices, the *21st Century Dictionary of Quotations* provides a myriad of thought-provoking avenues to the right quotation.

HOW TO SAY IT BEST

The *21st Century Dictionary of Quotations* is an indispensable addition to any personal reference library. To find inspiration or garner substantiation, to narrow your thoughts or expand your thinking, to find good company or extreme contradiction, users will discover how to say it best every time in the pages of this 21st century dictionary compiled with *their* needs in mind.

Consider **Woody Allen** and **Nathaniel Hawthorne** on **Afterlife**. Or **Benjamin Franklin** and **Jesse Jackson** on **Opportunity**. Or **Dostoyevsky** and **Liza Minelli** on **Realism**. Unlikely and unexpected quotations from cutting-edge contemporary sources, not included in any other quotation collection, share the page here with timeless classics from humanity's greatest thinkers to give depth and definition to subjects old and new. The *21st Century Dictionary of Quotations* represents a new reference standard for today's—and tomorrow's—readers, writers, and speakers.

SUBJECT INDEX

21st CENTURY
DICTIONARY OF QUOTATIONS

ABILITY

(also see concepts 178, 310, 327, 411, 440, 485, 605, 608, 720, 792)

The winds and waves are always on the side of the ablest navigators.
——EDWARD GIBBON

Ability is of little account without opportunity. ——NAPOLEON I

Ability is sexless. ——CHRISTABEL PANKHURST

Everyone must row with the oars he has. ——ENGLISH PROVERB

ABORTION

(also see concepts 69, 115, 160, 283)

Abortion doesn't belong in the political arena. It's a private right, like many other rights concerning the family. ——BELLA ABZUG

Abortion is a skillfully marketed product sold to a woman at a crisis time in her life. If the product is defective, she can't return it for a refund. ——CAROL EVERETT

...nothing more than mechanical rape. ——OLIVIA GANS

If men could get pregnant, abortion would be a sacrament.
——FLORYNCE KENNEDY

Both sides, pro-life, pro-abortion...care simply about winning: winning each court case, each legislative battle, each electoral contest, each rally. They glare and shout at each other over an unbridgeable chasm....I wonder if each side has forgotten the human element that originally prompted the debate: the innocent unborn child, the agonized pregnant woman. ——C. EVERETT KOOP

Liberty finds no refuge in a jurisprudence of doubt....The essential holding of Roe v. Wade should be retained and once again reaffirmed. ——SANDRA DAY O'CONNOR

ABSENCE
(also see concepts 185, 465, 468, 569)

Absence sharpens love, presence strengthens it. —THOMAS FULLER

Those who are absent are always wrong. —ENGLISH PROVERB

Out of sight, out of mind. —PROVERB

When the cat's away, the mice will play. —PROVERB

Absences are a good influence in love and keep it bright and delicate. —ROBERT LOUIS STEVENSON

Greater things are believed of those who are absent. —TACITUS

ABSTINENCE
(also see concepts 12, 225, 226, 743)

My experience through life has convinced me that, while moderation and temperance in all things are commendable and beneficial, abstinence from spirituous liquors is the best safeguard of morals and health. —ROBERT E. LEE

The people who are regarded as moral luminaries are those who forego ordinary pleasures themselves and find compensation in interfering with the pleasures of others. —BERTRAND RUSSELL

ABSURDITY
(also see concepts 258, 658, 775, 818)

The privilege of absurdity; to which no living creature is subject but man only. —THOMAS HOBBES

Almost all absurdity of conduct arises from the imitation of those whom we cannot resemble. —SAMUEL JOHNSON

There is but one step from the sublime to the ridiculous.
—NAPOLEON I

People who cannot recognize a palpable absurdity are very much in the way of civilization. —AGNES REPPLIER

No one is laughable who laughs at himself. —SENECA

ACCIDENTS
(also see concepts 17, 279, 402, 471, 779)

Accident, n. an inevitable occurrence due to the action of immutable natural laws. —AMBROSE BIERCE

Accidents will occur in the best-regulated families.
—CHARLES DICKENS

The chapter of accidents is the longest chapter in the book.
—JOHN WILKES

ACCUSATION
(also see concepts 138, 332, 875)

When a man points a finger at someone else, he should remember that three of his fingers are pointing at himself. —ANONYMOUS

Even doubtful accusations leave a stain behind them.
—THOMAS FULLER

ACHIEVEMENT
(also see concepts 9, 50, 191, 234, 241, 253, 578, 630, 778, 841)

By their fruits ye shall know them. —BIBLE, MATTHEW 7:20

One never notices what has been done; one can only see what remains to be done.... —MARIE CURIE

The reward of a thing well done is to have done it.
—RALPH WALDO EMERSON

Success follows doing what you want to do. There is no other way to be successful. —MALCOLM FORBES

We never do anything well till we cease to think about the manner of doing it. —WILLIAM HAZLITT

Those who dare to fail miserably can achieve greatly.
——ROBERT F. KENNEDY

Who begins too much accomplishes little. ——GERMAN PROVERB

You must do the thing you think you cannot do.
——ELEANOR ROOSEVELT

It had long since come to my attention that people of accomplishment rarely sat back and let things happen to them. They went out and happened to things. ——ELINOR SMITH

There's nothing half so real in life as the things you've done...inexorably, unalterably done. ——SARA TEASDALE

To achieve great things we must live as though we were never going to die. ——MARQUIS DE VAUVENARGUES

ACTION
(also see concepts 25, 63, 191, 241, 256)

Effective action is always unjust. ——JEAN ANOUILH

Action is the antidote to despair. ——JOAN BAEZ

Action should culminate in wisdom. ——BHAGAVADGITA

Inaction may be the biggest form of action. ——JERRY BROWN

Great actions are not always true sons / Of great and mightly resolutions. ——SAMUEL BUTLER

He that has done nothing has known nothing. ——THOMAS CARLYLE

In action, be primitive; in foresight, a strategist. ——RENÉ CHAR

A man's most open actions have a secret side to them.
——JOSEPH CONRAD

A man is not good or bad for one action. ——THOMAS FULLER

Action is the only reality, not only reality but morality as well.
——ABBIE HOFFMAN

When action grows unprofitable, gather information; when information grows unprofitable, sleep. ——URSULA K. LE GUIN

No action is in itself good or bad, but only such according to convention. —W. SOMERSET MAUGHAM

The stellar universe is not so difficult of comprehension as the real actions of other people. —MARCEL PROUST

Act quickly, think slowly. —GREEK PROVERB

Barking dogs seldom bite. —PROVERB

ACTIVITY
(also see concepts 9, 58, 63, 191, 241, 256, 292, 379, 447, 762)

He that is everywhere is nowhere. —THOMAS FULLER

If you want work well done, select a busy man: the other kind has no time. —ELBERT HUBBARD

Our nature consists in motion; complete rest is death. —BLAISE PASCAL

Men need some kind of external activity, because they are inactive within. —ARTHUR SCHOPENHAUER

In a word, I am always busy, which is perhaps the chief reason why I am always well. —ELIZABETH CADY STANTON

ACTORS AND ACTING
(also see concepts 53, 90, 223, 351, 521, 801)

Don't use your conscious past. Use your creative imagination to create a past that belongs to your characters. —STELLA ADLER

Acting is a matter of giving away secrets. —ELLEN BARKIN

For an actress to be a success she must have the face of Venus, the brains of Minerva, the grace of Terpsichore, the memory of Macaulay, the figure of Juno, and the hide of a rhinoceros. —ETHEL BARRYMORE

An actor's a guy who, if you ain't talking about him, he ain't listening. —MARLON BRANDO

Every actor has a natural animosity toward every other actor, present or absent, living or dead. —LOUISE BROOKS

Never meddle with play-actors, for they're a favoured race. —MIGUEL DE CERVANTES

Attempt the impossible in order to improve your work. —BETTE DAVIS

Do your job and demand your compensation–but in that order. —CARY GRANT

Acting is happy agony. —ALEC GUINNESS

It's such a cuckoo business. And it's a business you go into because you are an egocentric. It's a very embarrassing profession. —KATHARINE HEPBURN

It's not true that I said "actors are cattle." I said "they should be treated like cattle." —ALFRED HITCHCOCK

I'm no actor. And I have sixty-four pictures to prove it. —VICTOR MATURE

Actors die so loud. —HENRY MILLER

I have to act to live. —LAURENCE OLIVIER

A lot of what acting is is paying attention. —ROBERT REDFORD

Just learn your lines and don't bump into the furniture. —SPENCER TRACY

Every actor in his heart believes everything bad that's printed about him. —ORSON WELLES

ADJUSTMENT
(also see concepts 27, 140, 147, 337)

Since the house is on fire let us warm ourselves. —ITALIAN PROVERB

I dance to the tune that is played. —SPANISH PROVERB

There are no conditions to which a man cannot become accustomed, especially if he sees that all those around him live the same way. —LEO TOLSTOY

Adapt or perish, now as ever, is Nature's inexorable imperative. —H. G. WELLS

ADMIRATION
(also see concepts 40, 41, 176, 237, 601, 675)

Admiration, n. our polite recognition of another's resemblance to ourselves. —AMBROSE BIERCE

A fool always finds a greater fool to admire him. —NICOLAS BOILEAU

Always we like those who admire us, but we do not always like those whom we admire. —FRANÇOIS DE LA ROCHEFOUCAULD

ADVANTAGE
(also see concepts 260, 264, 337, 344, 413, 684)

It's them as take advantage that get advantage i' this world. —GEORGE ELIOT

Every advantage has its tax. —RALPH WALDO EMERSON

He that has one eye is a prince among those that have none. —THOMAS FULLER

ADVENTURE
(also see concepts 75, 167, 248)

To die will be an awfully big adventure. —J. M. BARRIE

It is only in adventure that some people succeed in knowing themselves–in finding themselves. —ANDRÉ GIDE

Life is either a daring adventure, or nothing. —HELEN KELLER

They sicken of the calm, who know the storm. —DOROTHY PARKER

ADVERSITY

(also see concepts 6, 206, 506, 757, 812)

Prosperity doth best discover vice; but adversity doth best discover virtue. —FRANCIS BACON

Calamities are of two kinds: misfortune to ourselves and good fortune to others. —AMBROSE BIERCE

Adversity is the first path to Truth. —LORD BYRON

There are three modes of bearing the ills of life: by indifference, by philosophy, and by religion. —CHARLES CALEB COLTON

Every calamity is a spur and valuable hint. —RALPH WALDO EMERSON

Troubles, like babies, grow larger by nursing. —CAROLINE HOLLAND

He knows not his own strength that hath not met adversity. —BEN JONSON

In the misfortune of our best friends, we always find something which is not displeasing to us. —FRANÇOIS DE LA ROCHEFOUCAULD

Let us be of good cheer, however, remembering that the misfortunes hardest to bear are those which never come. —JAMES RUSSELL LOWELL

The world is quickly bored by the recital of misfortune, and willingly avoids the sight of distress. —W. SOMERSET MAUGHAM

That which does not kill me makes me stronger. —FRIEDRICH WILHELM NIETZSCHE

When you fight something long enough, it becomes a center pole right in your life and you count on it to be there to fight with. —MARSHA NORMAN

It is easy to bear the misfortunes of others. —PROVERB

It never rains but it pours. —PROVERB

Misery acquaints a man with strange bedfellows. —WILLIAM SHAKESPEARE

ADVERTISING

(also see concepts 400, 627, 637, 639, 818, 819)

It pays to advertise. —ANONYMOUS

Publicity is the life of this culture–in so far as without publicity capitalism could not survive–and at the same time publicity is its dream. —JOHN BERGER

We grew up founding our dreams on the infinite promise of American advertising. I still believe that one can learn to play the piano by mail and that mud will give you a perfect complexion. —ZELDA FITZGERALD

Promise, large promise, is the soul of an advertisement. —SAMUEL JOHNSON

I think that I shall never see/ A billboard lovely as a tree. / Indeed, unless the billboards fall / I'll never see a tree at all. —OGDEN NASH

Advertising is the rattling of a stick inside a swill bucket. —GEORGE ORWELL

Any publicity is good publicity. —PROVERB

One Ad is worth more to a paper than forty Editorials. —WILL ROGERS

ADVICE

(also see concepts 344, 612)

There is nothing which we receive with so much reluctance as advice. —JOSEPH ADDISON

We ask advice, but we mean approbation. —CHARLES CALEB COLTON

A word to the wise ain't necessary–it's the stupid ones who need the advice. —BILL COSBY

He that won't be counselled can't be helped. —BENJAMIN FRANKLIN

Advice is what we ask for when we already know the answer but wish we didn't. —ERICA JONG

We give nothing so freely as advice.
——FRANÇOIS DE LA ROCHEFOUCAULD

Remember that to change your mind and follow him who sets you right is to be none the less free than you were before.
——MARCUS AURELIUS

This is the gist of what I know: / Give advice and buy a foe.
——PHYLLIS MCGINLEY

I give myself sometimes admirable advice, but I am incapable of taking it. ——MARY WORTLEY MONTAGU

Everybody knows good counsel except him that has need of it.
——GERMAN PROVERB

A good scare is worth more than good advice. ——PROVERB

He that has no children brings them up well. ——PROVERB

The true secret of giving advice, is after you have honestly given it, to be perfectly indifferent whether it is taken or not and never persist in trying to set people right. ——HANNAH WHITALL SMITH

No one wants advice—only corroboration. ——JOHN STEINBECK

It's a sad commentary on our times when our young must seek advice and counsel from "Dear Abby" instead of going to Mom and Dad. ——ABIGAIL VAN BUREN

The counsels of old age give light without heat, like the sun in winter. ——MARQUIS DE VAUVENARGUES

AFFECTION
(also see concepts 237, 300, 341, 439, 466, 469, 687)

Most people would rather get than give affection. ——ARISTOTLE

Whatever pretext we may give for our affections, often it is only interest and vanity which cause them.
——FRANÇOIS DE LA ROCHEFOUCAULD

Talk not of wasted affection! Affection never was wasted....
——HENRY WADSWORTH LONGFELLOW

A mixture of admiration and pity is one of the surest recipes for affection. —ANDRÉ MAUROIS

Most affections are habits or duties we lack the courage to end. —HENRY DE MONTHERLANT

I never met a man I didn't like. —WILL ROGERS

AFRICA AND THE AFRICANS
(also see concept 529)

She was back in Africa. And that felt like fresh honey on the tongue: a mixture of complete sweetness and smokey roughage. Below was home with its unavoidable warmth. Oh Africa! Crazy continent. —AMA ATA AIDOO

Certain older women in villages become very independent and respected. Christianity shook this attitude very badly; it was not considered nice or feminine to speak out. But the dignity which African woman has and which was lost through colonisation is coming back. —BUCHI EMECHETA

When a white man in Africa by accident looks into the eyes of a native and sees the human being (which it is his chief preoccupation to avoid), his sense of guilt, which he denies, fumes up in resentment and he brings down the whip. —DORIS LESSING

Together, hand in hand, with our matches and our necklaces, we shall liberate this country. —WINNIE MANDELA

There is always something new out of Africa. —PLINY THE ELDER

AFRICAN AMERICANS
(also see concepts 32, 522, 650)

Black women have not historically stood in the pulpit, but that doesn't undermine the fact that they built the churches and maintain the pulpits. —MAYA ANGELOU

The future is...black. —JAMES BALDWIN

Black women do not yet love ourselves as women. We've been taught to love everyone else; we've been taught, in fact, that it's shameful to love ourselves. —ALEXIS DE VEAUX

The *Titanic* was a great ship, but it was captained by one depicted as being arrogant, and warnings of an iceberg were not heeded. America is like that great ship. Unfortunately, at the helm may be a proud captain. And black people could become the iceberg that causes the sinking of this great ship called the United States of America. —LOUIS FARRAKHAN

When I drive to my house and go through the black neighborhood that's between two white neighborhoods, I don't see black kids packing books at five o'clock. They have a basketball, and they're going down to the courts. We have to change the erroneous assumption that you have a better chance of being Magic Johnson than you do of being a brain surgeon. —HENRY LOUIS GATES, JR.

We have allowed death to change its name from Southern rope to Northern dope. Too many black youths have been victimized by pushing dope into their veins instead of hope into their brains. —JESSE JACKSON

If you are black the only roads into the mainland of American life are through subservience, cowardice, and loss of manhood. These are the white man's roads. —LEROI JONES

It is not the destiny of Black America to repeat white Americans' mistakes. But we will, if we mistake the trappings of success in a sick society for the signs of a meaningful life. —AUDRE LORDE

Some years ago I said in an opinion that if this country is a melting pot, then either the Afro-American didn't get in the pot or he didn't get melted down. —THURGOOD MARSHALL

There is an incredible amount of magic and feistiness in black men that nobody has been able to wipe out. But everybody has tried. —TONI MORRISON

If you are going to think black, think positive about it. Don't think down on it, or think it is something in your way. And this way, when you really do want to stretch out, and express how beautiful black is, everybody will hear you....How can you not stand tall?–because you are saying who you are. ——LEONTYNE PRICE

Black women as a group have never been fools. We couldn't afford to be. ——BARBARA SMITH

Black women have never had an opportunity of displaying our talents; therefore the world thinks we know nothing.
——MARIA STEWART

AFTERLIFE
(also see concepts 185, 203, 246, 342, 343, 385, 453, 833)

The chief problem about death, incidentally, is the fear that there may be no afterlife–a depressing thought, particularly for those who have bothered to shave. Also, there is the fear that there is an afterlife but no one will know where it's being held. ——WOODY ALLEN

We sometimes congratulate ourselves at the moment of waking from a troubled dream; it may be so the moment after death.
——NATHANIEL HAWTHORNE

Is there another life? Shall I awake and find all this a dream? There must be, we cannot be created for this sort of suffering.
——JOHN KEATS

After your death you will be what you were before your birth.
——ARTHUR SCHOPENHAUER

Never did Christ utter a single word attesting to a personal resurrection and a life beyond the grave. ——LEO TOLSTOY

Heaven for climate, hell for society. ——MARK TWAIN

AGE
(also see concepts 69, 245, 308, 455, 463, 485, 497, 552, 876, 877)

Age will not be defied. ——FRANCIS BACON

Man arrives as a novice at each age of his life. ——NICOLAS CHAMFORT

Nature gives you the face you have at twenty; it is up to you to merit the face you have at fifty. —COCO CHANEL

We turn not older with years, but newer every day.
—EMILY DICKINSON

I have no romantic feelings about age. Either you are interesting at any age or you are not. There is nothing particularly interesting about being old–or being young, for that matter.
—KATHARINE HEPBURN

I have everything now I had twenty years ago–except now it's all lower. —GYPSY ROSE LEE

But at my back I always hear / Time's winged chariot hurrying near; / And yonder all before us lie / Deserts of vast eternity.
—ANDREW MARVELL

Age is not a handicap. Age is nothing but a number. It is how you use it. —ETHEL PAYNE

Never too late to learn. —PROVERB

AGGRESSION

(also see concepts 36, 183, 193, 237, 414, 415, 499, 693, 842, 850, 857)

The fourth [essential human freedom] is freedom from fear–which, translated into world terms, means a world-wide reduction of armaments to such a point and in such a thorough fashion that no nation will be in a position to commit an act of physical aggression against any neighbor–anywhere in the world. —FRANKLIN D. ROOSEVELT

To knock a thing down, especially if it is cocked at an arrogant angle, is a deep delight to the blood. —GEORGE SANTAYANA

Men must have corrupted nature a little, for they were not born wolves, and they have become wolves. —VOLTAIRE

AGNOSTICISM
(see also concepts 222, 378, 585)

If only God would give me some clear sign! Like making a large deposit in my name at a Swiss bank. —WOODY ALLEN

I do not pretend to know what many ignorant men are sure of–that is all agnosticism means. —CLARENCE DARROW

Question with boldness even the existence of God; because, if there be one, he must more approve of the homage of reason, than that of blindfolded fear. —THOMAS JEFFERSON

O Lord, if there is a Lord, save my soul, if I have a soul. —ERNEST RENAN

A faith which does not doubt is a dead faith. —MIGUEL DE UNAMUNO

AGREEMENT
(also see concepts 13, 140, 143, 147, 545, 626, 631, 662, 741, 790)

Elinor agreed with it all, for she did not think he deserved the compliment of rational opposition. —JANE AUSTEN

We are more inclined to hate one another for points on which we differ, than to love one another for points on which we agree. —CHARLES CALEB COLTON

Three may keep counsel, if two be away. —JOHN HEYWOOD

We seldom attribute common sense except to those who agree with us. —FRANÇOIS DE LA ROCHEFOUCAULD

If all pulled in one direction, the world would keel over. —YIDDISH PROVERB

Agreement is made more precious by disagreement. —PUBLILIUS SYRUS

AIDS

(also see concepts 340, 738)

I'm not asking that we be able to live in a risk-free world. I want people to be able to choose their risks. I didn't have a choice to walk out of the office and seek another dentist. —KIMBERLY BERGALIS

Everyone detected with AIDS should be tattooed in the upper forearm, to protect common needle-users, and on the buttocks, to prevent the victimization of other homosexuals.
—WILLIAM F. BUCKLEY

Stealing the lives of our friends and our loved ones, AIDS steals our dialogue, or poisons it with inhibited self-consciousness.
—MICHAEL FEINGOLD

People justify it–"I'm not going to promote finding a cure for it because it was started by these people and I don't like their sexual politics."–How do you tell that to a four-year-old who has no sexual politics, who doesn't even know what a sexual politic is?
—WHOOPI GOLDBERG

I think we sometimes think only gay people can get it; "it's not going to happen to me." And here I am saying that it can happen to anybody, even Magic Johnson. —EARVIN "MAGIC" JOHNSON

Syphilitics can be cured, alcoholics can be rescued, highway daredevils can be healed and reformed, coronary victims can change their diet and lifestyle. But AIDS has arrived on the scene and has become the first serious wedge to be driven into our remarkable public health compact because of general disapproval of the high-risk behavior responsible for most AIDS infection.
—C. EVERETT KOOP

I've spent fifteen years of my life fighting for our right to be free and make love whenever, wherever....And you're telling me that all those years of what being gay stood for is wrong...and I'm a murderer. We have been so oppressed! Don't you remember how it was? Can't you see how important it is for us to love openly, without hiding and without guilt? —LARRY KRAMER

What AIDS shows us is the limits of tolerance, that it's not enough to be talented, because when the shit hits the fan you find out how much tolerance is worth. Nothing. —TONY KUSHNER

Any important disease whose causality is murky, and for which treatment is ineffectual, tends to be awash in significance. —SUSAN SONTAG

When it happened to me, I sat in my apartment minutes after getting diagnosed, I'd come home–I'm looking out of the window and what's happened? What's changed? Absolutely nothing's changed; the world is still going on....That's what is amazing about suddenly developing a heightened sense of mortality–really, nothing changes. I have the same appetite I've always had. I have the same needs I've always had. —DAVID WOJNAROWICZ

AIRPLANES
(also see concepts 474, 814, 820)

Airline travel is hours of boredom interrupted by moments of stark terror. —AL BOLISKA

Lovers of air travel find it exhilarating to hang poised between the illusion of immortality and the fact of death. —ALEXANDER CHASE

I feel about airplanes the way I feel about diets: It seems to me that they are wonderful things for other people to go on. —JEAN KERR

ALIENATION
(also see concepts 218, 392, 462, 569, 622, 706, 756, 771, 833)

It's an abnormal world I live in. I don't belong anywhere. It's like I'm floating down the middle. I'm never quite sure where I am. —ARTHUR ASHE

What is a rebel? A man who says no. —ALBERT CAMUS

When one realizes that his life is worthless he either commits suicide or travels. —EDWARD DAHLBERG

Everything intercepts us from ourselves. —RALPH WALDO EMERSON

As this is the simple truth–that to live is to feel oneself lost–he who accepts it has already begun to find himself, to be on firm ground. —JOSÉ ORTEGA Y GASSET

AMBITION
(also see concepts 8, 237, 519, 618, 647, 865)

Man partly is and wholly hopes to be. —ROBERT BROWNING

Hitch your wagon to a star. —RALPH WALDO EMERSON

Nothing is so common-place as to wish to be remarkable. —OLIVER WENDELL HOLMES, SR.

Most people would succeed in small things, if they were not troubled with great ambitions. —HENRY WADSWORTH LONGFELLOW

Ambition is the grand enemy of all peace. —JOHN COWPER POWYS

If you take big paces you leave big spaces. —BURMESE PROVERB

He who would rise in the world should veil his ambition with the forms of humanity. —CHINESE PROVERB

He who rides a tiger is afraid to dismount. —PROVERB

He is much to be dreaded who stands in dread of poverty. —PUBLILIUS SYRUS

Ambition should be made of sterner stuff. —WILLIAM SHAKESPEARE

I do want to get rich but I never want to do what there is to do to get rich. —GERTRUDE STEIN

Ambition often puts men upon doing the meanest offices; so climbing is performed in the same posture with creeping. —JONATHAN SWIFT

This is the posture of fortune's slave: one foot in the gravy, one foot in the grave. —JAMES THURBER

Too low they build, who build beneath the stars. —EDWARD YOUNG

AMERICA AND THE AMERICANS
(also see concepts 22, 49, 79, 87, 105, 347, 522, 529, 530, 536, 537)

In America you watch TV and think that's totally unreal, then you step outside and it's just the same. —JOAN ARMATRADING

We must stop talking about the American dream and start listening to the dreams of the Americans. —REUBIN ASKEW

America is the country where you buy a lifetime supply of aspirin for one dollar, and use it up within two weeks. —JOHN BARRYMORE

America is like an unfaithful lover who promised us more than we got. —CHARLOTTE BUNCH

Americans think of themselves collectively as a huge rescue squad on twenty-four-hour call to any spot on the globe where dispute and conflict may erupt. —ELDRIDGE CLEAVER

America is the only nation in history which miraculously has gone directly from barbarism to degeneration without the usual interval of civilization. —GEORGES CLEMENCEAU

I have news for the forces of greed and the defenders of the status quo: your time has come–and gone. It's time for change in America. —BILL CLINTON

Patriotism is easy to understand in America; it means looking out for yourself while looking out for your country. —CALVIN COOLIDGE

As we have lost our economic dominance the sure promise of the American dream–built by the power of our ideas and industries, sustained by strong hands and bright minds–has dissipated gradually. If we lose that vision of the American dream, we lose the nation as we have known it. —MARIO CUOMO

Americans are uneasy with their possessions, guilty about power, all of which is difficult for me to perceive because they are themselves so truly materialistic, so versed in the use of power. —JOAN DIDION

America is woven of many strands; I would recognize them and let it so remain....Our fate is to become one, and yet many–This is not prophecy, but description. —RALPH ELLISON

The real death of the United States will come when everyone is just alike. —RALPH ELLISON

America is so vast that almost everything said about it is likely to be true, and the opposite is probably equally true. —JAMES T. FARRELL

Americans are not intuitive enough. We have to be feminized. The national identity is an erect penis. The national ideology is to go for it, no matter what. We rape women and other countries. The way we treat the earth is the way we treat women. We have no cultural experiences, no place for the imagination. —KAREN FINLEY

America is a mistake, a giant mistake. —SIGMUND FREUD

America is not a blanket woven from one thread, one color, one cloth. —JESSE JACKSON

I tremble for my country when I reflect that God is just. —THOMAS JEFFERSON

What the people want is very simple. They want an America as good as its promise. —BARBARA JORDAN

The United States has to move very fast to even stand still. —JOHN F. KENNEDY

For other nations, utopia is a blessed past never to be recovered; for Americans it is just beyond the horizon. —HENRY KISSINGER

If you're going to America, bring your own food. —FRAN LEBOWITZ

Action, swiftness, violence, power: these are native, homegrown America qualities, derived from the vast continent that has been ours to pen up, and the big prizes that have made our economy into a jungle where the law is eat or be eaten. —MAX LERNER

If destruction be our lot we must ourselves be its author and finisher. As a nation of free men we must live through all time, or die by suicide. —ABRAHAM LINCOLN

America, which has the most glorious present still existing in the world today, hardly stops to enjoy it, in her insatiable appetite for the future. —ANNE MORROW LINDBERGH

Sitting at the table doesn't make you a diner, unless you eat some of what's on that plate. Being here in America doesn't make you an American. Being born here in America doesn't make you an American. —MALCOLM X

I wish I could say that racism and prejudice were only distant memories. We must dissent from the indifference. We must dissent from the apathy. We must dissent from the fear, the hatred and the mistrust....We must dissent because America can do better, because America has no choice but to do better. —THURGOOD MARSHALL

American youth attributes much more importance to arriving at driver's license age than at voting age. —MARSHALL MCLUHAN

The pursuit of happiness, which American citizens are obliged to undertake, tends to involve them in trying to perpetuate the moods, tastes and aptitudes of youth. —MALCOLM MUGGERIDGE

We talk about the American Dream, and want to tell the world about the American Dream, but what is that Dream, in most cases, but the dream of material things? I sometimes think that the United States for this reason is the greatest failure the world has ever seen. —EUGENE O'NEILL

Coming to America has always been hard. Thriving in America is harder than ever. But so many things remain the same. And one of them is that the people who, generation to generation, believe America is a finished product are habitually revealed as people whose ideas would have impoverished this country beyond measure. It is foolish to forget where you come from, and that, in the case of the United States, is almost always somewhere else. The true authentic American is a pilgrim with a small "p" armed with little more than the phrase "I wish..." —ANNA QUINDLEN

America is gangsterism for the private profit of the few. —VANESSA REDGRAVE

I sometimes think that the saving grace of America lies in the fact that the overwhelming majority of Americans are possessed of two great qualities–a sense of humor and a sense of proportion. —FRANKLIN D. ROOSEVELT

Since the 1960s, we have seen the failure of the melting pot ideology. This ideology suggested that different historical, cultural and socioeconomic backgrounds could be subordinated to a larger ideology or social amalgam which is "America." This concept obviously did not work, because paradoxically America encourages a politics of contestation. —EDWARD SAID

In the United States there is more space where nobody is than where anybody is. That is what makes America what it is. —GERTRUDE STEIN

America...just a nation of two hundred million used-car salesmen with all the money we need to buy guns and no qualms about killing anybody else in the world who tries to make us uncomfortable. —HUNTER S. THOMPSON

There isn't a single human characteristic that can be safely labeled as "American." —MARK TWAIN

Americans have been conditioned to respect newness, whatever it costs them. —JOHN UPDIKE

In order to be able to live at all in America I must be unafraid to live anywhere in it, and I must be able to live in the fashion and with whom I choose. —ALICE WALKER

The American landscape has no foreground and the American mind has no background. —EDITH WHARTON

In nothing is there more evolution than the American mind. —WALT WHITMAN

Of course, America had often been discovered before, but it had always been hushed up. —OSCAR WILDE

AMUSEMENT
(also see concepts 58, 77, 237, 413, 447, 568, 592)

We never respect those who amuse us, however we may smile at their comic powers. —LADY MARGUERITE BLESSINGTON

I am a great friend to public amusements, for they keep people from vice. —SAMUEL JOHNSON

The real character of a man is found out by his amusements. —JOSHUA REYNOLDS

ANARCHY
(also see concepts 99, 148, 394, 659)

Anarchism is the only philosophy which brings to man the consciousness of himself; which maintains that God, the State, and society are non-existent, that their promises are null and void, since they can be fulfilled only through man's subordination. —EMMA GOLDMAN

Anarchy is the stepping stone to absolute power. —NAPOLEON I

ANCESTRY
(also see concepts 44, 320, 345, 511, 654)

I don't have to look up my family tree, because I know that I'm the sap. —FRED ALLEN

Heredity is nothing but stored environment. —LUTHER BURBANK

I don't know who my grandfather was; I am much more concerned to know what his grandson will be. —ABRAHAM LINCOLN

Birth is nothing without virtue, and we have no claim to share in the glory of our ancestors unless we strive to resemble them. —MOLIÉRE

...we are linked by blood, and blood is memory without language. —JOYCE CAROL OATES

Good birth is a fine thing, but the merit is our ancestors'. —PLUTARCH

To forget one's ancestors is to be a brook without a source, a tree without a root. ——CHINESE PROVERB

Noble and common blood is of the same color. ——GERMAN PROVERB

ANGER
(also see concepts 237, 393, 426, 557, 798)

Bitterness is like cancer. It eats upon the host. But anger is like fire. It burns it all clean. ——MAYA ANGELOU

No man is angry that feels not himself hurt. ——FRANCIS BACON

A man that does not know how to be angry does not know how to be good. ——HENRY WARD BEECHER

Let not the sun go down upon your wrath. ——BIBLE, EPHESIANS 4:26

Many people lose their tempers merely from seeing you keep yours. ——FRANK MOORE COLBY

Anger as soon as fed is dead / 'Tis starving makes it fat. ——EMILY DICKINSON

Never go to bed mad. Stay up and fight. ——PHYLLIS DILLER

Beware the fury of a patient man. ——JOHN DRYDEN

A man in a passion rides a horse that runs away with him. ——THOMAS FULLER

Grab the broom of anger and drive off the beast of fear. ——ZORA NEALE HURSTON

To be angry is to revenge the fault of others upon ourselves. ——ALEXANDER POPE

There is no old age for a man's anger, / Only death. ——SOPHOCLES

When angry, count four; when very angry, swear. ——MARK TWAIN

I have a right to my anger, and I don't want anybody telling me I shouldn't be, that it's not nice to be, and that something's wrong with me because I get angry. ——MAXINE WATERS

ANIMALS
(also see concepts 92, 221, 230, 250, 275, 359, 372, 517)

The zoo cannot but disappoint. The public purpose of zoos is to offer visitors the opportunity of looking at animals. Yet nowhere in a zoo can a stranger encounter the look of an animal. At the most, the animal's gaze flickers and passes on. They look sideways. They look blindly beyond. —JOHN BERGER

Whenever you observe an animal closely, you feel as if a human being sitting inside were making fun of you. —ELIAS CANETTI

Animals are such agreeable friends–they ask no questions, they pass no criticisms. —GEORGE ELIOT

If animals are deprived of hope (as well as of fear), they are compensated by being given an almost endless patience for enduring, or simply for waiting. —JOSEPH WOOD KRUTCH

The cow is of the bovine ilk; / One end is moo, the other, milk. —OGDEN NASH

Nothing can be more obvious than that all animals were created solely and exclusively for the use of man. —THOMAS LOVE PEACOCK

Those who wish to pet and baby wild animals, "love" them. But those who respect their natures and wish to let them live normal lives, love them more. —EDWIN WAY TEALE

We can no longer afford to neglect animals of vital ecological importance just because they don't initially appeal to our emotions. If people only understood bats, they would appreciate them as gentle and essential allies. —MERLIN D. TUTTLE

There are two things for which animals are to be envied: they know nothing of future evils, or of what people say about them. —VOLTAIRE

I think I could turn and live with animals, they're so placid and self-contained, / I stand and look at them long and long. —WALT WHITMAN

The best thing about animals is that they don't talk much. —THORNTON WILDER

APOLOGY

(also see concepts 193, 255, 263, 670)

Never make a defence or apology before you be accused.
—KING CHARLES I

A stiff apology is a second insult. —G. K. CHESTERTON

Apologies only account for that which they do not alter.
—BENJAMIN DISRAELI

Apology is only egotism wrong side out.
—OLIVER WENDELL HOLMES, SR.

It is a good rule in life never to apologize. The right sort of people do not want apologies, and the wrong sort take a mean advantage of them. —P. G. WODEHOUSE

APPEARANCE

(also see concepts 47, 59, 73, 74, 124, 165, 266, 277, 278, 336, 504, 547, 822)

Outside show is a poor substitute for inner worth. —AESOP

It is the common wonder of all men, how among so many million of faces, there should be none alike. —THOMAS BROWNE

Things are seldom what they seem, / Skim milk masquerades as cream. —W. S. GILBERT

Personal appearance is looking the best you can for the money.
—VIRGINIA CARY HUDSON

The Lord prefers common-looking people. That is why he makes so many of them. —ABRAHAM LINCOLN

It is easy to be beautiful; it is difficult to appear so. —FRANK O'HARA

An ox with long horns, even if he does not butt, will be accused of butting. —MALAY PROVERB

Be careless in your dress if you must, but keep a tidy soul.
—MARK TWAIN

It is only shallow people who do not judge by appearances.
—OSCAR WILDE

APPRECIATION
(also see concepts 326, 675, 724, 837)

Neither cast ye pearls before swine, lest they trample them under their feet, and turn again and rend you. —BIBLE, MATTHEW 7:6

Is there some principle of nature which states that we never know the quality of what we have until it is gone? —RICHARD HOFSTADTER

I would rather be able to appreciate things I can not have than to have things I am not able to appreciate. —ELBERT HUBBARD

Hay is more acceptable to an ass than gold. —LATIN PROVERB

APPROVAL
(also see concepts 14, 139, 237, 601, 610, 790, 837)

Please all, and you will please none. —AESOP

When we want to please in the world, we must resign ourselves to learning many things from people who are ignorant of them. —NICOLAS CHAMFORT

ARCHITECTURE
(also see concepts 46, 362)

Architecture, unlike poetry and painting, is a particularly fragile, vulnerable, and ephemeral art form. The greater the architect, the stronger the repressive forces that mean to see to it that the work lasts no longer than a generation at most. —JOHN ASHBERY

Architecture is inhabited sculpture. —CONSTANTIN BRANCUSI

We shape our buildings: thereafter they shape us. —WINSTON CHURCHILL

A modern, harmonic and lively architecture is the visible sign of an authentic democracy. —WALTER GROPIUS

Less is more. —LUDWIG MIES VAN DER ROHE

Every construction is in some way an attempt to create an artificial world away from a man's origin in the woman's body.
—CAMILLE PAGLIA

When we build, let us think that we build for ever. —JOHN RUSKIN

Architecture in general is frozen music. —FRIEDRICH WILHELM JOSEPH VON SCHELLING

The physician can bury his mistakes, but the architect can only advise his client to plant vines. —FRANK LLOYD WRIGHT

ARGUMENT
(also see concept 285)

Positive, adj. mistaken at the top of one's voice. —AMBROSE BIERCE

If you would convince others, seem open to conviction yourself.
—EARL OF CHESTERFIELD

Argument seldom convinces anyone contrary to his inclinations.
—THOMAS FULLER

Most quarrels amplify a misunderstanding. —ANDRÉ GIDE

The aim of argument, or of discussion, should not be victory, but progress. —JOSEPH JOUBERT

Anyone who in discussion relies upon authority uses, not his understanding, but rather his memory. —LEONARDO DA VINCI

True disputants are like true sportsmen; their whole delight is in the pursuit. —ALEXANDER POPE

Least said soonest mended. —PROVERB

The most savage controversies are those about matters as to which there is no good evidence either way. —BERTRAND RUSSELL

It was completely fruitless to quarrel with the world, whereas the quarrel with oneself was occasionally fruitful and always, she had to admit, interesting. —MAY SARTON

In a false quarrel there is no true valour. —WILLIAM SHAKESPEARE

Arguments only confirm people in their own opinions.
—BOOTH TARKINGTON

Arguments are to be avoided; they are always vulgar and often convincing. —OSCAR WILDE

ARISTOCRACY
(also see concepts 35, 118, 320, 345, 473, 498, 511, 542, 783, 861)

Like many of the upper class / He liked the sound of broken glass.
—HILAIRE BELLOC

There are bad manners everywhere, but an aristocracy is bad manners organised. —HENRY JAMES

There is a natural aristocracy among men. The grounds of this are virtue and talent. —THOMAS JEFFERSON

What is the use of your pedigrees? —JUVENAL

An aristocracy in a republic is like a chicken whose head has been cut off: it may run about in a lively way, but in fact it is dead.
—NANCY MITFORD

The true policy of a government is to make use of aristocracy, but under the forms and in the spirit of democracy. —NAPOLEON I

Aristocracy is always cruel. —WENDELL PHILLIPS

ARROGANCE
(also see concepts 237, 750, 783, 838)

The arrogance of age must submit to be taught by youth.
—EDMUND BURKE

The need to be right–the sign of a vulgar mind. —ALBERT CAMUS

ART

(also see concepts 11, 42, 169, 223, 284, 459, 565, 586, 595, 686, 801, 845)

The object of art is to give life a shape. —JEAN ANOUILH

Art distills sensation and embodies it with enhanced meaning in memorable form–or else it is not art. —JACQUES BARZUN

Art is an attempt to integrate evil. —SIMONE DE BEAUVOIR

When the age of mechanical reproduction separated art from its basis in cult, the semblance of its autonomy disappeared forever. —WALTER BENJAMIN

What is more natural in a democratic age than that we should begin to measure the stature of a work of art–especially of a painting–by how widely and how well it is reproduced? —DANIEL J. BOORSTIN

Art is the only thing that can go on mattering once it has stopped hurting. —ELIZABETH BOWEN

Art is meant to disturb. Science reassures. —GEORGES BRAQUE

With an apple I will astonish Paris. —PAUL CÉZANNE

Without tradition, art is a flock of sheep without a shepherd. Without innovation, it is a corpse. —WINSTON CHURCHILL

Art is a marriage of the conscious and the unconscious. —JEAN COCTEAU

It's either easy or impossible. —SALVADOR DALI

It depends little on the object, much on the mood, in art. —RALPH WALDO EMERSON

In art, as in love, instinct is enough. —ANATOLE FRANCE

The work of art is the exaggeration of an idea. —ANDRÉ GIDE

Art is not for the cultivated taste. It is to cultivate taste. —NIKKI GIOVANNI

There is no "must" in art, because art is free. —WASSILY KANDINSKY

Art changes all the time, but it never "improves." It may go down, or up, but it never improves as technology and medicine improve. —ALFRED KAZIN

We must never forget that art is not a form of propaganda; it is a form of truth. —JOHN F. KENNEDY

Art does not reproduce the visible; rather, it makes visible. —PAUL KLEE

The more minimal the art, the more maximum the explanation. —HILTON KRAMER

In art, there are tears that do often lie too deep for thoughts. —LOUIS KRONENBERGER

Art is not a mirror to reflect the world, but a hammer with which to shape it. —VLADIMIR MAYAKOVSKY

Art teaches nothing, except the significance of life. —HENRY MILLER

One puts into one's art what one has not been capable of putting into one's existence. It is because he was unhappy that God created the world. —HENRY DE MONTHERLANT

I am thinking of aurochs and angels, the secret of durable pigments, prophetic sonnets, the refuge of art. —VLADIMIR NABOKOV

Art raises its head where creeds relax. —FRIEDRICH WILHELM NIETZSCHE

Art is a form of catharsis. —DOROTHY PARKER

All art constantly aspires towards the condition of music. —WALTER PATER

Art is a lie that makes us realize the truth. —PABLO PICASSO

If we could but understand Gothic art, we should be irresistibly led back to the truth. —AUGUSTE RODIN

Art, like life, should be free, since both are experimental. —GEORGE SANTAYANA

Without art, the crudeness of reality would make the world unbearable. —GEORGE BERNARD SHAW

Not everything has a name. Some things lead us into a realm beyond words....By means of art we are sometimes sent–dimly, briefly–revelations unattainable by reason.
——ALEXANDER SOLZHENITSYN

Contemporary art, no matter how much it has defined itself by a taste for negation, can still be analyzed as a set of assertions of a formal kind. ——SUSAN SONTAG

Art is the only way to run away without leaving home.
——TWYLA THARP

Art imitates Nature in this: not to dare is to dwindle. ——JOHN UPDIKE

Art is the most intense mode of individualism that the world has known. ——OSCAR WILDE

ARTIFICIALITY

(also see concepts 59, 165, 383)

Men often applaud an imitation and hiss the real thing. ——AESOP

True eloquence makes light of eloquence, true morality makes light of morality. ——BLAISE PASCAL

Natural beauty is essentially temporary and sad; hence the impression of obscene mockery which artificial flowers give us.
——JOHN UPDIKE

The first duty in life is to be as artificial as possible. What the second duty is no one has yet discovered. ——OSCAR WILDE

ARTISTS

(also see concepts 11, 42, 128, 223, 310, 565, 594)

All art is a kind of confession, more or less oblique. All artists, if they are to survive, are forced, at last, to tell the whole story, to vomit the anguish up. ——JAMES BALDWIN

The artistic temperament is a disease that afflicts amateurs.
——G. K. CHESTERTON

An artist carries on throughout his life a mysterious, uninterrupted conversation with his public. —MAURICE CHEVALIER

As a citizen, of course. As a parent, of course. But as an artist, that's where the paradox is—your responsibility is to be irresponsible. As soon as you talk about social or political responsibility, you've amputated the best limbs you've got as an artist. —DAVID CRONENBERG

The attitude that nature is chaotic and that the artist puts order into it is a very absurd point of view, I think. All that we can hope for is to put some order into ourselves. —WILLEM DE KOONING

No poet, no artist of any art, has his complete meaning alone. His significance, his appreciation is the appreciation of his relation to the dead poets and artists. —T. S. ELIOT

An artist is a creature driven by demons. He doesn't know why they choose him and he's usually too busy to wonder why. —WILLIAM FAULKNER

I'm an artist; art has no color and no sex. —WHOOPI GOLDBERG

The moment you cheat for the sake of beauty, you know you're an artist. —MAX JACOB

They thought I was a surrealist, but I wasn't. I never painted dreams. I painted my own reality. —FRIDA KAHLO

Thought that can merge wholly into feeling, feeling that can merge wholly into thought—these are the artist's highest joy. —THOMAS MANN

The art of being an artist, if you weren't born in the right place, is to be able to live through rejections. A lot of them. To be able to speak when silenced. To be able to hear when not being heard. To be able to see and make seen. —GABRIELA MÜLLER

The people who make art their business are mostly imposters. —PABLO PICASSO

All artists, in whatever medium, in fact work largely through the feminine side of their personalities. This is because works of art are essentially formed and created inside the mind of the maker, and

are hardly at all dependent on external circumstances.
—JOAN RIVIERE

The artist needs but a roof, a crust of bread, and his easel, and all the rest God gives him in abundance. —ALBERT PINKHAM RYDER

The artist is the child of his time; but woe to him if he is also its disciple, or even its favorite. —JOHANN FRIEDRICH VON SCHILLER

A painter should not paint what he sees, but what will be seen. —PAUL VALÉRY

An artist is somebody who produces things that people don't need to have. —ANDY WARHOL

No great artist ever sees things as they really are. If he did he would cease to be an artist. —OSCAR WILDE

This is the artist, then–life's hungry man, the glutton of eternity, beauty's miser, glory's slave. —THOMAS WOLFE

If you ask me what I came to do in this world, I, an artist, I will answer you: "I am here to live out loud." —ÉMILE ZOLA

ASIAN AMERICANS
(also see concepts 32, 522, 650)

There's the stereotype of the Asian as quiet, courtly, yet not particularly introspective–I've felt compelled to say, "That's not me." —DAVID HENRY HWANG

As soon as my feet touched China, I became Chinese. —AMY TAN

ASPIRATION
(also see concepts 8, 31, 198, 234, 375, 519, 618, 647, 865)

What you are must always displease you, if you would attain to that which you are not. —ST. AUGUSTINE OF HIPPO

I might have been born in a hovel, but I determined to travel with the wind and the stars. —JACQUELINE COCHRAN

Slight not what's near through aiming at what's far. —EURIPIDES

I drink the wine of aspiration and the drug of illusion. Thus I am never dull. —JOHN GALSWORTHY

Mama exhorted her children at every opportunity to "jump at de sun." We might not land on the sun, but at least we would get off the ground. —ZORA NEALE HURSTON

From a certain point onward there is no longer any turning back. That is the point that must be reached. —FRANZ KAFKA

I do not want to die until I have faithfully made the most of my talent and cultivated the seed that was placed in me until the last small twig has grown. —KÄTHE KOLLWITZ

Not failure, but low aim, is crime. —JAMES RUSSELL LOWELL

Be wicked, be brave, be drunk, be reckless, be dissolute, be despotic, be an anarchist, be a suffragette, be anything you like–but for pity's sake be it to the top of your bent. —VIOLET TREFUSIS

We are all in the gutter, but some of us are looking at the stars. —OSCAR WILDE

ASSOCIATION

(also see concept 666)

Tell me thy company, and I'll tell thee what thou art.
—MIGUEL DE CERVANTES

If you live with a cripple, you will learn to limp. —PLUTARCH

He that lies down with dogs shall rise up with fleas.
—LATIN PROVERB

It is better to weep with wise men than to laugh with fools.
—SPANISH PROVERB

To take refuge with an inferior is to betray one's self.
—PUBLILIUS SYRUS

ATHEISM

(also see concepts 64, 316, 378, 585, 668)

They now have a 900 number for atheists. When you call, nobody answers and you get charged for the call. —ANONYMOUS

Atheism is rather in the lip than in the heart of man. —FRANCIS BACON

An atheist is a man who has no invisible means of support. —JOHN BUHAN

If there is a God, atheism must strike Him as less of an insult than religion. —EDMOND AND JULES DE GONCOURT

By night an atheist half believes a God. —EDWARD YOUNG

AUDIENCES

(also see concepts 48, 76, 521)

Every crowd has a silver lining. —P. T. BARNUM

Those in the cheaper seats clap. The rest of you rattle your jewellery. —JOHN LENNON

If one talks to more than four people, it is an audience; and one cannot really think or exchange thoughts with an audience. —ANNE MORROW LINDBERGH

Audiences are the same all over the world, and if you entertain them, they'll respond. —LIZA MINNELLI

I know two kinds of audience only—one coughing and one not coughing. —ARTUR SCHNABEL

It's the admirer and the watcher who provoke us to all the insanities we commit. —SENECA

Every successful creative person creates with an audience of one in mind. —KURT VONNEGUT

To have great poets, there must be great audiences too. —WALT WHITMAN

AUTHORITY

(also see concepts 95, 172, 211, 262, 323, 400, 445, 548, 596, 608, 654, 666)

Authority is never without hate. —EURIPIDES

Authority has every reason to fear the skeptic, for authority can rarely survive in the face of doubt. —ROBERT LINDNER

I am a woman in the prime of life, with certain powers and those powers severely limited by authorities whose faces I rarely see. —ADRIENNE RICH

AUTOBIOGRAPHY

(also see concepts 76, 204, 874)

Just as there is nothing between the admirable omelette and the intolerable, so with autobiography. —HILAIRE BELLOC

Autobiography is an obituary in serial form with the last installment missing. —QUENTIN CRISP

There ain't nothing that breaks up homes, country, and nations like somebody publishing their memoirs. —WILL ROGERS

Only when one has lost all curiosity about the future has one reached the age to write an autobiography. —EVELYN WAUGH

A poet's autobiography is his poetry. Anything else can only be a footnote. —YEVGENY YEVTUSHENKO

AUTOMOBILES

(also see concepts 474, 814, 820)

I think that cars today are almost the exact equivalent of the great Gothic cathedrals: I mean the supreme creation of an era, conceived in image if not in usage by a whole population which appropriates them as a purely magical object. —ROLAND BARTHES

The car has become a secular sanctuary for the individual, his shrine to the self, his mobile Walden Pond. —EDWARD MCDONAGH

The car has become an article of dress without which we feel uncertain, unclad, and incomplete. —MARSHALL MCLUHAN

Our national flower is the concrete cloverleaf. —LEWIS MUMFORD

We are the first nation in the history of the world to go to the poorhouse in an automobile. —WILL ROGERS

I don't even like old cars...I'd rather have a goddam horse. A horse is at least human, for God's sake. —J. D. SALINGER

Everything in life is somewhere else, and you get there in a car. —E. B. WHITE

BANKS AND BANKING
(also see concepts 10, 78, 85, 88, 421, 512)

It is easier to rob by setting up a Bank than by holding up a bank clerk. —BERTOLT BRECHT

Banking may well be a career from which no man really recovers. —JOHN KENNETH GALBRAITH

Put not your trust in money, but put your money in trust. —OLIVER WENDELL HOLMES, SR.

A bank is a place that will lend you money if you can prove that you don't need it. —BOB HOPE

It is better that a man should tyrannize over his bank balance than over his fellow citizens. —JOHN MAYNARD KEYNES

A banker is a fellow who lends his umbrella when the sun is shining and wants it back the minute it begins to rain. —MARK TWAIN

BASEBALL
(also see concepts 10, 256, 292, 305, 765)

You can't think and hit at the same time. —YOGI BERRA

Back then, if you had a sore arm, the only people concerned were you and your wife. Now it's you, your wife, your agent, your

investment counselor, your stockbroker, and your publisher.
——JIM BOUTON

A ball player's got to be kept hungry to become a big-leaguer.
That's why no boy from a rich family ever made the big leagues.
——JOE DIMAGGIO

Being an umpire is like being a king. It prepares you for nothing.
——RON LUCIANO

Never bet on baseball. ——PETE ROSE

Managing is getting paid for home runs someone else hits.
——CASEY STENGEL

BEAUTY

(also see concepts 39, 46, 165, 266, 822)

Beauty–the adjustment of all parts proportionately so that one
cannot add or subtract or change without impairing the harmony of
the whole. ——LEON BATTISTA ALBERTI

Things are beautiful if you love them. ——JEAN ANOUILH

Beauty is unbearable, drives us to despair, offering us for a minute
the glimpse of an eternity that we should like to stretch out over the
whole of time. ——ALBERT CAMUS

Love built on beauty, soon as beauty, dies. ——JOHN DONNE

I don't think of all the misery, but of all the beauty that still remains.
——ANNE FRANK

'Beauty is truth, truth beauty,'–that is all / Ye know on earth, and
all ye need to know. ——JOHN KEATS

A thing of beauty is a joy for ever: / Its loveliness increases; it will
never / pass into nothingness. ——JOHN KEATS

All God's children are not beautiful. Most of God's children are,
in fact, barely presentable. ——FRAN LEBOWITZ

Anything in any way beautiful derives its beauty from itself, and asks nothing beyond itself. Praise is no part of it, for nothing is made worse or better by praise. —MARCUS AURELIUS

Beauty is an ecstasy; it is as simple as hunger. There is really nothing to be said about it. —W. SOMERSET MAUGHAM

Beauty is everlasting / and dust is for a time. —MARIANNE MOORE

Judgment of beauty can err, what with the wine and the dark. —OVID

'Tis not a lip or eye we beauty call, / But the joint force and full result of all. —ALEXANDER POPE

Beauty is only skin-deep. —PROVERB

Remember that the most beautiful things in the world are the most useless: peacocks and lilies, for instance. —JOHN RUSKIN

I always say beauty is only sin deep. —SAKI

The beauty that addresses itself to the eyes is only the spell of the moment; the eye of the body is not always that of the soul. —GEORGE SAND

To keep beauty in its place is to make all things beautiful. —GEORGE SANTAYANA

Beauty more than bitterness / Makes the heart break. —SARA TEASDALE

Wrinkles should merely indicate where smiles have been. —MARK TWAIN

Ask a toad what is beauty...;he will answer that it is a female with two great round eyes coming out of her little head, a large flat mouth, a yellow belly and a brown back. —VOLTAIRE

They are the elect to whom beautiful things mean only Beauty. —OSCAR WILDE

BED
(also see concepts 73, 352, 361, 362, 541, 731, 748)

Bed is a bundle of paradoxes: we go to it with reluctance, yet we quit it with regret. —CHARLES CALEB COLTON

Early to bed and early to rise, makes a man healthy, wealthy, and wise. —BENJAMIN FRANKLIN

He that riseth late must trot all day. —BENJAMIN FRANKLIN

Believe me, you have to get up early if you want to get out of bed. —GROUCHO MARX

It was such a lovely day I thought it was a pity to get up. —W. SOMERSET MAUGHAM

What does "good in bed" mean to me? When I'm sick and I stay home from school propped up with lots of pillows watching TV and my mom brings me soup–that's good in bed. —BROOKE SHIELDS

BEGINNING
(also see concepts 69, 93)

The great majority of men are bundles of beginnings. —RALPH WALDO EMERSON

With the possible exception of the equator, everything begins somewhere. —PETER FLEMING

We stand today on the edge of a new frontier. —JOHN F. KENNEDY

A journey of a thousand miles must begin with a single step. —CHINESE PROVERB

From small beginnings come great things. —PROVERB

BEGINNING AND ENDING
(also see concepts 93, 454, 877)

In my beginning is my end. —T. S. ELIOT

A hard beginning maketh a good ending. —JOHN HEYWOOD

The truth is that the beginning of anything and its end are alike touching. —YOSHIDA KENKO

Great is the art of beginning, but greater is the art of ending.
—HENRY WADSWORTH LONGFELLOW

A good beginning makes a good ending. —ENGLISH PROVERB

Every exit is an entry somewhere else. —TOM STOPPARD

BEHAVIOR
(also see concept 478)

Our humanity rests upon a series of learned behaviors, woven together into patterns that are infinitely fragile and never directly inherited. —MARGARET MEAD

Physics does not change the nature of the world it studies, and no science of behavior can change the essential nature of man, even though both sciences yield technologies with a vast power to manipulate their subject matters. —B. F. SKINNER

I don't say we all ought to misbehave, but we ought to look as if we could. —ORSON WELLES

BELIEF
(also see concepts 26, 52, 64, 96, 145, 222, 259, 333, 585, 620, 674, 785)

It is always easier to believe than to deny. Our minds are naturally affirmative. —JOHN BURROUGHS

Sometimes I've believed as many as six impossible things before breakfast. —LEWIS CARROLL

Believe only half of what you see and nothing that you hear.
—DINAH MULOCK CRAIK

He does not believe that does not live according to his belief.
—THOMAS FULLER

We are so constitued that we believe the most incredible things; and, once they are engraved upon the memory, woe to him who would endeavor to erase them. —JOHANN WOLFGANG VON GOETHE

Loving is half of believing. —VICTOR HUGO

Believe that life is worth living, and your belief will help create the fact. —WILLIAM JAMES

There seems to be a terrible misunderstanding on the part of a great many people to the effect that when you cease to believe you may cease to behave. —LOUIS KRONENBERGER

Nothing is so firmly believed, as what we least know.
—MICHEL DE MONTAIGNE

Convictions are more dangerous foes of truth than lies.
—FRIEDRICH WILHELM NIETZSCHE

Of what worth are convictions that bring not suffering?
—ANTOINE DE SAINT-EXUPÉRY

You believe easily that which you hope for earnestly. —TERENCE

I believe because it is impossible. —TERTULLIAN

That which has been believed by everyone, always and everywhere, has every chance of being false. —PAUL VALÉRY

BETRAYAL

(also see concepts 216, 826)

It is all right to rat, but you can't re-rat. —WINSTON CHURCHILL

They talk of a man betraying his country, his friends, his sweetheart. There must be a moral bond first. All a man can betray is his conscience. —JOSEPH CONRAD

If I had to choose between betraying my country and betraying my friend, I hope I should have the guts to betray my country.
—E. M. FORSTER

To betray you must first belong. —HAROLD PHILBY

You too, Brutus? —WILLIAM SHAKESPEARE

THE BIBLE
(also see concepts 250, 269, 459, 629, 632, 668, 743, 802, 868)

I have spent a lot of time searching through the Bible for loopholes.
——W. C. FIELDS

The Good Book—one of the most remarkable euphemisms ever coined. ——ASHLEY MONTAGU

The Scripture in time of disputes is like an open town in time of war, which serves indifferently the occasions of both parties.
——ALEXANDER POPE

There's a Bible on that shelf there. But I keep it next to Voltaire –poison and antidote. ——BERTRAND RUSSELL

The Bible is literature, not dogma. ——GEORGE SANTAYANA

The Christian's Bible is a drug store. Its contents remain the same, but the medical practice changes. ——MARK TWAIN

BIGOTRY
(also see concepts 123, 213, 374, 555, 613, 732)

Bigot, n. one who is obstinately and zealously attached to an opinion that you do not entertain. ——AMBROSE BIERCE

The man who never alters his opinion is like standing water, and breeds reptiles of the mind. ——WILLIAM BLAKE

Religion is as effectually destroyed by bigotry as by indifference.
——RALPH WALDO EMERSON

Bigotry is the sacred disease. ——HERACLITUS

We are least open to precise knowledge concerning the things we are most vehement about. ——ERIC HOFFER

BIOGRAPHY
(also see concepts 204, 874)

History is the essence of innumerable biographies.
——THOMAS CARLYLE

There is properly no history; only biography.
—RALPH WALDO EMERSON

I have not much interest in anyone's personal history after the tenth year, not even my own. Whatever one was going to be was all prepared before that. —KATHERINE ANNE PORTER

Biographies are but the clothes and buttons of the man–the biography of the man himself cannot be written. —MARK TWAIN

Just how difficult it is to write biography can be reckoned by anybody who sits down and considers just how many people know the real truth about his or her love affairs. —REBECCA WEST

Every great man nowadays has his disciples, and it is always Judas who writes the biography. —OSCAR WILDE

BIRTH
(also see concepts 2, 61, 62, 106, 160, 248, 353, 455)

When I was born I was so surprised I didn't talk for a year and a half.
—GRACIE ALLEN

We brought nothing into this world, and it is certain we can carry nothing out. —BIBLE, 1 TIMOTHY 6:7

I think of birth as the search for a larger apartment.
—RITA MAE BROWN

The day of our birth is one day's advance towards our death.
—THOMAS FULLER

One must mourn not the death of men, but their birth.
—BARON DE MONTESQUIEU

The hour which gives us life begins to take it away. —SENECA

When we are born we cry that we are come / To this great stage of fools. —WILLIAM SHAKESPEARE

Our birth is but a sleep and a forgetting. —WILLIAM WORDSWORTH

Our birth is nothing but our death begun. —EDWARD YOUNG

BLINDNESS

(also see concepts 184, 209)

It is we that are blind, not Fortune. —THOMAS BROWNE

He does not weep who does not see. —VICTOR HUGO

It is not miserable to be blind; it is miserable to be incapable of enduring blindness. —JOHN MILTON

He has the greatest blind side who thinks he has none.
—DUTCH PROVERB

BLUSHING

(also see concepts 9, 39, 266, 734, 737)

Blushing is the color of virtue. —DIOGENES THE CYNIC

We never forgive those who make us blush.
—JEAN-FRANÇOIS DE LA HARPE

Man is the only animal that blushes. Or needs to. —MARK TWAIN

BOASTING

(also see concepts 9, 63, 251, 610, 618, 721, 838, 841)

The noisiest drum has nothing in it but air. —ENGLISH PROVERB

Do not make yourself so big, you are not so small.
—JEWISH PROVERB

THE BODY

(also see concepts 39, 124, 219, 265, 266, 336, 341, 501, 547, 758, 849)

The body never lies. —MARTHA GRAHAM

Only death reveals what a nothing the body of man is. —JUVENAL

The abdomen is the reason why man does not easily take himself for a god. —FRIEDRICH WILHELM NIETZSCHE

What is more important in life than our bodies or in the world than what we look like? —GEORGE SANTAYANA

I know a lot of athletes and models are written off as just bodies. I never felt used for my body. —ARNOLD SCHWARZENEGGER

If anything is sacred the human body is sacred. —WALT WHITMAN

BODY IMAGE
(also see 39, 73, 124, 278)

Anybody who thinks that society pressures women to live up to our image should think of what we have to go through to maintain that image. —CAROL ALT

A woman obsessed with her body is also obsessed with the limitations of her emotional life. —KIM CHERNIN

I think women see me on the cover of magazines and think I never have a pimple or bags under my eyes. You have to realize that's after two hours of hair and makeup, plus retouching. Even *I* don't wake up looking like Cindy Crawford. —CINDY CRAWFORD

...the beauty industry helped to deepen the psychic isolation that so many women felt in the '80s, by reinforcing the representation of women's problems as purely personal ills, unrelated to social pressures and curable only to the degree that the individual woman succeeded in fitting the universal standard–by physically changing herself. —SUSAN FALUDI

We know that every woman wants to be thin. Our images of womanhood are almost synonymous with thinness. —SUSIE ORBACH

Surgical expectations and weight fluctuations subject women to weak body boundaries. The stress on appearance gives them erratic, extremely negative or positive views of themselves. A torrent of media images show the female face and body split into pieces...Is it possible that by submitting women to the experiences symptomatic of mental illness, we are more likely to become mentally ill? —NAOMI WOLF

Taught from infancy that beauty is a woman's sceptre, the mind shapes itself to the body, and roaming round its gilt cage, only seeks to adorn its prison. —MARY WOLLSTONECRAFT

BOLDNESS

(also see concepts 63, 145, 167, 202, 237)

Boldness, without the rules of propriety, becomes insubordination. —CONFUCIUS

The people I respect most behave as if they were immortal and as if society was eternal. —E. M. FORSTER

You must either conquer and rule or serve and lose, suffer or triumph, be the anvil or the hammer. —JOHANN WOLFGANG VON GOETHE

A decent boldness ever meets with friends. —HOMER

If the creator had a purpose in equipping us with a neck, he surely meant us to stick it out. —ARTHUR KOESTLER

With audacity one can undertake anything, but not do everything. —NAPOLEON I

Audacity augments courage; hesitation, fear. —PUBLILIUS SYRUS

BOOKS AND READING

(also see concepts 10, 46, 53, 55, 66, 232, 233, 451, 458, 459, 874)

A man is known by the company his mind keeps. —THOMAS BAILEY ALDRICH

Some books are undeservedly forgotten; none are undeservedly remembered. —W. H. AUDEN

Some books are to be tasted, others to be swallowed, and some few to be chewed and digested. —FRANCIS BACON

Books succeed, / And lives fail. —ELIZABETH BARRETT BROWNING

The possession of a book becomes a substitute for reading it. —ANTHONY BURGESS

Books, books, books. It was not that I read so much. I read and re-read the same ones. But all of them were necessary to me. Their presence, their smell, the letters of their titles, and the texture of their leather bindings. —COLETTE

Some read to think–these are rare; some to write, these are common; and some read to talk, and these form the great majority. —CHARLES CALEB COLTON

The reading of all good books is like conversation with the finest men of past centuries. —RENÉ DESCARTES

A book is not harmless merely because no one is consciously offended by it. —T. S. ELIOT

What's a book? Everything or nothing. The eye that sees it is all. —RALPH WALDO EMERSON

How our life has been warped by books! We are not contented with realities: we crave conclusions. —DAVID GRAYSON

Reading is sometimes an ingenious device for avoiding thought. —ARTHUR HELPS

A bad book is as much of a labour to write as a good one; it comes as sincerely from the author's soul. —ALDOUS HUXLEY

A book must be an ice ax to break the frozen sea within us. —FRANZ KAFKA

All books are either dreams or swords. —AMY LOWELL

To read too many books is harmful. —MAO TSE-TUNG

I would sooner read a timetable or a catalogue than nothing at all. —W. SOMERSET MAUGHAM

I have never known any distress that an hour's reading did not relieve. —BARON DE MONTESQUIEU

When we read too fast or too slowly, we understand nothing. —BLAISE PASCAL

How many good books suffer neglect through the inefficiency of their beginnings! —EDGAR ALLAN POE

When a new book is published, read an old one. —SAMUEL ROGERS

There are two motives for reading a book: one, that you enjoy it, the other that you can boast about it. —BERTRAND RUSSELL

People say that life is the thing, but I prefer reading.
—LOGAN PEARSALL SMITH

Books are...funny little portable pieces of thought. —SUSAN SONTAG

Books are good enough in their own way, but they are a mighty bloodless substitute for life. —ROBERT LOUIS STEVENSON

Books must be read as deliberately and reservedly as they are written. —HENRY DAVID THOREAU

It is with books as with men–a very small number play a great part; the rest are lost in the multitude. —VOLTAIRE

There is no such thing as a moral or an immoral book. Books are well written, or badly written. That is all. —OSCAR WILDE

BORES AND BOREDOM
(also see concepts 63, 386, 671, 749)

The man who suspects his own tediousness is yet to be born.
—THOMAS BAILEY ALDRICH

A yawn is a silent shout. —G. K. CHESTERTON

I wanted to be bored to death, as good a way to go as any.
—PETER DE VRIES

He'd be sharper than a serpent's tooth, if he wasn't as dull as ditch water. —CHARLES DICKENS

Millions long for immortality who do not know what to do with themselves on a rainy Sunday afternoon. —SUSAN ERTZ

Man is the only animal that can be bored. —ERICH FROMM

Is not life a hundred times too short for us to bore ourselves?
—FRIEDRICH WILHELM NIETZSCHE

One must choose in life between boredom and torment.
—GERMAINE DE STAËL

Boredom: the desire for desires. —LEO TOLSTOY

A healthy male adult bore consumes each year one and a half times his own weight in other people's patience. —JOHN UPDIKE

The secret of being a bore is to tell everything. —VOLTAIRE

Dullness is the coming of age of seriousness. —OSCAR WILDE

BORROWING AND LENDING
(also see concepts 9, 57, 84, 512)

The borrower is servant to the lender. —BIBLE, PROVERBS 22:7

Neither a borrower nor a lender be; For loan oft loses both itself and friend. —WILLIAM SHAKESPEARE

Let us all be happy, and live within our means, even if we have to borrow the money to do it with. —ARTEMUS WARD

I don't owe a penny to a single soul–not counting tradesmen, of course. —P. G. WODEHOUSE

BOSTON
(also see concepts 32, 113, 536)

Boston–a festering mud puddle. —ELLIS ARNALL

And this is good old Boston, / The home of the bean and the cod, / Where the Lowells talk only to Cabots, / And the Cabots talk only to God. —JOHN COLLINS BOSSIDY

Boston is a moral and intellectual nursery always busy applying first principles to trifles. —GEORGE SANTAYANA

BREVITY
(also see concepts 117, 456, 463)

Promise is most given when the least is said. —GEORGE CHAPMAN

Men are born with two eyes, but with one tongue, in order that they should see twice as much as they say. —CHARLES CALEB COLTON

Good things, when short, are twice as good. —BALTASAR GRACIÁN

I strive to be brief, and I become obscure. —HORACE

Brevity is the soul of wit. —WILLIAM SHAKESPEARE

All pleasantry should be short; and it might even be as well were the serious short also. —VOLTAIRE

BRIBERY
(also see concepts 85, 164, 170, 840)

To a shower of gold most things are penetrable. —THOMAS CARLYLE

He that bringeth a present findeth the door open. —THOMAS FULLER

Though authority be a stubborn bear, yet he is oft led by the nose with gold. —WILLIAM SHAKESPEARE

A conscience which has been bought once will be bought twice. —NORBERT WIENER

BRITAIN AND THE BRITISH
(also see concepts 247, 423, 461, 529, 703)

I like the English. They have the most rigid code of immorality in the world. —MALCOLM BRADBURY

Without class differences, England would cease to be the living theatre it is. —ANTHONY BURGESS

The British love permanence more than they love beauty. —HUGH CASSON

The maxim of the British people is "Business as usual." —WINSTON CHURCHILL

The English think incompetence is the same thing as sincerity. —QUENTIN CRISP

Contrary to popular belief, English women do not wear tweed nightgowns. —HERMIONE GINGOLD

We may be a small island, but we are not a small people. —EDWARD HEATH

When two Englishmen meet, their first talk is of the weather. —SAMUEL JOHNSON

Curse the blasted, jelly-boned swines, the slimy, the belly-wriggling invertebrates, the miserable sodding rutters, the flaming sods, the snivelling, dribbling, dithering, palsied, pulse-less lot that make up England today. They've got white of egg in their veins and their spunk is that watery it's a marvel they can breed. —D. H. LAWRENCE

In England there is only silence or scandal. —ANDRÉ MAUROIS

It has to be admitted that we English have sex on the brain, which is a very unsatisfactory place to have it. —MALCOLM MUGGERIDGE

Remember that you are an Englishman, and have consequently won first prize in the lottery of life. —CECIL RHODES

It is equality of monotony which makes the strength of the British Isles. —ELEANOR ROOSEVELT

England is the paradise of individuality, eccentricity, heresy, anomalies, hobbies, and humours. —GEORGE SANTAYANA

This blessed plot, this earth, this realm, this England. —WILLIAM SHAKESPEARE

An Englishman thinks he is moral when he is only uncomfortable. —GEORGE BERNARD SHAW

What two ideas are more inseparable than Beer and Britannia? —SYDNEY SMITH

I'm in favor of liberalized immigration because of the effect it would have on restaurants. I'd let just about everybody in except the English. —CALVIN TRILLIN

Other nations use "force"; we Britons alone use "Might." —EVELYN WAUGH

To disagree with three-fourths of the British public is one of the first requisites of sanity. —OSCAR WILDE

BUREAUCRACY
(also see concepts 84, 111, 130, 323, 407)

Bureacracies are designed to perform public business. But as soon as a bureaucracy is established, it develops an autonomous spiritual life and comes to regard the public as its enemy.
—BROOKS ATKINSON

Bureaucracy is a giant mechanism operated by pygmies.
—HONORÉ DE BALZAC

Large organization is loose organization. Nay, it would be almost as true to say that organization is always disorganization.
—G. K. CHESTERTON

The longer the title, the less important the job. —GEORGE MCGOVERN

People who claw their way to the top are not likely to find very much wrong with the system that enabled them to rise.
—ARTHUR SCHLESINGER, JR.

There is something about a bureaucrat that does not like a poem.
—GORE VIDAL

BUSINESS
(also see concepts 9, 78, 85, 88, 135, 231, 241, 661)

Time is the measure of business. —FRANCIS BACON

No matter who reigns, the merchant reigns. —HENRY WARD BEECHER

The commerce of the world is conducted by the strong, and usually it operates against the weak. —HENRY WARD BEECHER

Here's the rule for bargains: "Do other men, for they would do you." That's the true business precept. —CHARLES DICKENS

A business that makes nothing but money is a poor kind of business. —HENRY FORD

Remember that time is money. —BENJAMIN FRANKLIN

There's no such thing as a free lunch. —MILTON FRIEDMAN

Production only fills a void that it has itself created.
—JOHN KENNETH GALBRAITH

It is difficult but not impossible to conduct strictly honest business.
What is true is that honesty is incompatible with the amassing of
a large fortune. —MOHANDAS K. GANDHI

Business is other people's money. —DELPHINE DE GIRARDIN

Honour sinks where commerce long prevails. —OLIVER GOLDSMITH

It is true that America produces and consumes more cars, soap, and
bathtubs than any other nation, but we live among these objects
rather than by them. —MARY MCCARTHY

A financier is a pawn-broker with imagination.
—ARTHUR WING PINERO

The customer is always right. —H. GORDON SELFRIDGE

BUYING AND SELLING

(also see concepts 9, 81, 84, 88)

The urge to consume is fathered by the value system which
emphasizes the ability of the society to produce.
—JOHN KENNETH GALBRAITH

America is a consumer culture, and when we change what we
buy–and how we buy it–we'll change who we are. —FAITH POPCORN

A miser and a liar bargain quickly. —GREEK PROVERB

Everyone lives by selling something. —ROBERT LOUIS STEVENSON

Through want of enterprise and faith men are where they are,
buying and selling, and spending their lives like serfs.
—HENRY DAVID THOREAU

CALMNESS

(also see concepts 604, 709, 728, 740, 771)

Tranquility! thou better name / Than all the family of Fame.
—SAMUEL TAYLOR COLERIDGE

Like water which can clearly mirror the sky and the trees only so long as its surface is undisturbed, the mind can only reflect the true image of the Self when it is tranquil and wholly relaxed.
—INDRA DEVI

Calmness is always Godlike. —RALPH WALDO EMERSON

You will find that deep place of silence right in your room, your garden or even your bathtub. —ELISABETH KÜBLER-ROSS

We are used to the actions of human beings, not to their stillness.
—V. S. PRITCHETT

There is no joy but calm. —ALFRED, LORD TENNYSON

CANADA AND THE CANADIANS

(also see concepts 32, 529)

A Canadian is someone who knows how to make love in a canoe.
—PIERRE BERTON

Americans are benevolently ignorant about Canada, while Canadians are malevolently well informed about the United States.
—J. BARTLET BREBNER

I don't even know what street Canada is on. —AL CAPONE

Canada has never been a melting-pot; more like a tossed salad.
—ARNOLD EDINBOROUGH

In any world menu, Canada must be considered the vichyssoise of nations—it's cold, half-Franch, and difficult to stir. —STUART KEATE

Geography has made us [America and Canada] neighbors. History has made us friends. Economics has made us partners. And necessity has made us allies. Those whom nature hath so joined together, let no man put asunder. —JOHN F. KENNEDY

If Canada is underdeveloped, so is Brigitte Bardot. —H. R. MACMILLAN

When they said Canada, I thought it would be up in the mountains somewhere. —MARILYN MONROE

Canada is useful only to provide me with furs.
—MADAME DE POMPADOUR

CAPITALISM
(also see concepts 231, 628)

Freedom in economic arrangements is itself a component of freedom broadly understood, so economic freedom is an end in itself....Economic freedom is also an indispensable means toward the achievement of political freedom. —MILTON FRIEDMAN

Under capitalism we have a state in the proper sense of the word, that is, a special machine for the suppression of one class by another. —V. I. LENIN

You show me a capitalist, I'll show you a bloodsucker.
—MALCOLM X

Man is the only creature that consumes without producing.
—GEORGE ORWELL

Every man, as long as he does not violate the laws of justice, is left perfectly free to pursue his own interest his own way, and to bring both his industry and capital into competition with those of any other man or order of men. —ADAM SMITH

The trouble with the profit system has always been that it was highly unprofitable to most people. —E. B. WHITE

CAPTIVITY
(also see concepts 299, 747, 810)

If men and women are in chains, anywhere in the world, the freedom is endangered everywhere. —JOHN F. KENNEDY

The narrower the cage, the sweeter the liberty. —GERMAN PROVERB

Man is born free; and everywhere he is in chains.
——JEAN JACQUES ROUSSEAU

He who is conceived in a cage / yearns for the cage.
——YEVGENY YEVTUSHENKO

CAREERS
(also see concepts 11, 232, 443, 829, 846, 869, 870)

The price one pays for pursuing any profession, or calling, is an intimate knowledge of its ugly side. ——JAMES BALDWIN

Blessed is he who has found his work; let him ask no other blessedness. ——THOMAS CARLYLE

The secret of long life is double careers. One to about age sixty, then another for the next thirty years. ——DAVID OGILVY

It's necessary to be slightly underemployed if you are to do something significant. ——JAMES WATSON

CAREFULNESS
(also see concepts 153, 311, 624, 633, 694, 863)

Look twice before you leap. ——CHARLOTTE BRONTË

Avoiding danger is no safer in the long run than outright exposure. The fearful are caught as often as the bold. ——HELEN KELLER

The torment of precautions often exceeds the dangers to be avoided. It is sometimes better to abandon one's self to destiny.
——NAPOLEON I

Measure a thousand times and cut once. ——TURKISH PROVERB

CATS
(also see concepts 37, 221)

Cats are intended to teach us that not everything in nature has a purpose. ——GARRISON KEILLOR

Cats seem to go on the principle that it never does any harm to ask for what you want. —JOSEPH WOOD KRUTCH

If a fish is the movement of water embodied, given shape, then a cat is a diagram and pattern of subtle air. —DORIS LESSING

No matter how much cats fight, there always seem to be plenty of kittens. —ABRAHAM LINCOLN

If a dog jumps onto your lap it is because he is fond of you; but if a cat does the same thing it is because your lap is warmer. —ALFRED NORTH WHITEHEAD

CAUSE AND EFFECT
(also see concepts 62, 97, 152, 488)

Nothing comes from nothing. —LUCRETIUS

Every why hath a wherefore. —WILLIAM SHAKESPEARE

There's no limit to how complicated things can get, on account of one thing always leading to another. —E. B. WHITE

CAUSES
(also see concepts 61, 112, 152, 480, 519)

A just cause is not ruined by a few mistakes. —FYODOR DOSTOYEVSKY

He that hath the worst cause makes the most noise. —THOMAS FULLER

Truth never damages a cause that is just. —MOHANDAS K. GANDHI

It is characteristic of all movements and crusades that the psychopathic element rises to the top. —ROBERT LINDNER

In a just cause the weak will beat the strong. —SOPHOCLES

CENSORSHIP

(also see concepts 54, 171, 456, 706, 740)

Censorship is the tool of those who have the need to hide actualities from themselves and others. Their fear is only their inability to face what is real. Somewhere in their upbringing they were shielded against the total facts of our experience. They were only taught to look one way when many ways exist. —CHARLES BUKOWSKI

Literature is one of the few areas left where black and white feel some identity of purpose; we all struggle under censorship. —NADINE GORDIMER

Persons who undertake to pry into, or cleanse out all the filth of a common sewer, either cannot have very nice noses, or will soon lose them. —WILLIAM HAZLITT

Whenever books are burned men also in the end are burned. —HEINRICH HEINE

To limit the press is to insult a nation; to prohibit reading of certain books is to declare the inhabitants to be either fools or slaves. —CLAUDE-ADRIEN HELVÉTIUS

No government ought to be without censors; and where the press is free, no one ever will. —THOMAS JEFFERSON

They can't censor the gleam in my eye. —CHARLES LAUGHTON

The problem of freedom in America is that of maintaining a competition of ideas, and you do not achieve that by silencing one brand of idea. —MAX LERNER

Men in earnest have no time to waste / In patching fig leaves for the naked truth. —JAMES RUSSELL LOWELL

Censorship may be useful for the preservation of morality, but can never be so for its restoration. —JEAN JACQUES ROUSSEAU

I call upon the intellectual community in this country and abroad to stand up for freedom of imagination, an issue much larger than my book or indeed my life. —SALMAN RUSHDIE

Art made tongue-tied by authority. —WILLIAM SHAKESPEARE

Assassination is the extreme form of censorship.
——GEORGE BERNARD SHAW

I believe in censorship. After all, I made a fortune out of it.
——MAE WEST

God forbid that any book should be banned. The practice is as indefensible as infanticide. ——REBECCA WEST

The books that the world calls immoral are the books that show the world its own shame. ——OSCAR WILDE

CERTAINTY
(also see concepts 145, 153, 202, 222, 279, 397, 579, 694)

There is one thing certain, namely, that we can have nothing certain; therefore it is not certain that we can have nothing certain.
——SAMUEL BUTLER

One certainty we all accept is the condition of being uncertain and insecure. ——DORIS LESSING

Certainties are arrived at only on foot. ——ANTONIO PORCHIA

He who knows nothing doubts nothing. ——SPANISH PROVERB

CHANCE
(also see concepts 279, 471, 556, 808)

Accident counts for as much in companionship as in marriage.
——HENRY BROOKS ADAMS

Of all the gin joints in all the towns in the world, she walks into mine. ——HUMPHREY BOGART

Living at risk is jumping off the cliff and building your wings on the way down. ——RAY BRADBURY

They who lose today may win tomorrow. ——MIGUEL DE CERVANTES

And the trouble is, if you don't risk anything, you risk even more.
——ERICA JONG

Fortune and humour govern the world.
——FRANÇOIS DE LA ROCHEFOUCAULD

There is many a slip 'twixt the cup and the lip. ——PALLADIUS

CHANGE

(also see concepts 250, 389, 669)

The absurd man is he who never changes. ——AUGUSTE BARTHÉLEMY

Change your life today. Don't gamble on the future, act now, without delay. ——SIMONE DE BEAUVOIR

I reject get-it-done, make-it-happen thinking. I want to slow things down so I understand them better. ——JERRY BROWN

All is change; all yields its place and goes. ——EURIPIDES

All changes, even the most longed for, have their melancholy; for what we leave behind us is a part of ourselves; we must die to one life before we can enter into another! ——ANATOLE FRANCE

Most of the change we think we see in life / Is due to truths being in and out of favor. ——ROBERT FROST

With me a change of trouble is as good as a vacation.
——WILLIAM LLOYD GEORGE

Nobody told me how hard and lonely change is. ——JOAN GILBERTSON

Nothing is permanent but change. ——HERACLITUS

There is a certain relief in change, even though it be from bad to worse. ——WASHINGTON IRVING

The more things change, the more they remain the same.
——ALPHONSE KARR

The moment of change is the only poem. ——ADRIENNE RICH

Things do not change, we do. ——HENRY DAVID THOREAU

There is a time for departure even when there's no certain place to go. ——TENNESSEE WILLIAMS

CHAOS
(also see concepts 34, 148, 217, 561)

There is nothing stable in the world; uproar's your only music.
—JOHN KEATS

Chaos in the midst of chaos isn't funny, but chaos in the midst of order is. —STEVE MARTIN

CHARACTER
(also see concepts 207, 364, 531, 580, 708, 843)

Character builds slowly, but it can be torn down with incredible swiftness. —FAITH BALDWIN

As he thinketh in his heart, so is he. —BIBLE, PROVERBS 23:7

Character contributes to beauty. It fortifies a woman as her youth fades. —JACQUELINE BISSET

Every man is as Heaven made him, and sometimes a great deal worse. —MIGUEL DE CERVANTES

Character–the willingness to accept responsibility for one's own life–is the source from which self-respect springs. —JOAN DIDION

People seem not to see that their opinion of the world is also a confession of character. —RALPH WALDO EMERSON

As if they were our own handiwork, we place a high value on our characters. —EPICURUS

...the final forming of a person's character lies in their own hands.
—ANNE FRANK

Old age and sickness bring out the essential characteristics of a man. —FELIX FRANKFURTER

Talent develops in quiet places, character in the full current of human life. —JOHANN WOLFGANG VON GOETHE

You can't go around hoping that most people have sterling moral characters. The most you can hope for is that people will pretend that they do. —FRAN LEBOWITZ

Character is much easier kept than recovered. —THOMAS PAINE

Character is injured habit. —PLUTARCH

Character is an essential tendency. It can be covered up, it can be messed with, it can be screwed around with, but it can't be ultimately changed. It's like the structure of our bones, the blood that runs through our veins. —SAM SHEPARD

CHARITY
(also see concepts 295, 309, 314, 367, 438, 588, 660, 735, 809)

The living need charity more than the dead. —GEORGE ARNOLD

In charity there is no excess. —FRANCIS BACON

Did a universal charity prevail, earth would be a heaven, and hell a fable. —CHARLES CALEB COLTON

Charity begins at home, but should not end there. —THOMAS FULLER

Charity begins at home. —PROVERB

The white man knows how to make everything, but he does not know how to distribute it. —SITTING BULL

To keep a lamp burning we have to keep putting oil in it.
—MOTHER TERESA

Charity and personal force are the only investments worth anything.
—WALT WHITMAN

I have always depended on the kindness of strangers.
—TENNESSEE WILLIAMS

CHARM
(also see concepts 324, 776, 799)

Charm: that quality in others of making us more satisfied with ourselves. —HENRI FRÉDÉRIC AMIEL

All charming people have something to conceal, usually their total dependence on the appreciation of others. —CYRIL CONNOLLY

Charm is a product of the unexpected. —JOSÉ MARTÍ

It's absurd to divide people into good and bad. People are either charming or tedious. —OSCAR WILDE

CHASTITY
(also see concepts 127, 188, 404, 731, 843)

Give me chastity and continence, but not yet.
—ST. AUGUSTINE OF HIPPO

Be warm, but pure; be amorous, but be chaste. —LORD BYRON

Chastity is not chastity in an old man, but a disability to be unchaste. —JOHN DONNE

It is fatally easy for Western folk, who have discarded chastity as a value for themselves, to suppose that it can have no value for anyone else. At the same time as Californians try to re-invent "celibacy," by which they seem to mean perverse restraint, the rest of us call societies which place a high value on chastity "backward."
—GERMAINE GREER

CHEERFULNESS
(also see concepts 237, 337, 433)

Good nature is worth more than knowledge, more than money, more than honor, to the persons who possess it.
—HENRY WARD BEECHER

Of cheerfulness, or a good temper–the more it is spent, the more it remains. —RALPH WALDO EMERSON

Cheerfulness, sir, is the principle ingredient in the composition of health. —ARTHUR MURPHY

CHICAGO
(also see concepts 32, 113)

This is virgin territory for whorehouses. —AL CAPONE

Chicago has a strange metaphysical elegance of death about it.
——CLAES OLDENBURG

CHILDREN
(also see concepts 24, 69, 160, 273, 280, 384, 518, 566, 876)

It was no wonder that people were so horrible when they started life as children. ——KINGSLEY AMIS

Children sweeten labours, but they make misfortunes more bitter. ——FRANCIS BACON

Children have never been very good at listening to their elders, but they have never failed to imitate them. ——JAMES BALDWIN

It goes without saying that you should never have more children than you have car windows. ——ERMA BOMBECK

Our children are not treated with sufficient respect as human beings, and yet from the moment they are born they have this right to respect. We keep them children far too long, their world separate from the real world of life. ——PEARL S. BUCK

There is no finer investment for any community than putting milk into babies. ——WINSTON CHURCHILL

When I was a kid my parents moved a lot–but I always found them. ——RODNEY DANGERFIELD

Every baby born into the world is a finer one than the last. ——CHARLES DICKENS

One of the things I've discovered in general about raising kids is that they really don't give a damn if you walked five miles to school. They want to deal with what's happening now. ——PATTY DUKE

There never was child so lovely but his mother was glad to get him asleep. ——RALPH WALDO EMERSON

Anybody who hates children and dogs can't be all bad. ——W. C. FIELDS

Let your children go if you want to keep them. ——MALCOLM FORBES

Children are completely egoistic; they feel their needs intensely and strive ruthlessly to satisfy them. —SIGMUND FREUD

Your children are not your children. / They are the sons and daughters of Life's longing for itself. —KAHLIL GIBRAN

No one has yet fully realized the wealth of sympathy, kindness and generosity hidden in the soul of a child. The effort of every true education should be to unlock that treasure... —EMMA GOLDMAN

Pretty much all the honest truth telling there is in the world is done by children. —OLIVER WENDELL HOLMES, SR.

Families with babies and families without babies are sorry for each other. —EDGAR WATSON HOWE

One of the most obvious facts about grown-ups to a child is that they have forgotten what it is like to be a child. —RANDALL JARRELL

Children need models rather than critics. —JOSEPH JOUBERT

What its children become, that will the community become. —SUZANNE LAFOLLETTE

A sweet child is the sweetest thing in nature. —CHARLES LAMB

A child is fed with milk and praise. —MARY LAMB

Even when freshly washed and relieved of all obvious confections, children tend to be sticky. —FRAN LEBOWITZ

A torn jacket is soon mended; but hard words bruise the heart of a child. —HENRY WADSWORTH LONGFELLOW

Everywhere, everywhere, children are the scorned people of the earth. —TONI MORRISON

Who knows the thoughts of a child? —NORA PERRY

Children are poor men's riches. —ENGLISH PROVERB

Spare the rod and spoil the child. —PROVERB

Some of my best friends are children. In fact, all of my best friends are children. —J. D. SALINGER

Children are natural mythologists: they beg to be told tales, and love not only to invent but to enact falsehoods. —GEORGE SANTAYANA

Parents learn a lot from their children about coping with life. —MURIEL SPARK

Children require guidance and sympathy far more than instruction. —ANNE SULLIVAN

Don't set your wit against a child. —JONATHAN SWIFT

An ugly baby is a very nasty object, and the prettiest is frightful when undressed. —QUEEN VICTORIA

Never have children, only grandchildren. —GORE VIDAL

My children weary me. I can only see them as defective adults: feckless, destructive, frivolous, sensual, humorless. —EVELYN WAUGH

Children begin by loving their parents. After a time they judge them. Rarely, if ever, do they forgive them. —OSCAR WILDE

We are given children to test us and make us more spiritual. —GEORGE F. WILL

CHOICE
(also see concepts 189, 200, 299, 555, 847)

What man wants is simply independent choice, whatever that may cost and wherever it may lead. —FYODOR DOSTOYEVSKY

It is your own conviction which compels you; that is, choice compels choice. —EPICTETUS

The difficulty in life is the choice. —GEORGE MOORE

We have to believe in free will. We've got no choice. —ISAAC BASHEVIS SINGER

CHRISTIANITY

(also see concepts 101, 109, 110, 121, 269, 295, 316, 317, 369, 668, 696, 802)

The glory of Christianity is to conquer by forgiveness.
——WILLIAM BLAKE

How very hard it is / To be a Christian! ——ROBERT BROWNING

The three great elements of modern civilization, gunpowder, printing, and the Protestant religion. ——THOMAS CARLYLE

Christianity has done a great deal for love by making a sin of it.
——ANATOLE FRANCE

Almost every sect of Christianity is a perversion of its essence, to accommodate it to the prejudices of the world. ——WILLIAM HAZLITT

The Papacy is not other than the Ghost of the deceased Roman Empire, sitting crowned upon the grave therof. ——THOMAS HOBBES

Christianity supplies a Hell for the people who disagree with you and Heaven for your friends. ——ELBERT HUBBARD

The chief contribution of Protestantism to human thought is its massive proof that God is a bore. ——H. L. MENCKEN

No kingdom has ever had as many civil wars as the kingdom of Christ. ——BARON DE MONTESQUIEU

One cannot really be a Catholic and grown-up. ——GEORGE ORWELL

Christianity has made of death a terror which was unknown to the gay calmness of the Pagan. ——OUIDA

The Catholic must adopt the decision handed down to him; the Protestant must learn to decide for himself. ——JEAN JACQUES ROUSSEAU

Christianity is the most materialistic of all great religions.
——WILLIAM TEMPLE

CHRISTMAS

(also see concepts 108, 309, 314, 349, 660)

How many observe Christ's birthday! How few, his precepts! O! 'tis easier to keep holidays than commandments.
—BENJAMIN FRANKLIN

At Christmas play and make good cheer, / For Christmas comes but once a year. —THOMAS TUSSER

To perceive Christmas through its wrapping becomes more difficult with every year. —E. B. WHITE

CHURCH

(also see concepts 108, 121, 176, 407, 431, 668, 802, 873)

I have no objections to churches so long as they do not interfere with God's work. —BROOKS ATKINSON

And of all plagues with which mankind are curst, / Ecclesiastic tyranny's the worst. —DANIEL DEFOE

No temple can still the personal griefs and strifes in the breasts of its visitors. —MARGARET FULLER

Many come to bring their clothes to church rather than themselves.
—THOMAS FULLER

My own mind is my own church. —THOMAS PAINE

He who is near the Church is often far from God. —FRENCH PROVERB

She say, Celie, tell the truth, have you ever found God in church? I never did. I just found a bunch of folks hoping for him to show. Any God I ever felt in church I brought in with me. And I think all the other folks did too. They come to church to share God, not find God. —ALICE WALKER

CHURCH AND STATE
(also see concepts 83, 407, 767)

Render to Caesar the things that are Ceasar's, and to God the things that are God's. —BIBLE, MARK 12:17

All religions united with government are more or less inimical to liberty. All separated from government are compatible with liberty. —HENRY CLAY

In all ages, hypocrites, called priests, have put crowns upon the heads of thieves, called kings. —ROBERT G. INGERSOLL

CIRCUMSTANCE
(also see concepts 94, 200, 248, 556, 654)

Man is not the creature of circumstances. Circumstances are the creatures of men. —BENJAMIN DISRAELI

It is nice to make heroic decisions and to be prevented by "circumstances beyond your control" from ever trying to execute them. —WILLIAM JAMES

Circumstances! I make circumstances! —NAPOLEON I

If all our happiness is bound up entirely in our personal circumstances it is difficult not to demand of life more than it has to give. —BERTRAND RUSSELL

The people who get on in this world are the people who get up and look for the circumstances they want, and, if they can't find them, make them. —GEORGE BERNARD SHAW

CITIES
(also see concepts 79, 105, 116, 416, 461, 537, 567, 589, 777)

A great city is not be confounded with a populous one. —ARISTOTLE

A ghetto can be improved in one way only: out of existence. —JAMES BALDWIN

If you would be known, and not know, vegetate in a village; if you would know, and not be known, live in a city.
—CHARLES CALEB COLTON

The big cities of America are becoming Third World countries.
—NORA EPHRON

The planner's problem is to find ways of creating, within the urban environment, the sense of belonging. —LEO MARX

I'd rather wake up in the middle of nowhere than in any city on earth. —STEVE MCQUEEN

The city is not a concrete jungle. It is a human zoo.
—DESMOND MORRIS

What is the city but the people? —WILLIAM SHAKESPEARE

City Life. Millions of people being lonesome together.
—HENRY DAVID THOREAU

The thing generally raised on city land is taxes.
—CHARLES DUDLEY WARNER

Commuters give the city its tidal restlessness; natives give it solidity and continuity; but the settlers give it passion. —E. B. WHITE

A great city is that which has the greatest men and women.
—WALT WHITMAN

CITIZENSHIP

(also see concepts 134, 195, 323, 602, 767, 794, 847)

It is not always the same thing to be a good man and a good citizen.
—ARISTOTLE

Man exists for his own sake and not to add a laborer to the State.
—RALPH WALDO EMERSON

The job of a citizen is to keep his mouth open. —GÜNTER GRASS

To establish a state on any other principle than the civic principle –on the principle of ideology, of nationality or religion for instance –means making one aspect of our home superior to all the others, and thus reduces us as people, reduces our natural world. And that hardly ever leads to anything good. —VÁCLAV HAVEL

In America there must be only citizens, not divided by grade, first and second, but citizens, east, west, north, and south. —JOHN F. KENNEDY

The citizen is influenced by principle in direct proportion to his distance from the political situation. —MILTON RAKOVE

The first requisite of a good citizen in this republic of ours is that he shall be able and willing to pull his weight. —THEODORE ROOSEVELT

Every subject's duty is the King's, but every subject's soul is his own. —WILLIAM SHAKESPEARE

All the citizens of a state cannot be equally powerful, but they may be equally free. —VOLTAIRE

CIVIL RIGHTS
(also see concepts 2, 157, 283, 298, 365, 617)

There was a whole human rights movement happening. It was called various things, but we always had the concerns of all oppressed people in mind. We focused on race, because of the phenomenon of black people in America. But we had always worked with poor whites, with Native Americans here in California, with Latinos here and in New York. This is what drew me to the Blank Panther Party–that expansive understanding. All power to the people really meant that. —ERIKA HUGGINS

A lot of things happened after the civil rights movement, where we were making great strides and progress. Somewhere from the end of the Sixties up to now, we got off the path. Or we were led off the path. —SPIKE LEE

CIVILIZATION

(also see concepts 99, 177, 190, 368, 416, 531, 597, 625, 754)

We are born princes and the civilizing process makes us frogs.
—ERIC BERNE

The test of a civilization is in the way that it cares for its helpless members. —PEARL BUCK

The three great elements of modern civilization, Gunpowder, Printing and the Protestant Religion. —THOMAS CARLYLE

The modern world...has no notion except that of simplifying something by destroying nearly everything. —G. K. CHESTERTON

The civilization of one epoch becomes the manure of the next.
—CYRIL CONNOLLY

Increased means and increased leisure are the two civilisers of man. —BENJAMIN DISRAELI

In a state of nature, the weakest go to the wall; in a state of over-refinement, both the weak and the strong go to the gutter.
—ELBERT HUBBARD

Civilization is a perishable commodity. —HELEN MACINNES

We are all born charming, fresh, and spontaneous and must be civilized before we are fit to participate in society. —JUDITH MARTIN

The degree of a nation's civilization is marked by its disregard for the necessities of existence. —W. SOMERSET MAUGHAM

You can't say civilization don't advance...for in every war they kill you a new way. —WILL ROGERS

Civilization is the making of civil persons. —JOHN RUSKIN

Every advance in civilization has been denounced as unnatural while it was recent. —BERTRAND RUSSELL

A civilization is built on what is required of men, not on that which is provided for them. —ANTOINE DE SAINT-EXUPÉRY

Soap and education are not as sudden as a massacre, but they are more deadly in the long run. —MARK TWAIN

The glossy surface of our civilization hides a real intellectual decadence. —SIMONE WEIL

CLARITY
(also see concepts 80, 440, 553, 646, 742)

Besides learning to see, there is another art to be learned–not to see what is not. —MARIA MITCHELL

A matter that becomes clear ceases to concern us.
—FRIEDRICH WILHELM NIETZSCHE

CLASS
(also see concepts 44, 498, 606, 607, 654, 753, 776)

All the world over, I will back the masses against the classes.
—WILLIAM EWART GLADSTONE

Dialect words–those terrible marks of the beast to the truly genteel.
—THOMAS HARDY

In class society everyone lives as a member of a particular class, and every kind of thinking, without exception, is stamped with the brand of class. —MAO TSE-TUNG

The history of all hitherto existing society is the history of class struggles. —KARL MARX

There's one law for the rich, and another for the poor. —PROVERB

The upper classes are merely a nation's past; the middle class is its future. —AYN RAND

We must be thoroughly democratic and patronise everybody without distinction of class. —GEORGE BERNARD SHAW

The constitution does not provide for first and second class citizens. —WENDELL LEWIS WILLKIE

THE CLASSICS
(also see concepts 46, 328, 459, 811)

The praise of ancient authors proceeds not from the reverence of the dead, but from the competition and mutual envy of the living. —THOMAS HOBBES

What a sense of security in an old book which Time has criticized for us! —JAMES RUSSELL LOWELL

Every man with a belly full of the classics is an enemy of the human race. —HENRY MILLER

Classic. A book which people praise and don't read. —MARK TWAIN

In Art, the public accept what has been, because they cannot alter it, not because they appreciate it. They swallow their classics whole, and never taste them. —OSCAR WILDE

CLEANLINESS
(also see concepts 95, 363, 515, 600, 646, 742, 843)

Cleanliness is not next to godliness nowadays, for cleanliness is made an essential and godliness is regarded as an offence. —G. K. CHESTERTON

People who wash much have a high mind about it, and talk down to those who wash little. —RALPH WALDO EMERSON

Hygiene is the corruption of medicine by morality. —H. I. MENCKEN

What separates two people most profoundly is a different sense and degree of cleanliness. —FRIEDRICH WILHELM NIETZSCHE

CLERGY
(also see concepts 4, 108, 110, 431, 611, 668, 802)

The clergyman is expected to be a kind of human Sunday. —SAMUEL BUTLER

For clergy are men as well as other folks. —HENRY FIELDING

A broad hat does not always cover a venerable head.
—THOMAS FULLER

Priests are no more necessary to religion than politicians to patriotism. —JOHN HAYNES HOLMES

A man who is good enough to go to heaven is good enough to be a clergyman. —SAMUEL JOHNSON

Satan hasn't a single salaried helper; the Opposition employ a million. —MARK TWAIN

CLEVERNESS
(also see concepts 128, 131, 178, 411, 644, 649, 863, 866)

It is a profitable thing, if one is wise, to seem foolish. —AESCHYLUS

The bold are helpless without cleverness. —EURIPIDES

The height of cleverness is to be able to conceal it.
—FRANÇOIS DE LA ROCHEFOUCAULD

Here's a good rule of thumb: / Too clever is dumb. —OGDEN NASH

Some people will never learn anything, for this reason, because they understand every thing too soon. —ALEXANDER POPE

The devil can cite Scripture for his purpose. —WILLIAM SHAKESPEARE

It is never wise to try to appear to be more clever than you are. It is sometimes wise to appear slightly less so. —WILLIAM WHITELAW

CLOSED-MINDEDNESS
(also see concepts 220, 237, 774, 775)

A closed mind is a dying mind. —EDNA FERBER

He who knows only his own side of the case, knows little of that.
—JOHN STUART MILL

It is with narrow-souled people as with narrow-necked bottles: the less they have in them, the more noise they make in pouring it out.
—ALEXANDER POPE

All living souls welcome whatsoever they are ready to cope with; all else they ignore, or pronounce to be monstrous and wrong, or deny to be possible. —GEORGE SANTAYANA

Beware of the man of one book. —ST. THOMAS AQUINAS

CLOTHES AND CLOTHING
(also see concepts 39, 74, 277, 547)

It is not only fine feathers that make fine birds. —AESOP

From the cradle to the coffin underwear comes first.
—BERTOLT BRECHT

Know, first, who you are; and then adorn yourself accordingly.
—EPICTETUS

Good clothes open all doors. —THOMAS FULLER

Those who make their dress a principal part of themselves, will, in general, become of no more value than their dress.
—WILLIAM HAZLITT

Fine clothes are good only as they supply the want of other means of procuring respect. —SAMUEL JOHNSON

The apparel oft proclaims the man. —WILLIAM SHAKESPEARE

Beware of all enterprises that require new clothes, and not rather a new wearer of clothes. —HENRY DAVID THOREAU

Let me be dressed fine as I will, / Flies, worms, and flowers, exceed me still. —ISAAC WATTS

You can say what you like about long dresses, but they cover a multitude of shins. —MAE WEST

COFFEE
(also see concepts 12, 225, 226, 516, 677)

The morning cup of coffee has an exhilaration about it which the cheering influence of the afternoon or evening cup of tea cannot be expected to reproduce. —OLIVER WENDELL HOLMES, SR.

Coffee should be black as Hell, strong as death, and sweet as love.
——TURKISH PROVERB

THE COLD WAR
(also see concepts 133, 378, 415, 546, 691)

Let us not be deceived–we are today in the midst of a cold war.
——BERNARD M. BARUCH

An iron curtain has descended across the continent.
——WINSTON CHURCHILL

The Cold War supplied both the economic and iconographic
staples of American politics, and the belief in the Soviet Union as
the Land of Mordor furnished the cover story for official sleights
of hand that otherwise might have been seen as dishonest, stingy,
or murderous. ——LEWIS H. LAPHAM

COLDNESS
(also see concepts 103, 174, 237, 392, 771)

To spare oneself from grief at all cost can be achieved only at the
price of total detachment, which excludes the ability to experience
happiness. ——ERICH FROMM

By keeping men off, you keep them on. ——JOHN GAY

Are you then unable to recognize a sob unless it has the same sound
as yours? ——ANDRÉ GIDE

Reserve is an artificial quality that is developed in most of us but
as the result of innumerable rebuffs. ——W. SOMERSET MAUGHAM

You do not see the river of mourning because it lacks one tear of
your own. ——ANTONIO PORCHIA

For an impenetrable shield, stand inside yourself.
——HENRY DAVID THOREAU

COMEDY

(also see concepts 48, 370, 424, 442, 699)

Comedy is tragedy plus time. —CAROL BURNETT

In the end, everything is a gag. —CHARLIE CHAPLIN

It is very difficult to be wholly joyous or wholly sad on this earth. The comic, when it is human, soon takes upon itself the face of pain. —JOSEPH CONRAD

Who are a little wise, the best fools be. —JOHN DONNE

Comedy, like sodomy, is an unnatural act. —MARTY FELDMAN

We participate in a tragedy; at a comedy we only look. —ALDOUS HUXLEY

The funny bone is universal. —BERNARD MALAMUD

Comedy may be big business, but it isn't pretty. —STEVE MARTIN

Comedy is the last refuge of the nonconformist mind. —GILBERT SELDES

If tragedy is an experience of hyperinvolvement, comedy is an experience of underinvolvement, of detachment. —SUSAN SONTAG

The only rules comedy can tolerate are those of taste, and the only limitations those of libel. —JAMES THURBER

COMMITMENT

(also see concepts 20, 421, 549, 626, 676)

Something must happen—that explains most human commitments. Something must happen, even servitude without love, even war, or death. —ALBERT CAMUS

He is poor indeed that can promise nothing. —THOMAS FULLER

COMMITTEES
(also see concept 83)

Committee–a group of men who keep minutes and waste hours.
—MILTON BERLE

A committee is a thing which takes a week to do what one good man can do in an hour. —ELBERT HUBBARD

The heaping together of paintings by Old Masters in museums is a catastrophe; likewise, a collection of a hundred Great Brains makes one big fathead. —CARL JUNG

COMMON SENSE
(also see concepts 122, 791, 843, 863)

Nothing astonishes men so much as common sense and plain dealing. —RALPH WALDO EMERSON

The best prophet is common sense, our native wit. —EURIPIDES

Common sense is not so uncommon. —HORACE GREELEY

COMMUNICATION
(also see concepts 7, 27, 38, 43, 162, 441, 449, 457, 662, 761)

Much unhappiness has come into the world because of bewilderment and things left unsaid. —FYODOR DOSTOYEVSKY

When the eyes say one thing, and the tongue another, a practiced man relies on the language of the first. —RALPH WALDO EMERSON

No one would talk so much in society, if he only knew how often he misunderstands others. —JOHANN WOLFGANG VON GOETHE

Unless one is a genius, it is best to aim at being intelligible.
—ANTHONY HOPE HAWKINS

The opposite of talking isn't listening. The opposite of talking is waiting. —FRAN LEBOWITZ

Good communication is as stimulating as black coffee, and just as hard to sleep after. —ANNE MORROW LINDBERGH

I distrust the incommunicable; it is the source of all violence.
——JEAN-PAUL SARTRE

COMMUNISM

(also see concepts 126, 231, 378, 810)

Communism is like one big phone company. ——LENNY BRUCE

One strength of the communist system of the East is that it has some of the character of a religion and inspires the emotions of a religion.
——ALBERT EINSTEIN

What is a communist? One who hath yearnings / For equal division of unequal earnings. ——EBENEZER ELLIOTT

Communists have committed great crimes, but at least they have not stood aside, like an established society, and been indifferent. I would rather have blood on my hands than water like Pilate.
——GRAHAM GREENE

Every year humanity takes a step towards Communism. Maybe not you, but at all events your grandson will surely be a Communist.
——NIKITA KHRUSHCHEV

Communism is Soviet power plus the electrification of the whole country. ——V. I. LENIN

Cow of many—well milked and badly fed. ——SPANISH PROVERB

Communism is like Prohibition, it's a good idea but it won't work.
——WILL ROGERS

For us in Russia communism is a dead dog, while, for many people in the West, it is still a living lion. ——ALEXANDER SOLZHENITSYN

Every communist has a fascist frown, every fascist a communist smile. ——MURIEL SPARK

Communism is the corruption of a dream of justice.
——ADLAI STEVENSON

COMMUNITY

(also see concepts 30, 135, 300, 394, 533, 576, 589, 602, 754)

When the head aches, all the members partake of the pain.
——MIGUEL DE CERVANTES

No man is an island, entire of itself; every man is a piece of the continent. ——JOHN DONNE

Life is lived in common, but not in the community.
——MICHAEL HARRINGTON

Your own safety is at stake when your neighbor's wall is ablaze.
——HORACE

What is not good for the swarm is not good for the bee.
——MARCUS AURELIUS

There can be no vulnerability without risk; there can be no community without vulnerability; there can be no peace, and ultimately no life, without community. ——M. SCOTT PECK

An isolated individual does not exist. He who is sad, saddens others. ——ANTOINE DE SAINT-EXUPÉRY

I am part of all that I have met. ——ALFRED, LORD TENNYSON

COMPANY

(also see concepts 134, 173, 300, 568, 754)

Not only is there no question of solitude, but in the long run we may not choose our company. ——ELIZABETH BOWEN

To be social is to be forgiving. ——ROBERT FROST

I live in the crowd of jollity, no so much to enjoy company as to shun myself. ——SAMUEL JOHNSON

Society in shipwreck is a comfort to all. ——PUBLILIUS SYRUS

What men call social virtues, good fellowship, is commonly but the virtue of pigs in a litter, which lie close together to keep each other warm. ——HENRY DAVID THOREAU

COMPARISON

(also see concepts 161, 244, 396, 741)

In the country of the blind, the one-eyed man is king.
——MICHAEL APOSTOLIUS

Analogies, it is true, decide nothing, but they can make one feel more at home. ——SIGMUND FREUD

Nothing is good or bad but by comparison. ——THOMAS FULLER

I murmured because I had no shoes, until I met a man who had no feet. ——PERSIAN PROVERB

The man with toothache thinks everyone happy whose teeth are sound. The poverty stricken man makes the same mistake about the rich man. ——GEORGE BERNARD SHAW

COMPETITION

(also see concepts 15, 192, 285, 430, 557, 765)

Competitions are for horses, not artists. ——BÉLA BARTÓK

He may well win the race that runs by himself.
——BENJAMIN FRANKLIN

Man is a gaming animal. He must be always trying to get the better in something or other. ——CHARLES LAMB

A horse never runs so fast as when he has other horses to catch up and outpace. ——OVID

The combative instinct is a savage prompting by which one man's good is found in another's evil. ——GEORGE SANTAYANA

COMPLAINTS

(also see concepts 520, 631)

Those who do not complain are never pitied. ——JANE AUSTEN

The wheel that squeaks the loudest / Is the one that gets the grease.
——JOSH BILLINGS

The world is disgracefully managed, one hardly knows to whom to complain. —RONALD FIRBANK

When people cease to complain, they cease to think.
—NAPOLEON I

The dog barks, but the caravan moves on. —ARABIC PROVERB

He that falls by himself never cries. —TURKISH PROVERB

COMPLIMENTS
(also see concepts 41, 288, 494, 610)

Nothing is so silly as the expression of a man who is being complimented. —ANDRÉ GIDE

A compliment is something like a kiss through a veil.
—VICTOR HUGO

When you cannot get a compliment in any other way pay yourself one. —MARK TWAIN

Women are never disarmed by compliments. Men always are.
—OSCAR WILDE

COMPROMISE
(also see concepts 13, 27, 143, 545, 662)

If one could recover the uncompromising spirit of one's youth, one's greatest indignation would be for what one has become.
—ANDRÉ GIDE

A lean compromise is better than a fat lawsuit. —GEORGE HERBERT

Compromise, if not the spice of life, is its solidity.
—PHYLLIS MCGINLEY

COMPUTERS

(also see concepts 460, 474, 796, 820)

The computer is only a fast idiot, it has no imagination; it cannot originate action. It is, and will remain, only a tool to man.
—AMERICAN LIBRARY ASSOCIATION STATEMENT ON UNIVAC COMPUTER EXHIBITED AT NEW YORK WORLD'S FAIR, 1964.

One of the most feared expressions in modern times is "The computer is down." —NORMAN AUGUSTINE

Man is still the most extraordinary computer of all.
—JOHN F. KENNEDY

Computers are useless. They can only give you answers.
—PABLO PICASSO

We live in a time when automation is ushering in a second industrial revolution. —ADLAI STEVENSON

Personal computer security is still an oxymoron. —DANIEL WHITE

If it keeps up, man will atrophy all his limbs but the push-button finger. —FRANK LLOYD WRIGHT

CONCENTRATION

(also see concepts 8, 500, 772, 831)

A straight path never leads anywhere except to the objective.
—ANDRÉ GIDE

...when a man knows he is to be hanged in a fortnight, it concentrates his mind wonderfully. —SAMUEL JOHNSON

When you are at sea, keep clear of the land. —PUBLILIUS SYRUS

CONCILIATION

(also see concepts 27, 140, 208, 575, 755, 824)

Be swift to hear, slow to speak, slow to wrath. —BIBLE, JAMES 1:19

It behooves a prudent person to make trial of everything before arms. —TERENCE

CONFESSION
(also see concepts 7, 263, 743, 875)

A generous confession disarms slander. —THOMAS FULLER

Confession of our faults is the next thing to innocence.
—PUBLILIUS SYRUS

It is not the criminal things which are hardest to confess, but the ridiculous and shameful. —JEAN JACQUES ROUSSEAU

CONFIDENCE
(also see concepts 1, 96, 196, 237, 259, 262, 357, 720, 722, 817)

Danger breeds best on too much confidence. —PIERRE CORNEILLE

Good swimmers are oftenest drowned. —THOMAS FULLER

As is our confidence, so is our capacity. —WILLIAM HAZLITT

It generally happens that assurance keeps an even pace with ability.
—SAMUEL JOHNSON

There's one blessing only, the source and cornerstone of beatitude
–confidence in self. —SENECA

They can do all because they think they can. —VIRGIL

CONFLICT, INNER
(also see concepts 557, 564, 634, 635, 714, 718)

No, when the fight begins within himself, / A man's worth something. —ROBERT BROWNING

Two souls dwell, alas, in my breast.
—JOHANN WOLFGANG VON GOETHE

Let me say to begin with: It is not neurotic to have conflicts....
Conflicts within ourselves are an integral part of human life.
—KAREN HORNEY

Sometimes I want to clean up my desk and go out and say, respect me, I'm a respectable grown-up, and other times I just want to jump

into a paper bag and shake and bake myself to death.
—WENDY WASSERSTEIN

CONFORMITY
(also see concepts 13, 54, 217, 394, 548, 741, 770, 830)

Take the tone of the company you are in. —EARL OF CHESTERFIELD

Conformity is the ape of harmony. —RALPH WALDO EMERSON

Conformity is the jailer of freedom and the enemy of growth.
—JOHN F. KENNEDY

Conformity, humility, acceptance–with these coins we are to pay
our fares to paradise. —ROBERT LINDNER

The strongest bulwark of authority is uniformity; the least divergence
from it is the greatest crime. —WALTER LIPPMANN

Why do you have to be a nonconformist like everybody else?
—JAMES THURBER

I think it would be terrific if everybody was alike. —ANDY WARHOL

We are half ruined by conformity, but we should be wholly ruined
without it. —CHARLES DUDLEY WARNER

CONFUSION
(also see concepts 99, 237, 301, 391, 507, 561, 714)

I never said I had no idea about most of the things you said I had
no idea about. —ELLIOTT ABRAMS

I'm not confused, I'm just well-mixed. —ROBERT FROST

I had nothing to offer anybody except my own confusion.
—JACK KEROUAC

Confusion is a word we have invented for an order which is not
understood. —HENRY MILLER

Have a place for everything and keep the thing somewhere else.
This is not advice, it is merely custom. —MARK TWAIN

CONGRESS

(also see concepts 157, 195, 323, 847, 852)

Large legislative bodies resolve themselves into coteries, and coteries into jealousies. —NAPOLEON I

It is the duty of the President to propose and it is the privilege of the Congress to dispose. —FRANKLIN D. ROOSEVELT

It could probably be shown by facts and figures that there is no distinctly native American criminal class except Congress. —MARK TWAIN

CONSCIENCE

(also see concepts 7, 144, 332, 549, 665, 670, 717, 844)

Conscience is thoroughly well-bred and soon leaves off talking to those who do not wish to hear it. —SAMUEL BUTLER

Conscience is the internal perception of the rejection of a particular wish operating within us. —SIGMUND FREUD

A good conscience is the best divinity. —THOMAS FULLER

Conscience is a just but a weak judge. Weakness leaves it powerless to execute its judgment. —KAHLIL GIBRAN

Everyone has his own conscience, and there should be no rules about how a conscience should function. —ERNEST HEMINGWAY

Conscience is a treacherous thing, and mine behaves badly whenever there is a serious danger of being found out. —MARGARET LANE

The one thing that doesn't abide by majority rule is a person's conscience. —HARPER LEE

A state of conscience is higher than a state of innocence. —THOMAS MANN

Conscience is the inner voice which warns us that someone may be looking. —H. L. MENCKEN

A guilty conscience needs no accuser. —ENGLISH PROVERB

Even when there is no law, there is conscience. —PUBLILIUS SYRUS

Conscience does make cowards of us all. —WILLIAM SHAKESPEARE

The more estimable the offender, the greater the torment. —VOLTAIRE

Conscience and cowardice are really the same things. Conscience is the trade name of the firm. —OSCAR WILDE

CONSCIOUSNESS
(also see concepts 226, 492, 717, 719, 724)

That's one reason there's so much drug abuse: people are not shown other ways to alter their consciousness. All we have is the mall and the video rental shop; that's our cultural experience, our museums. —KAREN FINLEY

Consciousness...is the phenomenon whereby the universe's very existence is made known. —ROGER PENROSE

Renounce your consciousness and you become a brute.
—AYN RAND

CONSEQUENCES
(also see concepts 62, 93)

A mighty flame followeth a tiny spark. —DANTE

A bad beginning makes a bad ending. —EURIPIDES

You can do anything in this world if you are prepared to take the consequences. —W. SOMERSET MAUGHAM

The consequences of our actions take hold of us quite indifferent to our claim that meanwhile we have "improved."
—FRIEDRICH WILHELM NIETZSCHE

Half of the results of a good intention are evil; half the results of an evil intention are good. —MARK TWAIN

CONSERVATION

(also see concept 230)

It's a morbid observation, but if every one on earth just stopped breathing for an hour, the greenhouse effect would no longer be a problem. —JERRY ADLER

We must find methods of saving our forests, of saving threatened species, of maintaining a healthy ecological balance on earth. If there is any spare effort left over from these absolute necessities of scientific advance, we can put them into other projects–otherwise not. —ISAAC ASIMOV

Saving the planet has never been an issue of money, but rather a matter of resourcefulness and motivation of individuals. —SPENCER BEEBE

In its deepest sense, the environmentalism that concerns itself with the ecology of the whole earth is rising powerfully from the part of our being that knows better, that knows to consolidate, protect, and conserve those things we care about before we manipulate and change them, perhaps irrevocably. —AL GORE

It is our task in our time and in our generation to hand down undiminished to those who come after us, as was handed down to us by those who went before, the natural wealth and beauty which is ours. —JOHN F. KENNEDY

Conservation is a state of harmony between men and land. —ALDO LEOPOLD

If a tree dies, plant another in its place. —LINNAEUS

Something will have gone out of us as a people if we ever let the remaining wilderness be destroyed; if we permit the last virgin forest to be turned into comic books and plastic cigarette cases: if we drive the few remaining members of the wild species into zoos or to extinction; if we pollute the last clear air and dirty the last clean streams and push our paved roads through the last of the silence, so that never again will Americans be free in their own country from the noise, the exhausts, the stinks of human and automotive wastes. —WALLACE STEGNER

CONSERVATISM

(also see concepts 378, 394, 450, 510, 652, 811)

When a nation's young men are conservative, its funeral bell is already rung. —HENRY WARD BEECHER

A conservative government is an organised hypocrisy. —BENJAMIN DISRAELI

There is always a certain meanness in the argument of conservatism, joined with a certain superiority in its fact. —RALPH WALDO EMERSON

All reactionaries are paper tigers. —MAO TSE-TUNG

A conservative is a man with two perfectly good legs who, however, has never learned to walk forward. —FRANKLIN D. ROOSEVELT

The radical invents the views. When he has worn them out the conservative adopts them. —MARK TWAIN

CONSISTENCY AND INCONSISTENCY

(also see concepts 156, 490, 544, 579, 844)

A foolish consistency is the hobgoblin of little minds, adored by little statesman and philosophers and divines. —RALPH WALDO EMERSON

People who honestly mean to be true really contradict themselves much more rarely than those who try to be "consistent." —OLIVER WENDELL HOLMES, SR.

Consistency is contrary to nature, contrary to life. The only completely consistent people are the dead. —ALDOUS HUXLEY

It is not best to swap horses while crossing the river. —ABRAHAM LINCOLN

There are those who would misteach us that to stick in a rut is consistency–and a virtue, and that to climb out of the rut is inconsistency–and a vice. —MARK TWAIN

Do I contradict myself? / Very well then I contradict myself, / (I am large, I contain multitudes). —WALT WHITMAN

CONSTANCY AND INCONSTANCY
(also see concepts 155, 579, 647, 855)

One man; two loves. No good ever comes of that. —EURIPIDES

Only the person who has faith in himself is able to be faithful to others. —ERICH FROMM

The more things change, the more they remain the same.
—ALPHONSE KARR

The violence we do to ourselves in order to remain faithful to the one we love is hardly better than an act of infidelity.
—FRANÇOIS DE LA ROCHEFOUCAULD

He wears his faith but as the fashion of his hat.
—WILLIAM SHAKESPEARE

There is nothing in this world constant but inconstancy.
—JONATHAN SWIFT

Faithfulness is to the emotional life what consistency is to the life of the intellect–simply a confession of failures. —OSCAR WILDE

CONSTITUTIONS
(also see concepts 298, 323, 365, 617, 847)

The Constitution gives every American the inalienable right to make a damn fool of himself. —JOHN CIARDI

Our constitution is in actual operation; everything appears to promise that it will last; but in this world nothing is certain but death and taxes. —BENJAMIN FRANKLIN

Some men look at constitutions with sanctimonious reverence, and deem them like the ark of the covenant, too sacred to be touched.
—THOMAS JEFFERSON

Constitutions are good only as we make progress under them.
—NAPOLEON I

A Constitution should be short and obscure. —NAPOLEON I

It is very doubtful whether man is enough of a political animal to produce a good, sensible, serious and efficient constitution. All the evidence is against it. —GEORGE BERNARD SHAW

CONTEMPT
(also see concepts 237, 689, 698, 734)

The great despisers are the great reverers.
—FRIEDRICH WILHELM NIETZSCHE

Who can refute a sneer? —WILLIAM PALEY

Silence is the most perfect expression of scorn.
—GEORGE BERNARD SHAW

Everything can be borne except contempt. —VOLTAIRE

CONTENTMENT
(also see concepts 237, 337, 433, 575, 593)

Be content with your lot; one cannot be first in everything. —AESOP

I have learned, in whatsoever state I am, therewith to be content.
—BIBLE, PHILIPPIANS 4:11

Give me neither poverty nor riches; feed me with food convenient for me. —BIBLE, PROVERBS 30:8

The seat of perfect contentment is in the head; for every individual is thoroughly satisfied with his own proportion of brains.
—CHARLES CALEB COLTON

Better a little fire to warm us than a great one to burn us.
—THOMAS FULLER

Four things impair the strength of man: sin, journeying, fasting, and royalty. —HAGGADAH, PALESTINIAN TALMUD

Most human beings have an almost infinite capacity for taking things for granted. —ALDOUS HUXLEY

Complacency is the enemy of study. We cannot really learn anything until we rid ourselves of complacency. —MAO TSE-TUNG

Nothing will content him who is not content with a little. —GREEK PROVERB

Poor and content is rich, and rich enough. —WILLIAM SHAKESPEARE

Good friends, good books and a sleepy conscience: this is the ideal life. —MARK TWAIN

CONTRACEPTION

(also see concepts 2, 283)

Vasectomy means not ever having to say you're sorry. —LARRY ADLER

I want to tell you a terrific story about oral contraception. I asked this girl to sleep with me and she said "no." —WOODY ALLEN

To label family planning and legal abortion programs "genocide" is male rhetoric, for male ears. —SHIRLEY CHISHOLM

We think women should have a choice when it comes to being pregnant. Barefoot is another story. —KENNETH COLE

The management of fertility is one of the most important functions of adulthood. —GERMAINE GREER

We all worry about the population explosion, but we don't worry about it at the right time. —ARTHUR HOPPE

It is now quite lawful for a Catholic woman to avoid pregnancy by a resort to mathematics, though she is still forbidden to resort to physics and chemistry. —H. L. MENCKEN

Contraceptives should be used on every conceivable occasion. —SPIKE MILLIGAN

We want far better reasons for having children than not knowing how to prevent them. —DORA RUSSELL

No woman can call herself free who does not own and control her body. No woman can call herself free until she can choose consciously whether she will or will not be a mother.
—MARGARET H. SANGER

CONTRAST
(also see concepts 205, 467, 557)

Without contraries is no progression. Attraction and repulsion, reason and energy, love and hate, are necessary to human existence.
—WILLIAM BLAKE

We are so made that we can derive intense enjoyment only from a contrast and very little from a state of things. —SIGMUND FREUD

Sleep, riches, and health, to be truly enjoyed, must be interrupted.
—JEAN PAUL RICHTER

CONVERSATION
(also see concepts 132, 322, 457)

Good-nature is more agreeable in conversation than wit, and gives a certan air to the countenance which is more amiable than beauty.
—JOSEPH ADDISON

Too much agreement kills a chat. —ELDRIDGE CLEAVER

The best of life is conversation, and the greatest success is confidence, or perfect understanding between sincere people.
—RALPH WALDO EMERSON

If to talk to oneself when alone is folly, it must be doubly unwise to listen to oneself in the presence of others. —BALTASAR GRACIÁN

Inject a few raisins of conversation into the tasteless dough of existence. —O. HENRY

Conversation is not a search after knowledge, but an endeavour at effect. —JOHN KEATS

The more the pleasures of the body fade away, the greater to me is the pleasure and charm of conversation. —PLATO

Whoever interrupts the conversation of others to make a display of his fund of knowledge, makes notorious his own stock of ignorance. —SA'DI

Conversation has a kind of charm about it, an insinuating and insidious something that elicits secrets from us just like love or liquor. —SENECA

There is no such thing as conversation. It is an illusion. There are intersecting monologues, that is all. —REBECCA WEST

When people talk to us about others they are usually dull. When they talk to us about themselves they are nearly always interesting. —OSCAR WILDE

COOKS AND COOKING
(also see concepts 90, 275, 278, 290, 296, 363, 371)

Men do not have to cook their food; they do so for symbolic reasons to show they are men and not beasts. —EDMUND LEACH

Kissing don't last; cookery do! —GEORGE MEREDITH

Bad cooks–and the utter lack of reason in the kitchen– have delayed human development longest and impaired it most. —FRIEDRICH WILHELM NIETZSCHE

Cooking is like love. It should be entered into with abandon or not at all. —HARRIET VAN HORNE

A good cook is a certain slow poisoner, if you are not temperate. —VOLTAIRE

CORRUPTION
(also see concepts 81, 85, 170, 186, 487, 600, 707)

Among a people generally corrupt, liberty cannot long exist. —EDMUND BURKE

Where God hath a temple, the Devil will have a chapel. —ROBERT BURTON

Our worst enemies here are not the ignorant and the simple, however cruel; our worst enemies are the intelligent and the corrupt. —GRAHAM GREENE

Power corrupts the few, while weakness corrupts the many. —ERIC HOFFER

The corruption of every government begins nearly always with that of principles. —BARON DE MONTESQUIEU

Lilies that fester smell far worse than weeds. —WILLIAM SHAKESPEARE

COSMETICS
(also see concepts 47, 59, 381)

I always wear boot polish on my eyelashes, because I am a very emotional person and it doesn't run when I cry.
—BARBARA CARTLAND

In the factory we make cosmetics. In the store we sell hope.
—CHARLES REVSON

God hath given you one face, and you make yourselves another.
—WILLIAM SHAKESPEARE

Women are feeding their skins as a way to feed themselves the love of which many are deprived. —NAOMI WOLF

THE COUNTRY AND THE COUNTRYSIDE
(also see concepts 275, 289, 531, 589, 777)

To sit in the shade on a fine day and look upon verdure is the most perfect refreshment. —JANE AUSTEN

It is only in the country that we can get to know a person or a book.
—CYRIL CONNOLLY

God made the country, and man made the town. —WILLIAM COWPER

I lived in solitude in the country and noticed how the monotony of a quiet life stimulates the creative mind. —ALBERT EINSTEIN

It is quiet here and restful and the air is delicious. There are gardens everywhere, nightingales sing in the gardens and police spies lie in the bushes. —MAXIM GORKY

When I am in the country I wish to vegetate like the country. —WILLIAM HAZLITT

The city has a face, the country has a soul. —JACQUES DE LACRETELLE

I have no relish for the country; it is a kind of healthy grave. —SYDNEY SMITH

The country has its charms–cheapness for one. —ROBERT SMITH SURTEES

COURAGE
(also see concepts 75, 237, 860)

It is easy to be brave from a safe distance. —AESOP

Until the day of his death, no man can be sure of his courage. —JEAN ANOUILH

All bravery stands upon comparisons. —FRANCIS BACON

Courage is the thing. All goes if courage goes. —J. M. BARRIE

The paradox of courage is that a man must be a little careless of his life even in order to keep it. —G. K. CHESTERTON

Between cowardice and despair, valour is gendred. —JOHN DONNE

None but the brave deserves the fair. —JOHN DRYDEN

Courage is the price that Life exacts for granting peace. —AMELIA EARHART

Without justice, courage is weak. —BENJAMIN FRANKLIN

People with courage and character always seem sinister to the rest. —HERMANN HESSE

It is better to die on your feet than to live on your knees. —DOLORES IBARRURI

There is plenty of courage among us for the abstract but not for the concrete. —HELEN KELLER

Perfect valour consists in doing without witnesses that which we would be capable of doing before everyone.
—FRANÇOIS DE LA ROCHEFOUCAULD

The only courage that matters is the kind that gets you from one minute to the next. —MIGNON MCLAUGHLIN

Courage is like love; it must have hope for nourishment.
—NAPOLEON I

Everyone becomes brave when he observes one who despairs.
—FRIEDRICH WILHELM NIETZSCHE

Courage is a kind of salvation. —PLATO

Sometimes even to live is an act of courage. —SENECA

Considering how dangerous everything is nothing is really very frightening. —GERTRUDE STEIN

Courage is resistance to fear, mastery of fear–not absence of fear.
—MARK TWAIN

All serious daring starts from within. —EUDORA WELTY

COWARDICE

(also see concepts 237, 282, 855)

Optimism and self-pity are the positive and negative poles of modern cowardice. —CYRIL CONNOLLY

None but a coward dares to boast that he has never known fear.
—MARSHAL FOCH

Many would be cowards if they had courage enough.
—THOMAS FULLER

Cowardice, as distinguished from panic, is almost always simply a lack of ability to suspend the functioning of the imagination.
—ERNEST HEMINGWAY

Perfect courage and utter cowardice are two extremes which rarely occur. —FRANÇOIS DE LA ROCHEFOUCAULD

Cowards die many times before their deaths; / The valiant never taste of death but once. —WILLIAM SHAKESPEARE

The human race is a race of cowards: and I am not only marching in that procession but carrying a banner. —MARK TWAIN

CREATION AND CREATIVITY
(also see concepts 48, 61, 75, 562, 565, 832, 845)

Don't think! Thinking is the enemy of creativity. It's self-conscious, and anything self-conscious is lousy. You can't try to do things; you simply must do them. —RAY BRADBURY

Every production must resemble its author. —MIGUEL DE CERVANTES

With the offspring of genius, the law of parturition is reversed: the throes are in the conception, the pleasure in the birth. —CHARLES CALEB COLTON

Our inventions mirror our secret wishes. —LAWRENCE DURRELL

Creative minds have always been known to survive any kind of bad training. —ANNA FREUD

Man unites himself with the world in the process of creation. —ERICH FROMM

We can invent only with memory. —ALPHONSE KARR

One must die to life in order to be utterly a creator. —THOMAS MANN

We are traditionally rather proud of ourselves for having slipped creative work in there between the domestic chores and obligations. I'm not sure we deserve such a big A-plus for all that. —TONI MORRISON

In life it is more necessary to lose than to gain. A seed will only germinate if it dies. —BORIS PASTERNAK

A creative artist works on his next composition because he was not satisfied with his previous one. —DMITRI SHOSTAKOVICH

In order to create there must be a dynamic force, and what force is more potent than love? —IGOR STRAVINSKY

God made everything out of nothing. But the nothingness shows through. —PAUL VALÉRY

The art of creation / is older than the art of killing.
—ANDREI VOZNESENSKY

CRIMINALS AND CRIME
(also see concepts 81, 164, 437, 596, 621, 642, 656, 769, 875)

There is hardly any deviancy, no matter how reprehensible in one context, which is not extolled as a virtue in another. There are no natural crimes, only legal ones. —FREDA ADLER

Commit a crime, and the earth is made of glass. There is no such thing as concealment. —RALPH WALDO EMERSON

He'd forgotten just how addictive crime can be. Repeat offenders are motivated more by withdrawal symptoms than necessity. —SUE GRAFTON

The study of crime begins with the knowledge of oneself.
—HENRY MILLER

Crime, like virtue, has its degrees. —JEAN RACINE

Successful and fortunate crime is called virtue. —SENECA

Fear succeeds crime–it is punishment. —VOLTAIRE

CRITICISM
(also see concepts 138, 172, 435, 555, 730)

Criticism and dissent are the indispensable antidote to major delusions. —ALAN BARTH

Criticism is like champagne: nothing more execrable if bad, nothing more excellent if good. —CHARLES CALEB COLTON

Men in authority will always think that criticism of their policies is dangerous. They will always equate their policies with patriotism, and find criticism subversive. —HENRY STEELE COMMAGER

Criticism is easy, art is difficult. —PHILIPPE DESTOUCHES

One must first learn to live oneself before one blames others. —FYODOR DOSTOYEVSKY

I have never found, in a long experience of politics, that criticism is ever inhibited by ignorance. —HAROLD MACMILLAN

People ask you for criticism, but they only want praise. —W. SOMERSET MAUGHAM

Anyone can be accurate and even profound, but it is damned hard work to make criticism charming. —H. L. MENCKEN

Every place swarms with commentaries; of authors there is great scarcity. —MICHEL DE MONTAIGNE

We find fault with perfection itself. —BLAISE PASCAL

Take each man's censure, but reserve thy judgment. —WILLIAM SHAKESPEARE

A bad review is like baking a cake with all the best ingredients and having someone sit on it. —DANIELLE STEEL

I am sorry to think that you do not get a man's most effective criticism until you provoke him. —HENRY DAVID THOREAU

CRITICS
(also see concepts 171, 262, 435, 555)

They who are to be judges must also be performers. —ARISTOTLE

One cannot review a bad book without showing off. —W. H. AUDEN

Critics are like eunuchs in a harem. They're there every night, they see how it should be done every night, but they can't do it themselves. —BRENDAN BEHAN

Of all fatiguing, futile, empty trades, the worst, I suppose, is writing about writing. —HILAIRE BELLOC

Judge not, that ye be not judged. —BIBLE, MATTHEW 7:1

I don't read my reviews, I measure them. —JOSEPH CONRAD

It is much easier to be critical than to be correct.
—BENJAMIN DISRAELI

Taking to pieces is the trade of those who cannot construct.
—RALPH WALDO EMERSON

I was so long writing my review that I never got around to reading
the book. —GROUCHO MARX

A critic is a gong at a railroad crossing clanging loudly and vainly
as the train goes by. —CHRISTOPHER MORLEY

Critics sometimes appear to be addressing themselves to works
other than those I remember writing. —JOYCE CAROL OATES

A book reviewer is usually a barker before the door of a publisher's
circus. —AUSTIN O'MALLEY

I love every bone in their heads. —EUGENE O'NEILL

They have a right to censure that have a heart to help.
—WILLIAM PENN

'Tis hard to say, if greater want of skill / Appear in writing or in
judging ill. —ALEXANDER POPE

The greater part of critics are parasites, who, if nothing had been
written, would find nothing to write. —J. B. PRIESTLEY

It is folly to censure him whom all the world adores.
—PUBLILIUS SYRUS

A drama critic is a man who leaves no turn unstoned.
—GEORGE BERNARD SHAW

Unless the bastards have the courage to give you unqualified
praise, I say ignore them. —JOHN STEINBECK

Time is the only critic without ambition. —JOHN STEINBECK

Critics are like pigs at the pastry cart. —JOHN UPDIKE

Any reviewer who expresses rage and loathing for a novel is preposterous. He or she is like a person who has put on full armor and attacked a hot fudge sundae. —KURT VONNEGUT

A critic is a necessary evil, and criticism is an evil necessity. —CAROLYN WELLS

When critics disagree, the artist is in accord with himself. —OSCAR WILDE

CROWDS
(also see concept 576)

A crowd is not company, and faces are but a gallery of pictures. —FRANCIS BACON

Observe any meetings of people, and you will always find their eagerness and impetuosity rise or fall in proportion to their numbers. —EARL OF CHESTERFIELD

Nothing is so uncertain or unpredictable as the feelings of a crowd. —LIVY

I would rather sit on a pumpkin and have it all to myself than to be crowded on a velvet cushion. —HENRY DAVID THOREAU

Great bodies of people are never responsible for what they do. —VIRGINIA WOOLF

CRUELTY
(also see concept 127, 237, 558, 680, 693, 730, 821)

Cruelty ever proceeds from a vile mind, and often from a cowardly heart. —LUDOVICO ARIOSTO

Cruelty, like every other vice, requires no motive outside of itself; it only requires opportunity. —GEORGE ELIOT

Fear is the parent of cruelty. —J. A. FROUDE

All the world will beat the man whom fortune buffets. —THOMAS FULLER

Cruelty is the law pervading all nature and society; and we can't get out of it if we would. —THOMAS HARDY

I must be cruel only to be kind. —WILLIAM SHAKESPEARE

CRYING
(also see concepts 9, 302, 520, 718, 757, 827)

I wept not, so to stone within I grew. —DANTE

Waste not fresh tears over old griefs. —EURIPIDES

It is only to the happy that tears are a luxury. —THOMAS MOORE

Let tears flow of their own accord: their flowing is not inconsistent with inward peace and harmony. —SENECA

How much better is it to weep at joy than to joy at weeping! —WILLIAM SHAKESPEARE

CULTS
(also see concept 274)

What's a cult? It just means not enough people to make a minority. —ROBERT ALTMAN

As long as we continue to do that and make cults around our leaders, all they have to do to stop it any time we're making ground is just kill us off, kill off that leader. —SPIKE LEE

A cult is a religion with no political power. —TOM WOLFE

CULTURE
(also see concept 116, 180, 335, 416, 485, 597, 754, 811)

Culture opens the sense of beauty. —RALPH WALDO EMERSON

Man is born a barbarian and raises himself above the beast by culture. —BALTASAR GRACIÁN

Culture is simply how one lives and is connected to history by habit. —LEROI JONES

Culture is half-way to heaven. —GEORGE MEREDITH

Culture is an instrument wielded by professors to manufacture professors, who when their turn comes will manufacture professors. —SIMONE WEIL

CUNNING
(also see concepts 1, 122, 131, 260, 411, 864, 866)

The weak in courage is strong in cunning. —WILLIAM BLAKE

With foxes we must play the fox. —THOMAS FULLER

There is great ability in knowing how to conceal one's ability. —FRANÇOIS DE LA ROCHEFOUCAULD

The greatest cunning is to have none at all. —CARL SANDBURG

CURIOSITY
(also see concepts 237, 413)

Only that mind draws me which I cannot read. —RALPH WALDO EMERSON

Enquire not what boils in another's pot. —THOMAS FULLER

Curiosity is one of the permanent and certain characteristics of a vigorous intellect. —SAMUEL JOHNSON

I think "more" is the cry of the curious person. —BETTE MIDLER

The world is but a school of inquiry. —MICHEL DE MONTAIGNE

Curiosity killed the cat. —PROVERB

He that breaks a thing to find out what it is has left the path of wisdom. —J. R. R. TOLKIEN

CUSTOM
(also see concepts 177, 335, 671, 690, 770, 811)

Custom reconciles us to everything. —EDMUND BURKE

Most of the things we do, we do for no better reason than that our fathers have done them or our neighbors do them, and the same is true of a larger part than what we suspect of what we think.
—OLIVER WENDELL HOLMES, JR.

Custom, then, is the great guide of human life. —DAVID HUME

He who does anything because it is the custom, makes no choice.
—JOHN STUART MILL

There is nothing so extreme that is not allowed by the custom of some nation or other. —MICHEL DE MONTAIGNE

Custom is the guide of the ignorant. —ENGLISH PROVERB

How many things, both just and unjust, are sanctioned by custom!
—TERENCE

CYNICISM
(also see concepts 216, 237, 559, 560)

One is not superior merely because one sees the world in an odious light. —VICOMTE DE CHATEAUBRIAND

We can destroy ourselves by cynicism and disillusion just as effectively as by bombs. —KENNETH CLARK

A cynic is not merely one who reads bitter lessons from the past; he is one who is prematurely disappointed in the future.
—SYDNEY J. HARRIS

Cynicism is an unpleasant way of saying the truth.
—LILLIAN HELLMAN

The worst cynicism: a belief in luck. —JOYCE CAROL OATES

The only deadly sin I know is cynicism. —HENRY L. STIMSON

What is a cynic? A man who knows the price of everything, and the value of nothing. —OSCAR WILDE

DANCING
(also see concepts 9, 256, 524)

I just put my feet in the air and move them around. —FRED ASTAIRE

I don't want people who want to dance, I want people who have to dance. —GEORGE BALANCHINE

I have discovered the dance. I have discovered the art which has been lost for two thousand years. —ISADORA DUNCAN

Dancing is the loftiest, the most moving, the most beautiful of the arts, because it is no mere translation or abstraction from life; it is life itself. —HAVELOCK ELLIS

Come, and trip it as you go / On the light fantastic toe. —JOHN MILTON

My feet are dogs. —RUDOLF NUREYEV

A perpendicular expression of a horizontal desire. —GEORGE BERNARD SHAW

DANGER
(also see concepts 282, 694, 800, 805, 842)

Those who'll play with cats must expect to be scratched. —MIGUEL DE CERVANTES

However well organized the foundations of life may be, life must always be full of risks. —HAVELOCK ELLIS

Great perils have this beauty, that they bring to light the fraternity of stangers. —VICTOR HUGO

To be alive at all involves some risk. —HAROLD MACMILLAN

Only an awareness of the dangers menacing what we love allows us to sense the dimension of time and to feel in everything we see and touch the presence of past generations. —CZESLAW MILOSZ

Believe me! The secret of reaping the greatest fruitfulness and the greatest enjoyment from life is to live dangerously! —FRIEDRICH WILHELM NIETZSCHE

Any port in a storm. —PROVERB

The path is smooth that leadeth on to danger. —WILLIAM SHAKESPEARE

Everything is sweetened by risk. —ALEXANDER SMITH

DEAFNESS
(also see concept 209)

I need to know what is being said. Always. Anywhere. Not just a word now and then. —ELEANORE DEVINE

Deafness has left me acutely aware of both the duplicity that language is capable of and the many expressions the body cannot hide. —TERRY GALLOWAY

The inability to hear is a nuisance; the inability to communicate is the tragedy. —LOU ANN WALKER

DEATH
(also see concepts 3, 23, 62, 238, 246, 302, 313, 425, 453, 455, 480, 517, 520, 552, 713, 781, 813)

It's not that I'm afraid to die. I just don't want to be there when it happens. —WOODY ALLEN

Death cancels everything but truth. —ANONYMOUS

Man dies when he wants, as he wants, of what he chooses. —JEAN ANOUILH

It is as natural to die as to be born. —FRANCIS BACON

Dust thou art, and unto dust shalt thou return. —BIBLE, GENESIS 3:19

Though it be in the power of the weakest arm to take away life, it is not in the strongest to deprive us of death. —THOMAS BROWNE

Men are convinced of your arguments, your sincerity, and the seriousness of your efforts only by your death. —ALBERT CAMUS

Death eats up all things, both the young lamb and old sheep. —MIGUEL DE CERVANTES

Alack he's gone the way of all flesh. —WILLIAM CONGREVE

Because I could not stop for Death, / He kindly stopped for me; / The carriage held but just ourselves / And Immortality.
—EMILY DICKINSON

Any man's death diminishes me, because I am involved in mankind; and therefore never send to know for whom the bell tolls; it tolls for thee. —JOHN DONNE

All human things are subject to decay, / And when fate summons, monarchs must obey. —JOHN DRYDEN

It is possible to provide security against other ills, but as far as death is concerned, we men all live in a city without walls. —EPICURUS

It hath often been said, that it is not death, but dying, which is terrible. —HENRY FIELDING

Death destroys a man, the idea of Death saves him. —E. M. FORSTER

To die is poignantly bitter, but the idea of having to die without having lived is unbearable. —ERICH FROMM

Do not seek death. Death will find you. But seek the road which makes death a fulfillment. —DAG HAMMARSKJÖLD

Our repugnance to death increases in proportion to our consciousness of having lived in vain. —WILLIAM HAZLITT

To die is to go into the Collective Unconscious, to lose oneself in order to be transformed into form, pure form. —HERMANN HESSE

Death has but one terror, that it has no tomorrow. —ERIC HOFFER

Death....It's the only thing we haven't succeeded in completely vulgarizing. —ALDOUS HUXLEY

Death is simply a shedding of the physical body, like the butterfly coming out of a cocoon....It's like putting away your winter coat when spring comes. —ELISABETH KÜBLER-ROSS

Neither the sun nor death can be looked at steadily.
—FRANÇOIS DE LA ROCHEFOUCAULD

While I thought that I was learning how to live, I have been learning how to die. —LEONARDO DA VINCI

The grave's a fine and private place, / But none, I think, do there embrace. —ANDREW MARVELL

Dying is a very dull, dreary affair. And my advice to you is to have nothing whatever to do with it. —W. SOMERSET MAUGHAM

Even Rome cannot grant us a dispensation from death. —MOLIÉRE

The perpetual work of your life is but to lay the foundation of death. —MICHEL DE MONTAIGNE

One should die proudly when it is no longer possible to live proudly. —FRIEDRICH WILHELM NIETZSCHE

I postpone death by living, by suffering, by error, by risking, by giving, by losing. —ANAÏS NIN

Death always comes too early or too late. —ENGLISH PROVERB

Our last garment is made without pockets. —ITALIAN PROVERB

Death is a distant rumor to the young. —ANDY ROONEY

Death is a punishment to some, to some a gift, and to many a favour. —SENECA

He that dies pays all debts. —WILLIAM SHAKESPEARE

For the dead there are no more toils. —SOPHOCLES

Go and try to disprove death. Death will disprove you and that's all! —IVAN TURGENEV

Let us endeavor so to live that when we come to die even the undertaker will be sorry. —MARK TWAIN

To die is different from what any one supposed, and luckier. —WALT WHITMAN

DEBAUCHERY
(also see concepts 164, 707, 731, 840)

Here's a rule I recommend. Never practice two vices at once.
—TALLULAH BANKHEAD

It is the hour to be drunken! To escape being the martyred slaves of time, be ceaselessly drunk. On wine, on poetry, or on virtue, as you wish. —CHARLES BAUDELAIRE

My main problem is reconciling my gross habits with my net income. —ERROL FLYNN

A libertine life is not a life of liberty. —THOMAS FULLER

An orgy looks particularly alluring seen through the mists of righteous indignation. —MALCOLM MUGGERIDGE

Not joy but joylessness is the mother of debauchery.
—FRIEDRICH WILHELM NIETZSCHE

An improper mind is a perpetual feast. —LOGAN PEARSALL SMITH

DEBT
(also see concepts 512, 549, 574, 606)

Man was lost if he went to a usurer, for the interest ran faster than a tiger upon him. —PEARL BUCK

There are but two ways of paying debt: increase of industry in raising income, increase of thrift in laying out. —THOMAS CARLYLE

Debt is the worst poverty. —THOMAS FULLER

I've often known people more shocked because you are not bankrupt than because you are. —MARGARET BAILLIE SAUNDERS

Words pay no debts. —WILLIAM SHAKESPEARE

DECENCY

(also see concepts 103, 120, 214, 587)

A private sin is not so prejudicial in this world as a public indecency. —MIGUEL DE CERVANTES

Nature knows no indecencies; man invents them. —MARK TWAIN

There are few things that so touch us with instinctive revulsion as a breach of decorum. —THORSTEIN VEBLEN

DECISION

(also see concepts 107, 202)

Decisiveness is often the art of timely cruelty. —HENRY BECQUE

Nothing is more difficult, and therefore more precious, than to be able to decide. —NAPOLEON I

DECLINE

(also see concepts 192, 238, 664)

Ruin is the destination toward which all men rush....
—GARRETT HARDIN

The passing years steal from us one thing after another. —HORACE

The wolf loses his teeth, but not his inclinations. —SPANISH PROVERB

Apples taste sweetest when they're going. —SENECA

Men shut their doors against a setting sun. —WILLIAM SHAKESPEARE

I shall be like that tree; I shall die from the top. —JONATHAN SWIFT

Like our shadows, / Our wishes lengthen as our sun declines.
—EDWARD YOUNG

DEEDS
(also see concepts 9, 10, 25, 234)

Every man feels instinctively that all the beautiful sentiments in the world weigh less than a single lovely action.
——JAMES RUSSELL LOWELL

Whatever is done for love always occurs beyond good and evil.
——FRIEDRICH WILHELM NIETZSCHE

Noble deeds are most estimable when hidden. ——BLAISE PASCAL

Ugly deeds are taught by ugly deeds. ——SOPHOCLES

DEFEAT
(also see concepts 190, 201, 215, 268, 841)

Defeat is a school in which truth always grows strong.
——HENRY WARD BEECHER

Never confuse a single defeat with a final defeat.
——F. SCOTT FITZGERALD

A man can be destroyed but not defeated. ——ERNEST HEMINGWAY

The important thing is to learn a lesson every time you lose.
——JOHN MCENROE

There are defeats more triumphant than victories.
——MICHEL DE MONTAIGNE

Defeat is a thing of weariness, of incoherence, of boredom. And above all futility. ——ANTOINE DE SAINT-EXUPÉRY

DEFENSE
(also see concepts 255, 263, 557)

I think you know that I believe we must be strong militarily, but beyond a certain point military strength can become a national weakness. ——DWIGHT D. EISENHOWER

The contention that a standing army and navy is the best security of peace is about as logical as the claim that the most peaceful citizen is he who goes about heavily armed. —EMMA GOLDMAN

One sword keeps another in the sheath. —GEORGE HERBERT

It is an unfortunate fact that we can secure peace only by preparing for war. —JOHN F. KENNEDY

Isn't the best defense always a good attack? —OVID

To be prepared for war is one of the most effectual means of preserving peace. —GEORGE WASHINGTON

DELAY
(also see concept 624)

Defer not till to-morrow to be wise, / To-morrow's sun to thee may never rise. —WILLIAM CONGREVE

What may be done at any time will be done at no time. —THOMAS FULLER

Delay is preferable to error. —THOMAS JEFFERSON

Life, as it is called, is for most of us one long postponement. —HENRY MILLER

Procrastination is the thief of time. —EDWARD YOUNG

DEMOCRACY
(also see concepts 114, 298, 299, 323, 328, 576, 767, 847, 852)

Democracy is the form of government in which the free are rulers. —ARISTOTLE

In a democracy the general good is furthered only when the special interests of competing minorities accidentally coincide–or cancel each other out. —ALEXANDER CHASE

It has been said that Democracy is the worst form of government except all those other forms that have been tried from time to time. —WINSTON CHURCHILL

The most may err as grossly as the few. —JOHN DRYDEN

Democracy is a form of government which may be rationally defended, not as being good, but as being less bad than any other. —WILLIAM RALPH INGE

A democracy is the most difficult kind of government to operate. It represents the last flowering, really, of the human experience. —JOHN F. KENNEDY

The taste of democracy becomes a bitter taste when the fullness of democracy is denied. —MAX LERNER

The blind lead the blind. It's the democratic way. —HENRY MILLER

Democracy is good. I say this because other systems are worse. —JAWAHARLAL NEHRU

Let the people think they govern and they will be governed. —WILLIAM PENN

Democracy passes into despotism. —PLATO

Democracy is not a static thing. It is an everlasting march. —FRANKLIN D. ROOSEVELT

Envy is the basis of democracy. —BERTRAND RUSSELL

It's not the voting that's democracy; it's the counting. —TOM STOPPARD

We are called a democracy, for the administration is in the hands of the many and not of the few. —THUCYDIDES

When the people rule, they must be rendered happy, or they will overturn the state. —ALEXIS DE TOCQUEVILLE

That a peasant may become king does not render the kingdom democratic. —WOODROW WILSON

A democracy cannot endure long with the head of a God and the tail of a demon. —JOSEPHINE SILONE YATES

DEPENDENCE

(also see concepts 89, 747, 755, 817)

Nothing is more desirable than to be released from an affliction, but nothing is more frightening than to be divested of a crutch.
——JAMES BALDWIN

No one can build his security upon the nobleness of another person.
——WILLA CATHER

It is easier to live through someone else than to become complete yourself. ——BETTY FRIEDAN

We often have to put up with most from those on whom we most depend. ——BALTASAR GRACIÁN

Independence? That's middle-class blasphemy. We are all dependent on one another, every soul of us on earth.
——GEORGE BERNARD SHAW

DEPRIVATION

(also see concepts 465, 606)

We know well only what we are deprived of. ——FRANÇOIS MAURIAC

To be without some of the things you want is an indispensable part of happiness. ——BERTRAND RUSSELL

DESIRES

(also see concepts 243, 430, 472, 647, 673, 726, 793, 799, 860, 865)

We would often be sorry if our wishes were gratified. ——AESOP

Make us, not fly to dreams, but moderate desire.
——MATTHEW ARNOLD

He who desires but acts not, breeds pestilence. ——WILLIAM BLAKE

If you desire many things, many things will seem but a few.
——BENJAMIN FRANKLIN

Other people's appetites easily appear excessive when one doesn't share them. ——ANDRÉ GIDE

The act of longing for something will always be more intense than the requiting of it. —GAIL GODWIN

We are never further from our wishes than when we imagine that we possess what we have desired. —JOHANN WOLFGANG VON GOETHE

When desire dies, fear is born. —BALTASAR GRACIÁN

Life is a progress from want to want, not from enjoyment to enjoyment. —SAMUEL JOHNSON

There is wishful thinking in Hell as well as on earth. —C. S. LEWIS

A little of what you fancy does you good. —MARIE LLOYD

Granting our wish one of Fate's saddest jokes is! —JAMES RUSSELL LOWELL

Desire creates desire and then feels pain. —MICHELANGELO

We do not succeed in changing things according to our desire, but gradually our desire changes. —MARCEL PROUST

Appetite comes with eating. —FRANÇOIS RABELAIS

All impediments in fancy's course / Are motives of more fancy. —WILLIAM SHAKESPEARE

There are two tragedies in life. One is to lose your heart's desire. The other is to gain it. —GEORGE BERNARD SHAW

DESPAIR

(also see concepts 237, 491, 506, 584, 872)

You may not know it, but at the far end of despair, there is a white clearing where one is almost happy. —JEAN ANOUILH

Action is the antidote to despair. —JOAN BAEZ

To eat bread without hope is still slowly to starve to death. —PEARL S. BUCK

In despair there are the most intense enjoyments, especially when one is very acutely conscious of the hopelessness of one's position. —FYODOR DOSTOYEVSKY

Despair is the price one pays for setting oneself an impossible aim.
——GRAHAM GREENE

Don't despair, not even over the fact that you don't despair.
——FRANZ KAFKA

The mass of men lead lives of quiet desperation.
——HENRY DAVID THOREAU

Lord save us all from old age and broken health and a hope tree that
has lost the faculty of putting out blossoms. ——MARK TWAIN

DESTINY
(also see concepts 97, 112, 279, 397, 471)

It is a mistake to look too far ahead. Only one link of the chain of
destiny can be handled at a time. ——WINSTON CHURCHILL

The efforts which we make to escape from our destiny only serve
to lead us into it. ——RALPH WALDO EMERSON

Anatomy is destiny. ——SIGMUND FREUD

Destiny grants us our wishes, but in its own way, in order to give
us something beyond our wishes. ——JOHANN WOLFGANG VON GOETHE

We are not permitted to choose the frame of our destiny. But what
we put into it is ours. ——DAG HAMMARSKJÖLD

Our destiny rules over us, even when we are not yet aware of it; it
is the future that makes laws for us today.
——FRIEDRICH WILHELM NIETZSCHE

Everything comes gradually and at its appointed hour. ——OVID

What must be, must be. ——PROVERB

DESTRUCTION
(also see concepts 192, 238, 842)

When one builds and another tears down, what do they gain but
toil? ——APOCRYPHA

There is nothing we value and hunt and cultivate and strive to draw to us, but in some hour we turn and rend it. —RALPH WALDO EMERSON

After all, to make a beautiful omelet, you have to break an egg. —SPANISH PROVERB

DETERMINATION

(also see concepts 107, 189, 237, 579, 647, 674, 720, 722, 774, 860)

Whatever I engage in, I must push inordinately. —ANDREW CARNEGIE

You have to...learn the rules of the game. And then you have to play better than anyone else. —DIANNE FEINSTEIN

Where there's a will there's a way. —PROVERB

If I have to, I can do anything. —HELEN REDDY

I don't think of myself as a poor deprived ghetto girl who made good. I think of myself as somebody who from an early age knew I was responsible for myself, and I had to make good. —OPRAH WINFREY

THE DEVIL

(also see concept 343)

The world is all the richer for having the devil in it, so long as we keep our foot upon his neck. —WILLIAM JAMES

To insure our sense of mystery, we need a sense of evil which sees the devil as a real spirit who must be made to name himself as vague evil, but to name himself with his specific personality for every occasion. —FLANNERY O'CONNOR

I believe that there is a devil, and here's Satan's agenda. First, he doesn't want anyone having kids. Secondly, if they do conceive, he wants them killed. If they're not killed through abortion, he wants them neglected or abused, physically, emotionally, sexually. Barring that, he wants to get them into some godless curriculum or setting, where their minds are filled with pollution. —RANDALL TERRY

We may not pay Satan reverence, for that would be indiscreet, but we can at least respect his talents. —MARK TWAIN

DIARIES
(also see concepts 449, 622, 874)

A Japanese company now provides a diary service for people who just can't find the time every day to write down their entries. They can phone the company to tape record their day's activities and at the end of the month receive a nicely bounded transcription of their musings. —HARRIET BLODGETT

I suppose this is the reason why diaries are so rarely kept nowadays –that nothing ever happens to anybody. —A. A. MILNE

When all is said and done, leading a good life is more important than keeping a good diary. —SIEGFRIED SASSOON

It would be curious to discover who it is to whom one writes in a diary. Possibly to some mysterious personification of one's own identity. —BEATRICE WEBB

I always say, keep a diary and someday it'll keep you. —MAE WEST

As I think, this diary writing has greatly helped my style; loosened the ligatures. —VIRGINIA WOOLF

DIFFERENCE
(also see concepts 136, 161, 217, 294, 418, 830)

At this point it seems impossible to think difference without thinking it aggressively or defensively. But think it we must, because if we don't, it will continue to think us, as it has since genesis at the very least. —ALICE JARDINE

If we cannot now end our differences, at least we can help make the world safe for diversity. —JOHN F. KENNEDY

One man's meat is another man's poison. —PROVERB

There is more than one way to skin a cat. —PROVERB

Differences challenge assumptions. —ANNE WILSON SCHAEF

DIFFICULTY

(also see concepts 17, 623, 648, 757, 779)

In the face of an obstacle which is impossible to overcome, stubbornness is stupid. —SIMONE DE BEAUVOIR

Nothing is easy to the unwilling. —THOMAS FULLER

Many things difficult to design prove easy to performance.
—SAMUEL JOHNSON

I walk firmer and more secure up hill than down.
—MICHEL DE MONTAIGNE

DIGNITY

(also see conept 542)

I'll keep my personal dignity and pride to the very end–it's all I have left and it's a possession that only myself can part with.
—DAISY BATES

The only kind of dignity which is genuine is that which is not diminished by the indifference of others. —DAG HAMMARSKJÖLD

Dignity is a matter which concerns only mankind. —LIVY

Our dignity is not in what we do, but in what we understand.
—GEORGE SANTAYANA

No race can prosper till it learns that there is as much dignity in tilling a field as in writing a poem. —BOOKER T. WASHINGTON

DIPLOMATS AND DIPLOMACY

(also see concepts 90, 143, 294, 415, 791, 851)

All diplomacy is a continuation of war by other means.
—CHOU EN-LAI

To jaw-jaw is better than to war-war. —WINSTON CHURCHILL

Diplomacy is the police in grand costume. —NAPOLEON I

A diplomat is a person who can tell you to go to hell in such a way that you actually look forward to the trip. —CASKIE STINNETT

An ambassador is an honest man sent to lie abroad for the good of his country. —HENRY WOTTON

DISABILITY
(also see concepts 70, 184, 402)

If there are any of you at the back who do not hear me, please don't raise your hands because I am also nearsighted. —W. H. AUDEN

Though people with disabilities have become more vocal in recent years, we still constitute a very small minority. Yet the Beautiful People–the slender, fair and perfect ones–form a minority that may be even smaller. —DEBRA KENT

DISAPPOINTMENT
(also see concepts 215, 301, 734)

Disappointment tears the bearable film of life. —ELIZABETH BOWEN

Are you angry that others disappoint you? Remember you cannot depend upon yourself. —BENJAMIN FRANKLIN

He who expects much can expect little. —GABRIEL GARCIÁ MÁRQUEZ

In education, in marriage, in religion, in everything, disappointment is the lot of women. It shall be the business of my life to deepen this disappointment in every woman's heart until she bows down to it no longer. —LUCY STONE

DISCIPLINE
(also see concepts 234, 239, 709)

Some people regard discipline as a chore. For me, it is a kind of order that sets me free to fly. —JULIE ANDREWS

He who requires much from himself and little from others, will keep himself from being the object of resentment. —CONFUCIUS

Do not consider painful what is good for you. —EURIPIDES

Better a little chiding than a great deal of heartbreak.
—WILLIAM SHAKESPEARE

I'm all for bringing back the birch, but only between consenting adults. —GORE VIDAL

DISCOVERY
(also see concepts 10, 406, 420, 562, 760, 786)

Time is the greatest innovator. —FRANCIS BACON

At first people refuse to believe that a strange new thing can be done, then they begin to hope it can be done, then they see it can be done–then it is done and all the world wonders why it was not done centuries ago. —FRANCES HODGSON BURNETT

Inventors and men of genius have almost always been regarded as fools at the beginning (and very often at the end) of their careers.
—FYODOR DOSTOYEVSKY

I just invent, then wait until man comes around to needing what I've invented. —R. BUCKMINSTER FULLER

One doesn't discover new lands without consenting to lose sight of the shore for a very long time. —ANDRÉ GIDE

The vitality of a new movement in art or letters can be pretty accurately gauged by the fury it arouses. —LOGAN PEARSALL SMITH

Discovery consists of seeing what everybody has seen and thinking what nobody has thought. —ALBERT SZENT-GYÖRGYI

DISCRIMINATION
(also see concepts 396, 613)

In the end antiblack, antifemale, and all forms of discrimination are equivalent to the same thing–antihumanism. —SHIRLEY CHISHOLM

If we even tolerate any oppression of gay and lesbian Americans, if we join those who would intrude upon the choices of our hearts, then who among us shall be free? —JUNE JORDAN

Given the ethnic and racial hierarchies of American life, there are those who dish it out and those who have to take it...Some find themselves in the position of always having to take it. Such a position is, psychologically and emotionally speaking, almost unbearable. Rage and despair accumulate with no place to go. —ELIZABETH STONE

DISHONESTY
(also see concepts 374, 452, 711, 819, 826)

Man is practised in disguise; / He cheats the most discerning eyes. —JOHN GAY

One deceit needs many others, and so the whole house is built in the air and must soon come to the ground. —BALTASAR GRACIÁN

We are never so easily deceived as when we imagine we are deceiving others. —FRANÇOIS DE LA ROCHEFOUCAULD

You can fool some of the people all the time and all the people some of the time; but you can't fool all the people all the time. —ABRAHAM LINCOLN

It is more tolerable to be refused than deceived. —PUBLILIUS SYRUS

One may smile, and smile, and be a villain. —WILLIAM SHAKESPEARE

Hatred of dishonesty generally arises from fear of being deceived. —MARQUIS DE VAUVENARGUES

DISILLUSIONMENT
(also see concepts 210, 237, 375, 401, 781)

If you live long enough, you'll see that every victory turns into a defeat. —SIMONE DE BEAUVOIR

The flowers of life are but illusions. How many fade away and leave no trace; how few yield any fruit; and the fruit itself, how rarely does it ripen! —JOHANN WOLFGANG VON GOETHE

Every real object must cease to be what it seemed, and none could ever be what the whole soul desired. —GEORGE SANTAYANA

Things sweet to taste prove in digestion sour. —WILLIAM SHAKESPEARE

Hope is the only good thing that disillusion respects.
—MARQUIS DE VAUVENARGUES

DISTRUST
(also see concepts 41, 65, 181, 222, 333, 648, 826)

The lion and the calf shall lie down together but the calf won't get much sleep. —WOODY ALLEN

At the gate which suspicion enters, love goes out. —THOMAS FULLER

Trust the friends to-day as if they will be enemies to-morrow.
—BALTASAR GRACIÁN

Silence is the best tactic for him who distrusts himself.
—FRANÇOIS DE LA ROCHEFOUCAULD

Trust in God, but tie your camel. —PERSIAN PROVERB

Suspicion begets suspicion. —PUBLILIUS SYRUS

We are always paid for our suspicion by finding what we suspect.
—HENRY DAVID THOREAU

An ally has to be watched just like an enemy. —LEON TROTSKY

DIVERSITY
(also see concepts 34, 205, 414)

There are no elements so diverse that they cannot be joined in the heart of a man. —JEAN GIRAUDOUX

Let a hundred flowers bloom. Let a hundred schools of thought contend. —MAO TSE-TUNG

If we are to achieve a richer culture, rich in contrasting values, we must recognize the whole gamut of human potentialities, and so weave a less arbitrary social fabric, one in which each diverse human gift will find a fitting place. —MARGARET MEAD

There never were, in the world, two opinions alike, no more than two hairs, or two grains; the most universal quality is diversity. —MICHEL DE MONTAIGNE

DIVORCE

(also see concepts 465, 468, 479, 569, 831)

Divorce is defeat. —LUCILLE BALL

You never realize how short a month is until you pay alimony. —JOHN BARRYMORE

Divorce is the one human tragedy that reduces everything to cash. —RITA MAE BROWN

The only solid and lasting peace between a man and his wife is doubtless a separation. —EARL OF CHESTERFIELD

You never really know a man until you have divorced him. —ZSA ZSA GABOR

Divorce is a game played by lawyers. —CARY GRANT

After years of advising other people on their personal problems, I was stunned by my own divorce. I only wish I had someone to write to for help. —ANN LANDERS

However often marriage is dissolved, it remains indissoluble. Real divorce, the divorce of heart and nerve and fiber, does not exist, since there is no divorce from memory. —VIRGILIA PETERSON

In Biblical times, a man could have as many wives as he could afford. Just like today. —ABIGAIL VAN BUREN

Divorce is probably of nearly the same date as marriage. I believe, however, that marriage is some weeks the more ancient. —VOLTAIRE

Judges, as a class, display, in the matter of arranging alimony, that reckless generosity which is found only in men who are giving away someone else's cash. ——P. G. WODEHOUSE

DOCTORS
(also see concepts 340, 341, 350, 489, 738)

Physician, heal thyself. ——BIBLE, LUKE 4:23

Doctors are just the same as lawyers; the only difference is that lawyers merely rob you, whereas doctors rob you and kill you, too. ——ANTON CHEKHOV

Physicians must discover the weaknesses of the human mind, and even condescend to humour them, or they will never be called in to cure the infirmities of the body. ——CHARLES CALEB COLTON

God heals, and the doctor takes the fees. ——BENJAMIN FRANKLIN

I suppose one has a greater sense of intellectual degradation after an interview with a doctor than from any human experience. ——ALICE JAMES

As long as men are liable to die and are desirous to live, a physician will be made fun of, but he will be well paid. ——JEAN DE LA BRUYÈRE

The best surgeon is he that hath been hacked himself. ——ENGLISH PROVERB

The best doctor in the world is the Veterinarian. He can't ask his patients what is the matter—he's got to just know. ——WILL ROGERS

A physician is one who pours drugs of which he knows little into a body of which he knows less. ——VOLTAIRE

DOGMATISM
(also see concepts 64, 123, 378)

In this unbelievable universe in which we live there are no absolutes. Even parallel lines, reaching into infinity, meet somewhere yonder. ——PEARL BUCK

Dogma can in no way limit a limitless God. —FLANNERY O'CONNOR

You can't teach an old dogma new tricks. —DOROTHY PARKER

DOGS
(also see concepts 37, 92)

The dog was created specially for children. He is the god of frolic.
—HENRY WARD BEECHER

The great pleasure of a dog is that you may make a fool of yourself with him and not only will he not scold you, he will make a fool of himself too. —SAMUEL BUTLER

Histories are more full of examples of the fidelity of dogs than of friends. —ALEXANDER POPE

Don't make the mistake of treating your dogs like humans, or they'll treat you like dogs. —MARTHA SCOTT

I loathe people who keep dogs. They are cowards who haven't got the guts to bite people themselves. —AUGUST STRINDBERG

DOUBT
(also see concepts 26, 216, 237, 391, 648)

Doubt is not below knowledge, but above it. —ALAIN

Doubt of the reality of love ends by making us doubt everything.
—HENRI FRÉDÉRIC AMIEL

Without measureless and perpetual uncertainty the drama of human life would be destroyed. —WINSTON CHURCHILL

Just think of the tragedy of teaching children not to doubt.
—CLARENCE DARROW

Man's most valuable trait / is a judicious sense of what not to believe. —EURIPIDES

There seems to be a terrible misunderstanding on the part of a great many people to the effect that when you cease to believe you may cease to behave. —LOUIS KRONENBERGER

A wise skepticism is the first attribute of a good critic.
——JAMES RUSSELL LOWELL

The only limit to our realization of tomorrow will be our doubts of today. ——FRANKLIN D. ROOSEVELT

The trouble with the world is that the stupid are cocksure and the intelligent full of doubt. ——BERTRAND RUSSELL

Our doubts are traitors / And make us lose the good we oft might win / By fearing to attempt. ——WILLIAM SHAKESPEARE

DRAMATISTS AND DRAMA
(also see concepts 11, 48, 53, 90, 592, 801, 812, 874)

Drama is life with the dull bits cut out. ——ALFRED HITCHCOCK

The theatre, so called, can flourish on barbarism, but any drama worth speaking of can develop but in the air of civilisation. ——HENRY JAMES

Drama—what literature does at night. ——GEORGE JEAN NATHAN

Drama is action, sir, action and not confounded philosophy. ——LUIGI PIRANDELLO

A novelist may lose his readers for a few pages; a playwright never dares lose his audience for a minute. ——TERENCE RATTIGAN

I see the playwright as a lay preacher peddling the ideas of his time in popular form. ——AUGUST STRINDBERG

Show me a congenital eavesdropper with the instincts of a Peeping Tom and I will show you the makings of a dramatist. ——KENNETH TYNAN

A talent for drama is not a talent for writing, but is an ability to articulate human relationships. ——GORE VIDAL

DREAMS

(also see concepts 381, 591, 748)

If one is lucky, a solitary fantasy can totally transform one million realities. —MAYA ANGELOU

Dreamers are insatiable expansionists, and the space of dreams rapidly becomes overcrowded. —JOHN ASHBERY

Dreaming men are haunted men. —STEPHEN VINCENT BENÉT

Dreams are, by definition, cursed with short life spans.
—CANDICE BERGEN

Dreams have only one owner at a time. That's why dreamers are lonely. —ERMA BOMBECK

When we can't dream any longer, we die. —EMMA GOLDMAN

We are not hypocrites in our sleep. —WILLIAM HAZLITT

The waking have one world in common; sleepers have each a private world of his own. —HERACLITUS

We do not really feel grateful toward those who make our dreams come true; they ruin our dreams. —ERIC HOFFER

Dreams are faithful interpreters of our inclinations; but there is art required to sort and understand them. —MICHEL DE MONTAIGNE

To believe in one's dreams is to spend all of one's life asleep.
—CHINESE PROVERB

Keep true to the dreams of thy youth.
—JOHANN FRIEDRICH VON SCHILLER

I talk of dreams; / Which are the children of an idle brain, / Begot of nothing but vain fantasy. —WILLIAM SHAKESPEARE

It is in our idleness, in our dreams, that the submerged truth sometimes comes to the top. —VIRGINIA WOOLF

DRINKS AND DRINKING

(also see concepts 4, 12, 125, 412, 854)

Drink no longer water, but use a little wine for thy stomach's sake and thine often infirmities. —BIBLE, I TIMOTHY 5:23

Man, being reasonable, must get drunk; / The best of Life is but intoxication. —LORD BYRON

Drink moderately, for drunkenness neither keeps a secret, nor observes a promise. —MIGUEL DE CERVANTES

The secret of drunkenness is, that it insulates us in thought, whilst it unites us in feeling. —RALPH WALDO EMERSON

I am as sober as a judge. —HENRY FIELDING

First you take a drink, then the drink takes a drink, then the drink takes you. —F. SCOTT FITZGERALD

Best while you have it use your breath / There is no drinking after death. —JOHN FLETCHER

Bacchus hath drowned more men than Neptune. —THOMAS FULLER

Although it is better to hide our ignorance, this is hard to do when we relax over wine. —HERACLITUS

He that goes to bed thirsty rises healthy. —GEORGE HERBERT

Who, after wine, talks of war's hardships or of poverty? —HORACE

God made only water, but man made wine. —VICTOR HUGO

We drink one another's healths and spoil our own.
—JEROME K. JEROME

Wine is only sweet to happy men. —JOHN KEATS

I can't look forward to going out and getting drunk on a given night anymore, which I used to love. That was the way to get back to oneself, and I can't do it. Because I wake up in the morning and I can't get out of bed. —NORMAN MAILER

I'd hate to be a teetotaler. Imagine getting up in the morning and knowing that's as good as you're going to feel all day.
—DEAN MARTIN

Better sleep with a sober cannibal than a drunken Christian.
——HERMAN MELVILLE

When there is plenty of wine, sorrow and worry take wing. ——OVID

One more drink and I'd be under the host. ——DOROTHY PARKER

In wine there is truth. ——PLINY THE ELDER

There are more old drunkards than old doctors. ——PROVERB

To dispute with a drunkard is to debate with an empty house.
——PUBLILIUS SYRUS

Drunkenness is simply voluntary insanity. ——SENECA

It provokes the desire, but it takes away the performance. Therefore
much drink may be said to be an equivocator with lechery.
——WILLIAM SHAKESPEARE

An alcoholic is someone you don't like who drinks as much as you
do. ——DYLAN THOMAS

DRUGS

(also see concepts 4, 12, 151, 669, 738)

Cocaine isn't habit-forming. I should know–I've been using it for
years. ——TALLULAH BANKHEAD

I'll die young, but it's like kissing God. ——LENNY BRUCE

And the answer on drugs is, again, education–until some genius
finds an antidote that you can stick in your arm and it does away
with all addictions. ——MARIO CUOMO

Thou hast the keys of Paradise, oh, just, subtle, and mighty opium!
——THOMAS DE QUINCEY

If God wanted us high, He would have given us wings.
——ARSENIO HALL

Every form of addiction is bad, no matter whether the narcotic be
alcohol or morphine or idealism. ——CARL JUNG

One man's poison is another man's drug. ——RONALD KNOX

Turn on, tune in, drop out. —TIMOTHY LEARY

We black people aren't the only people on drugs. The reason you've got drugs on the so-called agenda is because you've got young white kids in middle-class America and white suburbia who are doing crack and whatever. Then it becomes a national problem. As long as it was contained within the black ghettos, you would never see the problem being dealt with on the covers of *Time* or *Newsweek*. —SPIKE LEE

The only reason that cocaine is such a rage today is that people are too dumb and lazy to get themselves together to roll a joint. —JACK NICHOLSON

Just say no. —NANCY REAGAN

To tell the story of Coleridge without the opium is to tell the story of Hamlet without mentioning the ghost. —LESLIE STEPHEN

DUTY
(also see concepts 150, 375, 549, 676, 729)

Our duty is to be useful, not according to our desires but according to our powers. —HENRI FRÉDÉRIC AMIEL

Do your duty, and leave the rest to the gods. —PIERRE CORNEILLE

You will always find those who think they know that is your duty better than you know it. —RALPH WALDO EMERSON

Oh! Duty is an icy shadow. —AUGUSTA EVANS

What, then, is your duty? What the day demands. —JOHANN WOLFGANG VON GOETHE

The last pleasure in life is the sense of discharging our duty. —WILLIAM HAZLITT

What is the use of such terrible diligence as many tire themselves out with, if they always postpone their exchange of smiles with Beauty and Joy to cling to irksome duties and relations? —HELEN KELLER

The path of duty lies in the thing that is nearby, but men seek it in things far off. —CHINESE PROVERB

A sense of duty is useful in work, but offensive in personal relations. People wish to be liked, not endured with patient resignation. —BERTRAND RUSSELL

Alas! when duty grows thy law, enjoyment fades away.
—JOHANN FRIEDRICH VON SCHILLER

There is no duty we so much underrate as the duty of being happy.
—ROBERT LOUIS STEVENSON

Duty is what one expects from others, it is not what one does one's self. —OSCAR WILDE

EARTH

(also see concepts 230, 815, 839, 871)

Earth being so good, would Heaven seem best? —ROBERT BROWNING

The lunatic asylum of the solar system. —SAMUEL PARKS CADMAN

The earth is given as a common for men to labor and live in.
—THOMAS JEFFERSON

Take what you can use and let the rest go by. —KEN KESEY

I should like the green earth not to feel my step as a heavy burden. I should like her to forgive that she for my sake is wounded by plow and harrow, and willingly to open for my dead body.
—SELMA LAGERLÖF

EATING DISORDERS

(also see concepts 290, 340)

I know I could never/with such ease allow another to put food into my mouth:/happily *myself* put food into another's mouth–;/I knew that to become a wife I would have to give up my ideal.
—FRANK BIDART

We cannot even begin to think about self-healing until we stop using the words "eating disorder" to hide from ourselves the formidable struggle for a self in which every woman suffering in her relationship to food is secretly engaged. We are in trouble (and how else could it be, considering the magnitude of our task?) as we attempt to shape ourselves for a future unprecedented in what has been, indeed, until now, a history of man. Clearly, we need every bit of help and divine guidance and practical cunning we can find. For in our hands, these hands that lift children to our breasts and open books and pull us up unconquered mountains and cut wood and spice food and place that food in our mouths and in the mouths of our children, the future identity of generations of women is being prepared. —KIM CHERNIN

It seems to me that our three basic needs, for food and security and love, are so mixed and mingled and entwined that we cannot straightly think of one without the others. —M.F.K. FISHER

Anorexia marks a girl's move from the conscious underground where she is connected to her feelings but strategically protects them from view, into a psychological resistance where she struggles to remain in touch with herself and her feelings. Girls' healthy resistance, once underground, may turn into a psychological resistance as girls become reluctant to know what they know and fear that their experience if spoken will endanger their relationships and threaten survival. —CAROL GILLIGAN

Women with body-image or eating disorders are not a special category, just more extreme in their response to a culture that emphasizes thinness and impossible standards of appearance for women instead of individuality and health. —GLORIA STEINEM

How would America react to the mass self-immolation by hunger of its favorite sons? —NAOMI WOLF

ECOLOGY
(see also concepts 153, 228, 600, 815)

The current collapse of industrial society may well be the planet's way of avoiding a larger death. —MORRIS BERMAN

As soils are depleted, human health, vitality and intelligence go with them. —LOUIS BROMFIELD

The universe is like a safe to which there is a combination. But the combination is locked up in the safe. —PETER DE VRIES

The sun, the moon and the stars would have disappeared long ago, had they happened to be within reach of predatory human hands. —HAVELOCK ELLIS

After all, the men and women of every generation must share the same earth–the only earth we have–and so we also share a responsibility to ensure that what one generation calls the future will be able to mature safely into what another generation will call the present. —AL GORE

The struggle to save the global environment is in one way much more difficult than the struggle to vanquish Hitler, for this time the war is with ourselves. We are the enemy, just as we have only ourselves as allies. In a war such as this, then, what is victory and how will we recognize it? —AL GORE

Man is not an omnipotent master of the universe, allowed to do with impunity whatever he thinks, or whatever suits him at the moment. The world we live in is made of an immensely complex and mysterious tissue about which we know very little and which we must treat with utmost humility. —VÁCLAV HAVEL

Everyone has gone back to a place that they remember from childhood and seen an apartment complex or a K-mart. When I was growing up we were on the edge of the Everglades. Now we're in the middle of mall hell. —CARL HIAASEN

The crisis of life grows greater and ever more insistent, like an environmental *Bolero*. I used to think the tragedy was that so much would be lost and nobody would notice a century from now. I now believe the impact on society could be so great that it will be remembered if we do not speak out and act. —THOMAS LOVEJOY

If we think of nothing but selfish human greed and ignore the natural life of the Earth, we have set the scene for our own destruction and that of the comfortable Earth we know. Just now, we seem like the gaderene swine driving our polluting cars down to a sea rising to meet us. —JAMES LOVELOCK

We are living beyond our means. As a people we have developed a life-style that is draining the earth of its priceless and irreplaceable resources without regard for the future of our children and people all around the world. —MARGARET MEAD

We won't have a society if we destroy the environment.
—MARGARET MEAD

Obviously, the answer to oil spills is to paper-train the tankers.
—RALPH NADER

We do not inherit the land from our ancestors; we borrow it from our children. —NATIVE AMERICAN PROVERB

We've always thought of climate as an act of God. It requires an enormous shift in the way we think of the world and our place in it to understand that we have already moved into an era in which we are actually responsible for managing climatic parameters.
—ROBERT REDFORD

...the thickness of the air, compared to the size of the Earth, is something like the thickness of a coat of shellac on a schoolroom globe. Many astronauts have reported seeing that delicate, thin, blue aura at the horizon of daylit hemisphere and immediately, unbidden, thinking about its fragility and vulnerability. They have reason to worry. —CARL SAGAN

Man did not weave this web of life. He is merely a strand of it. Whatever he does to the web, he does to himself. —CHIEF SEATTLE

ECONOMICS
(also see concepts 57, 88, 133, 399, 421, 512, 628, 661, 768, 806)

In economics the majority is always wrong.
—JOHN KENNETH GALBRAITH

I learned more about the economy from one South Dakota dust storm than I did in all my years at college. —HUBERT HUMPHREY

Economic growth without social progress lets the great majority of the people remain in poverty, while a privileged few reap the benefits of rising abundance. —JOHN F. KENNEDY

Just as men cannot now escape taking on collective responsibility for peace, neither can they escape taking on collective responsibility for economic plenty. —MAX LERNER

A nation is not in danger of financial disaster merely because it owes itself money. —ANDREW WILLIAM MELLON

If all economists were laid end to end, they would not reach a conclusion. —GEORGE BERNARD SHAW

Give me a one-handed economist! All my economists say, "on the one hand...on the other." —HARRY S TRUMAN

EDITORS AND EDITING
(also see concepts 90, 325, 476, 540, 640)

Art should simplify...finding what convention of form and what detail one can do without and yet preserve the spirit of the whole–so that all that one has suppressed and cut away is there to the reader's consciousness as much as if it were in type on the page. —WILLA CATHER

My definition of a good editor is a man I think charming, who sends me large checks, praises my work, my physical beauty, and my sexual prowess, and who has a stranglehold on the publisher and the bank. —JOHN CHEEVER

An editor should tell the author his writing is better than it is. Not a lot better, a little better. —T. S. ELIOT

Yes, I suppose some editors are failed writers–but so are most writers. —T. S. ELIOT

Great editors do not discover nor produce great authors; great authors create and produce great publishers. —JOHN FARRAR

I usually have poor to absent relations with editors because they have a habit of desiring changes and I resist changes. —WILLIAM GASS

Editing is the same as quarreling with writers–same thing exactly.
——HAROLD ROSS

An editor is one who separates the wheat from the chaff and prints the chaff. ——ADLAI STEVENSON

Editing is the most companionable form of education.
——EDWARD WEEKS

No passion in the world is equal to the passion to alter someone else's draft. ——H. G. WELLS

EDUCATION
(also see concepts 116, 177, 325, 446, 458, 614, 700, 795)

They know enough who know how to learn.
——HENRY BROOKS ADAMS

Life is my college. May I graduate well, and earn some honours!
——LOUISA MAY ALCOTT

Education is an ornament in prosperity and a refuge in adversity.
——ARISTOTLE

Studies serve for delight, for ornament, and for ability.
——FRANCIS BACON

A child cannot be taught by anyone who despises him, and a child cannot afford to be fooled. ——JAMES BALDWIN

Those who trust us educate us. ——GEORGE ELIOT

I pay the schoolmaster, but 'tis the schoolboys that educate my son.
——RALPH WALDO EMERSON

Only the educated are free. ——EPICTETUS

Public schools are the nurseries of all vice and immorality.
——HENRY FIELDING

Education is hanging around until you've caught on.
——ROBERT FROST

The ability to think straight, some knowledge of the past, some vision of the future, some urge to fit that service into the well-being of the community—these are the most vital things education must try to produce. —VIRGINIA GILDERSLEEVE

It is not who you attend school with but who controls the school you attend. —NIKKI GIOVANNI

Education makes us more stupid than the brutes. A thousand voices call to us on every hand, but our ears are stopped with wisdom. —JEAN GIRAUDOUX

They teach in academies far too many things, and far too much that is useless. —JOHANN WOLFGANG VON GOETHE

Much learning does not teach understanding. —HERACLITUS

The main part of intellectual education is not the acquisition of facts but learning how to make facts live. —OLIVER WENDELL HOLMES, JR.

Education is what you learn in books, and nobody knows you know it but your teacher. —VIRGINIA CARY HUDSON

Education is not a *product*: mark, diploma, job, money—in that order; it is a *process*, a never-ending one. —BEL KAUFMAN

Like most Americans, I believed in the myth of progress: If you don't hear anything about it for ten years, it must have gotten better. But the schools are more crowded, the black children are more segregated, their health is worse, their nutrition is worse. The schools are more like garrisons or outposts or prisons than places of education. —JONATHAN KOZOL

More money is put into prison construction than into schools. That, in itself, is the description of a nation bent on suicide. I mean, what's more precious to us than our own children? We're going to build a lot more prisons if we don't deal with the schools and their inequalities. —JONATHAN KOZOL

We are dealing with the best-educated generation in history. But they've got a brain dressed up with nowhere to go. —TIMOTHY LEARY

We only labor to stuff the memory, and leave the conscience and the understanding unfurnished and void. —MICHEL DE MONTAIGNE

The first idea that the child must acquire in order to be actively disciplined is that of the difference between good and evil; and the task of the education lies in seeing that the child does not confound good with immobility, and evil with activity. —MARIA MONTESSORI

Knowledge which is acquired under compulsion obtains no hold on the mind. —PLATO

When you do know something about the reality of the world that those who stand in ignorance do not know, then you can't not educate. —BETTY POWELL

It is only the ignorant who despise education. —PUBLILIUS SYRUS

The great difficulty in education is to get experience out of ideas. —GEORGE SANTAYANA

Education is what survives when what has been learned has been forgotten. —B. F. SKINNER

To throw obstacles in the way of a complete education is like putting out the eyes. —ELIZABETH CADY STANTON

The schools of the country are its future in miniature. —TEHYI HSIEH

What does education often do? It makes a straight-cut ditch of a free, meandering brook. —HENRY DAVID THOREAU

In the first place God made idiots. This was for practice. Then he made school boards. —MARK TWAIN

Theories and goals of education don't matter a whit if you don't consider your students to be human beings. —LOU ANN WALKER

EFFORT
(also see concepts 8, 50, 241)

The bitter and the sweet come from the outside, the hard from within, from one's own efforts. —ALBERT EINSTEIN

Much effort, much prosperity. —EURIPIDES

Just don't give up trying to do what you really want to do. Where there is love and inspiration, I don't think you can go wrong. —ELLA FITZGERALD

To win one's joy through struggle is better than to yield to melancholy. —ANDRÉ GIDE

What we hope ever to do with ease, we must learn first to do with diligence. —SAMUEL JOHNSON

When we do the best we can, we never know what miracle is wrought in our life, or in the life of another. —HELEN KELLER

Effort is only effort when it begins to hurt. —JOSÉ ORTEGA Y GASSET

The struggle alone pleases us, not the victory. —BLAISE PASCAL

If a job's worth doing, it's worth doing well. —PROVERB

Nothing can come of nothing. —WILLIAM SHAKESPEARE

You may be disappointed if you fail, but you are doomed if you don't try. —BEVERLY SILLS

EGOTISM
(also see concepts 45, 708, 715, 721, 723, 838)

Our own self-love draws a thick veil between us and our faults. —EARL OF CHESTERFIELD

What, will the world be quite overturned when you die?—EPICTETUS

Self-love depressed becomes self-loathing. —SALLY KEMPTON

We would rather speak badly of ourselves than not talk about ourselves at all. —FRANÇOIS DE LA ROCHEFOUCAULD

Egotism is the anesthetic that dulls the pain of stupidity. —FRANK LEAHY

Listen, everyone is entitled to my opinion. —MADONNA

One must learn to love oneself...with a wholesome and healthy love, so that one can bear to be with oneself and need not roam. —FRIEDRICH WILHELM NIETZSCHE

If someone as blessed as I am is not willing to clean out the barn, who will? —ROSS PEROT

Self-love, my liege, is not so vile a sin / As self-neglecting.
—WILLIAM SHAKESPEARE

Egotism—usually just a case of mistaken nonentity.
—BARBARA STANWYCK

If only I had a little humility, I'd be perfect. —TED TURNER

I'm in trouble because I'm normal and slightly arrogant. A lot of people don't like themselves and I happen to be totally in love with myself. —MIKE TYSON

It is not love we should have painted as blind, but self-love.
—VOLTAIRE

To love oneself is the beginning of a life-long romance.
—OSCAR WILDE

ELOQUENCE
(also see concepts 400, 582, 594, 638, 649, 761)

There is no more sovereign eloquence than the truth in indignation.
—VICTOR HUGO

True eloquence consists in saying all that should be said, and that only. —FRANÇOIS DE LA ROCHEFOUCAULD

Continuous eloquence wearies. —BLAISE PASCAL

A thing said walks in immortality / if it has been said well.
—PETER PINDAR

EMOTIONS
(also see concepts 14, 20, 36, 146, 210, 467, 534, 570, 634, 635, 725, 726, 798, 823)

We are adhering to life now with our last muscle—the heart.
—DJUNA BARNES

It is not our exalted feelings, it is our sentiments that build the necessary home. —ELIZABETH BOWEN

Where the heart lies, let the brain lie also. —ROBERT BROWNING

It is as healthy to enjoy sentiment as to enjoy jam.
—G. K. CHESTERTON

The important thing is being capable of emotions, but to experience only *one's own* would be a sorry limitation. —ANDRÉ GIDE

All the knowledge I possess everyone else can acquire, but my heart is all my own. —JOHANN WOLFGANG VON GOETHE

If you would have me weep, you must first of all feel grief yourself.
—HORACE

One ought to hold on to one's heart; for if one lets it go, one soon loses control of the head too. —FRIEDRICH WILHELM NIETZSCHE

The direct speech of feeling is allegorical and cannot be replaced by anything. —BORIS PASTERNAK

In a full heart there is room for everything, and in an empty heart there is room for nothing. —ANTONIO PORCHIA

The heart is half a prophet. —YIDDISH PROVERB

Nothing vivifies, and nothing kills, like the emotions.
—JOSEPH ROUX

Whatever makes an impression on the heart seems lovely in the eye. —SA`DI

Emotion is primarily about nothing and much of it remains about nothing to the end. —GEORGE SANTAYANA

The heart is forever inexperienced. —HENRY DAVID THOREAU

Emotion has taught mankind to reason. —MARQUIS DE VAUVENARGUES

For years I have endeavored to calm an impetuous tide–laboring to make my feelings take an orderly course–it was striving against the stream. —MARY WOLLSTONECRAFT

ENDING

(also see concepts 93, 152, 190, 425, 456)

This is the way the world ends / Not with a bang but a whimper.
——T. S. ELIOT

All good things must come to an end. ——PROVERB

God alone can finish. ——JOHN RUSKIN

It's the job that's never started as takes longest to finish.
——J. R. R. TOLKIEN

ENDURANCE

(also see concepts 772, 779, 787, 849)

People are too durable, that's their main trouble. They can do too much to themselves, they last too long. ——BERTOLT BRECHT

To bear is to conquer our fate. ——THOMAS CAMPBELL

What cannot be altered must be borne, not blamed.
——THOMAS FULLER

Know how sublime a thing it is / To suffer and be strong.
——HENRY WADSWORTH LONGFELLOW

Nothing happens to any man that he is not formed by nature to bear.
——MARCUS AURELIUS

People have to learn sometimes not only how much the heart, but how much the head, can bear. ——MARIA MITCHELL

What can't be cured, must be endured. ——PROVERB

Happy he who learns to bear what he cannot change!
——JOHANN FRIEDRICH VON SCHILLER

Many can brook the weather that love not the wind.
——WILLIAM SHAKESPEARE

ENEMIES

(also see concepts 36, 285, 339, 414, 499)

Enemies' promises were made to be broken. —AESOP

Pay attention to your enemies, for they are the first to discover your mistakes. —ANTISTHENES

A strong foe is better than a weak friend. —EDWARD DAHLBERG

A wise man gets more use from his enemies than a fool from his friends. —BALTASAR GRACIÁN

Enemies are so stimulating. —KATHARINE HEPBURN

Even a paranoid can have enemies. —HENRY KISSINGER

Our enemies approach nearer to truth in their judgements of us than we do ourselves. —FRANÇOIS DE LA ROCHEFOUCAULD

The real enemy can always be met and conquered, or won over. Real antagonism is based on love, a love which has not recognized itself. —HENRY MILLER

He who lives by fighting with an enemy has an interest in the preservation of the enemy's life. —FRIEDRICH WILHELM NIETZSCHE

ENTERPRISE

(also see concept 8, 9, 10, 167, 234, 720)

None will improve your lot / If you yourselves do not.
—BERTOLT BRECHT

The passion to get ahead is sometimes born of the fear lest we be left behind. —ERIC HOFFER

Nothing will ever be attempted, if all possible objections must be first overcome. —SAMUEL JOHNSON

Go and wake up your luck. —PERSIAN PROVERB

ENTHUSIASM

(also see concepts 525, 786, 878, 880)

In things pertaining to enthusiasm, no man is sane who does not know how to be insane on proper occasions.
——HENRY WARD BEECHER

You will do foolish things, but do them with enthusiasm. ——COLETTE

You can't sweep other people off their feet, if you can't be swept off your own. ——CLARENCE DAY

Nothing great was ever achieved without enthusiasm.
——RALPH WALDO EMERSON

The love of life is necessary to the vigorous prosecution of any undertaking. ——SAMUEL JOHNSON

The world belongs to the enthusiast who keeps cool.
——WILLIAM MCFEE

ENVY

(also see concepts 237, 329, 430)

He who goes unenvied shall not be admired. ——AESCHYLUS

As iron is eaten away by rust, so the envious are consumed by their own passion. ——ANTISTHENES

Let age, not envy, draw wrinkles on thy cheeks. ——THOMAS BROWNE

Envy is the tax which all distinction must pay.
——RALPH WALDO EMERSON

Nothing sharpens sight like envy. ——THOMAS FULLER

Envy's a sharper spur than pay. ——JOHN GAY

The envious die not once, but as oft as the envied win applause.
——BALTASAR GRACIÁN

How much better a thing it is to be envied than to be pitied.
——HERODOTUS

Envy is more irreconcilable than hatred.
—FRANÇOIS DE LA ROCHEFOUCAULD

Even success softens not the heart of the envious. —PETER PINDAR

Whenever a friend succeeds, a little something in me dies.
—GORE VIDAL

A show of envy is an insult to oneself. —YEVGENY YEVTUSHENKO

EQUALITY

(also see concepts 136, 365, 436)

Equality consists in the same treatment of similar persons.
—ARISTOTLE

Equality may perhaps be a right, but no power on earth can ever turn it into a fact. —HONORÉ DE BALZAC

The most mediocre of males feels himself a demigod as compared with women. —SIMONE DE BEAUVOIR

The defect of equality is that we only desire it with our superiors.
—HENRY BECQUE

Equality is a mortuary word. —CHRISTOPHER FRY

That all men are equal is a proposition to which, at ordinary times, no sane individual has ever given his assent. —ALDOUS HUXLEY

We hold these truths to be self-evident, that all men are created equal, that they are endowed by their creator with certain unalienable Rights, that among these are Life, Liberty, and the pursuit of happiness. —THOMAS JEFFERSON

It is better that some should be unhappy than that none should be happy, which would be the case in a general state of equality.
—SAMUEL JOHNSON

I have a dream that one day this nation will rise up, live out the true meaning of its creed: we hold these truths to be self-evident, that all men are created equal. —MARTIN LUTHER KING, JR.

Whether women are better than men I cannot say—but I can say they are certainly no worse. —GOLDA MEIR

It is the American vice, the democratic disease which expresses its tyranny by reducing everything unique to the level of the herd. —HENRY MILLER

Weariness is the shortest path to equality and fraternity—and finally liberty is bestowed by sleep. —FRIEDRICH WILHELM NIETZSCHE

On the road to equality there is no better place for blacks to detour around American values than in foregoing its example in the treatment of its women and the organization of its family life. —ELEANOR HOLMES NORTON

All animals are equal, but some animals are more equal than others. —GEORGE ORWELL

I never doubted that equal rights was the right direction. Most reforms, most problems, are complicated. But to me there is nothing complicated about ordinary equality. —ALICE PAUL

The liberation of women is above all based on their capacity to think their own problems through and to link them to the total progress of the society and the world in which they live, to their capacity to develop a political and cultural consciousness. —NAWAL EL SAADAWI

A friend to everybody and to nobody is the same thing. —SPANISH PROVERB

Life levels all men: death reveals the eminent. —GEORGE BERNARD SHAW

The principle of equality does not destroy the imagination, but lowers its flight to the level of the earth. —ALEXIS DE TOCQUEVILLE

We cannot expect in the immediate future that all women who seek it will achieve full equality of opportunity. But if women are to start moving towards that goal, we must believe in ourselves or no one else will believe in us; we must match our aspirations with the competence, courage and determination to succeed. —ROSALYN YALOW

ERAS
(also see concepts 308, 513, 552, 571, 807)

The men who come on the stage at one period are all found to be related to each other. Certain ideas are in the air.
——RALPH WALDO EMERSON

Woe to these people who have no appetite for the very dish that their age serves up. ——ANDRÉ GIDE

The man who thinks only of his own generation is born for few.
——SENECA

ETERNITY
(also see concepts 23, 385, 463)

Our theories of the eternal are as valuable as are those which a chick which has not broken its way through its shell might form of the outside world. ——BUDDHA

Happiness is never really so welcome as changelessness.
——GRAHAM GREENE

Reversion to destiny is called eternity. ——LAO-TZU

Everything that has been is eternal: the sea will wash it up again.
——FRIEDRICH WILHELM NIETZSCHE

Eternity is a terrible thought. I mean, where's it going to end?
——TOM STOPPARD

Time's violence rends the soul; by the rent eternity enters.
——SIMONE WEIL

EUROPE
(also see concepts 82, 296, 312, 328, 423, 428, 461, 567, 691, 703, 760, 789)

Europe has what we do not have yet, a sense of the mysterious and inexorable limits of life, a sense, in a word, of tragedy. And we have

what they sorely need: a sense of life's possibilities.
—JAMES BALDWIN

We came over here to find culture, and if this is it I'll not take a second helping. —DJUNA BARNES

Can we never extract the tapeworm of Europe from the brain of our countrymen? —RALPH WALDO EMERSON

I am inclined to notice the ruin in things, perhaps because I was born in Italy. —ARTHUR MILLER

That Europe is nothin' on earth but a great big auction.
—TENNESSEE WILLIAMS

EVENTS
(also see concepts 16, 112, 137, 261, 432, 539, 556, 571)

People to whom nothing has ever happened / Cannot understand the unimportance of events. —T. S. ELIOT

Events expand with the character. —RALPH WALDO EMERSON

The enemy of the conventional wisdom is not ideas but the march of events. —JOHN KENNETH GALBRAITH

The greatest events–they are not our loudest but our stillest hours.
—FRIEDRICH WILHELM NIETZSCHE

EVIL
(also see concepts 164, 186, 203, 321, 477, 743, 840)

No notice is taken of a little evil, but when it increases it strikes the eye. —ARISTOTLE

A belief in a supernatural source of evil is not necessary; men alone are quite capable of every wickedness. —JOSEPH CONRAD

All evils are equal when they are extreme. —PIERRE CORNEILLE

Wicked is not much worse than indiscreet. —JOHN DONNE

It is by its promise of a sense of power that evil often attracts the weak. —ERIC HOFFER

He who passively accepts evil is as much involved in it as he who helps to perpetrate it. —MARTIN LUTHER KING, JR.

When you choose the lesser of two evils, always remember that it is still an evil. —MAX LERNER

There is no explanation for evil. It must be looked upon as a necessary part of the order of the universe. To ignore it is childish; to bewail it senseless. —W. SOMERSET MAUGHAM

Evil alone has oil for every wheel. —EDNA ST. VINCENT MILLAY

Submit to the present evil, lest a greater one befall you. —PHAEDRUS

Evil enters like a needle and spreads like an oak tree. —ETHIOPIAN PROVERB

Our greatest evils flow from ourselves. —JEAN JACQUES ROUSSEAU

There's small choice in rotten apples. —WILLIAM SHAKESPEARE

Between two evils, I always pick the one I never tried before. —MAE WEST

EVOLUTION
(also see concepts 98, 316, 330, 454, 787)

We must, however, acknowledge, as it seems to me, that man with all his noble qualities, still bears in his bodily frame the indelible stamp of his lowly origin. —CHARLES DARWIN

How like us is that ugly brute, the ape! —ENNIUS

Darwinian Man, though well-behaved, / At best is only a monkey shaved. —W. S. GILBERT

Evolution is not a force but a process; not a cause but a law. —JOHN MORLEY

All the evolution we know of proceeds from the vague to the definite. —CHARLES SANDERS PEIRCE

The tide of evolution carries everything before it, thoughts no less than bodies, and persons no less than nations. —GEORGE SANTAYANA

I believe that our Heavenly Father invented man because he was disappointed in the monkey. —MARK TWAIN

EXAGGERATION
(also see concepts 72, 254, 399, 711)

To exaggerate is to weaken. —JEAN-FRANÇOIS DE LA HARPE

Camp is a vision of the world in terms of style–but a particular style. It is the love of the exaggerated. —SUSAN SONTAG

Exaggeration, the inseparable companion of greatness. —VOLTAIRE

EXAMPLE
(also see concepts 263, 383)

Example is the best precept. —AESOP

Example is the school of mankind, and they will learn at no other. —EDMUND BURKE

What you do not want done to yourself, do not do to others. —CONFUCIUS

He teaches me to be good that does me good. —THOMAS FULLER

Practice what you preach. —PROVERB

Few things are harder to put up with than the annoyance of a good example. —MARK TWAIN

EXCELLENCE
(also see concepts 310, 327, 578, 783, 830, 835)

There is none who cannot teach somebody something, and there is none so excellent but he is excelled. —BALTASAR GRACIÁN

One shining quality lends a lustre to another, or hides some glaring defect. —WILLIAM HAZLITT

EXCESS
(also see concepts 251, 399, 412, 654, 806, 853)

Nothing in excess. —ANONYMOUS

Riches are for spending. —FRANCIS BACON

The road to excess leads to the palace of wisdom. —WILLIAM BLAKE

All progress is based upon a universal innate desire on the part of every organism to live beyond its income. —SAMUEL BUTLER

To go beyond is as wrong as to fall short. —CONFUCIUS

Excess on occasion is exhilarating. It prevents moderation from acquiring the deadening effect of a habit. —W. SOMERSET MAUGHAM

They are as sick that surfeit with too much as they that starve with nothing. —WILLIAM SHAKESPEARE

Modern life is given over to immoderation. Immoderation invades everything: actions and thought, public and private life.
—SIMONE WEIL

EXCUSES
(also see 38, 193, 263, 295, 556, 664)

Bad excuses are worse than none. —THOMAS FULLER

And oftentimes excusing of a fault / Doth make the fault worse by the excuse. —WILLIAM SHAKESPEARE

Two wrongs don't make a right, but they make a good excuse.
—THOMAS SZASZ

EXERCISE
(also see 58, 182, 229, 292, 318, 340)

The only reason I would take up jogging is so that I could hear heavy breathing again. —ERMA BOMBECK

Nothing lifts me out of a bad mood better than a hard workout on my treadmill. It never fails: to us, exercise is nothing short of a miracle. —CHER

Use it or lose it. —JIMMY CONNORS

Exercise is bunk. If you are healthy you don't need it: if you are sick you shouldn't take it. —HENRY FORD

If we could give every individual the right amount of nourishment and exercise, not too little and not too much, we would have found the safest way to health. —HIPPOCRATES

We are under-exercised as a nation. We look instead of play. We ride instead of walk. Our existence deprives us of the minimum of physical activity essential for healthy living. —JOHN F. KENNEDY

The human body has the performance capability of a Ferrari, and the durability of the Chevy. Although we need to put ourselves through the human equivalent of an all-out lap at Le Mons from time to time, we can also idle along for thirty years before we start having serious maintenance problems. No machine was ever designed to compare with this combination of performance and durability. —ARNOLD SCHWARZENEGGER

Regimen is superior to medicine, especially as, from time immemorial, out of every hundred physicians, ninety-eight are charlatans. —VOLTAIRE

EXISTENCE
(also see concepts 453, 585, 802)

Let us be moral. Let us contemplate existence. —CHARLES DICKENS

Man is the only animal for whom his own existence is a problem which he has to solve. —ERICH FROMM

Every life is its own excuse for being. —ELBERT HUBBARD

We spend our lives talking about this mystery: our life. —JULES RENARD

That I exist is a perpetual surprise which is life.
—RABINDRANATH TAGORE

Being is the great explainer. —HENRY DAVID THOREAU

I can, therefore I am. —SIMONE WEIL

EXISTENTIALISM
(also see concepts 30, 378, 453, 585)

Ultimately, if you are an existentialist and you don't believe in God and the judgment after death, then you can do anything you want: You can kill, you can do whatever society considers the most taboo thing. —DAVID CRONENBERG

Man is nothing else but what he makes of himself. Such is the first principle of existentialism. —JEAN-PAUL SARTRE

Existentialism is possible only in a world where God is dead or a luxury, and where Christianity is dead. —GABRIEL VAHANIAN

EXPECTATION
(also see concepts 210, 357, 786)

Don't count your chickens before they are hatched. —AESOP

Life is so constructed, that the event does not, cannot, will not, match the expectation. —CHARLOTTE BRONTË

What we anticipate seldom occurs, what we least expected generally happens. —BENJAMIN DISRAELI

Nothing is so good as it seems beforehand. —GEORGE ELIOT

How much of human life is lost in waiting! —RALPH WALDO EMERSON

Prospect is often better than possession. —THOMAS FULLER

The hours we pass with happy prospects in view are more pleasing than those crowned with fruition. —OLIVER GOLDSMITH

The best part of our lives we pass in counting on what is to come.
—WILLIAM HAZLITT

Don't cross the bridge till you come to it. —PROVERB

Even if it is to be, what end do you serve by running to distress?
—SENECA

EXPEDIENCY
(also see concepts 488, 532, 633)

Nobody is forgotten when it is convenient to remember him.
—BENJAMIN DISRAELI

We do what we must, and call it by the best names.
—RALPH WALDO EMERSON

You can't learn too soon that the most useful thing about a principle
is that it can always be sacrificed to expediency.
—W. SOMERSET MAUGHAM

The end justifies the means. —PROVERB

No man is justified in doing evil on the ground of expediency.
—THEODORE ROOSEVELT

Policy sits above conscience. —WILLIAM SHAKESPEARE

Custom adapts itself to expediency. —TACITUS

EXPERIENCE
(also see concepts 16, 239, 248, 262, 272, 614, 735, 793, 863, 864)

I am not afraid of storms for I am learning how to sail my ship.
—LOUISA MAY ALCOTT

Experience, which destroys innocence, also leads one back to it.
—JAMES BALDWIN

Experience isn't interesting until it begins to repeat itself–in fact,
till it does that, it hardly *is* experience. —ELIZABETH BOWEN

I don't have to have faith, I have experience. —JOSEPH CAMPBELL

You cannot create experience. You must undergo it.
—ALBERT CAMUS

Experience which was once claimed by the aged is now claimed exclusively by the young. —G. K. CHESTERTON

I have but one lamp by which my feet are guided, and that is the lamp of experience. I know of no way of judging of the future but by the past. —PATRICK HENRY

The fool knows after he's suffered. —HESIOD

A moment's insight is sometimes worth a life's experience. —OLIVER WENDELL HOLMES, SR.

Experience is not what happens to you; it is what you do with what happens to you. —ALDOUS HUXLEY

It's all right letting yourself go, as long as you can get yourself back. —MICK JAGGER

I am too long in the tooth to think you can make demands on life and expect that they will be granted, like waving a magic fairy wand. —ANNIE LENNOX

Experience does not err; only your judgments err by expecting from her what is not in her power. —LEONARDO DA VINCI

Adventure is something you seek for pleasure, or even for profit, like a gold rush or invading a country;...but experience is what really happens to you in the long run; the truth that finally overtakes you. —KATHERINE ANNE PORTER

I know by my own pot how the others boil. —FRENCH PROVERB

He who has been bitten by a snake fears a piece of string. —PERSIAN PROVERB

Everything happens to everybody sooner or later if there is time enough. —GEORGE BERNARD SHAW

Experience is in the fingers and head. The heart is inexperienced. —HENRY DAVID THOREAU

If we could sell our experiences for what they cost us we'd be millionaires. —ABIGAIL VAN BUREN

Experience is the name everyone gives to their mistakes. —OSCAR WILDE

EXPERTS
(also see concepts 172, 261, 272, 390, 792)

Do not be bullied out of your common sense by the specialist; two to one, he is a pedant. ——OLIVER WENDELL HOLMES, SR.

One who limits himself to his chosen mode of ignorance. ——ELBERT HUBBARD

Specialized meaninglessness has come to be regarded, in certain circles, as a kind of hall mark of true science. ——ALDOUS HUXLEY

Given one well-trained physician of the highest type he will do better work for a thousand people than ten specialists. ——WILLIAM J. MAYO

No man can be a pure specialist without being in the strict sense an idiot. ——GEORGE BERNARD SHAW

EXPLANATION
(also see concepts 38, 94, 193, 255)

There is no waste of time in life like that of making explanations. ——BENJAMIN DISRAELI

Never explain. Your friends do not need it and your enemies will not believe it anyway. ——ELBERT HUBBARD

I am one of those unfortunates to whom death is less hideous than explanations. ——D. B. WYNDHAM LEWIS

There is occasions and causes why and wherefore in all things. ——WILLIAM SHAKESPEARE

EXPLOITATION
(also see concepts 18, 329)

Never give a sucker an even break. ——W. C. FIELDS

The human being as a commodity is the disease of our age. ——MAX LERNER

EYES

(also see concepts 70, 266, 504, 551, 724, 739, 797, 845)

I have eyes like those of a dead pig. —MARLON BRANDO

The soul, fortunately, has an interpreter–often an unconscious, but still a truthful interpreter–in the eye. —CHARLOTTE BRONTÉ

The eyes indicate the antiquity of the soul. —RALPH WALDO EMERSON

The eyes have one language everywhere. —GEORGE HERBERT

The eyes are the window of the soul. —PROVERB

Eyes lie if you ever look into them for the character of a person.
—STEVIE WONDER

FACES

(also see concepts 39, 59, 71, 165, 265, 336)

My face looks like a wedding cake that has been left out in the rain.
—W. H. AUDEN

I guess I look like a rock quarry that someone has dynamited.
—CHARLES BRONSON

He had a face like a benediction. —MIGUEL DE CERVANTES

I have always considered my face a convenience rather than an ornament. —OLIVER WENDELL HOLMES, SR.

At fifty everyone has the face he deserves. —GEORGE ORWELL

After a certain number of years, our faces become our biographies.
—CYNTHIA OZICK

I'm not a dictator. It's just that I have a grumpy face.
—AUGUSTO PINOCHET

FACTS

(also see concepts 112, 284, 440, 446, 768)

Conclusive facts are inseparable from inconclusive except by a head that already understands and knows. —THOMAS CARLYLE

If a man will kick a fact out of the window, when he comes back he finds it again in the chimney corner. —RALPH WALDO EMERSON

Facts and truth really don't have much to do with each other. —WILLIAM FAULKNER

Facts do not cease to exist because they are ignored. —ALDOUS HUXLEY

It is the spirit of the age to believe that any fact, no matter how suspect, is superior to any imaginative exercise, no matter how true. —GORE VIDAL

The Doctor said that Death was but / A scientific fact. —OSCAR WILDE

FAILURE

(also see concepts 301, 390, 464, 507, 812)

There is much to be said for failure. It is more interesting than success. —MAX BEERBOHM

I don't know the key to success, but the key to failure is trying to please everybody. —BILL COSBY

There is no failure except in no longer trying. —ELBERT HUBBARD

There is not a fiercer hell than the failure in a great object. —JOHN KEATS

Show me a good and gracious loser and I'll show you a failure. —KNUTE ROCKNE

I would prefer even to fail with honor than win by cheating. —SOPHOCLES

FAITH

(also see concepts 96, 145, 222, 237, 357, 701, 817)

To believe only possibilities is not faith, but mere philosophy. —THOMAS BROWNE

I feel no need for any other faith than my faith in human beings.
——PEARL S. BUCK

No one thinks of how much blood it costs. ——DANTE

As he that fears God fears nothing else, so, he that sees God sees every thing else. ——JOHN DONNE

Be a sinner and sin strongly, but more strongly have faith and rejoice in Christ. ——MARTIN LUTHER

Faith may be defined briefly as an illogical belief in the occurrence of the improbable. ——H. L. MENCKEN

Not Truth but Faith, it is / That keeps the world alive.
——EDNA ST. VINCENT MILLAY

Faith embraces many truths which seem to contradict each other.
——BLAISE PASCAL

All outward forms of religion are almost useless, and are the causes of endless strife....Believe there is a great power silently working all things for good, behave yourself and never mind the rest.
——BEATRIX POTTER

Neither reproaches nor encouragements are able to revive a faith that is waning. ——NATHALIE SARRAUTE

Faith is believing what you know ain't so. ——MARK TWAIN

FAITHFULNESS
(also see concepts 96, 156, 470, 548, 676, 826)

It is better to be unfaithful than faithful without wanting to be.
——BRIGITTE BARDOT

Be faithful to that which exists nowhere but in yourself–and thus make yourself indispensable. ——ANDRÉ GIDE

Those who are faithful know only the trivial side of love: it is the faithless who know love's tragedies. ——OSCAR WILDE

FAME

(also see concepts 315, 346, 351, 601, 639, 672, 778)

A celebrity is a person who works hard all his life to be known, then wears dark glasses to avoid being recognized. —FRED ALLEN

We movie stars all end up by ourselves. Who knows? Maybe we want to. —BETTE DAVIS

It's either vilification or sanctification, and both piss me off. —BOB GELDOF

Fame is a powerful aphrodisiac. —GRAHAM GREENE

How vain, without the merit, is the name. —HOMER

A sex symbol becomes a thing. I hate being a thing. —MARILYN MONROE

It's a short walk from the hallelujah to the hoot. —VLADIMIR NABOKOV

The charm of fame is so great that we like every object to which it is attached, even death. —BLAISE PASCAL

Fame is a constant effort. —JULES RENARD

The highest form of vanity is love of fame. —GEORGE SANTAYANA

I think that some public figures are more fair game than others. It's gloves off on politicians and people whose public image is perfection, like the televangelists–Jim Bakker–people who claim to be spiritual or moral leaders. They are the whited sepulchers waiting for our graffiti. —LIZ SMITH

Love of fame is the last thing even learned men can bear to be parted from. —TACITUS

The fame you earn has a different taste from the fame that is forced upon you. —GLORIA VANDERBILT

In the future, everyone will be famous for fifteen minutes. —ANDY WARHOL

FAMILIARITY

(also see concepts 51, 261, 262, 601, 824)

A shocking occurrence ceases to be shocking when it occurs daily.
——ALEXANDER CHASE

The hues of the opal, the light of the diamond, are not to be seen if the eye is too near. ——RALPH WALDO EMERSON

Sweets grown common lose their dear delight.
——WILLIAM SHAKESPEARE

Familiarity breeds contempt–and children. ——MARK TWAIN

FAMILY

(also see concepts 35, 106, 566, 667)

To separate from my culture (as from my family) I had to feel competent enough on the outside and secure enough inside to live life on my own. Yet in leaving home I did not lose touch with my origins because *lo mexicano* is in my system. I am a turtle, wherever I go I carry "home" on my back. ——GLORIA ANZALDUA

Cruel is the strife of brothers. ——ARISTOTLE

If Absolute Sovereignty be not necessary in a State, how comes it to be so in a family? ——MARY ASTELL

I think the family is the place where the most ridiculous and least respectable things in the world go on. ——UGO BETTI

Happiness is having a large, loving, caring, close-knit family in another city. ——GEORGE BURNS

The parents' age must be remembered, both for joy and anxiety.
——CONFUCIUS

Families are about love overcoming emotional torture.
——MATT GROENING

Roots is not just the saga of my family. It is the symbolic saga of a people. ——ALEX HALEY

There is little less trouble in governing a private family than a whole kingdom. —MICHEL DE MONTAIGNE

Blood is thicker than water. —PROVERB

Big sisters are the crab grass in the lawn of life. —CHARLES M. SCHULTZ

There is no such thing as fun for the whole family. —JERRY SEINFELD

But there were years when, in search of what I thought was better, nobler things I denied these, my people, and my family. I forgot the songs they sung–and most of those songs are now dead; I erased their dialect from my tongue; I was ashamed of them and their ways of life. But now–yes, I love them; they are a part of my blood; they, with all their virtues and their faults, played a great part in forming my way of looking at life. —AGNES SMEDLEY

Absence is one of the most useful ingredients of family life, and to dose it rightly is an art like any other. —FREYA STARK

The biological family isn't the only important unit in society; we have needs and longings that our families cannot meet. Indeed, in some cultures, community is more important than the family. —GLORIA STEINEM

Happy families are all alike; every unhappy family is unhappy in its own way. —LEO TOLSTOY

FANATICISM

(also see concepts 64, 176, 378, 480)

A fanatic is one who can't change his mind and won't change the subject. —WINSTON CHURCHILL

Defined in psychological terms, a fanatic is a man who consciously overcompensates a secret doubt. —ALDOUS HUXLEY

There is no place in a fanatic's head where reason can enter. —NAPOLEON I

Without fanaticism we cannot accomplish anything. —EVA PERÓN

Fanaticism consists in redoubling your efforts when you have forgotten your aim. —GEORGE SANTAYANA

FARMS AND FARMING
(also see concepts 90, 163, 166, 653)

It is thus with farming; if you do one thing late, you will be late in all your work. —CATO THE ELDER

A plow on a field arable is the most honorable of ancient arms. —ABRAHAM COWLEY

Farming looks mighty easy when your plow is a pencil, and you're a thousand miles from the corn field. —DWIGHT D. EISENHOWER

The first farmer was the first man; all historic nobility rests on the possession and use of land. —RALPH WALDO EMERSON

The farmer is the only man in our economy who buys everything he buys at retail, sells everything he sells at wholesale, and pays the freight both ways. —JOHN F. KENNEDY

A farmer is dependent on too many things outside his control; it makes for modesty. —BHARATI MUKHERJEE

A farm is an irregular patch of nettles, bounded by short-term notes, containing a fool and his wife who didn't know enough to stay in the city. —S. J. PERELMAN

Farmers are philosophical; they have learned that it is less wearing to shrug than to beat their breasts. —RUTH STOUT

When tillage begins, other arts follow. The farmers therefore are the founders of human civilization. —DANIEL WEBSTER

There is no doubt about it, the basic satisfaction in farming is manure, that always suggests that life can be cyclic and chemically perfect and aromatic and continuous. —E. B. WHITE

A good farmer is nothing more nor less than a handy man with a sense of humus. —E. B. WHITE

FASCISM

(also see concepts 312, 378, 428, 558, 810, 821)

Because Fascism is a lie, it is condemned to literary sterility. And when it is past, it will have no history, except the bloody history of murder. —ERNEST HEMINGWAY

Fascism is a religion; the twentieth century will be known in history as the century of Fascism. —BENITO MUSSOLINI

Fascism is Capitalism plus murder. —UPTON SINCLAIR

Fascism is nothing but capitalist reaction. —LEON TROTSKY

That which the Fascists hate above all else, is intelligence. —MIGUEL DE UNAMUNO

FASHION

(also see concepts 124, 296, 776, 793, 808)

Fashion is architecture: it is a matter of proportions. —COCO CHANEL

My weakness is wearing too much leopard print. —JACKIE COLLINS

Fashion is more powerful than any tyrant. —LATIN PROVERB

I base most of my fashion taste on what doesn't itch. —GILDA RADNER

Fashions, after all, are only induced epidemics. —GEORGE BERNARD SHAW

Nothing is so hideous as an obsolete fashion. —STENDHAL

Every generation laughs at the old fashions, but follows religiously the new. —HENRY DAVID THOREAU

You don't have to signal a social conscience by looking like a frump. Lace knickers won't hasten the holocaust, you can ban the bomb in a feather boa just as well as without, and a mild interest in the length of hemlines doesn't necessarily disqualify you from reading *Das Kapital* and agreeing with every word. —JILL TWEEDIE

It is fancy rather than taste which produces so many new fashions. —VOLTAIRE

FAT AND FATNESS
(also see concepts 73, 74, 163, 290)

Women should try to increase their size rather than decrease it, because I believe the bigger we are, the more space we'll take up, and the more we'll have to be reckoned with. —ROSEANNE BARR

Imprisoned in every fat man a thin one is wildly signalling to be let out. —CYRIL CONNOLLY

Gluttony is an emotional escape, a sign something is eating us. —PETER DE VRIES

A big man has no time really to do anything but just sit and be big. —F. SCOTT FITZGERALD

More die in the United States of too much food than of too little. —JOHN KENNETH GALBRAITH

I find no sweeter fat than sticks to my own bones. —WALT WHITMAN

FATE
(also see concepts 6, 97, 200, 397, 471)

Fate is not an eagle, it creeps like a rat. —ELIZABETH BOWEN

Whatever limits us, we call Fate. —RALPH WALDO EMERSON

Many men would take the death-sentence without a whimper to escape the life-sentence which fate carries in her other hand. —T. E. LAWRENCE

Fate keeps on happening. —ANITA LOOS

We may become the makers of our fate when we have ceased to pose as its prophets. —KARL POPPER

Fate leads the willing, and drags along the reluctant. —SENECA

FATHERS

(also see concepts 106, 273, 493, 518, 566, 667)

Fathers, provoke not your children to anger, lest they be discouraged.
—BIBLE, COLOSSIANS 3:21

My father was frightened of his father, I was frightened of my father, and I am damned well going to see to it that my children are frightened of me. —KING GEORGE V

To be a successful father, there's one absolute rule. When you have a kid, don't look at it for the first two years. —ERNEST HEMINGWAY

The son offers the father his life as a vessel for carrying forth his father's dream. —TONY KUSHNER

The worst misfortune that can happen to an ordinary man is to have an extraordinary father. —AUSTIN O'MALLEY

An angry father is most cruel toward himself. —PUBLILIUS SYRUS

The kind of man who thinks that helping with the dishes is beneath him will also think than helping with the baby is beneath him, and then he certainly is not going to be a very successful father.
—ELEANOR ROOSEVELT

The fundamental defect of fathers is that they want their children to be a credit to them. —BERTRAND RUSSELL

It is a wise father that knows his own child. —WILLIAM SHAKESPEARE

FAULTS

(also see concepts 387, 507, 855)

The real fault is to have faults and not amend them. —CONFUCIUS

Certain defects are necessary for the existence of individuality.
—JOHANN WOLFGANG VON GOETHE

We forget our faults easily when they are known to ourselves alone. —FRANÇOIS DE LA ROCHEFOUCAULD

We confess to little faults, only to persuade ourselves that we have no great ones. —FRANÇOIS DE LA ROCHEFOUCAULD

None of us can stand other people having the same faults as ourselves. —OSCAR WILDE

FEAR
(also see concepts 168, 237, 358, 785, 800, 805)

It is a miserable state of mind to have few things to desire and many things to fear. —FRANCIS BACON

Fear has many eyes and can see things underground.
—MIGUEL DE CERVANTES

Just as courage imperils life, fear protects it. —LEONARDO DA VINCI

Fear is well known as a cement of societies. —CZESLAW MILOSZ

Fear has the largest eyes of all. —BORIS PASTERNAK

Let me assert my firm belief that the only thing we have to fear is fear itself. —FRANKLIN D. ROOSEVELT

Where the fear is, happiness is not. —SENECA

If something makes me uncomfortable, or scares me, I have to surround myself with it and get to understand its shape. Then it can't affect me. —DAVID WOJNAROWICZ

Fear no more, says the heart. Fear no more, says the heart, committing its burden to some sea which sighs collectively for all sorrows, and renews, begins, collects, lets fall. —VIRGINIA WOOLF

FEMINISM
(also see concepts 2, 867)

Men, their rights and nothing more; women, their rights and nothing less. —SUSAN B. ANTHONY

Women get more unhappy the more they try to liberate themselves.
—BRIGITTE BARDOT

When an individual is kept in a situation of inferiority, the fact is that he does become inferior. —SIMONE DE BEAUVOIR

Feminism's agenda is basic: It asks that women not be forced to "choose" between public justice and private happiness. It asks that women be free to define themselves–instead of having their identity defined for them, time and again, by their culture and their men. —SUSAN FALUDI

There is a hidden fear that somehow, if they are only given a chance, women will suddenly do as they have been done by. —EVA FIGES

The extension of women's rights is the basic principle of all social progress. —CHARLES FOURIER

I didn't fight to get women out from behind the vacuum cleaner to get them onto the board of Hoover. —GERMAINE GREER

We might well long for the day when the knowledge of the debt all society owed to organized womanhood in bringing the human race closer together, not pushing it farther apart, will still the laughter in the throats of the now uninformed. —LORRAINE HANSBERRY

We haven't come a long way, we've come a short way. If we hadn't come a short way, no one would be calling us "baby." —ELIZABETH JANEWAY

Women really must have equal pay for equal work, equality in work at home, and reproductive choices. Men must press for these things also. They must cease to see them as "women's issues" and learn that they are everyone's issues–essential to survival on planet Earth. —ERICA JONG

Women who seek to be equal with men lack ambition. —TIMOTHY LEARY

But if God had wanted us to think with our wombs, why did He give us a brain? —CLARE BOOTHE LUCE

The only way a woman can marry now is to agree to become a charwoman, regardless of her education and skills. —MARGARET MEAD

The most important thing women have to do is to stir up the zeal of women themselves. —JOHN STUART MILL

The vote, I thought, means nothing to women. We should be armed. —EDNA O'BRIEN

There must be a world revolution which puts an end to all materialistic conditions hindering woman from performing her natural role in life and driving her to carry out man's duties in order to be equal in rights. —MUHAMMAR QADDAFI

Much male fear of feminism is the fear that, in becoming whole human beings, women will cease to mother men, to provide the breast, the lullaby, the continuous attention associated by the infant with the mother. Much male fear of feminism is infantilism–the longing to remain the mother's son, to possess a woman who exists purely for him. —ADRIENNE RICH

Feminism is doomed to failure because it is based on an attempt to repeal and restructure human nature. —PHYLLIS SCHLAFLY

The prolonged slavery of women is the darkest page in human history. —ELIZABETH CADY STANTON

A liberated woman is one who has sex before marriage and a job after. —GLORIA STEINEM

Feminism is not antisexuality; on the contrary. It says that sexuality shouldn't be confused with violence and dominance and that it should be a matter of free choice. It shouldn't be forced on you by economics, including dependence on a husband, or by pressure. —GLORIA STEINEM

One of the things about equality is not just that you be treated equally to a man, but that you treat yourself equally to the way you treat a man. —MARLO THOMAS

I am glad to see that men are getting their rights, but I want women to get theirs, and while the water is stirring I will step into the pool. —SOJOURNER TRUTH

People call me a feminist whenever I express sentiments that differentiate me from a doormat or a prostitute. —REBECCA WEST

The history of men's opposition to women's emancipation is more interesting perhaps than the story of that emancipation itself. —VIRGINIA WOOLF

FICTION

(also see concepts 76, 382, 526, 727)

Good fiction is made of that which is real, and reality is difficult to come by. —RALPH ELLISON

Human beings have their great chance in the novel. —E. M. FORSTER

Fiction is history without tables, graphs, dates, imports, edicts, evidence, laws; history without hiatus–intelligible, simple, smooth. —WILLIAM GASS

All that non-fiction can do is answer questions. It's fiction's business to ask them. —RICHARD HUGHES

Far too many relied on the classic formula of a beginning, a muddle, and an end. —PHILIP LARKIN

I'm not interested in fiction. I want faithfulness. —ANAÏS NIN

The novel is practically a Protestant form of art; it is a product of the free mind, of the autonomous individual. —GEORGE ORWELL

A good novel is possible only after one has given up and let go. —WALKER PERCY

A novel is a mirror walking along a main road. —STENDHAL

The novel is something that never was before and will not be again. —EUDORA WELTY

All fiction for me is a kind of magic and trickery–a confidence trick, trying to make people believe something is true that isn't. —ANGUS WILSON

Fiction is like a spider's web, attached ever so slightly perhaps, but still attached to life at all four corners. —VIRGINIA WOOLF

FIGHTS AND FIGHTING

(also see concepts 25, 36, 43, 193, 248, 499, 557)

What counts is not necessarily the size of the dog in the fight–it's the size of the fight in the dog. —DWIGHT D. EISENHOWER

Never contend with a man who has nothing to lose.
——BALTASAR GRACIÁN

I have not yet begun to fight. ——JOHN PAUL JONES

There is such a thing as a man being too proud to fight.
——WOODROW WILSON

FISH AND FISHING
(also see concepts 10, 37, 704, 736, 765)

Fish die belly-upward and rise to the surface; it is their way of falling. ——ANDRÉ GIDE

Fishing is a delusion entirely surrounded by liars in old clothes.
——DON MARQUIS

No human being, however great, or powerful, was ever so free as a fish. ——JOHN RUSKIN

Angling may be said to be so like the mathematics that it can never be fully learnt. ——IZAAK WALTON

THE FLAG
(also see concepts 528, 573)

How about American flag napkins? What if you blow your nose in one? Have you broken the law? ——GARY L. ACKERMAN

Punishing desecration of the flag dilutes the very freedom that makes this emblem so revered, and worth revering.
——WILLIAM J. BRENNAN, JR.

If anyone attempts to haul down the American flag, shoot him on the spot. ——JOHN A. DIX

Patriotic societies seem to think that the way to educate school children in a democracy is to stage bigger and better flag-saluting.
——S. I. HAYAKAWA

Let us raise a standard to which the wise and honest can repair.
——GEORGE WASHINGTON

"Shoot if you must, this old grey head, / But spare your country's flag," she said. —JOHN GREENLEAF WHITTIER

FLATTERY
(also see concepts 139, 405, 610)

Flattery is a juggler, and no kin unto sincerity. —THOMAS BROWNE

Flattery sits in the parlour when plain dealing is kicked out of doors. —THOMAS FULLER

Be advised that all flatterers live at the expense of those who listen to them. —JEAN DE LA FONTAINE

I will praise any man that will praise me. —WILLIAM SHAKESPEARE

Flattery is all right so long as you don't inhale. —ADLAI STEVENSON

FLOWERS AND PLANTS
(also see concepts 166, 228, 306, 815, 839)

God gave us our memories so that we might have roses in December. —J. M. BARRIE

You cannot forget if you would those golden kisses all over the cheeks of the meadow, queerly called dandelions. —HENRY WARD BEECHER

I like to see flowers growing, but when they are gathered they cease to please. I never offer flowers to those I love; I never wish to receive them from hands dear to me. —CHARLOTTE BRONTË

Art is the unceasing effort to compete with the beauty of flowers –and never succeeding. —MARC CHAGALL

The rose, wherein, the word divine makes itself flesh. —DANTE

It has always pleased me to exalt plants in the scale of organized beings. —CHARLES DARWIN

Earth laughs in flowers. —RALPH WALDO EMERSON

Flowers are restful to look at. They have neither emotions nor conflicts. —SIGMUND FREUD

The Amen! of Nature is always a flower.
—OLIVER WENDELL HOLMES, SR.

The greatest service which can be rendered any country is to add a useful plant to its culture. —THOMAS JEFFERSON

If I had but two loaves of bread, I would sell one and buy hyacinths, for they would feed my soul. —KORAN

The fairest thing in nature, a flower, still has its roots in earth and manure. —D. H. LAWRENCE

Can we conceive what humanity would be if it did not know the flowers? —MAURICE MAETERLINCK

...roses are the only flowers at garden-parties; the only flowers that everybody is certain of knowing. —KATHERINE MANSFIELD

I perhaps owe having become a painter to flowers. —CLAUDE MONET

Sweet flowers are slow and weeds make haste.
—WILLIAM SHAKESPEARE

A slight, pretty flower that grows on any ground, and flowers pledge no allegiance to banners of any man. —ALICE WALKER

A morning glory at my window satisfies me more than the metaphysics of books. —WALT WHITMAN

Flowers are as common in the country as people are in London.
—OSCAR WILDE

Flowers are happy things. —P. G. WODEHOUSE

To me the meanest flower that blows can give / Thoughts that do often lie too deep for tears. —WILLIAM WORDSWORTH

FOOD AND EATING
(also see concepts 163, 229, 275, 278, 296, 371, 793, 839)

Tell me what you eat and I will tell you who you are.
—ANTHELME BRILLAT-SAVARIN

I do not like broccoli. And I haven't liked it since I was a little kid and my mother made me eat it. And I'm President of the United States, and I'm not going to eat any more broccoli! —GEORGE BUSH

Eating is touch carried to the bitter end. —SAMUEL BUTLER

To eat is human, to digest divine. —CHARLES T. COPELAND

When a man's stomach is full it makes no difference whether he is rich or poor. —EURIPIDES

Cheese–milk's leap toward immortality. —CLIFTON FADIMAN

The way to a man's heart is through his stomach. —FANNY FERN

A man seldom thinks with more earnestness of anything than he does of his dinner. —SAMUEL JOHNSON

Everything you see I owe to spaghetti. —SOPHIA LOREN

You can travel fifty thousand miles in America without once tasting a piece of good bread. —HENRY MILLER

One should eat to live, not live to eat. —MOLIÉRE

This is my clam theory: Eating clams is extremely sensuous. It's not just cutting something very neatly with a knife and fork; you're actually picking up the clam and getting into the shapelessness and the marine character of it. —CAMILLE PAGLIA

Strange to see how a good dinner and feasting reconciles everybody. —SAMUEL PEPYS

A good meal ought to begin with hunger. —FRENCH PROVERB

There is nothing to which men, while they have food and drink, cannot reconcile themselves. —GEORGE SANTAYANA

Training is everything. The peach was once a bitter almond; cauliflower is nothing but cabbage with a college education. —MARK TWAIN

One cannot think well, love well, sleep well, if one has not dined well. —VIRGINIA WOOLF

FOOLS AND FOOLISHNESS
(also see concepts 5, 380, 544, 864)

Even a fool, when he holdeth his peace, is counted wise.
—BIBLE, PROVERBS 17:28

Those who realize their folly are not true fools. —CHUANG-TZU

Mix a little foolishness with your serious plans: it's lovely to be silly at the right moment. —HORACE

Fools rush in where angels fear to tread. —ALEXANDER POPE

A fool and his money are soon parted. —PROVERB

Folly is perennial and yet the human race has survived.
—BERTRAND RUSSELL

Lord, what fools these mortals be! —WILLIAM SHAKESPEARE

FOOTBALL
(also see concepts 256, 765)

Pro football is like nuclear warfare. There are no winners, only survivors. —FRANK GIFFORD

NFL owners should quit worrying about silly things like players celebrating in the end zone. They should give them something to really celebrate. Get rid of those artificial surfaces. —O. J. SIMPSON

FORCE
(also see concepts 173, 558, 772, 773)

Force is not a remedy. —JOHN BRIGHT

The one means that wins the easiest victory over reason: terror and force. —ADOLF HITLER

Force works on servile natures, not the free. —BEN JONSON

Whatever needs to be maintained through force is doomed.
—HENRY MILLER

FOREIGNERS AND FOREIGNNESS

(also see concepts 208, 418, 563)

He will deal harshly by a stranger who has not been himself often a traveller and stranger. —SA'DI

Don't imagine I regard foreigners as inferior–they fascinate me. —HAROLD WILSON

FORGIVENESS

(also see concepts 101, 237)

Forgive us our debts, as we forgive our debtors. —BIBLE, MATTHEW 6:12

Once a woman has forgiven her man, she must not reheat his sins for breakfast. —MARLENE DIETRICH

Forgotten is forgiven. —F. SCOTT FITZGERALD

The weak can never forgive. Forgiveness is the attribute of the strong. —MOHANDAS K. GANDHI

Only lies and evil come from letting people off. —IRIS MURDOCH

To err is human, to forgive divine. —ALEXANDER POPE

Forgive and forget. —PROVERB

FRANCE AND THE FRENCH

(also see concepts 247, 529, 567)

A relatively small and eternally quarrelsome country in Western Europe, fountainhead of rationalist political manias, militarily impotent, historically inglorious during the past century, democratically bankrupt, Communist-infiltrated from top to bottom. —WILLIAM F. BUCKLEY

There's always something fishy about the French. —NOËL COWARD

How can anyone govern a nation that has two hundred and forty different kinds of cheese? —CHARLES DE GAULLE

Boy, those French–they have a different word for everything. —STEVE MARTIN

Frenchmen have an unlimited capacity for gallantry and indulge it on every occasion. —MOLIÉRE

The French complain of everything, and always. —NAPOLEON I

France has neither winter nor summer nor morals–apart from these drawbacks it is a fine country. —MARK TWAIN

France is the country where the money falls apart and you can't tear the toilet paper. —BILLY WILDER

FRANKNESS
(also see concepts 355, 818)

The great consolation in life is to say what one thinks. —VOLTAIRE

All faults may be forgiven of him who has perfect candor. —WALT WHITMAN

All cruel people describe themselves as paragons of frankness. —TENNESSEE WILLIAMS

FREE SPEECH
(also see concepts 115, 157, 299, 365, 617)

The very aim and end of our institutions is just this: that we may think what we like and say what we think. —OLIVER WENDELL HOLMES, SR.

A people which is able to say everything becomes able to do everything. —NAPOLEON I

The only way to make sure people you agree with can speak is to support the rights of people you don't agree with. —ELEANOR HOLMES NORTON

The sound of tireless voices is the price we pay for the right to hear the music of our own opinions. —ADLAI STEVENSON

I disapprove of what you say, but I will defend to the death your right to say it. —VOLTAIRE

FREEDOM
(also see concepts 89, 157, 195, 200, 258, 298, 456, 684, 821)

Eternal vigilance is the price of liberty. —JOHN PHILPOT CURRAN

Liberty is a different kind of pain from prison. —T. S. ELIOT

If you cannot be free, be as free as you can. —RALPH WALDO EMERSON

Freedom is fragile and must be protected. To sacrifice it, even as a temporary measure, is to betray it. —GERMAINE GREER

The love of liberty is the love of others; the love of power is the love of ourselves. —WILLIAM HAZLITT

Freedom is a condition of mind, and the best way to secure it is to breed it. —ELBERT HUBBARD

Liberation is not deliverance. —VICTOR HUGO

It is better to die on your feet than to live on your knees.
—DOLORES IBARRURI

It's often safer to be in chains than to be free. —FRANZ KAFKA

Freedom's just another word for nothing left to lose.
—KRIS KRISTOFFERSON

Until economic freedom is attained for everybody, there can be no real freedom for anybody. —SUZANNE LA FOLLETTE

It is true that liberty is precious–so precious that it must be rationed.
—V. I. LENIN

Those who deny freedom to others, deserve it not for themselves.
—ABRAHAM LINCOLN

Freedom is always and exclusively for one who thinks differently.
—ROSA LUXEMBURG

There's something contagious about demanding freedom.
—ROBIN MORGAN

...the function of freedom is to free somebody else. —TONI MORRISON

I sometimes think that the price of liberty is not so much eternal vigilance as eternal dirt. —GEORGE ORWELL

I know but one freedom and that is the freedom of the mind. —ANTOINE DE SAINT-EXUPÉRY

Man is condemned to be free. —JEAN-PAUL SARTRE

I do desire we may be better strangers. —WILLIAM SHAKESPEARE

A nation has character only when it is free. —GERMAINE DE STAËL

We have confused the free with the free and easy. —ADLAI STEVENSON

If the world knew how to use freedom without abusing it, tyranny would not exist. —TEHYI HSIEH

The true character of liberty is independence, maintained by force. —VOLTAIRE

Independence I have long considered the grand blessing of life, the basis of every virtue–and independence I will ever secure by contracting my wants, though I were to live on a barren heath. —MARY WOLLSTONECRAFT

FRIENDS AND FRIENDSHIP
(also see concepts 20, 51, 134, 135, 221, 270, 417, 533, 568, 666, 754)

One friend in a lifetime is much; two are many; three are hardly possible. —HENRY BROOKS ADAMS

That's what friendship means: sharing the prejudice of experience. —CHARLES BUKOWSKI

My friends, there are no friends. —COCO CHANEL

Every murderer is probably somebody's old friend. —AGATHA CHRISTIE

And what a delight it is to make friends with someone you have despised! —COLETTE

True friendship is like sound health; the value of it is seldom known until it be lost. —CHARLES CALEB COLTON

Have no friends not equal to yourself. —CONFUCIUS

My friends are my estate. —EMILY DICKINSON

It is one of the blessings of old friends that you can afford to be stupid with them. —RALPH WALDO EMERSON

Only friends will tell you the truths you need to hear to make the last part of your life bearable. —FRANCINE DU PLESSIX GRAY

Friendship is by its very nature freer of deceit than any other relationship we can know because it is the bond least affected by striving for power, physical pleasure, or material profit, most liberated from any oath of duty or constancy.
—FRANCINE DU PLESSIX GRAY

Sir, I look upon every day to be lost, in which I do not make a new acquaintance. —SAMUEL JOHNSON

However rare true love may be, it is less so than friendship.
—FRANÇOIS DE LA ROCHEFOUCAULD

We know our friends by their defects rather than their merits.
—W. SOMERSET MAUGHAM

Love demands infinitely less than friendship. —GEORGE JEAN NATHAN

What I cannot love, I overlook. Is that real friendship? —ANAÏS NIN

Each friend represents a world in us, a world possibly not born until they arrive, and it is only by this meeting that a new world is born.
—ANAÏS NIN

I have always made a distinction between my friends and my confidants. I enjoy the conversation of the former; from the latter I hide nothing. —EDITH PIAF

These can never be true friends: hope, dice, a prostitute, a robber, a cheat, a goldsmith, a monkey, a doctor, a distiller.
—HINDU PROVERB

We die as often as we lose a friend. —PUBLILIUS SYRUS

Champagne for my real friends and real pain for my sham friends. —TOM WAITS

FRUSTRATION

(also see concepts 148, 192, 199, 206, 210, 303)

Not to get what you have set your heart on is almost as bad as getting nothing at all. —ARISTOTLE

FUNERALS

(also see concepts 175, 520)

Nature is honest, we aren't; we embalm our dead. —UGO BETTI

Epitaph, n. an inscription on a tomb, showing that virtues acquired by death have a retroactive effect. —AMBROSE BIERCE

The chief mourner does not always attend the funeral. —RALPH WALDO EMERSON

It makes small difference to the dead if they / are buried in the tokens of luxury. All this / is an empty glorification left for those who live. —EURIPIDES

The pomp of funerals has more regard to the vanity of the living than the honour of the dead. —FRANÇOIS DE LA ROCHEFOUCAULD

FUTILITY

(also see concepts 301, 836)

So we beat on, boats against the current, borne back ceaselessly into the past. —F. SCOTT FITZGERALD

As futile as a clock in an empty house. —JAMES THURBER

THE FUTURE

(also see concepts 238, 259, 357, 571, 615, 625, 629, 807)

The future is like heaven—everyone exalts it but no one wants to go there now. —JAMES BALDWIN

Future, n. that period of time in which our affairs prosper, our friends are true and our happiness is assured. —AMBROSE BIERCE

But now all I need in order to have a future, is to design a future I can manage to get inside of. —FRANCINE JULIAN CLARK

What the 21st century will be like depends on whether we learn the lessons of the 20th century and avoid repeating its worst mistakes....For example, it would be disastrous if we began to renew our entire system of social relations by acting like a bull in a china shop. —MIKHAIL GORBACHEV

Things which matter cost money, and we've got to spend the money if we don't want to have generations of parasites rather than generations of citizens. —BARBARA JORDAN

We should all be concerned about the future because we will have to spend the rest of our lives there. —CHARLES F. KETTERING

The future will one day be the present and will seem as unimportant as the present does now. —W. SOMERSET MAUGHAM

Tomorrow never comes. —PROVERB

The future belongs to those who believe in the beauty of their dreams. —ELEANOR ROOSEVELT

As for the Future, your task is not to foresee, but to enable it. —ANTOINE DE SAINT-EXUPÉRY

We know what we are, but know not what we may be. —WILLIAM SHAKESPEARE

It is extraordinary that whole populations have no projects for the future, none at all. It certainly is extraordinary, but it is certainly true. —GERTRUDE STEIN

The future is made of the same stuff as the present. —SIMONE WEIL

When I look into the future, it's so bright it burns my eyes.
—OPRAH WINFREY

GAMBLING

(also see concepts 9, 97, 359, 765)

Cards are war, in disguise of a sport. —CHARLES LAMB

Gambling promises the poor what property performs for the rich –something for nothing. —GEORGE BERNARD SHAW

It is the child of avarice, the brother of iniquity, and the father of mischief. —GEORGE WASHINGTON

Time spent in a casino is time given to death, a foretaste to the hour when one's flesh will be diverted to the purposes of the worm and not the will. —REBECCA WEST

GARDENS AND GARDENING

(also see concepts 10, 289, 447)

And the Lord God planted a garden eastward in Eden.
—BIBLE, GENESIS 2:8

A garden is a lovesome thing, God wot! —THOMAS EDWARD BROWN

The ancients venially delighted in flourishing gardens.
—THOMAS BROWNE

Though I've wandered along many a shady lane, and down several primrose paths, I can't pretend to know much about gardening.
—TRUMAN CAPOTE

To lift and punctuate and tear apart the soil is a labor–of pleasure–always accompanied by an exultation that no unprofitable exercise can ever provide. —COLETTE

God the first garden made, and the first city Cain.
—ABRAHAM COWLEY

It is good to be alone in a garden at dawn or dark so that all its shy presences may haunt you and possess you in a reverie of suspended thought. —JAMES DOUGLAS

I have never had so many good ideas day after day as when I worked in the garden. —JOHN ERSKINE

A garden must be looked into, and dressed as the body. —GEORGE HERBERT

No occupation is so delightful to me as the culture of the earth, and no culture comparable to that of the garden. —THOMAS JEFFERSON

A little thin, flowery border, round, neat, not gaudy. —CHARLES LAMB

Gardening has its compensations out of all proportion to its goals. It is creation in the pore sense. —PHYLLIS MCGINLEY

The more one gardens, the more one learns; the more one learns, the more one realizes how little one knows. —VITA SACKVILLE-WEST

A garden is a delight to the eye, and a solace to the soul; it soothes angry passions, and produces that pleasure which is a foretaste of paradise. —SA'DI

Nothing is more completely the child of art than a garden. —WALTER SCOTT

The best place to seek God is in a garden. You can dig for him there. —GEORGE BERNARD SHAW

The works of a person that builds begin immediately to decay; while those of him who plants begin directly to improve. In this, planting promises a more lasting pleasure than building. —WILLIAM SHENSTONE

The cottage garden; most for use designed, yet not of beauty destitute. —CHARLOTTE SMITH

It is a golden maxim to cultivate the garden for the nose, and the eyes will take care of themselves. —ROBERT LOUIS STEVENSON

Within the garden there is healthfulness. —ÉMILE VERHAEREN

What a man needs in gardening is a cast-iron back, with a hinge in it. —CHARLES DUDLEY WARNER

GENERALIZATION
(also see concepts 376, 803)

To generalize is to be an idiot. —WILLIAM BLAKE

All generalizations are false, including this one.
—ALEXANDER CHASE

Any general statement is like a cheque drawn on a bank. Its value depends on what is there to meet it. —EZRA POUND

GENERATIONS
(also see concepts 245, 463, 497, 552, 571, 877)

We have to hate our immediate predecessors to get free of their authority. —D. H. LAWRENCE

Every generation revolts against its fathers and makes friends with its grandfathers. —LEWIS MUMFORD

Each generation imagines itself to be more intelligent than the one that went before it, and wiser than the one that comes after it.
—GEORGE ORWELL

The weeks slide by like a funeral procession, but generations pass like a snowstorm. —NED ROREM

That's what you are. That's what you all are. All of you young people who served in the war. You are a lost generation.
—GERTRUDE STEIN

Amongst democratic nations, each new generation is a new people.
—ALEXIS DE TOCQUEVILLE

GENEROSITY
(also see concepts 109, 314, 360, 367, 438, 495, 660, 712, 834)

Lavishness is not generosity. —THOMAS FULLER

Generosity is the flower of justice. —NATHANIEL HAWTHORNE

Liberality consists less in giving a great deal than in gifts well-timed. —JEAN DE LA BRUYÉRE

As for the largest-hearted of us, what is the word we write most often in our chequebooks?–"Self." —EDEN PHILLPOTTS

No one would remember the Good Samaritan if he'd only had good intentions. He had money as well. —MARGARET THATCHER

GENIUS
(also see concepts 1, 48, 253, 327, 578, 792)

Genius is sorrow's child. —JOHN ADAMS

It takes people a long time to learn the difference between talent and genius, especially ambitious young men and women. —LOUISA MAY ALCOTT

Geniuses are the luckiest of mortals because what they must do is the same as what they most want to do. —W. H. AUDEN

Since when was genius found respectable? —ELIZABETH BARRETT BROWNING

Patience is a necessary ingredient of genius. —BENJAMIN DISRAELI

Genius is one percent inspiration and ninety-nine percent perspiration. —THOMAS EDISON

Coffee is good for talent, but genius wants prayer. —RALPH WALDO EMERSON

Genius means little more than the faculty of perceiving in an unhabitual way. —WILLIAM JAMES

No one can arrive from being talented alone. God gives talent, work transforms talent into genius. —ANNA PAVLOVA

There is no great genius without some touch of madness. —SENECA

It takes a lot of time to be a genius–you have to sit around so much doing nothing, really doing nothing. —GERTRUDE STEIN

When a true genius appears in the world, you may know him by this sign, that the dunces are all in the confederacy against him. —JONATHAN SWIFT

The divine egoism that is genius. —MARY WEBB

The public is wonderfully tolerant. It forgives everything except genius. —OSCAR WILDE

GENTLENESS
(also see concepts 86, 369, 438, 495, 572, 597)

Fair and softly goes far. —MIGUEL DE CERVANTES

My feeling is that there is nothing in life but refraining from hurting others, and comforting those that are sad. —OLIVE SCHREINER

GERMANY AND THE GERMANS
(also see concepts 247, 276, 529)

The German's wit is in his fingers. —GEORGE HERBERT

Germany will be either a world power or will not be at all. —ADOLF HITLER

At issue is the moral strength of our people. Have we lost some of that during the years of affluence and prosperity? I don't think so. But a layer of butter and kiwi and shrimp has covered our moral strength. It will reappear when we remove that layer. —HELMUT KOHL

Everything ponderous, viscous, and solemnly clumsy, all long-winded and boring types of style are developed in profuse variety among Germans. —FRIEDRICH WILHELM NIETZSCHE

Whenever the literary German dives into a sentence, that is the last you are going to see of him till he emerges on the other side of his Atlantic with his verb in his mouth. —MARK TWAIN

The German Empire has become a world empire. —KING WILHELM II

GHOSTS
(also see concepts 23, 758, 763, 784)

Ghosts remind me of men's smart crack about women, you can't live with them and can't live without them. —EUGENE O'NEILL

He who does not fill his world with phantoms remains alone.
—ANTONIO PORCHIA

GIFTS AND GIVING
(also see concepts 109, 309, 349, 660)

It is more blessed to give than to receive. —BIBLE, ACTS 20:35

The manner of giving is worth more than the gift.
—PIERRE CORNEILLE

One must be poor to know the luxury of giving. —GEORGE ELIOT

The only gift is a portion of thyself. —RALPH WALDO EMERSON

Presents, I often say, endear absents. —CHARLES LAMB

When I give I give myself. —WALT WHITMAN

GLORY
(also see concepts 271, 346, 356, 542)

The paths of glory lead but to the grave. —THOMAS GRAY

Glory is largely a theatrical concept. There is no striving for glory without a vivid awareness of an audience. —ERIC HOFFER

GOD
(also see concepts 26, 52, 66, 108, 203, 246, 257, 258, 269, 321, 424, 427, 431, 611, 668, 701, 832, 833, 873)

A God who let us prove his existence would be an idol.
—DIETRICH BONHOEFFER

God is the Celebrity-Author of the World's Best Seller. We have made God into the biggest celebrity of all, to contain our own emptiness. —DANIEL J. BOORSTIN

Though God's attributes are equal, yet his mercy is more attractive and pleasing in our eyes than his justice. —MIGUEL DE CERVANTES

If God is male, then male is God. The divine patriarch castrates women as long as he is allowed to live on in the human imagination. —MARY DALY

God is clever, but not dishonest. —ALBERT EINSTEIN

At bottom God is nothing more than an exalted father. —SIGMUND FREUD

An honest God is the noblest work of man. —ROBERT G. INGERSOLL

God has been replaced, as he has all over the West, with respectability and air conditioning. —LEROI JONES

God is but a word invented to explain the world. —ALPHONSE DE LAMARTINE

God is a gentleman. He prefers blondes. —JOE ORTON

It is the heart which experiences God, and not the reason. —BLAISE PASCAL

It is fear that first brought gods into the world. —PETRONIUS

God always has another custard pie up his sleeve. —LYNN REDGRAVE

God, that dumping ground of our dreams. —JEAN ROSTAND

Respectable society believed in God in order to avoid having to speak about him. —JEAN-PAUL SARTRE

By the year 2000 we will, I hope, raise our children to believe in human potential, not God. —GLORIA STEINEM

Your idol is shattered in the dust to prove that God's dust is greater than your idol. —RABINDRANATH TAGORE

The experience of God, or in any case the possibility of experiencing God, is innate. —ALICE WALKER

All your Western theologies, the whole mythology of them, are based on the concept of God as a senile delinquent.
—TENNESSEE WILLIAMS

THE GOLDEN RULE
(also see concept 620)

What you do not want done to yourself, do not do to others.
—CONFUCIUS

Do not do unto others as you would that they should do unto you. Their tastes may not be the same. —GEORGE BERNARD SHAW

GOLF
(also see concepts 10, 256, 447, 765)

Have you ever noticed what golf spells backwards? —AL BOLISKA

Golf is a game whose aim is to hit a very small ball into an even smaller hole, with weapons singularly ill-designed for the purpose.
—WINSTON CHURCHILL

If you watch a game, it's fun. If you play it, it's recreation. If you work at it, it's golf. —BOB HOPE

Drive for show. But putt for dough. —BOBBY LOCKE

Anyone who likes golf on television would enjoy watching the grass grow on the greens. —ANDY ROONEY

Golf is a good walk spoiled. —MARK TWAIN

A day spent in a round of strenuous idleness. —WILLIAM WORDSWORTH

GOOD AND EVIL
(also see concepts 515, 802)

Evil comes at leisure like the disease; good comes in a hurry like the doctor. —G. K. CHESTERTON

The meaning of good and bad, of better and worse, is simply helping or hurting. —RALPH WALDO EMERSON

Non-cooperation with evil is as much a duty as is cooperation with good. —MOHANDAS K. GANDHI

The web of our life is of a mingled yarn, good and ill together. —WILLIAM SHAKESPEARE

The only good is knowledge and the only evil is ignorance. —SOCRATES

GOOD   BREEDING
(also see concepts 35, 44, 478)

The scholar without good breeding is a pedant; the philosopher, a cynic. —EARL OF CHESTERFIELD

Good breeding, a union of kindness and independence. —RALPH WALDO EMERSON

The test of a man or woman's breeding is how they behave in a quarrel. —GEORGE BERNARD SHAW

Good breeding consists in concealing how much we think of ourselves and how little we think of other persons. —MARK TWAIN

GOODNESS
(also see concepts 515, 843)

It is easy to perform a good action, but not easy to acquire a settled habit of performing such actions. —ARISTOTLE

It is very hard to be simple enough to be good. —RALPH WALDO EMERSON

Goodness is uneventful. It does not flash, it glows. —DAVID GRAYSON

The greatest pleasure I know, is to do a good action by stealth, and to have it found out by accident. —CHARLES LAMB

Live not as though there were a thousand years ahead of you. Fate is at your elbow; make yourself good while life and power are still yours. —MARCUS AURELIUS

Our will is always for our own good, but we do not always see what that is. —JEAN JACQUES ROUSSEAU

Beauty endures only for as long as it can be seen; goodness, beautiful today, will remain so tomorrow. —SAPPHO

How far that little candle throws its beams! / So shines a good deed in a naughty world. —WILLIAM SHAKESPEARE

There is nothing either good or bad but thinking makes it so. —WILLIAM SHAKESPEARE

Goodness is the only investment that never fails. —HENRY DAVID THOREAU

To be good is noble; but to show others how to be good is nobler and no trouble. —MARK TWAIN

GOSSIP
(also see concepts 10, 162, 477, 746)

The idea of strictly minding our own business is moldy rubbish. Who could be so selfish? —MYRTLE BARKER

Love and scandal are the best sweeteners of tea. —HENRY FIELDING

A lie has no leg, but a scandal has wings. —THOMAS FULLER

Nobody's interested in sweetness and light. —HEDDA HOPPER

For prying into any human affairs, none are equal to those whom it does not concern. —VICTOR HUGO

Gossip is the opiate of the oppressed. —ERICA JONG

Gossip isn't scandal and it's not merely malicious. It's chatter about the human race by lovers of the same. —PHYLLIS MCGINLEY

Whoever gossips to you will gossip about you. —SPANISH PROVERB

Count not him among your friends who will retail your privacies to the world. —PUBLILIUS SYRUS

No one gossips about other people's secret virtues.
—BERTRAND RUSSELL

Show me someone who never gossips, and I'll show you someone who isn't interested in people. —BARBARA WALTERS

There is only one thing in the world worse than being talked about, and that is not being talked about. —OSCAR WILDE

GOVERNMENT
(also see concepts 83, 114, 149, 195, 208, 407, 445, 511, 598, 599, 616, 636, 753, 767, 794, 810, 847, 852)

You talk about capitalism and communism and all that sort of thing, but the important thing is the struggle everybody is engaged in to get better living conditions, and they are not interested too much in the form of government. —BERNARD M. BARUCH

The insatiable appetite for campaign dollars virtually has turned the government into a Stop & Shop for every greed and special interest in the country. —JERRY BROWN

Too bad all the people who know how to run the country are busy driving cabs and cutting hair. —GEORGE BURNS

In a healthy nation there is a kind of dramatic balance between the will of the people and the government, which prevents its degeneration into tyranny. —ALBERT EINSTEIN

It is hard to feel individually responsible with respect to the invisible processes of a huge and distant government.
—JOHN GARDNER

Even to observe neutrality you must have a strong government.
—ALEXANDER HAMILTON

There are no necessary evils in government. Its evils exist only in its abuses. —ANDREW JACKSON

It is a function of government to invent philosophies to explain the demands of its own convenience. —MURRAY KEMPTON

The basis of effective government is public confidence.
—JOHN F. KENNEDY

Any cook should be able to run the country. —V. I. LENIN

It is perfectly true that that government is best which governs least. It is equally true that that government is best which provides most.
—WALTER LIPPMANN

It is very easy to accuse a government of imperfection, for all mortal things are full of it. —MICHEL DE MONTAIGNE

Government is like a baby. An alimentary canal with a big appetite at one end and no sense of responsibility at the other.
—RONALD REAGAN

The body politic, as well as the human body, begins to die as soon as it is born, and carries itself the causes of its destruction.
—JEAN JACQUES ROUSSEAU

Government is at best but an expedient; but most governments are usually, and all governments are sometimes, inexpedient.
—HENRY DAVID THOREAU

Whenever you have an efficient government, you have a dictatorship. —HARRY S TRUMAN

Governments need to have both shepherds and butchers. —VOLTAIRE

GRACE
(also see concepts 102, 326, 776, 809)

Gracefulness is to the body what understanding is to the mind.
—FRANÇOIS DE LA ROCHEFOUCAULD

Without grace beauty is an unbaited hook. —FRENCH PROVERB

GRAMMAR

(also see concepts 232, 441, 874)

No iron can pierce the heart with such force as a period put just at the right place. —ISAAC BABEL

Grammar is a piano I play by ear. All I know about grammar is its power. —JOAN DIDION

You can be a little ungrammatical if you come from the right part of the country. —ROBERT FROST

Grammar is the grave of letters. —ELBERT HUBBARD

Is sloppiness in speech caused by ignorance or apathy? I don't know and I don't care. —WILLIAM SAFIRE

I never made a mistake in grammar but one in my life and as soon as I done it I seen it. —CARL SANDBURG

I am the Roman emperor, and am above grammar. —SIGISMUND

Damn the subjunctive. It brings all our writers to shame.
—MARK TWAIN

English usage is sometimes more than mere taste, judgment, and education—sometimes it's sheer luck, like getting across a street.
—E. B. WHITE

I used to be adjective-happy. Now I cut them with so much severity that I find I have to put a few adjectives back. —FRANK YERBY

GRATITUDE

(also see concept 40, 549)

It is not possible to eat me without insisting that I sing praises of my devourer? —FYODOR DOSTOYEVSKY

Maybe the only thing worse than having to give gratitude constantly...is having to accept it. —WILLIAM FAULKNER

Revenge is profitable, gratitude is expensive. —EDWARD GIBBON

Gratitude is the most exquisite form of courtesy. —JACQUES MARITAIN

Gratitude is a sickness suffered by dogs. —JOSEPH STALIN

GREATNESS
(also see concepts 207, 253, 542)

All your youth you want to have your greatness taken for granted; when you find it taken for granted, you are unnerved.
—ELIZABETH BOWEN

All great deeds and all great thoughts have a ridiculous beginning.
—ALBERT CAMUS

Greatness and goodness are not means, but ends.
—SAMUEL TAYLOR COLERIDGE

To be great is to be misunderstood. —RALPH WALDO EMERSON

No great thing is created suddenly. —EPICTETUS

The privilege of the great is to see catastrophes from a terrace.
—JEAN GIRAUDOUX

The herd seek out the great, not for their sake but for their influence; and the great welcome them out of vanity or need. —NAPOLEON I

I will be small in small things, great among great. —PINDAR

Do not despise the bottom rungs in the ascent to greatness.
—PUBLILIUS SYRUS

The loftiest edifices need the deepest foundations.
—GEORGE SANTAYANA

Some are born great, some achieve greatness, and some have greatness thrust upon 'em. —WILLIAM SHAKESPEARE

GREECE AND THE GREEKS
(also see concepts 247, 529)

To the Greeks the muse gave native wit, to the Greeks the gift of graceful eloquence. —HORACE

GREED

(also see concepts 237, 243, 264, 487, 505, 723, 780, 806)

Avarice is the vice of declining years. —GEORGE BANCROFT

If your desires be endless, your cares and fears will be so too.
—THOMAS FULLER

More die in the United States of too much food than of too little.
—JOHN KENNETH GALBRAITH

To hazard much to get much has more of avarice than wisdom.
—WILLIAM PENN

Big mouthfuls often choke. —ITALIAN PROVERB

Wealth is like sea-water; the more we drink, the thirstier we
become; and the same is true of fame. —ARTHUR SCHOPENHAUER

For greed all nature is too little. —SENECA

GROWTH AND DEVELOPMENT

(also see concepts 98, 177, 250, 389, 485)

Some people are molded by their admirations, others by their
hostilities. —ELIZABETH BOWEN

It is necessary to try to surpass one's self always; this occupation
ought to last as long as life. —QUEEN CHRISTINA OF SWEDEN

All growth is a leap in the dark, a spontaneous, unpremeditated act
without benefit of experience. —HENRY MILLER

Growth is the only evidence of life. —JOHN HENRY NEWMAN

No single event can awaken within us a stranger totally unknown
to us. To live is to be slowly born. —ANTOINE DE SAINT-EXUPÉRY

GUESTS

(also see concepts 135, 360, 361, 478)

My evening visitors, if they cannot see the clock should find the
time in my face. —RALPH WALDO EMERSON

A guest never forgets the host who had treated him kindly.
—HOMER

To be an ideal guest, stay at home. —EDGAR WATSON HOWE

Some people can stay longer in an hour than others can in a week.
—WILLIAM DEAN HOWELLS

Superior people never make long visits. —MARIANNE MOORE

Fish and guests smell at three days old. —DANISH PROVERB

GUILT
(also see concepts 71, 144, 150, 670, 734)

There may be responsible persons, but there are no guilty ones.
—ALBERT CAMUS

The guilty think all talk is of themselves. —GEOFFREY CHAUCER

I'm an Irish Catholic and I have a long iceberg of guilt.
—EDNA O'BRIEN

GULLIBILITY
(also see concepts 216, 375, 817)

There's a sucker born every minute. —P. T. BARNUM

A man is his own easiest dupe, for what he wishes to be true he
generally believes to be true. —DEMOSTHENES

Fame is proof that the people are gullible. —RALPH WALDO EMERSON

A certain portion of the human race has certainly a taste for being
diddled. —THOMAS HOOD

We are inclined to believe those whom we do not know because
they have never deceived us. —SAMUEL JOHNSON

GUNS AND GUN CONTROL
(also see concepts 372, 842)

You can get more with a kind word and a gun than you can with a kind word alone. —JOHNNY CARSON

Guns have a way of materializing more readily than the commodities that sustain life. —NORMAN COUSINS

Based on some estimates, guns are statistically like rats. They outnumber our population. —EDWARD M. KENNEDY

With all the violence and murder and killings we've had in the United States, I think you will agree that we must keep firearms from people who have no business with guns. —ROBERT F. KENNEDY

As long as there are guns, the individual that wants a gun for a crime is going to have one and going to get it. The only person who's going to be penalized and have difficulty is the law-abiding citizen, who then cannot have [it] if he wants protection–the protection of a weapon in his home, for home protection. —RONALD REAGAN

HABIT
(also see concepts 180, 671, 690, 770)

Habit is a great deadener. —SAMUEL BECKETT

Habit, n. a shackle for the free. —AMBROSE BIERCE

Habit is not mere subjugation, it is a tender tie; when one remembers habit it seems to have been happiness. —ELIZABETH BOWEN

Curious things, habits. People themselves never knew they had them. —AGATHA CHRISTIE

The evolution from happiness to habit is one of death's best weapons. —JULIO CORTÁZAR

Laws are never as effective as habits. —ADLAI STEVENSON

HAIR
(also see concepts 73, 266)

A haircut is a metaphysical operation. —JULIO CORTÁZAR

It is an ill wind that blows when you leave the hairdresser. —PHYLLIS DILLER

The hair in the head is worth two in the brush. —OLIVER HERFORD

The only thing that can stop hair falling is the floor. —WILL ROGERS

It [a moustache] keeps the water out of my nose. —MARK SPITZ

HAPPINESS
(also see concepts 104, 159, 433, 442, 592, 619)

Happiness depends upon ourselves. —ARISTOTLE

Happiness is good health and a bad memory. —INGRID BERGMAN

The bird of paradise alights only upon the hand that does not grasp. —JOHN BERRY

He that is of a merry heart hath a continual feast. —BIBLE, PROVERBS 15:15

The right to happiness is fundamental: / Men live so little time and die alone. —BERTOLT BRECHT

Follow your bliss. —JOSEPH CAMPBELL

To be happy, we must not be too concerned with others. —ALBERT CAMUS

Happiness does not lie in happiness, but in the achievement of it. —FYODOR DOSTOYEVSKY

Whoever is happy will make others happy too. —ANNE FRANK

Happiness makes up in height for what it lacks in length. —ROBERT FROST

Nothing is more fatal to happiness than the remembrance of happiness. —ANDRÉ GIDE

I used to think it was great to disregard happiness, to press on to a high goal, careless, disdainful of it. But now I see that there is nothing so great as to be capable of happiness. —ANNE GILCHRIST

Joys divided are increased. —JOSIAH GILBERT HOLLAND

Keep your face to the sunshine and you cannot see the shadow. —HELEN KELLER

We are never so happy nor so unhappy as we imagine. —FRANÇOIS DE LA ROCHEFOUCAULD

We possess only the happiness we are able to understand. —MAURICE MAETERLINCK

Ask yourself whether you are happy, and you cease to be so. —JOHN STUART MILL

The most profound joy has more of gravity than of gaiety in it. —MICHEL DE MONTAIGNE

What happiness is there which is not purchased with more or less of pain? —MARGARET OLIPHANT

When a small child...I thought that success spelled happiness. I was wrong, happiness is like a butterfly which appears and delights us for one brief moment, but soon flits away. —ANNA PAVLOVA

It is not enough to be happy, it is also necessary that others not be. —JULES RENARD

Happiness is not best achieved by those who seek it directly. —BERTRAND RUSSELL

We have no more right to consume happiness without producing it than to consume wealth without producing it. —GEORGE BERNARD SHAW

It is God's giving if we laugh or weep. —SOPHOCLES

Happiness is mostly a by-product of doing what makes us feel fulfilled. —BENJAMIN SPOCK

So long as we can lose any happiness, we possess some. —BOOTH TARKINGTON

Joy is a net of love by which you can catch souls. —MOTHER TERESA

That which makes people dissatisfied with their condition, is the chimerical idea they form of the happiness of others.
—JAMES THOMSON

If you want to be happy, be. —LEO TOLSTOY

If only we'd stop trying to be happy, we could have a pretty good time. —EDITH WHARTON

HASTE
(also see concepts 91, 386, 624, 762)

One of the great disadvantages of hurry is that it takes such a long time. —G. K. CHESTERTON

Take time for all things: great haste makes great waste.
—BENJAMIN FRANKLIN

Do nothing hastily but catching of fleas. —THOMAS FULLER

The greatest assassin of life is haste, the desire to reach things before the right time which means overreaching them.
—JUAN RAMÓN JIMÉNEZ

For fools rush in where angels fear to tread. —ALEXANDER POPE

Wisely, and slow. They stumble that run fast. —WILLIAM SHAKESPEARE

HATE
(also see concepts 36, 158, 237, 240, 418, 477, 570)

The price of hating other human beings is loving oneself less.
—ELDRIDGE CLEAVER

I am free of all prejudice. I hate everyone equally. —W. C. FIELDS

If you hate a person, you hate something in him that is part of yourself. What isn't part of ourselves doesn't disturb us.
—HERMANN HESSE

An intellectual hatred is the worst. —WILLIAM BUTLER YEATS

HEALTH
(also see concepts 28, 219, 229, 697, 772)

Health is not a condition of matter, but of Mind.
—MARY BAKER EDDY

The first wealth is health. —RALPH WALDO EMERSON

If you mean to keep as well as possible, the less you think about your health the better. —OLIVER WENDELL HOLMES, SR.

We should pray for a sane mind in a sound body. —JUVENAL

Preserving the health by too severe a rule is a wearisome malady.
—FRANÇOIS DE LA ROCHEFOUCAULD

We are not sensible of the most perfect health, as we are of the least sickness. —MICHEL DE MONTAIGNE

Attention to health is the greatest hindrance to life. —PLATO

We have to act now to make sure you don't have to be a Rockefeller to afford decent health care in this country.
—JAY ROCKEFELLER

'Tis healthy to be sick some times. —HENRY DAVID THOREAU

THE HEART
(also see concepts 73, 219, 340, 727)

What comes from the heart, goes to the heart.
—SAMUEL TAYLOR COLERIDGE

The heart has its reasons which reason does not know.
—BLAISE PASCAL

HEAVEN
(also see concepts 23, 203, 246, 316, 343, 385, 514, 751, 759, 766, 782, 784)

Earth's crammed with heaven. —ELIZABETH BARRETT BROWNING

Do not ask God the way to heaven; he will show you the hardest way. —STANISLAW LEC

Probably no invention came more easily to man than Heaven. —GEORG CHRISTOPH LICHTENBERG

The heaven of each is but what each desires. —THOMAS MOORE

Men have feverishly conceived a heaven only to find it insipid, and a hell to find it ridiculous. —GEORGE SANTAYANA

HELL
(also see concepts 23, 203, 246, 249, 342, 784)

Hell has three gates: lust, anger, and greed. —BHAGAVADGITA, CH. 16

Hell is paved with priests' skulls. —JOHN CHRYSOSTOM

The merit of Mahomet is that he founded a religion with an inferno. —NAPOLEON I

Hell is other people. —JEAN-PAUL SARTRE

HELP
(also see concepts 15, 51, 669, 729, 835)

People must help one another; it is nature's law. —JEAN DE LA FONTAINE

Many hands make light work. —PROVERB

God helps them that help themselves. —PROVERB

HEREDITY
(also see concepts 35, 44, 320, 511, 861)

With him for a sire and her for a dam. / What should I be but just what I am? —EDNA ST. VINCENT MILLAY

Just as you inherit your mother's brown eyes, you inherit part of yourself. —ALICE WALKER

HEROES AND HEROISM

(also see concepts 75, 167, 315, 356, 672, 783)

Unhappy the land that is in need of heroes. —BERTOLT BRECHT

Every hero becomes a bore at last. —RALPH WALDO EMERSON

Show me a hero and I will write you a tragedy.
—F. SCOTT FITZGERALD

A hero cannot be a hero unless in an heroic world.
—NATHANIEL HAWTHORNE

We are the hero of our own story. —MARY MCCARTHY

This thing of being a hero, about the main thing to it is to know when to die. —WILL ROGERS

HISPANIC AMERICANS

(also see concepts 32, 522, 650)

We're not undocumented people; we're from here. We have no work, 60 percent of the people are unemployed. Why is the government spending money to discover the moon, which is a piece of stone in the sky? —CARMEN ANAYA

One cannot observe Puerto Rican life close up without reaching the conclusion that every form of tutelage is morally degrading. As long as sovereignty does not reside in us, there will be genuflections and degradations before those in whom it does reside. This is the political illness of Puerto Rico and its only cure is a dose of unadulterated sovereignty. —LUIS MUÑOZ MARÍN

Ask me what it was like to have grown up a Mexican kid in Sacramento and I will think of my father's smile, its sweetness, its introspection, its weight of sobriety. Mexico was most powerfully my father's smile and not, as you might otherwise imagine, not language, not pigment. —RICHARD RODRIGUEZ

HISTORIANS AND HISTORY

(also see concepts 410, 571, 700)

Real solemn history, I cannot be interested in....The quarrels of popes and kings, with wars and pestilences in every page; the men all so good for nothing, and hardly any women at all. —JANE AUSTEN

People are trapped in history and history is trapped in them.
—JAMES BALDWIN

World history would be different if humanity did more sitting on its rear. —BERTOLT BRECHT

These gentle historians, on the contrary, dip their pens in nothing but the milk of human kindness. —EDMUND BURKE

God cannot alter the past, but historians can. —SAMUEL BUTLER

History, with all her volumes vast, / Hath but one page.
—LORD BYRON

The history of every country begins in the heart of a man or woman.
—WILLA CATHER

The historical sense involves a perception, not only of the pastness of the past, but of it presence. —T. S. ELIOT

History is more or less bunk. —HENRY FORD

So it is all the same day—the past, the present, and the future existing on the same plane—but you just have to change your drawers every couple of hours. —WHOOPI GOLDBERG

Peoples and governments never have learned anything from history, or acted on principles deduced from it.
—GEORG WILHELM FRIEDRICH HEGEL

It is not the neutrals or the lukewarm who make history.
—ADOLF HITLER

All things from eternity are of like forms and come round in a circle. —MARCUS AURELIUS

The history of the world is the history of a privileged few.
—HENRY MILLER

For a while I thought history was something bitter old men wrote. But Jack loved history so...for Jack history was full of heroes. ——JACQUELINE KENNEDY ONASSIS

A historian is a prophet in reverse. ——FRIEDRICH VON SCHLEGEL

History is the ship carrying living memories into the future. ——STEPHEN SPENDER

The very ink with which all history is written is merely fluid prejudice. ——MARK TWAIN

History is no more than a portrayal of crimes and misfortunes. ——VOLTAIRE

History is all explained by geography. ——ROBERT PENN WARREN

As soon as histories are properly told there is no more need of romances. ——WALT WHITMAN

HOLIDAYS
(also see concepts 109, 444, 677)

Now the New Year reviving old Desires, / The thoughtful Soul to Solitude retires. ——OMAR KHAYYÁM

Other holidays repose in the past; Arbor Day proposes for the future. ——STERLING MORTON

Labor Day symbolizes our determination to achieve an economic freedom for the average man which will give his political freedom reality. ——FRANKLIN D. ROOSEVELT

HOLISTIC   MEDICINE
(also see concepts 219, 340, 489, 501, 738)

A bodily disease, which we look upon as whole and entire within itself, may, after all, be but a symptom of some ailment in the spiritual part. ——NATHANIEL HAWTHORNE

Disease has social as well as physical, chemical, and biological causes. ——HENRY E. SIEGRIST

HOLLYWOOD

(also see concepts 11, 271, 521)

Hollywood is a place where people from Iowa mistake each other for a star. ——FRED ALLEN

Hollywood is like being nowhere and talking to nobody about nothing. ——MICHELANGELO ANTONIONI

Hollywood is the only place in the world where an amicable divorce means each one getting fifty percent of the publicity. ——LAUREN BACALL

The people are unreal. The flowers are unreal; they don't smell. The fruit is unreal; it doesn't taste of anything. The whole place is a glaring, gaudy, nightmarish set, built up in the desert. ——ETHEL BARRYMORE

Hollywood is a world with all the personality of a paper cup. ——RAYMOND CHANDLER

Living in Hollywood is like living in a lit cigar butt. ——PHYLLIS DILLER

If we have to kiss Hollywood goodbye, it may be with one of those tender, old-fashioned, seven-second kisses as exchanged between two people of the opposite sex with all their clothes on. ——ANITA LOOS

Hollywood's a place where they'll pay you a thousand dollars for a kiss, and fifty cents for your soul. ——MARILYN MONROE

A dreary industrial town controlled by hoodlums of enormous wealth, the ethical sense of a pack of jackals, and taste so degraded that it befouled everything to touch it. ——S. J. PERELMAN

Hollywood has done a sufficient job of showing the sexual positions of women. Now it has to explore the emotional and spiritual depths of women, as well as their intellectual and creative capabilities. ——SISTER SOULJAH

HOME

(also see concepts 60, 362, 363, 589, 604, 628)

The strength of a nation is derived from the integrity of its homes.
—CONFUCIUS

Charity begins at home, and justice begins next door.
—CHARLES DICKENS

The ornament of a house is the friends who frequent it.
—RALPH WALDO EMERSON

Home is the place where, when you have to go there, / They have
to take you in. —ROBERT FROST

Nobody soldiers a rifle in defense of a boarding house.
—BRET HARTE

But everybody needs a home so at least you can have some place
to leave which is where most other folks will say you must be
coming from. —JUNE JORDAN

East, west, home's best. —PROVERB

HOMELAND

(also see concepts 69, 528)

There is no sorrow above / The loss of a native land. —EURIPIDES

The accent of one's birthplace lingers in the mind and in the heart
as it does in one's speech. —FRANÇOIS DE LA ROCHEFOUCAULD

It is right to prefer our own country to all others, because we are
children and citizens before we can be travellers or philosophers.
—GEORGE SANTAYANA

HOMOSEXUALITY

(also see concepts 448, 493, 731)

There's this illusion that homosexuals have sex and heterosexuals
fall in love. That's completely untrue. Everybody wants to be
loved. —BOY GEORGE

This is a celebration of individual freedom, not of homosexuality. No government has the right to tell its citizens when or whom to love. The only queer people are those who don't love anybody.
——RITA MAE BROWN

If God had meant to have homosexuals he would have created Adam and Bruce. ——ANITA BRYANT

I don't think homosexuality is normal behavior and I oppose the codification of gay rights. But I wouldn't harass them and I wish they could know that. Actually, I wish the whole issue could be toned down. I wish it would go away, but, of course, I know it can't.
——GEORGE BUSH

Homosexuality is always elsewhere because it is everywhere.
——RENAUD CAMUS

I would not have come out of the closet if it were not for other people making space for me to accept myself. ——ROBERT CHESLEY

Let me say, a more artistic, appreciative group of people for the arts does not exist....They are more knowledgeable, more loving of the arts. They make the average male look stupid. ——BETTE DAVIS

Homosexuality is assuredly no advantage, but it is nothing to be ashamed of, no vice, no degradation, it cannot be classified as an illness....It is a great injustice to persecute homosexuality as a crime, and cruelty too. ——SIGMUND FREUD

It seems to me that the real clue to your sex-orientation lies in your romantic feelings rather than in your sexual feelings. If you are really gay, you are able to fall in love with a man, not just enjoy having sex with him. ——CHRISTOPHER ISHERWOOD

When you finally come out, there's a pain that stops, and you know it will never hurt like that again, no matter how bad you lose or how bad you die. ——PAUL MONETTE

...those who behave in a homosexual fashion...shall not enter the kingdom of God. ——POPE JOHN PAUL II

I believe that the masculine male homosexual is the ultimate symbol of human freedom, and that's why you have male homosexuality occurring at those great high points of culture such as classical Athens and Florence. Gay men and men in general have made astonishing contributions: haute cuisine, haute couture, the Pyramids, the George Washington Bridge. —CAMILLE PAGLIA

There is enormous pressure to keep gay people defined solely by our sexuality, which prevents us from presenting our existence in political terms. —VITO RUSSO

The big lie about lesbians and gay men is that we do not exist. —VITO RUSSO

What gay life does offer is some *give* in the social machine. If Americans, those least political of all social animals, must doubt the sexual given, then that skepticism may shift to other aspects of our national life. —EDMUND WHITE

We are not trying to imitate women. —TENNESSEE WILLIAMS

My attitude toward anybody's sexual persuasion is this: without deviation from the norm, progress is not possible. —FRANK ZAPPA

HONESTY

(also see concepts 188, 214, 297, 409, 620, 742, 744)

Honesty's praised, then left to freeze. —JUVENAL

Honesty has come to mean the privilege of insulting you to your face without expecting redress. —JUDITH MARTIN

Don't be ashamed to say what you are not ashamed to think. —MICHEL DE MONTAIGNE

Honesty is for the most part less profitable than dishonesty. —PLATO

Honesty is the best policy. —PROVERB

God looks at the clean hands, not the full ones. —PUBLILIUS SYRUS

To make your children capable of honesty is the beginning of education. —JOHN RUSKIN

No legacy is so rich as honesty. —WILLIAM SHAKESPEARE

If you do not tell the truth about yourself you cannot tell it about other people. —VIRGINIA WOOLF

HONOR

(also see concepts 100, 103, 139, 237, 315, 326, 346, 409, 619, 646, 675, 682, 744)

Honour and shame from no condition rise; / Act well your part, there all the honour lies. —ALEXANDER POPE

Without money, honor is a malady. —JEAN RACINE

It is sure that those are most desirous of honour or glory who cry out loudest of its abuse and the vanity of the world. —BENEDICT SPINOZA

Honor wears different coats to different eyes. —BARBARA TUCHMAN

A woman of honor should not suspect another of things she would not do herself. —MARGUERITE DE VALOIS

HOPE

(also see concepts 237, 259, 559, 560, 647)

Hope is a waking dream. —ARISTOTLE

While there's life there's hope. —CICERO

Death is the greatest evil, because it cuts off hope. —WILLIAM HAZLITT

We should not let our fears hold us back from pursuing our hopes. —JOHN F. KENNEDY

Hope is the feeling you have that the feeling you have isn't permanent. —JEAN KERR

Hope has as many lives as a cat or a king. —HENRY WADSWORTH LONGFELLOW

Hope says to us constantly, "Go on, go on," and leads us to the grave. —FRANÇOISE DE MAINTENON

Strong hope is a much greater stimulant of life than any single realised joy could be. —FRIEDRICH WILHELM NIETZSCHE

Hope for the best, but prepare for the worst. —ENGLISH PROVERB

The miserable have no other medicine / But only hope.
—WILLIAM SHAKESPEARE

Hope is a very unruly emotion. —GLORIA STEINEM

HORROR
(also see concepts 282, 800)

We make up horrors to help us cope with the real ones.
—STEPHEN KING

HORSES AND HORSE RACING
(also see concepts 37, 305)

A canter is the cure for every evil. —BENJAMIN DISRAELI

Every one knows that horse-racing is carried on mainly for the delight and profit of fools, ruffians, and thieves. —GEORGE GISSING

The horse, the horse! The symbol of surging potency and power of movement, of action, in man. —D. H. LAWRENCE

A horse! A horse! my kingdom for a horse. —WILLIAM SHAKESPEARE

I bet on a horse at ten to one. It didn't come in until half-past five.
—HENNY YOUNGMAN

HOSPITALITY
(also see concepts 331, 478)

When hospitality becomes an art, it loses its very soul.
—MAX BEERBOHM

Not many sounds in life, and I include all urban and all rural sounds, exceed in interest a knock at the door. —CHARLES LAMB

HOTELS

(also see concepts 60, 814)

Why do they put the Gideon Bibles only in the bedrooms, where it's usually too late? —CHRISTOPHER MORLEY

All saints can do miracles, but few of them can keep a hotel.
—MARK TWAIN

HOUSES

(also see concepts 42, 60, 352, 363, 589, 604, 628)

I don't want a house that has got over all its troubles; I don't want to spend the rest of my life bringing up a young and inexperienced house. —JEROME K. JEROME

A house is a machine for living in. —LE CORBUSIER

Small rooms or dwellings discipline the mind, large ones weaken it. —LEONARDO DA VINCI

Our houses are such unwieldy property that we are often imprisoned rather than housed in them. —HENRY DAVID THOREAU

HOUSEWORK

(also see concepts 10, 163, 352, 362)

Housekeeping ain't no joke. —LOUISA MAY ALCOTT

There was no need to do any housework at all. After the first four years the dirt doesn't get any worse. —QUENTIN CRISP

If a few lustful and erotic reveries make the housework go by "as if in a dream," why not? —NANCY FRIDAY

There are days when housework seems the only outlet.
—ADRIENNE RICH

I hate housework! You make the beds, you do the dishes–and six months later you have to start all over again. —JOAN RIVERS

Motherhood and homemaking are honorable choices for any woman, provided it is the woman who makes those decisions. —MOLLY YARD

HUMAN NATURE
(also see concepts 10, 16, 576, 580, 635)

Human nature is the same everywhere; the modes only are different. —EARL OF CHESTERFIELD

The perfect joys of heaven do not satisfy the cravings of nature. —WILLIAM HAZLITT

Most human beings have an almost infinite capacity for taking things for granted. —ALDOUS HUXLEY

Out of the crooked timber of humanity no straight thing can ever be made. —IMMANUEL KANT

Scenery is fine—but human nature is finer. —JOHN KEATS

The essence of being human is that one does not seek perfection. —GEORGE ORWELL

We ride through life on the beast within us. Beat the animal, but you can't make it think. —LUIGI PIRANDELLO

One touch of nature makes the whole world kin. —WILLIAM SHAKESPEARE

Nature has always had more power than education. —VOLTAIRE

HUMAN RIGHTS
(also see concepts 115, 157, 244, 298)

Rights that do not flow from duty well performed are not worth having. —MOHANDAS K. GANDHI

They have rights who dare maintain them. —JAMES RUSSELL LOWELL

There's no question in my mind but that rights are never won unless people are willing to fight for them. —ELEANOR SMEAL

All human beings are born free and equal in dignity and rights.
——UNIVERSAL DECLARATION OF HUMAN RIGHTS

A right is worth fighting for only when it can be put into operation.
——WOODROW WILSON

HUMANISM
(also see concepts 213, 378, 459, 834)

What the world needs is not redemption from sin but redemption from hunger and oppression; it has no need to pin its hopes upon Heaven, it has everything to hope for from this earth.
——FRIEDRICH DÜRRENMATT

We now no longer camp as for a night, but have settled down on earth and forgotten heaven. ——HENRY DAVID THOREAU

We are healthy only to the extent that our ideas are humane.
——KURT VONNEGUT

HUMANITARIANISM
(also see concepts 344, 375)

Social work is a Band-Aid on the festering wounds of society.
——ALEXANDER CHASE

In abstract love of humanity one almost always only loves oneself.
——FYODOR DOSTOYEVSKY

As often as we do good we sacrifice. ——THOMAS FULLER

A large part of altruism, even when it is perfectly honest, is grounded upon the fact that it is uncomfortable to have unhappy people about one. ——H. L. MENCKEN

A humanitarian is always a hypocrite. ——GEORGE ORWELL

HUMANKIND
(also see concepts 257, 517, 563, 576)

Either a beast or a god. ——ARISTOTLE

We drink without thirst and we make love anytime, madame; only this distinguishes us from the other animals.
——PIERRE DE BEAUMARCHAIS

Man is a noble animal, splendid in ashes, and pompous in the grave. ——THOMAS BROWNE

A single sentence will suffice for modern man: he fornicated and read the papers. ——ALBERT CAMUS

A wonderful fact to reflect upon, that every human creature is constituted to be that profound secret and mystery to every other.
——CHARLES DICKENS

We cannot despair of humanity, since we ourselves are human beings. ——ALBERT EINSTEIN

Human beings are like timid punctuation marks sprinkled among the incomprehensible sentences of life. ——JEAN GIRAUDOUX

Mankind are earthen jugs with spirits in them.
——NATHANIEL HAWTHORNE

There is nothing on earth divine except humanity.
——WALTER SAVAGE LANDOR

Human beings make a strange fauna and flora. From a distance they appear negligible; close up they are apt to appear ugly and malicious. More than anything they need to be surrounded with sufficient space–space even more than time. ——HENRY MILLER

I have never seen greater monster or miracle in the world than myself. ——MICHEL DE MONTAIGNE

Lord, what fools these mortals be! ——WILLIAM SHAKESPEARE

We're all of us guinea pigs in the laboratory of God. Humanity is just a work in progress. ——TENNESSEE WILLIAMS

HUMILITY
(also see concepts 237, 311, 510, 572, 737)

They are proud in humility; proud in that they are not proud.
——ROBERT BURTON

Don't be humble. You're not that great. —GOLDA MEIR

He that humbleth himself wishes to be exalted.
—FRIEDRICH WILHELM NIETZSCHE

The humble and meek are thirsting for blood. —JOE ORTON

Too humble is half proud. —YIDDISH PROVERB

Those who are believed to be most abject and humble are usually
most ambitious and envious. —BENEDICT SPINOZA

HUMOR

(also see concepts 128, 442, 644, 866)

I have a fine sense of the ridiculous, but no sense of humor.
—EDWARD ALBEE

A difference of taste in jokes is a great strain on the affections.
—GEORGE ELIOT

A jest often decides matters of importance more effectually and
happily than seriousness. —HORACE

Many a true word is spoken in jest. —ENGLISH PROVERB

The absolute truth is the thing that makes people laugh.
—CARL REINER

Everything is funny as long as it is happening to somebody else.
—WILL ROGERS

Humor is emotional chaos remembered in tranquility.
—JAMES THURBER

The secret source of humor itself is not joy but sorrow. There is no
humor in heaven. —MARK TWAIN

It's hard to be funny when you have to be clean. —MAE WEST

Humour is the first of the gifts to perish in a foreign tongue.
—VIRGINIA WOOLF

HUNGER

(also see concepts 163, 290, 606)

There's no sauce in the world like hunger. —MIGUEL DE CERVANTES

In general, mankind, since the improvement of cookery, eats twice as much as nature requires. —BENJAMIN FRANKLIN

Hunger can explain many acts. It can be said that all vile acts are done to satisfy hunger. —MAXIM GORKY

Love and business and family and religion and art and patriotism are nothing but shadows of words when a man's starving.
—O. HENRY

HUNTING

(also see concepts 9, 10, 37, 334, 437, 765)

I generally hate clubs, but in 1961 I formed my own. It's called the "Hunt the Hunters Club." After you've bagged your hunter, drape him over the hood of your car and mount him when you get home.
—CLEVELAND AMORY

Detested sport / That owes its pleasures to another's pain.
—WILLIAM COWPER

There is a passion for hunting something deeply implanted in the human breast. —CHARLES DICKENS

Hunting was the labour of the savages of North America, but the amusement of the gentlemen of England. —SAMUEL JOHNSON

When a man wantonly destroys one of the works of man we call him a vandal. When he destroys one of the works of God we call him a sportsman. —JOSEPH WOOD KRUTCH

HYPOCHONDRIA

(also see concepts 382, 500, 738)

An imaginary ailment is worse than a disease. —YIDDISH PROVERB

Hypochondria torments us not only with causeless irritation with the things of the present; not only with groundless anxiety on the score of future misfortunes entirely of our own manufacture; but also with unmerited self-reproach for our own past actions. ——ARTHUR SCHOPENHAUER

The imaginary complaints of indestructible old ladies. ——E. B. WHITE

Most of the time we think we're sick, it's all in the mind. ——THOMAS WOLFE

HYPOCRISY

(also see concepts 288, 405, 452, 711, 721)

We ought to see far enough into a hypocrite to see even his sincerity. ——G. K. CHESTERTON

Often a noble face hides filthy ways. ——EURIPIDES

Most people have seen worse things in private than they pretend to be shocked at in public. ——EDGAR WATSON HOWE

Hypocrisy is the homage that vice pays to virtue. ——FRANÇOIS DE LA ROCHEFOUCAULD

The hypocrite who always plays one and the same part ceases at last to be a hypocrite. ——FRIEDRICH WILHELM NIETZSCHE

It is with a pious fraud as with a bad action; it begets a calamitous necessity of going on. ——THOMAS PAINE

That character in conversation which commonly passes for agreeable is made up of civility and falsehood. ——ALEXANDER POPE

All are not saints that go to church. ——PROVERB

Men use thought only as authority for their injustice, and employ speech only to conceal their thoughts. ——VOLTAIRE

IDEALISM

(also see concepts 64, 215, 367, 378, 480, 525, 559, 560, 688)

No man or woman who tries to pursue an ideal in his or her own way is without enemies. —DAISY BATES

Idealism is fine, but as it approaches reality the cost becomes prohibitive. —WILLIAM F. BUCKLEY

The idealist walks on tiptoe, the materialist on his heels.
—MALCOLM DE CHAZAL

If two or three persons should come with a high spiritual aim and with great powers, the world would fall into their hands like a ripe peach. —RALPH WALDO EMERSON

Idealists...foolish enough to throw caution to the winds...have advanced mankind and have enriched the world. —EMMA GOLDMAN

Don't use that foreign word "ideals." We have that excellent native word "lies." —HENRIK IBSEN

If a man hasn't discovered something that he would die for, he isn't fit to live. —MARTIN LUTHER KING, JR.

Ideal mankind would abolish death, multiply itself million upon million, rear up city upon city, save every parasite alive, until the accumulation of mere existence is swollen to a horror.
—D. H. LAWRENCE

I'm not going to throw my imagination away. I refuse to live down to expectation. If I can just hold out 'til I'm thirty, I'll be incredible.
—WENDY WASSERSTEIN

IDEAS

(also see concepts 64, 307, 378, 406, 419, 519, 555, 674, 700, 795, 803, 804)

Ideas are fatal to caste. —E. M. FORSTER

Ideas move fast when their time comes. —CAROLYN HEILBRUN

If you want to kill any idea in the world today, get a committee working on it. —CHARLES F. KETTERING

A single idea, if it is right, saves us the labor of an infinity of experiences. —JACQUES MARITAIN

An idea isn't responsible for the people who believe in it. —DON MARQUIS

Human life is driven forward by its dim apprehension of notions too general for its existing language. —ALFRED NORTH WHITEHEAD

IDENTITY
(also see concepts 354, 527, 708, 741, 770, 831)

People remain what they are, even when their faces fall to pieces. —BERTOLT BRECHT

It is thus with most of us; we are what other people say we are. We know ourselves chiefly by hearsay. —ERIC HOFFER

Identity is what you can say you are according to what they say you can be. —JILL JOHNSTON

Rose is a rose is a rose is a rose. —GERTRUDE STEIN

IDEOLOGY
(also see concepts 64, 88, 133, 153, 154, 220, 274, 276, 283, 366, 376, 450, 753)

I am always easy of belief when the creed pleases me. —CHARLOTTE BRONTË

They were so strong in their beliefs that there came a time when it hardly mattered what exactly those beliefs were; they all fused into a single stubbornness. —LOUISE ERDRICH

Our blight is ideologies–they are the long-expected Antichrist! —CARL JUNG

IDLENESS

(also see concepts 10, 444, 447)

Expect poison from the standing water. —WILLIAM BLAKE

It is impossible to enjoy idling thoroughly unless one has plenty of work to do. —JEROME K. JEROME

If you are idle, be not solitary; if you are solitary, be not idle.
—SAMUEL JOHNSON

It is better to have loafed and lost than never to have loafed at all.
—JAMES THURBER

IGNORANCE

(also see concepts 116, 291, 390, 440, 689)

Ignorance is not innocence but sin. —ROBERT BROWNING

To be conscious that you are ignorant is a great step to knowledge.
—BENJAMIN DISRAELI

What you don't know can't hurt you. —PROVERB

Better to be ignorant of a matter than half know it.
—PUBLILIUS SYRUS

Ignorance is like a delicate exotic fruit; touch it, and the bloom is gone. —OSCAR WILDE

ILLUSION

(also see concepts 215, 382, 500, 507, 836)

Illusions are art, for the feeling person, and it is by art that we live, if we do. —ELIZABETH BOWEN

Obsessed by a fairy tale, we spend our lives searching for a magic door and a lost kingdom of peace. —EUGENE O'NEILL

IMAGINATION

(also see concepts 46, 75, 284, 381, 420)

Imagination is the highest kite one can fly. —LAUREN BACALL

People can die of mere imagination. —GEOFFREY CHAUCER

Art is ruled uniquely by the imagination. —BENEDETTO CROCE

With our progress we have destroyed our only weapon against tedium: that rare weakness we call imagination. —ORIANA FALLACI

Imagination is the first faculty wanting in those that do harm to their own kind. —MARGARET OLIPHANT

The eyes are not responsible when the mind does the seeing. —PUBLILIUS SYRUS

Imagination and fiction make up more than three quarters of our real life. —SIMONE WEIL

IMITATION

(also see concept 252)

No living person is sunk so low as not to be imitated by somebody. —WILLIAM JAMES

To refrain from imitation is the best revenge. —MARCUS AURELIUS

A mere copier of nature can never produce anything great. —JOSHUA REYNOLDS

IMMATURITY

(also see concepts 485, 876, 877)

Is life so wretched? Isn't it rather your hands which are too small, your vision which is muddied? You are the one who must grow up. —DAG HAMMARSKJÖLD

The mark of the immature man is that he wants to die nobly for a cause, while the mark of the mature man is that he wants to live humbly for one. —WILHELM STEKEL

IMMORTALITY

(also see concepts 23, 185, 246, 463)

To live in hearts we leave / Is not to die. —THOMAS CAMPBELL

He had decided to live forever or die in the attempt. —JOSEPH HELLER

I have good hope that there is something after death. —PLATO

We feel and know that we are eternal. —BENEDICT SPINOZA

IMPATIENCE

(also see concepts 237, 338, 798)

Impatience is the mark of independence, / not of bondage.
—MARIANNE MOORE

IMPERFECTION

(also see concepts 281, 398, 822, 836, 855)

When you have faults, do not fear to abandon them. —CONFUCIUS

Even imperfection itself may have its ideal or perfect state.
—THOMAS DE QUINCEY

A good garden may have some weeds. —THOMAS FULLER

IMPORTANCE

(also see concepts 207, 728, 773, 835, 837)

In heaven an angel is no one in particular. —GEORGE BERNARD SHAW

IMPROVEMENT

(also see concepts 625, 663)

If way to the Better there be, it exacts a full look at the Worst.
—THOMAS HARDY

Happy are they that hear their detractions and can put them to
mending. —WILLIAM SHAKESPEARE

INCOMPETENCE
(also see concepts 268, 380)

The worse the carpenter, the more the chips. —DUTCH PROVERB

Failure can get to be a rather comfortable old friend.
—MIGNON MCLAUGHLIN

INDECISION
(also see concepts 222, 550, 624)

How long halt ye between two opinions? —BIBLE, I KINGS 18:21

There is no more miserable human being than one in whom nothing is habitual but indecision. —WILLIAM JAMES

It is human nature to stand in the middle of a thing.
—MARIANNE MOORE

He who hesitates is sometimes saved. —JAMES THURBER

I must have a prodigious quantity of mind; it takes me as much as a week, sometimes, to make it up. —MARK TWAIN

INDIFFERENCE
(also see concepts 45, 77, 127, 174, 535, 551, 749, 771, 828)

But what is past my help is past my care. —FRANCIS BEAUMONT

Lukewarmness I account a sin as great in love as in religion.
—ABRAHAM COWLEY

Human indifference and passivity represent the greatest threats to planetary survival. The "ecological imperative" demands that we care and act. —TERRELL MINGER

Indifference is the invincible giant of the world. —OUIDA

I need not fear my enemies because the most they can do is attack me. I need not fear my friends because the most they can do is betray me. But I have much to fear from people who are indifferent.
—RUSSIAN PROVERB

The worst sin towards our fellow creatures is not to hate them, but to be indifferent to them: that's the essence of inhumanity.
—GEORGE BERNARD SHAW

I regard you with an indifference closely bordering on aversion.
—ROBERT LOUIS STEVENSON

INDIGNATION
(also see concepts 36, 237, 426)

A puritan's a person who pours righteous indignation into the wrong things. —G. K. CHESTERTON

Moral indignation is in most cases two percent moral, forty-eight percent indignation and fifty percent envy. —VITTORIO DE SICA

No one lies as much as the indignant do.
—FRIEDRICH WILHELM NIETZSCHE

Humanity is outraged in me and with me. We must not dissimilate nor try to forget this indignation which is one of the most passionate forms of love. —GEORGE SAND

INDIVIDUALISM
(also see concepts 100, 205, 830)

I wish that every human life might be pure transparent freedom.
—SIMONE DE BEAUVOIR

Meeting people unlike oneself does not enlarge one's outlook; it only confirms one's idea that one is unique. —ELIZABETH BOWEN

We boil at different degrees. —RALPH WALDO EMERSON

You are unique, and if that is not fulfilled, then something has been lost. —MARTHA GRAHAM

Woe to him inside a non-conformist clique who does not conform to non-conformity. —ERIC HOFFER

Individualism is rather like innocence; there must be something unconscious about it. —LOUIS KRONENBERGER

They will say that you are on the wrong road, if it is your own.
——ANTONIO PORCHIA

INDULGENCE

(also see concepts 473, 723)

Indulgences, not fulfillment, is what the world / Permits us.
——CHRISTOPHER FRY

The more you let yourself go, the less others let you go.
——FRIEDRICH WILHELM NIETZSCHE

INEQUALITY

(also see concepts 136, 205, 213, 403, 651)

We are all Adam's children, but silk makes the difference.
——THOMAS FULLER

If human equality is to be forever averted–if the High, as we have called them, are to keep their places permanently–then the prevailing mental condition must be controlled insanity. ——GEORGE ORWELL

True education makes for inequality; the inequality of individuality, the inequality of success; the glorious inequality of talent, of genius, for inequality, not mediocrity, individual superiority, not standardization, is the measure of the progress of the world.
——FELIX E. SCHELLING

Who ever walked behind anyone to freedom? If we can't go hand in hand, I don't want to go. ——HAZEL SCOTT

INEVITABILITY

(also see concepts 96, 200, 279)

Nothing is inevitable until it happens. ——A. J. P. TAYLOR

INFERIORITY

(also see concepts 387, 490)

Wherever an inferiority complex exists, there is a good reason for it. There is always something inferior there, although not just where we persuade ourselves that it is. —CARL JUNG

No one can make you feel inferior without your consent.
—ELEANOR ROOSEVELT

INFLATION

(also see concepts 231, 254)

Having a little inflation is like being a little pregnant.
—LEON HENDERSON

I haven't heard of anybody who wants to stop living on account of the cost. —KIN HUBBARD

The best way to destroy the capitalist system is to debauch the currency. By a continuing process of inflation governments can confiscate, secretly and unobserved, an important part of the wealth of their citizens. —JOHN MAYNARD KEYNES

Inflation in the Sixties was a nuisance to be endured, like varicose veins or French foreign policy. —BERNARD LEVIN

INFLUENCE

(also see concepts 43, 81, 236, 388, 582, 613, 627, 637, 728)

People exercise an unconscious selection in being influenced.
—T. S. ELIOT

We have met too late. You are too old for me to have any effect on you. —JAMES JOYCE

Half our standards come from our first masters, and the other half from our first loves. —GEORGE SANTAYANA

INGRATITUDE

(also see concepts 583, 689)

Eaten bread is forgotten. —THOMAS FULLER

Too great haste in paying off an obligation is a kind of ingratitude.
—FRANÇOIS DE LA ROCHEFOUCAULD

INJURY

(also see concepts 6, 183, 184, 201, 209, 613, 779)

Everyone suffers wrongs for which there is no remedy.
—EDGAR WATSON HOWE

Reject your sense of injury and the injury itself disappears.
—MARCUS AURELIUS

Wounds heal and become scars. But scars grow with us.
—KING STANISLAUS I

INJUSTICE

(also see concepts 396, 613, 651)

When one has been threatened with a great injustice, one accepts
a smaller as a favour. —JANE CARLYLE

Since when do you have to agree with people to defend them from
injustice? —LILLIAN HELLMAN

Undeservedly you will atone for the sins of your fathers. —HORACE

An unrectified case of injustice has a terrible way of lingering,
restlessly, in the social atmosphere like an unfinished question.
—MARY MCCARTHY

A hurtful act is the transference to others of the degradation which
we bear in ourselves. —SIMONE WEIL

One had better die fighting against injustice than die like a dog or
a rat in a trap. —IDA B. WELLS

Injustice which lasts for three long centuries and which exists among millions of people over thousands of square miles of territory, is injustice no longer; it is an accomplished fact of life. ——RICHARD WRIGHT

INNOCENCE

(also see concepts 103, 117, 120, 876)

Those who are incapable of committing great crimes do not readily suspect them in others. ——FRANÇOIS DE LA ROCHEFOUCAULD

If you would live innocently, seek solitude. ——PUBLILIUS SYRUS

Now my innocence begins to weigh me down. ——JEAN RACINE

INSECTS

(also see concepts 289, 426, 531)

The ant sets an example to us all, but it is not a good one. ——MAX BEERBOHM

Dost thou not see the little plants, the little birds, the ants, the spiders, the bees working together in order to put in order their several parts of the universe? ——MARCUS AURELIUS

Is there a polity better ordered, the offices better distributed, and more inviolably observed and maintained, than that of bees? ——MICHEL DE MONTAIGNE

God in His wisdom made the fly / And then forgot to tell us why. ——OGDEN NASH

We hope that, when the insects take over the world, they will remember with gratitude how we took them along on all our picnics. ——BILL VAUGHAN

INSINCERITY
(also see concepts 288, 374)

A false friend and a shadow attend only while the sun shines.
—BENJAMIN FRANKLIN

The most exhausting thing in life is being insincere.
—ANNE MORROW LINDBERGH

Most friendship is feigning, most loving mere folly.
—WILLIAM SHAKESPEARE

INSPIRATION
(also see concepts 94, 212, 419, 582, 764)

The unconscious mind has a habit of asserting itself in the afternoon.
—ANTHONY BURGESS

Listen to the voices. —WILLIAM FAULKNER

Deprivation is for me what daffodils were to Wordsworth.
—PHILIP LARKIN

You can't wait for inspiration. You have to go after it with a club.
—JACK LONDON

There is no wide road which leads to the Muses. —PROPERTIUS

Just as appetite comes by eating, so work brings inspiration, if inspiration is not discernible at the beginning. —IGOR STRAVINSKY

All you have to do is close your eyes and wait for the symbols.
—TENNESSEE WILLIAMS

INSTITUTIONS
(also see concepts 83, 111, 621, 754, 767, 770)

The test of political institutions is the condition of the country whose future they regulate. —BENJAMIN DISRAELI

We do not make a world of our own, but fall into institutions already made, and have to accommodate ourselves to them to be useful at all. —RALPH WALDO EMERSON

Every institution not only carries within it the seeds of its own dissolution, but prepares the way for its most hated rival. —WILLIAM RALPH INGE

In the infancy of societies, the chiefs of the state shape its institutions; later the institutions shape the chiefs of state. —BARON DE MONTESQUIEU

The working of great institutions is mainly the result of a vast mass of routine, petty malice, self-interest, carelessness, and sheer mistake. Only a residual fraction is thought. —GEORGE SANTAYANA

INSULTS
(also see concepts 689, 746)

There are two insults which no human will endure: the assertion that he hasn't a sense of humor, and the doubly impertinent assertion that he has never known trouble. —SINCLAIR LEWIS

A graceful taunt is worth a thousand insults. —LOUIS NIZER

Insults should be well avenged or well endured. —SPANISH PROVERB

INTEGRITY
(also see concepts 100, 355, 377, 488, 742, 744, 843)

I ran the wrong kind of business, but I did it with integrity. —SYDNEY BIDDLE BARROWS

Integrity without knowledge is weak and useless, and knowledge without integrity is dangerous and dreadful. —SAMUEL JOHNSON

A man should be upright, not be kept upright. —MARCUS AURELIUS

The courage of all one really knows comes but late in life. —FRIEDRICH WILHELM NIETZSCHE

Integrity is so perishable in the summer months of success. —VANESSA REDGRAVE

Few men have virtue to withstand the highest bidder. —GEORGE WASHINGTON

INTELLECTUALS AND INTELLECTUALISM

(also see concepts 348, 804)

An intellectual is a man who doesn't know how to park a bike.
——SPIRO AGNEW

I've been called many things, but never an intellectual.
——TALLULAH BANKHEAD

The intellectuals' chief cause of anguish are one another's works.
——JACQUES BARZUN

An intellectual is someone whose mind watches itself.
——ALBERT CAMUS

INTELLIGENCE

(also see concepts 1, 122, 131, 178, 410, 553, 605, 791, 804, 863)

It is not enough to have a good mind; the main thing is to use it well.
——RENÉ DESCARTES

There is nobody so irritating as somebody with less intelligence and more sense than we have. ——DON HEROLD

An honest heart being the first blessing, a knowing head is the second. ——THOMAS JEFFERSON

The height of cleverness is to be able to conceal it.
——FRANÇOIS DE LA ROCHEFOUCAULD

The sign of an intelligent people is their ability to control emotions by the application of reason. ——MARYA MANNES

Many complain of their looks, but none of their brains.
——YIDDISH PROVERB

Intelligence is quickness in seeing things as they are.
——GEORGE SANTAYANA

INTEMPERANCE

(also see concepts 225, 254, 652, 826)

Since the creation of the world there has been no tyrant like Intemperance, and no slaves so cruelly treated as his.
—WILLIAM LLOYD GARRISON

Intemperance is the physician's provider. —PUBLILIUS SYRUS

INTEREST

(also see concepts 15, 33, 179, 242, 388, 486, 728)

Interest speaks all sorts of tongues, and plays all sorts of parts, even that of disinterestedness. —FRANÇOIS DE LA ROCHEFOUCAULD

Do not confuse your vested interests with ethics. Do not identify the enemies of your privilege with the enemies of humanity.
—MAX LERNER

I don't believe in principle, but I do in interest.
—JAMES RUSSELL LOWELL

A man will fight harder for his interests than his rights.
—NAPOLEON I

INTERESTS, DIVIDED

(also see concepts 217, 240, 557)

The perplexity of life arises from there being too many interesting things in it for us to be interested properly in any of them.
—G. K. CHESTERTON

If you run after two hares, you will catch neither. —THOMAS FULLER

INTERNATIONAL RELATIONS

(also see concepts 208, 851)

We shall be judged more by what we do at home than what we preach abroad. —JOHN F. KENNEDY

That expression "positive neutrality" is a contradiction in terms. There can be no more positive neutrality than there can be a vegetarian tiger. —v. k. KRISHNA MENON

International incidents should not govern foreign policy, but foreign policy, incidents. —NAPOLEON I

There must be, not a balance of power, but a community of power; not organized rivalries, but an organized peace. —WOODROW WILSON

INTERNATIONALISM
(also see concepts 116, 177, 509)

I am a citizen of the world. —DIOGENES THE CYNIC

We deny your internationalism, because it is a luxury which only the upper classes can afford; the working people are hopelessly bound to their native shores. —BENITO MUSSOLINI

My country is the world, and my religion is to do good.
—THOMAS PAINE

A man's feet must be planted in his country, but his eyes should survey the world. —GEORGE SANTAYANA

INTIMACY
(also see concepts 439, 466)

You can do the most wonderful things when you're really close. It's hard to take showers with only one of the five men you're dating. —CHER

A man knows his companion in a long journey and a little inn.
—THOMAS FULLER

No stranger can get a great many notes of torture out of a human soul; it takes one that knows it well–parent, child, brother, sister, intimate. —OLIVER WENDELL HOLMES, SR.

To really know someone is to have loved and hated him in turn.
—MARCEL JOUHANDEAU

INTOLERANCE

(also see concepts 220, 294, 339)

No loss by flood and lightning, no destruction of cities and temples by the hostile forces of nature, has deprived man of so many noble lives and impulses as those which his intolerance has destroyed.
——HELEN KELLER

INTUITION

(also see concepts 406, 764, 824)

Intuition is a suspension of logic due to impatience.
——RITA MAE BROWN

It is the heart always that sees, before the head can see.
——THOMAS CARLYLE

Knowledge is the distilled essence of our intuitions, corroborated by experience. ——ELBERT HUBBARD

I don't believe in intuition. When you get sudden flashes of perception, it is just the brain working faster than usual. But you've been getting ready to know it for a long time, and when it comes, you feel you've known it always. ——KATHERINE ANN PORTER

Intuition is a spiritual faculty and does not explain, but simply points the way. ——FLORENCE SCOVEL SHINN

INVENTION

(also see concepts 212, 562)

Inventing is a combination of brains and materials. The more brains you use, the less materials you need. ——CHARLES F. KETTERING

Name the greatest of all the inventors. Accident. ——MARK TWAIN

Invention is the mother of necessity. ——THORSTEIN VEBLEN

It must be confessed that the inventors of the mechanical arts have been much more useful to men than the inventors of syllogisms.
——VOLTAIRE

INVESTMENT

(also see concepts 85, 129, 422, 628)

There is no finer investment for any community than putting milk into babies. —WINSTON CHURCHILL

We cannot eat the fruit while the tree is in blossom. —BENJAMIN DISRAELI

'Tis money that begets money. —THOMAS FULLER

Let Wall Street have a nightmare and the whole country has to help get them back in bed again. —WILL ROGERS

There are two times in a man's life when he should not speculate: when he can't afford it, and when he can. —MARK TWAIN

INVOLVEMENT

(also see concepts 129, 142, 242, 421, 535)

To say yes, you have to sweat and roll up your sleeves and plunge both hands into life up to the elbows. It is easy to say no, even if saying no means death. —JEAN ANOUILH

Do not fear death so much, but rather the inadequate life. —BERTOLT BRECHT

Walk the street with us into history. Get off the sidewalk. —DOLORES HUERTA

I postpone death by living, by suffering, by error, by risking, by giving, by losing. —ANAÏS NIN

IRELAND AND THE IRISH

(also see concepts 247, 529)

Other people have a nationality. The Irish and the Jews have a psychosis. —BRENDAN BEHAN

It is really astonishing of what various and comprehensive powers this neglected language [Irish] is possessed. In the pathetic it breathes the most beautiful and affecting simplicity; and in the

bolder species of composition it is distinguished by a freedom of expression, a sublime dignity, and rapid energy, which it is scarcely possible for any translation fully to convey.
——CHARLOTTE BROOKE

It is scarcely possible that an English or Irish Protestant of the present day can look back to the past history of Ireland, especially in connection with its terrible Penal Code, without a feeling of grief and of shame. The sleepless eyes of Justice have never ceased to watch throughout the long centuries of wrongs done to Ireland.
——JOSEPHINE BUTLER

Our Irish blunders are never blunders of the heart.
——MARIA EDGEWORTH

The English may batter us to pieces but they will never succeed in breaking our spirit. ——MAUD GONNE

The Irish are a fair people; they never speak well of one another.
——SAMUEL JOHNSON

Ireland is the old sow that eats her farrow. ——JAMES JOYCE

When anyone asks me about the Irish character, I say look at the trees. Maimed, stark and misshapen, but ferociously tenacious. The Irish have got gab but are too touchy to be humorous. Me too.
——EDNA O'BRIEN

Belfast is like an ugly child—you love it the most. ——STEPHEN REA

The English should give Ireland home rule—and reserve the motion picture rights. ——WILL ROGERS

IRREVERENCE
(also see concepts 128, 548)

Beware of the community in which blasphemy does not exist: underneath, atheism runs rampant. ——ANTONIO MACHADO

All great truths begin as blasphemies. ——GEORGE BERNARD SHAW

IRREVOCABILITY

(also see concepts 185, 517, 571)

A word and a stone let go cannot be called back. —THOMAS FULLER

Time flies, and what is past is done.
—JOHANN WOLFGANG VON GOETHE

Once the toothpaste is out of the tube, it is awfully hard to get it back in. —H. R. HALDEMAN

What's done cannot be undone. To bed, to bed, to bed.
—WILLIAM SHAKESPEARE

The Gods themselves cannot recall their gifts.
—ALFRED, LORD TENNYSON

Of all sad words of tongue or pen, / The saddest are these: "It might have been!" —JOHN GREENLEAF WHITTIER

IRRITATION

(also see 36, 393, 798)

Continual dripping wears away a stone. —LUCRETIUS

The point is that nobody likes having salt rubbed into their wounds, even if it is the salt of the earth. —REBECCA WEST

ISLAM

(also see concept 668)

There's plenty of sun in the lands of Islam: a sun that is white, violent, blinding. But Moslem women never see it–their eyes are conditioned to gloom like the eyes of moles. From the darkness of the mother's womb they pass into the darkness of the tomb. And in all this darkness nobody takes any notice of them.
—ORIANA FALLACI

Unlike Christianity, which preached a peace that it never achieved, Islam unashamedly came with a sword. —STEVE RUNCIMAN

ITALY AND THE ITALIANS
(also see concepts 247, 276, 529)

Everyone soon or late comes round by Rome. —ROBERT BROWNING

Midnight, and love, and youth, and Italy!
—EDWARD BULWER-LYTTON

Venice is like eating an entire box of chocolate liqueurs in one go.
—TRUMAN CAPOTE

A man who has not been in Italy, is always conscious of an inferiority. —SAMUEL JOHNSON

Thou Paradise of exiles, Italy! —PERCY BYSSHE SHELLEY

JAZZ
(also see concepts 32, 105, 524, 537, 655)

Jazz is the only music in which the same note can be played night after night but differently each time. —ORNETTE COLEMAN

I'll play it first and tell you what it is later. —MILES DAVIS

Playing "bop" is like playing Scrabble with all the vowels missing. —DUKE ELLINGTON

Jazz is the big brother of blues. If a guy's playing blues like we play, he's in high school. When he starts playing jazz it's like going on to college, to a school of higher learning. —B. B. KING

Jazz will endure just as long as people hear it through their feet instead of their brains. —JOHN PHILIP SOUSA

JEALOUSY
(also see concepts 237, 243)

Love is strong as death; jealousy is cruel as the grave.
—BIBLE, SONG OF SOLOMON 8:6

Jealousy is no more than feeling alone against smiling enemies.
—ELIZABETH BOWEN

Jealousy is not at all low, but it catches us humbled and bowed down, at first sight. —COLETTE

Jealousy, that dragon which slays love under the pretence of keeping it alive. —HAVELOCK ELLIS

There is never jealousy where there is not strong regard. —WASHINGTON IRVING

In jealousy there is more of self-love than love. —FRANÇOIS DE LA ROCHEFOUCAULD

To jealousy, nothing is more frightful than laughter. —FRANÇOISE SAGAN

O beware, my lord, of jealousy; It is the green-ey'd monster which doth mock the meat it feeds on. —WILLIAM SHAKESPEARE

JEWS AND JUDAISM
(also see concepts 110, 269, 668, 802)

The twentieth century ideals of America have been the ideals of the Jews for more than twenty centuries. —LOUIS D. BRANDEIS

The pursuit of knowledge for its own sake, an almost fanatical love of justice and the desire for personal independence—these are the features of the Jewish tradition which make me thank my stars that I belong to it. —ALBERT EINSTEIN

What one Christian does is his own responsibility. What one Jew does is thrown back at all Jews. —ANNE FRANK

Jews are the intensive form of any nationality whose language and customs they adopt. —EMMA LAZARUS

Pessimism is a luxury that a Jew can never allow himself. —GOLDA MEIR

With Judaism we have a relationship which we do not have with any other religion. You are our dearly beloved brothers and, in a certain way, it could be said that you are our elder brothers. —POPE JOHN PAUL II

The nations which have received and in any way dealt fairly and mercifully with the Jew have prospered, and the nations that have tortured and oppressed him have written out their own curse.
—OLIVE SCHREINER

The Jews are a frightened people. Nineteen centuries of Christian love have broken their nerves. —ISRAEL ZANGWILL

JOURNALISTS AND JOURNALISM
(also see concepts 90, 476, 539, 540, 874)

The very blood and semen of journalism...is a broad and successful form of lying. Remove that form of lying and you no longer have journalism. —JAMES AGEE

Literature is the art of writing something that will be read twice; journalism what will be grasped at once. —CYRIL CONNOLLY

Journalism will kill you, but it will keep you alive while you're at it. —HORACE GREELEY

Journalism is the entertainment business. —FRANK HERBERT

The distinction between literature and journalism is becoming blurred; but journalism gains as much as literature loses.
—WILLIAM RALPH INGE

Journalism—an ability to meet the challenge of filling the space.
—REBECCA WEST

Most rock journalism is people who can't write interviewing people who can't talk for people who can't read. —FRANK ZAPPA

JOY
(also see concepts 33, 104, 159, 182, 237, 337, 442, 593, 619)

Joy seems to me a step beyond happiness—happiness is a sort of atmosphere you can live in sometimes when you're lucky. Joy is a light that fills you with hope and faith and love.
—ADELA ROGERS ST. JOHNS

JUDGES

(also see concepts 95, 172, 435, 436, 443, 555)

That judges of important causes should hold office for life is a disputable thing, for the mind grows old as well as the body.
——ARISTOTLE

Having been appointed by a Republican president and being accused now of being a flaming liberal on the court, the Republicans think I'm a traitor, I guess, and the Democrats don't trust me. And so I twist in the wind, I hope, beholden to no one, and that's just exactly where I want to be. ——HARRY BLACKMUN

To an incompetent judge I must not lie, but I may be silent; to a competent I must answer. ——JOHN DONNE

JUDGMENT

(also see concepts 67, 95, 136, 171, 172, 189, 434, 555, 577, 791)

The ultimate cynicism is to suspend judgment so that you are not judged. ——MARYA MANNES

Make no judgments where you have no compassion.
——ANNE MCCAFFREY

'Tis with our judgements as our watches, none / Go just alike, yet each believes his own. ——ALEXANDER POPE

Don't judge any man until you have walked two moons in his moccasins. ——NATIVE AMERICAN PROVERB

A hasty judgment is a first step to recantation. ——PUBLILIUS SYRUS

Do not judge, and you will never be mistaken.
——JEAN JACQUES ROUSSEAU

JUSTICE

(also see concepts 244, 434, 443, 508, 642, 643, 680, 684, 744)

Children are innocent and love justice, while most adults are wicked and prefer mercy. ——G. K. CHESTERTON

Justice is not a mincing-machine but a compromise.
—FRIEDRICH DÜRRENMATT

Let justice be done, though the world will perish.
—KING FERDINAND I

Justice delayed is democracy denied. —ROBERT F. KENNEDY

We will not be satisfied until justice rolls down like waters and righteousness like a mighty stream. —MARTIN LUTHER KING, JR.

Injustice is relatively easy to bear; what stings is justice.
—H. L. MENCKEN

Be just before you're generous. —RICHARD BRINSLEY SHERIDAN

If they are just, they are better than clever. —SOPHOCLES

KILLING

(also see concepts 9, 185, 201, 334, 372, 643, 781)

The worst thing that can be said of the most powerful is that they can take your life; but the same thing can be said of the most weak.
—CHARLES CALEB COLTON

It takes two to make a murder. There are born victims, born to have their throats cut. —ALDOUS HUXLEY

...there's no difference between one's killing and one's making decisions that will send others to kill. It's exactly the same thing, or even worse. —GOLDA MEIR

One kills a man, one is an assassin; one kills millions, one is a conqueror; one kills everybody, one is a god. —JEAN ROSTAND

A sword never kills anybody; it's a tool in the killer's hand.
—SENECA

Other sins only speak, murder shrieks out. —JOHN WEBSTER

KINDNESS

(also see concepts 309, 311, 367, 495, 588, 735, 790, 834)

There is no sickness worse / for me than words that to be kind must lie. —AESCHYLUS

When kindness has left people for even a few moments, we become afraid of them as if their reason had left them. —WILLA CATHER

We live very close together. So, our prime purpose in this life is to help others. And if you can't help them, at least don't hurt them. —DALAI LAMA

Many think they have a kind heart who have only weak nerves. —MARIE VON EBNER-ESCHENBACH

Kindness can become its own motive. We are made kind by being kind. —ERIC HOFFER

You can accomplish by kindness what you cannot by force. —PUBLILIUS SYRUS

The purpose of human life is to serve and show compassion and the will to help others. —ALBERT SCHWEITZER

Kind words can be short and easy to speak, but their echoes are truly endless. —MOTHER TERESA

KISSING

(also see concepts 9, 417, 466, 469, 687)

What lies lurk in kisses. —HEINRICH HEINE

When a rogue kisses you, count your teeth. —HEBREW PROVERB

KNOWLEDGE

(also see concepts 116, 119, 177, 261, 262, 267, 272, 376, 380, 446, 700, 701, 702, 717, 719, 795, 803, 824)

He that increaseth knowledge increaseth sorrow. —BIBLE, ECCLESIASTES 1:18

Knowledge is knowing as little as possible. —CHARLES BUKOWSKI

A smattering of everything, and a knowledge of nothing.
——CHARLES DICKENS

To be proud of knowledge is to be blind with light.
——BENJAMIN FRANKLIN

Teach thy tongue to say 'I do not know.' ——MAIMONIDES

Without knowledge, life is not more than the shadow of death.
——MOLIÉRE

Knowledge is power, if you know it about the right person.
——ETHEL WATTS MUMFORD

A little learning is a dangerous thing. ——ALEXANDER POPE

Knowledge is recognition of something absent; it is a salutation,
not an embrace. ——GEORGE SANTAYANA

The things we know best are the things we haven't been taught.
——MARQUIS DE VAUVENARGUES

LANGUAGE

(also see concept 868)

Language is magic: it makes things appear and disappear.
——NICOLE BROSSARD

A silly remark can be made in Latin as well as in Spanish.
——MIGUEL DE CERVANTES

Language is the archives of history....Language is fossil poetry.
——RALPH WALDO EMERSON

I am always sorry when any language is lost, because languages are
the pedigree of nations. ——SAMUEL JOHNSON

I work with language. I love the flowers of afterthought.
——BERNARD MALAMUD

I live on good soup and not fine language. ——MOLIÉRE

No one sleeps in this room without the dream of a common
language. ——ADRIENNE RICH

Slang is a language that rolls up its sleeves, spits on its hands and goes to work. —CARL SANDBURG

England and America are two countries separated by the same language. —GEORGE BERNARD SHAW

LAUGHTER
(also see concepts 128, 370, 866)

And if I laugh at any mortal thing, / 'Tis that I may not weep. —LORD BYRON

The most wasted day of all is that on which we have not laughed. —NICOLAS CHAMFORT

Laughter is by definition healthy. —DORIS LESSING

You are not angry with people when you laugh at them. Humour teaches tolerance. —W. SOMERSET MAUGHAM

Not by wrath does one kill but by laughter. —FRIEDRICH WILHELM NIETZSCHE

Laughter restores the universe to its original state of indifference and strangeness: if it has a meaning, it is a divine one, not a human one. —OCTAVIO PAZ

Laughter is pleasant, but the exertion is too much for me. —THOMAS LOVE PEACOCK

No one is more profoundly sad than he who laughs too much. —JEAN PAUL RICHTER

One can never speak enough of the virtues, the dangers, the power of shared laughter. —FRANÇOISE SAGAN

LAWYERS AND LAW
(also see concepts 90, 218, 334, 434, 436, 599, 620)

Lawyers are the only persons in whom ignorance of the law is not punished. —JEREMY BENTHAM

All bad precedents began as justifiable measures. —JULIUS CAESAR

The more laws, the more offenders. —THOMAS FULLER

Laws grind the poor, and rich men rule the law. —OLIVER GOLDSMITH

Every new time will give its law. —MAXIM GORKY

In university they don't tell you that the greater part of the law is learning to tolerate fools. —DORIS LESSING

No law is quite appropriate for all. —LIVY

A man's respect for law and order exists in precise relationship to the size of his paycheck. —ADAM CLAYTON POWELL

A lawyer with his briefcase can steal more than a thousand men with guns. —MARIO PUZO

Good laws lead to the making of better ones; bad ones bring about worse. —JEAN JACQUES ROUSSEAU

It ain't no sin if you crack a few laws now and then, just so long as you don't break any. —MAE WEST

LAZINESS
(also see concepts 379, 447)

Laziness travels so slowly that poverty soon overtakes him.
—BENJAMIN FRANKLIN

The biggest sin is sitting on your ass. —FLORYNCE KENNEDY

The lazy are always wanting to do something.
—MARQUIS DE VAUVENARGUES

LEADERS AND LEADERSHIP
(also see concepts 388, 511, 616)

Every ruler is harsh whose rule is new. —AESCHYLUS

A leader who doesn't hesitate before he sends his nation into battle is not fit to be a leader. —GOLDA MEIR

The real leader has no need to lead–he is content to point the way.
—HENRY MILLER

A leader is a dealer in hope. —NAPOLEON I

What you cannot enforce, / Do not command. —SOPHOCLES

LEARNING
(also see concepts 9, 10, 233, 252, 325, 348, 440, 700, 795)

Learn as though you would never be able to master it; hold it as though you would be in fear of losing it. —CONFUCIUS

A university should be a place of light, of liberty, and of learning. —BENJAMIN DISRAELI

Everywhere, we learn only from those whom we love. —JOHANN WOLFGANG VON GOETHE

...that is what learning is. You suddenly understand something you've understood all your life, but in a new way. —DORIS LESSING

You have learnt something. That always feels at first as if you had lost something. —GEORGE BERNARD SHAW

The more we study the more we discover our ignorance. —PERCY BYSSHE SHELLEY

LEISURE
(also see concepts 10, 33, 58, 286, 292, 306, 318, 349, 379, 444, 592, 677, 825)

We are closer to the ants than to the butterflies. Very few people can endure much leisure. —GERALD BRENAN

To be at ease is better than to be at business. Nothing really belongs to us but time, which even he has who has nothing else. —BALTASAR GRACIÁN

It is the leisured, I have noticed, who rebel the most at an interruption of routine. —PHYLLIS MCGINLEY

LESBIANISM

(also see concepts 354, 731)

Love between women is seen as a paradigm of love between equals, and that is perhaps its greatest attraction.
—ELIZABETH JANEWAY

The love expressed between women is particular and powerful, because we have had to love in order to live; love has been our survival. —AUDRE LORDE

The women's movement has always had lesbians at its vanguard....The lesbian is the archetypal feminist, because she's not into men–she's the independent woman par excellence.
—KATE MILLETT

My lesbianism is the avenue through which I have learned the most about silence and oppression, and it continues to be the most tactile reminder to me that we are not free human beings.
—CHERRIE MORAGA

Being a lesbian is by definition an act of treason against our cultural values. —JUANITA RAMOS

It is the lesbian in every woman who is compelled by female energy, who gravitates toward strong women, who seeks a literature that will express that energy and strength. It is the lesbian in us who drives us to feel imaginatively, render in language, grasp, the full connection between woman and woman. —ADRIENNE RICH

LETTERS   AND   LETTER-WRITING

(also see concepts 10, 132, 204)

...a habit the pleasure of which increases with practice, but becomes more irksome with neglect. —ABIGAIL ADAMS

Sir, more than kisses, letters mingle souls; / For, thus friends absent speak. —JOHN DONNE

Why it should be such an effort to write to the people one loves I can't imagine. It's none at all to write to those who don't really count. —KATHERINE MANSFIELD

Correspondences are like small-clothes before the invention of suspenders: it is impossible to keep them up. —SYDNEY SMITH

I don't believe I ever wrote a literary letter–ever got discussing books or literary men or writers or artists of any sort in letters: the very idea of it makes me sick. I like letters to be personal–very personal–and then stop. —WALT WHITMAN

LIBERALISM
(also see concepts 154, 378, 553, 652, 663, 752)

The liberals can understand everything but people who don't understand them. —LENNY BRUCE

Hell hath no fury like a liberal scorned. —DICK GREGORY

Leftwingers are incapable of conspiring because they are all egomaniacs. —NORMAN MAILER

Liberal institutions straightway cease from being liberal the moment they are soundly established. —FRIEDRICH WILHELM NIETZSCHE

Liberalism...is the supreme form of generosity; it is the right which the majority concedes to minorities and hence it is *the noblest cry* that has ever resounded in this planet. —JOSÉ ORTEGA Y GASSET

Liberal–a power worshipper without the power. —GEORGE ORWELL

LIBRARIES
(also see concepts 76, 700)

A library is but the soul's burying ground. It is a land of shadows. —HENRY WARD BEECHER

Good as it is to inherit a library, it is better to collect one. —AUGUSTINE BIRRELL

To arrange a library is to practise / in a quiet and modest way / the art of criticism. —JORGE LUIS BORGES

A man's library is a sort of harem. —RALPH WALDO EMERSON

Every library should try to be complete on something, if it were only the history of pinheads. —OLIVER WENDELL HOLMES, SR.

A library implies an act of faith. —VICTOR HUGO

No place affords a more striking conviction of the vanity of human hopes, than a public library. —SAMUEL JOHNSON

My alma mater was books, a good library...I could spend the rest of my life reading, just satisfying my curiosity. —MALCOLM X

A library is thought in cold storage. —HERBERT SAMUEL

Come, and take choice of all my library, / And so beguile thy sorrow. —WILLIAM SHAKESPEARE

A circulating library in a town is an ever-green tree of diabolical knowledge! It blossoms through the year.
—RICHARD BRINSLEY SHERIDAN

LIES AND LYING
(also see concepts 214, 374, 711, 746, 819)

Nobody speaks the truth when there's something they must have.
—ELIZABETH BOWEN

Never to lie is to have no lock to your door, you are never wholly alone. —ELIZABETH BOWEN

Without lies humanity would perish of despair and boredom.
—ANATOLE FRANCE

It's not a lie, it's a terminological inexactitude. —ALEXANDER HAIG

Sin has many tools, but a lie is the handle that fits them all.
—OLIVER WENDELL HOLMES, SR.

The truth that survives is simply the lie that is pleasantest to believe. —H. L. MENCKEN

In our country the lie has become not just a moral category but a pillar of the State. —ALEXANDER SOLZHENITSYN

LIFE

(also see concepts 16, 68, 204, 258, 455, 517, 787)

I don't want to get to the end of my life and find that I just lived the length of it. I want to have lived the width of it as well.
——DIANE ACKERMAN

Life loves to be taken by the lapel and told: "I am with you kid. Let's go." ——MAYA ANGELOU

Life, the permission to know death. ——DJUNA BARNES

For everything that lives is holy, life delights in life.
——WILLIAM BLAKE

Men must live and create. Live to the point of tears.
——ALBERT CAMUS

If life was fair, Elvis would be alive and all the impersonators would be dead. ——JOHNNY CARSON

Don't drag the engine, like an ignoramus, but bring wood and water and flame, like an engineer. ——MARIA WESTON CHAPMAN

Life itself is the proper binge. ——JULIA CHILD

What a wonderful life I've had! I only wish I'd realised it sooner.
——COLETTE

Life was a funny thing that occurred on the way to the grave.
——QUENTIN CRISP

People do not live nowadays. They get about 10% out of life.
——ISADORA DUNCAN

Life is made up of marble and mud. ——NATHANIEL HAWTHORNE

Life is something to do when you can't get to sleep.
——FRAN LEBOWITZ

I have a simple philosophy. Fill what's empty. Empty what's full. And scratch where it itches. ——ALICE ROOSEVELT LONGWORTH

The art of living is more like wrestling than dancing.
——MARCUS AURELIUS

It is not true that life is one damn thing after another--it's one damn thing over and over. —EDNA ST. VINCENT MILLAY

Human affairs are not serious, but they have to be taken seriously. —IRIS MURDOCH

If you believed more in life you would fling yourself less to the moment. —FRIEDRICH WILHELM NIETZSCHE

Life is a process of becoming, a combination of states we have to go through. Where people fail is that they wish to elect a state and remain in it. This is a kind of death. —ANAÏS NIN

Between us and heaven or hell there is only life, which is the frailest thing in the world. —BLAISE PASCAL

Having grown up in a racist culture where two and two are not five, I have found life to be incredibly theatrical and theatre to be profoundly lifeless. —BEAH RICHARDS

There is no cure for birth and death save to enjoy the interval. —GEORGE SANTAYANA

There must be more to life than having everything. —MAURICE SENDAK

Life is a gamble, at terrible odds--if it was a bet you wouldn't take it. —TOM STOPPARD

Oh, isn't life a terrible thing, thank God? —DYLAN THOMAS

Life is better than death, I believe, if only because it is less boring, and because it has fresh peaches in it. —ALICE WALKER

The world is wide, and I will not waste my life in friction when it could be turned into momentum. —FRANCES WILLARD

Why is life so tragic; so like a little strip of pavement over an abyss. I look down; I feel giddy; I wonder how I am ever to walk to the end. —VIRGINIA WOOLF

LIFE AND DEATH
(also see concepts 185, 453, 517)

All our life is but a going out to the place of execution, to death.
——JOHN DONNE

Our final experience, like our first, is conjectural. We move between two darknesses. ——E. M. FORSTER

I'm not afraid of death. It's the stake one puts up in order to play the game of life. ——JEAN GIRAUDOUX

Our life is made by the death of others. ——LEONARDO DA VINCI

If you wish to live, you must first attend your own funeral.
——KATHERINE MANSFIELD

You will die not because you're ill, but because you're alive.
——SENECA

LIFE STAGES
(also see concepts 24, 98, 453, 454)

Every stage of human life, except the last, is marked out by certain and defined limits; old age alone has no precise and determinate boundary. ——CICERO

Youth is a blunder; manhood a struggle; old age a regret.
——BENJAMIN DISRAELI

It is in the thirties that we want friends. In the forties we know they won't save us any more than love did. ——F. SCOTT FITZGERALD

At twenty years of age, the will reigns; at thirty, the wit; and at forty, the judgement. ——BENJAMIN FRANKLIN

We arrive at the various stages of life quite as novices.
——FRANÇOIS DE LA ROCHEFOUCAULD

The four stages of man are infancy, childhood, adolescence, and obsolescence. ——ART LINKLETTER

As an infant, man is wrapped in his mother's womb; grown up, he is wrapped in custom; dead, he is wrapped in earth.
——MALAY PROVERB

LIMITATIONS
(also see concepts 95, 508)

Who ever is adequate? We all create situations each other can't live up to, then break our hearts at them because they don't.
——ELIZABETH BOWEN

I'm not going to limit myself just because people won't accept the fact that I can do something else. ——DOLLY PARTON

O my soul, do not aspire to immortal life, but exhaust the limits of the possible. ——PINDAR

Knowledge of what is possible is the beginning of happiness.
——GEORGE SANTAYANA

LISTENING
(also see concepts 9, 132, 761)

Listening, not imitation, may be the sincerest form of flattery.
——JOYCE BROTHERS

We only consult the ear because the heart is wanting.
——BLAISE PASCAL

Give every man thine ear, but few thy voice. ——WILLIAM SHAKESPEARE

LITERACY
(also see concepts 233, 795)

If there's one major cause for the spread of mass illiteracy, it's the fact that everybody can read and write. ——PETER DE VRIES

It is better to be able neither to read nor write than to be able to do nothing else. ——WILLIAM HAZLITT

One thing is certain today–the illiterates are definitely not the least intelligent among us. —HENRY MILLER

The ratio of literacy to illiteracy is constant, but nowadays the illiterates can read. —ALBERTO MORAVIA

I'm quite illiterate, but I read a lot. —J. D. SALINGER

LITERATURE
(also see concepts 76, 325, 366, 526, 594, 595, 640, 657, 688, 868)

Literature is the question minus the answer. —ROLAND BARTHES

All literature is gossip. —TRUMAN CAPOTE

The greatest masterpiece in literature is only a dictionary out of order. —JEAN COCTEAU

Only two classes of books are of universal appeal. The very best and the very worst. —FORD MADOX FORD

Literature flourishes best when it is half a trade and half an art. —WILLIAM RALPH INGE

Literature could be said to be a sort of disciplined technique for arousing certain emotions. —IRIS MURDOCH

There is only one school of literature–that of talent. —VLADIMIR NABOKOV

Literature is news that *stays* news. —EZRA POUND

Perversity is the muse of modern literature. —SUSAN SONTAG

Remarks are not literature. —GERTRUDE STEIN

A species living under the threat of obliteration is bound to produce obliterature–and that's what we are producing. —JAMES THURBER

LOGIC
(also see concepts 141, 804)

Reason can wrestle / And overthrow terror. —EURIPIDES

Reason also is choice. —JOHN MILTON

Pure logic is the ruin of the spirit. —ANTOINE DE SAINT-EXUPÉRY

There is occasions and causes why and wherefore in all things. —WILLIAM SHAKESPEARE

A mind all logic is like a knife all blade. It makes the hand bleed that uses it. —RABINDRANATH TAGORE

Logic must take care of itself. —LUDWIG WITTGENSTEIN

LONDON
(also see concepts 82, 113)

Nobody is healthy in London, nobody can be. —JANE AUSTEN

It is strange with how little notice, good, bad or indifferent, a man may live and die in London. —CHARLES DICKENS

London is a modern Babylon. —BENJAMIN DISRAELI

I think the full tide of human existence is at Charing-Cross. —SAMUEL JOHNSON

When a man is tired of London, he is tired of life; for there is in London all that life can afford. —SAMUEL JOHNSON

Dear damned distracting town. —ALEXANDER POPE

LONELINESS
(also see concepts 30, 237, 678, 756)

Pray that your loneliness may spur you into finding something to live for, great enough to die for. —DAG HAMMARSKJÖLD

The most I ever did for you was to outlive you. / But that is much. —EDNA ST. VINCENT MILLAY

For loneliness is but cutting adrift from our moorings and floating out to the open sea; an opportunity for finding ourselves, our real selves, what we are about, where we are heading during our little time on this beautiful earth. —ANNE SHANNON MONROE

Man's loneliness is but his fear of life. —EUGENE O'NEILL

If you are lonely while you are alone, you are in bad company.
——JEAN-PAUL SARTRE

Loneliness and the feeling of being unwanted is the most terrible poverty. ——MOTHER TERESA

LONGEVITY
(also see concepts 552, 877)

Longevity, n. uncommon extension of the fear of death.
——AMBROSE BIERCE

'Tis very certain the desire of life / Prolongs it. ——LORD BYRON

It is not the years in your life but the life in your years that counts!
——ADLAI STEVENSON

It is vanity to desire a long life and to take no heed of a good life.
——THOMAS Á KEMPIS

LOSERS
(also see concepts 268, 465, 502)

If a man once fall, all will tread upon him. ——THOMAS FULLER

Nobody ever chooses the already unfortunate as objects of his loyal friendship. ——LUCAN

Show me a good loser and I will show you a loser. ——PAUL NEWMAN

Fear of losing is what makes competitors so great. Show me a gracious loser and I'll show you a permanent loser. ——O. J. SIMPSON

LOSS
(also see concepts 3, 190, 192, 197, 302, 464, 468, 520, 569, 692, 853)

Loss is nothing else but change, and change is Nature's delight.
——MARCUS AURELIUS

Whatever you can lose, reckon of no account. ——PUBLILIUS SYRUS

LOVE

(also see concepts 3, 20, 237, 300, 341, 417, 430, 439, 469, 472, 479, 494, 570, 687, 726, 859)

Love is a great beautifier. —LOUISA MAY ALCOTT

Sex alleviates tension. Love causes it. —WOODY ALLEN

Love involves a peculiar unfathomable combination of understanding and misunderstanding. —DIANE ARBUS

Love has the quality of informing almost everything–even one's work. —SYLVIA ASHTON-WARNER

All the privilege I claim for my own sex...is that of loving longest, when existence or hope is gone. —JANE AUSTEN

To love without criticism is to be betrayed. —DJUNA BARNES

Love is just a system for getting someone to call you darling after sex. —JULIAN BARNES

The word "love" has by no means the same sense for both sexes, and this is one of the serious misunderstandings that divide them. —SIMONE DE BEAUVOIR

Love ceases to be a pleasure when it ceases to be a secret. —APHRA BEHN

To fall in love is to create a religion that has a fallible god. —JORGE LUIS BORGES

When you love someone all your saved-up wishes start coming out. —ELIZABETH BOWEN

To love without role, without power plays, is revolution. —RITA MAE BROWN

I truly feel that there are as many ways of loving as there are people in the world and as there are days in the lives of those people. —MARY CALDERONE

Love is a tyrant sparing none. —PIERRE CORNEILLE

The pain of love is the pain of being alive. It is a perpetual wound. —MAUREEN DUFFY

The richest love is that which submits to the arbitration of time.
—LAWRENCE DURRELL

We don't believe in rheumatism and true love until after the first attack. —MARIE VON EBNER-ESCHENBACH

All mankind love a lover. —RALPH WALDO EMERSON

...I don't want to live–I want to love first, and live incidentally.
—ZELDA FITZGERALD

Two persons love in one another the future good which they aid one another to unfold. —MARGARET FULLER

Even as love crowns you so shall he crucify you. Even as he is for your growth so is he for your pruning. —KAHLIL GIBRAN

Don't threaten me with love, baby. Let's just go walking in the rain.
—BILLIE HOLIDAY

Love, I find, is like singing. Everybody can do enough to satisfy themselves, though it may not impress the neighbors as being very much. —ZORA NEALE HURSTON

You can wish you were in love, but you have to wait until the object of your affection knocks on your door. —ANJELICA HUSTON

...it is not a question of passing through women like one passes through showers in the morning. An eight o'clock kiss is as important as a kiss at twelve o'clock at night. —JULIO IGLESIAS

True love is like ghosts, which everybody talks about and few have seen. —FRANÇOIS DE LA ROCHEFOUCAULD

Love just doesn't sit there, like a stone, it has to be made, like bread; re-made all the time, made new. —URSULA K. LE GUIN

How alike are the groans of love to those of the dying.
—MALCOLM LOWRY

Love's a disease. But curable. —ROSE MACAULAY

He who loves the more is the inferior and must suffer.
—THOMAS MANN

If only one could tell true love from false love as one can tell mushrooms from toadstools. —KATHERINE MANSFIELD

Love is many things. But more than anything it is a disturbance of the digestive system. —GABRIEL GARCÍA MÁRQUEZ

He that would eat of love must eat it where it hangs.
—EDNA ST. VINCENT MILLAY

I wish I'd a knowed more people. I would of loved 'em all. If I'd a knowed more, I woulda loved more. —TONI MORRISON

Falling out of love is very enlightening. For a short while you see the world with new eyes. —IRIS MURDOCH

In love there are two things—bodies and words.
—JOYCE CAROL OATES

Love is like quicksilver in the hand. Leave the fingers open and it stays. Clutch it, and it darts away. —DOROTHY PARKER

Cupid is naked and does not like artifices contrived of beauty.
—PROPERTIUS

Love is not love until love's vulnerable. —THEODORE ROETHKE

They do not love that do not show their love. —WILLIAM SHAKESPEARE

We cease loving ourselves if no one loves us. —GERMAINE DE STAËL

O tell her, brief is life but love is long. —ALFRED, LORD TENNYSON

Love is the only gold. —ALFRED, LORD TENNYSON

Those who have courage to love should have courage to suffer.
—ANTHONY TROLLOPE

I have learned not to worry about love; but to honor its coming with all my heart. —ALICE WALKER

When one is in love one begins by deceiving one's self. And one ends by deceiving others. That is what the world calls a romance.
—OSCAR WILDE

LOVE AND HATE
(also see concepts 237, 844)

I hate and I love. —CATULLUS

Hatred paralyzes life; love releases it. Hatred confuses life; love harmonizes it. Hatred darkens life; love illumines it.
—MARTIN LUTHER KING, JR.

Oh, I have loved him too much to feel no hate for him.
—JEAN RACINE

I love her and she loves me, and we hate each other with a wild hatred born of love. —AUGUST STRINDBERG

LOVE, LOSS OF
(also see concepts 3, 218, 464, 520)

Hunger stops love, or, if not hunger, Time. —CRATES

How do you know Love is gone? If you said that you would be there at seven and you get there by nine, and he or she has not called the police yet–it's gone. —MARLENE DIETRICH

A sharp knife cuts the quickest and hurts the least.
—KATHARINE HEPBURN

The great tragedy of life is not that men perish, but that they cease to love. —W. SOMERSET MAUGHAM

To find oneself jilted is a blow to one's pride. One must do one's best to forget it and if one doesn't succeed, at least one must pretend to. —MOLIÉRE

The heart that can no longer / Love passionately, must with fury hate. —JEAN RACINE

LOVERS
(also see concepts 422, 439, 466, 479, 687, 859)

Pity the selfishness of lovers: it is brief, a forlorn hope; it is impossible. —ELIZABETH BOWEN

Imparadised in one another's arms. —JOHN MILTON

Lovers. Not a soft word, as people thought, but cruel and tearing. —ALICE MUNRO

Scratch a lover and find a foe. —DOROTHY PARKER

Lovers know what they want, but not what they need. —PUBLILIUS SYRUS

And the lovers lie abed with all their griefs in their arms. —DYLAN THOMAS

LOYALTY
(also see concepts 65, 221, 237, 270, 300, 528, 548, 676, 817)

When young we are faithful to individuals, when older we grow more loyal to situations and to types. —CYRIL CONNOLLY

To be sure, the dog is loyal. But why, on that account, should we take him as an example? He is loyal to men, not to other dogs. —KARL KRAUS

LUCK
(also see concepts 6, 97, 279, 556)

Luck's always to blame. —JEAN DE LA FONTAINE

Luck is a matter of preparation meeting opportunity. —OPRAH WINFREY

LUST
(also see concepts 237, 570)

Let my lusts be my ruin, then, since all else is a fake and a mockery. —HART CRANE

No one ever suddenly became depraved. —JUVENAL

Home is heaven and orgies are vile / But you need an orgy, once in a while. —OGDEN NASH

LUXURY
(also see concepts 254, 395, 483, 606, 776)

The saddest thing I can imagine is to get used to luxury.
—CHARLIE CHAPLIN

The lust for comfort, that stealthy thing that enters the house a guest, and then becomes a host, and then a master. —KAHLIL GIBRAN

How many things I can do without! —SOCRATES

Give me the luxuries of life and I will willingly do without the necessities. —FRANK LLOYD WRIGHT

MACHINES
(also see concepts 29, 56, 141, 796)

You cannot endow even the best machine with initiative; the jolliest steamroller will not plant flowers. —WALTER LIPPMANN

Ever since our love for machines replaced the love we used to have for our fellow men, catastrophes proceed to increase. —MAN RAY

The machine threatens all achievement. —RAINER MARIA RILKE

The machine does not isolate man from the great problems of nature but plunges him more deeply into them.
—ANTOINE DE SAINT-EXUPÉRY

It is said that one machine can do the work of fifty ordinary men. No machine, however, can do the work of one extraordinary man.
—TEHYI HSIEH

On mechanical slavery, on the slavery of the machine, the future of the world depends. —OSCAR WILDE

MADNESS
(also see concepts 340, 534, 544, 634, 697)

We are all born mad. Some remain so. —SAMUEL BECKETT

I saw the best minds of my generation destroyed by madness, starving hysterical naked... —ALLEN GINSBERG

Better mad with the rest of the world than wise alone.
——BALTASAR GRACIÁN

Insanity is often logic of an accurate mind overtaxed.
——OLIVER WENDELL HOLMES, SR.

Everyone is more or less mad on one point. ——RUDYARD KIPLING

The great proof of madness is the disproportion of one's designs to one's means. ——NAPOLEON I

Whom God wishes to destroy, he first makes mad. ——PROVERB

A body seriously out of equilibrium, either with itself or with its environment, perishes outright. Not so a mind. Madness and suffering can set themselves no limit. ——GEORGE SANTAYANA

MAGAZINES
(also see concepts 76, 432, 482, 539)

Magazines all too frequently lead to books and should be regarded as the heavy petting of literature. ——FRAN LEBOWITZ

MALICE
(also see concepts 174, 237, 322, 339)

I am convinced that we have a degree of delight, and that no small one, in the real misfortunes and pains of others. ——EDMUND BURKE

If no action if to be deemed virtuous for which malice can imagine a sinister motive, then there never was a virtuous action.
——THOMAS JEFFERSON

Malice swallows the greater part of its own venom.
——PUBLILIUS SYRUS

One likes people much better when they're battered down by a prodigious siege of misfortune than when they triumph.
——VIRGINIA WOOLF

MANNERS

(also see concepts 320, 331, 360, 597, 689, 791, 848)

The hardest job kids face today is learning good manners without seeing any. —FRED ASTAIRE

Manners are the hypocrisy of a nation. —HONORÉ DE BALZAC

Manners require time, as nothing is more vulgar than haste.
—RALPH WALDO EMERSON

You've got to have something to eat and a little love in your life before you can hold still for any damn body's sermon on how to behave. —BILLIE HOLIDAY

I have always been of the mind that in a democracy manners are the only effective weapons against the bowie-knife.
—JAMES RUSSELL LOWELL

Manners are a sensitive awareness of the feelings of others. If you have that awareness, you have good manners, no matter what fork you use. —EMILY POST

Manners are not idle, but the fruit / Of loyal nature and of noble mind. —ALFRED, LORD TENNYSON

Manners are especially the need of the plain. The pretty can get away with anything. —EVELYN WAUGH

To the real artist in humanity, what are called bad manners are often the most picturesque and significant of all. —WALT WHITMAN

MARRIAGE

(also see concepts 218, 422, 469, 666, 859)

When a match has equal partners / then I fear not. —AESCHYLUS

Happiness in marriage is entirely a matter of chance. —JANE AUSTEN

A man who is compelled to go on materially and morally supporting a woman he no longer loves feels victimized; but if he abandons without resources the woman who has pledged her whole life to him, she will be quite as unjustly victimized. —SIMONE DE BEAUVOIR

The dread of loneliness is greater than the fear of bondage, so we get married. —CYRIL CONNOLLY

So that ends my first experience of matrimony, which I always thought a highly over-rated performance. —ISADORA DUNCAN

I would rather be a beggar and single than a queen and married. —QUEEN ELIZABETH I

Marriage could be the greatest success in the sociological history of humanity if the man would or could play fair. But, I believe any woman with independent instincts, with the dream of making her individual personality count for something in the world, might just as well shun marriage. —MAUD GONNE

It is not from reason and prudence that people marry, but from inclination. —SAMUEL JOHNSON

Any one must see at a glance that if men and women marry those whom they do not love, they must love those whom they do not marry. —HARRIET MARTINEAU

Quarrels are the dowry which married folk bring one another. —OVID

And I knew that in spite of all the roses and kisses and restaurant dinners a man showered on a woman before he married her, what he secretly wanted when the wedding ended was for her to flatten out underneath his feet like Mrs. Willard's kitchen mat. —SYLVIA PLATH

Oh, what a pother, she thought, women make about marriage! And yet who can blame them, when the marriage—and its consequences—is the only thing that women have to make a pother about in their whole lives?....Safeguarded, kept in the dark, hinted at, segregated, repressed, all so that at a given moment they may be delivered or may deliver their daughters over, to minister to a man? —VITA SACKVILLE-WEST

Chains do not hold a marriage together. It is threads, hundreds of tiny threads, which sew people together through the years. —SIMONE SIGNORET

The surest way to be alone is to get married. —GLORIA STEINEM

Both marriage and death ought to be welcome: the one promises happiness, doubtless the other assures it. —MARK TWAIN

Being married gives one one's position like nothing else can. —QUEEN VICTORIA

Marriage is the only adventure open to the cowardly. —VOLTAIRE

The best part about married life is the fights. The rest is merely so-so. —THORNTON WILDER

Marriage isn't a process of prolonging the life of love, but of mummifying the corpse. —P. G. WODEHOUSE

MARTYRS AND MARTYRDOM
(also see concepts 108, 431, 564, 692, 696, 712)

To die for a religion is easier than to live it absolutely. —JORGE LUIS BORGES

Martyrs, my friend, have to choose between being forgotten, mocked or used. As for being understood–never. —ALBERT CAMUS

Opposition may become sweet to a man when he has christened it persecution. —GEORGE ELIOT

Martyrdom does not end something, it is only a beginning. —INDIRA GANDHI

'Dying for an idea,' again, sounds well enough, but why not let the idea die instead of you? —WYNDHAM LEWIS

MASOCHISM
(also see concepts 174, 534, 564, 693, 710, 713, 716)

A hair shirt does not always render those chaste who wear it. —MICHEL DE MONTAIGNE

Troubles hurt the most / when they prove self-inflicted. —SOPHOCLES

MASS MEDIA
(also see concepts 132, 476, 539, 540, 797)

What the mass media offer is not popular art, but entertainment which is intended to be consumed like food, forgotten, and replaced by a new dish. —W. H. AUDEN

Media is just a word that has come to mean bad journalism. —GRAHAM GREENE

Each day a few more lies eat into the seed with which we are born, little institutional lies from the print of newspapers, the shock waves of television, and the sentimental cheats of the movie screen. —NORMAN MAILER

For the very first time the young are seeing history being made before it is censored by their elders. —MARGARET MEAD

Everybody gets so much information all day long that they lose their common sense. —GERTRUDE STEIN

MATERIALISM
(also see concepts 267, 313, 473, 604, 763)

We live in a world of things, and our only connection with them is that we know how to manipulate or to consume them. —ERICH FROMM

Increase of material comforts, it may be generally laid down, does not in any way whatsoever conduce to moral growth. —MOHANDAS K. GANDHI

We are the slaves of objects around us, and appear little or important according as these contract or give us room to expand. —JOHANN WOLFGANG VON GOETHE

Acquisition means life to miserable mortals. —HESIOD

In a consumer society there are inevitably two kinds of slaves: the prisoners of addiction and the prisoners of envy. —IVAN ILLICH

A woman who has no way of expressing herself and of realizing herself as a human being has nothing else to turn to but the owning of material things. ——ENRIQUETA LONGEAUX Y VASQUEZ

MATHEMATICS
(also see concepts 141, 623, 702, 768)

As far as the laws of mathematics refer to reality, they are not certain, and as far as they are certain, they do not refer to reality. ——ALBERT EINSTEIN

Stand firm in your refusal to remain conscious during algebra. In real life, I assure you, there is no such thing as algebra. ——FRAN LEBOWITZ

I have hardly ever known a mathematician who was capable of reasoning. ——PLATO

Mathematics possesses not only truth, but supreme beauty–a beauty cold and austere, like that of a sculpture. ——BERTRAND RUSSELL

What would life be without arithmetic, but a scene of horrors? ——SYDNEY SMITH

Numbers constitute the only universal language. ——NATHANAEL WEST

MATURITY
(also see concepts 384, 404, 497, 877)

It is sad to grow old but nice to ripen. ——BRIGITTE BARDOT

Where id was, there shall ego be. ——SIGMUND FREUD

How do you know that the fruit is ripe? Simply because it leaves the branch. ——ANDRÉ GIDE

To be adult is to be alone. ——JEAN ROSTAND

One of the signs of passing youth is the birth of a sense of fellowship with other human beings as we take our place among them. —VIRGINIA WOOLF

MEANING
(also see concepts 773, 802, 824, 837)

Take care of the sense, and the sounds will take care of themselves. —LEWIS CARROLL

The least of things with a meaning is worth more in life than the greatest of things without it. —CARL JUNG

There is not one big cosmic meaning for all, there is only the meaning we each give to our life....To give as much meaning to one's life as possible is right to me. —ANAÏS NIN

The meaning of things lies not in the things themselves but in our attitude towards them. —ANTOINE DE SAINT-EXUPÉRY

MEANNESS
(also see concepts 505, 723, 816, 822, 828)

To the mean eye all things are trivial, as certainly as to the jaundiced they are yellow. —THOMAS CARLYLE

Man hoards himself when he has nothing to give away. —EDWARD DAHLBERG

To the mean all becomes mean. —FRIEDRICH WILHELM NIETZSCHE

Small things make base men proud. —WILLIAM SHAKESPEARE

There are many things that we would throw away, if we were not afraid that others might pick them up. —OSCAR WILDE

MEANS AND ENDS
(also see concepts 93, 260, 496)

When we deliberate it is about means and not ends. —ARISTOTLE

Results! Why, man, I have gotten a lot of results. I know several thousand things that won't work. —THOMAS EDISON

Most of the great results of history are brought about by discreditable means. —RALPH WALDO EMERSON

It is not enough to take steps which may some day lead to a goal; each step must be itself a goal and a step likewise.
—JOHANN WOLFGANG VON GOETHE

Methods and means cannot be separated from the ultimate aim.
—EMMA GOLDMAN

MEDICINE
(also see concepts 28, 219, 226, 340, 341, 350, 501, 702, 738)

When you buy a pill and buy peace with it you get conditioned to cheap solutions instead of deep ones. —MAX LERNER

All interest in disease and death is only another expression of interest in life. —THOMAS MANN

Medicine heals doubts as well as diseases. —KARL MARX

Medicines are only fit for old people. —NAPOLEON I

It is medicine, not scenery, for which a sick man must go searching.
—SENECA

By medicine life may be prolonged, yet death / Will seize the doctor too. —WILLIAM SHAKESPEARE

Formerly, when religion was strong and science weak, men mistook magic for medicine, now, when science is strong and religion weak, men mistake medicine for magic. —THOMAS SZASZ

The art of medicine consists of amusing the patient while Nature cures the disease. —VOLTAIRE

MEDIOCRITY

(also see concepts 398, 508)

Only mediocrity can be trusted to be always at its best.
—MAX BEERBOHM

Good behavior is the last refuge of mediocrity. —HENRY S. HASKINS

In the republic of mediocrity genius is dangerous.
—ROBERT G. INGERSOLL

The general tendency of things throughout the world is to render mediocrity the ascendant power among mankind.
—JOHN STUART MILL

When small men attempt great enterprises, they always end by reducing them to the level of their mediocrity. —NAPOLEON I

MELANCHOLY

(also see concepts 237, 584, 718, 757, 827)

Nothing's so dainty sweet as melancholy. —FRANCIS BEAUMONT

If there is hell upon earth, it is to be found in a melancholy man's heart. —ROBERT BURTON

Melancholy, indeed, should be diverted by every means but drinking. —SAMUEL JOHNSON

MEMORY

(also see concepts 151, 313, 500)

Memories are hunting horns whose sound dies on the wind.
—GUILLAUME APOLLINAIRE

Some memories are realities, and are better than anything that can ever happen to one again. —WILLA CATHER

We forget all too soon the things we thought we could never forget.
—JOAN DIDION

We have all forgot more than we remember. —THOMAS FULLER

The things we remember best are those better forgotten.
——BALTASAR GRACIÁN

Memory is more indelible than ink. ——ANITA LOOS

I never forget a face, but I'll make an exception in your case.
——GROUCHO MARX

The memory represents to us not what we choose but what it pleases. ——MICHEL DE MONTAIGNE

We do not remember days, we remember moments.
——CESARE PAVESE

Reminiscences make one feel so deliciously aged and sad.
——GEORGE BERNARD SHAW

God created memory so that we might have roses in December.
——ITALO SVEVO

Memories are like mulligatawny soup in a cheap restaurant. It is best not to stir them. ——P. G. WODEHOUSE

MEN

(also see concepts 160, 354, 732, 733)

Can't anything be done about that klunky phrase *male bonding*? What kind of people invent phrases like *male bonding*?
——RUSSELL BAKER

We are living at an important and fruitful moment now, for it is clear to men that the images of adult manhood given by the popular culture are worn out; a man can no longer depend on them. By the time a man is thirty-five he knows that the images of the right man, the tough man, the true man which he received in high school do not work in life. ——ROBERT BLY

The journey many American men have taken into softness, or receptivity, or "development of the feminine side," has been an immensely valuable journey, but more travel lies ahead. No stage is the final stop. ——ROBERT BLY

It is men, not women, who have promoted the cult of brutal masculinity; and because men admire muscle and physical force, they assume that we do too. —ELIZABETH GOULD DAVIS

The beauty of stature is the only beauty of men.
—MICHEL DE MONTAIGNE

Man is not the enemy here, but the fellow victim. —BETTY FRIEDAN

One hell of an outlay for a very small return with most of them.
—GLENDA JACKSON

It's a man's world, and you men can have it.
—KATHERINE ANNE PORTER

The bravest thing that men do is love women. —MORT SAHL

It doesn't take a hero to order men into battle. It takes a hero to be one of those men who goes into battle.
—GENERAL H. NORMANN SCHWARZKOPF

Every man sees a little of himself in Rhett Butler. —TED TURNER

There is a period near the beginning of every man's life when he has little to cling to except his unmanageable dream, little to support him except good health, and nowhere to go but all over the place. —E.B. WHITE

Who goes there! hankering, gross, mystical, nude? / How is it I extract strength from the beef I eat? / What is a man anyhow? What am I? and what are you? —WALT WHITMAN

Men, since they made gods in their own image, feel that their bodies are essentially all right. Studies show that while women unrealistically distort their bodies negatively, men unrealistically distort theirs positively. —NAOMI WOLF

MEN AND WOMEN
(also see concepts 160, 479, 493, 666, 707, 731, 733, 859, 867)

The woman who is known only through a man is known wrong.
—HENRY BROOKS ADAMS

I don't know why women want any of the things men have when one of the things that women have is men. —COCO CHANEL

I'm not afraid to show my feminine side–it's part of what makes me a man. —GÉRARD DEPARDIEU

Man and woman are two locked caskets, of which each contains the key to the other. —ISAK DINESEN

The finest people marry the two sexes in their own person. —RALPH WALDO EMERSON

Right now the sweet white bush clover is blooming; but sooner or later winter will come, and the flowers and the stems will dry up. Just wait and see. The relationship between men and women is like this, I guess. —HAYASHI FUMIKO

Boys and girls are expected to behave differently to each other, and to people in general–a behavior to be briefly described in two words. To the boy we say "Do"; to the girl we say "Don't." —CHARLOTTE PERKINS GILMAN

A true conception of the relation of the sexes will not admit of conqueror and conquered; it knows of but one great thing; to give of one's self boundlessly, in order to find one's self richer, deeper, better. —EMMA GOLDMAN

Sometimes I wonder if men and women suit each other. Perhaps they should live next door and just visit now and then. —KATHARINE HEPBURN

The consequence of a very free commerce between the sexes, and of their living much together, will often terminate in intrigues and gallantry. —DAVID HUME

Men and women, women and men. It will never work. —ERICA JONG

Women are not men's equals in anything except responsibility. We are not their inferiors, either, or even their superiors. We are quite simply different races. —PHYLLIS MCGINLEY

I often want to cry. That is the only advantage women have over men–at least they can cry. —JEAN RHYS

There is only one sex....A man and a woman are so entirely the same thing that one can scarcely understand the subtle reasons for sex distinction with which our minds are filled. —GEORGE SAND

As far as I'm concerned, being any gender is a drag. —PATTI SMITH

What is most beautiful in virile men is something feminine; what is most beautiful in feminine women is something masculine. —SUSAN SONTAG

A woman without a man is like a fish without a bicycle. —GLORIA STEINEM

Instead of this absurd division into sexes they ought to class people as static and dynamic. —EVELYN WAUGH

Women are as old as they feel–and men are old when they lose their feelings. —MAE WEST

It is fatal to be a man or woman pure and simple: one must be a woman manly, or a man womanly. —VIRGINIA WOOLF

MERCY
(also see concepts 367, 588)

We hand folks over to God's mercy, and show none ourselves. —GEORGE ELIOT

Sweet mercy is nobility's true badge. —WILLIAM SHAKESPEARE

METHOD
(also see concepts 180, 488, 561, 609)

Little by little does the trick. —AESOP

There is always a best way of doing everything, if it be to boil an egg. —RALPH WALDO EMERSON

We often get in quicker by the back door than by the front. —NAPOLEON I

Divide the fire, and you will the sooner put it out. —PUBLILIUS SYRUS

MIDDLE AGE

(also see concepts 24, 485)

Youth is cause, effect is age; so with the thickening of the neck we get data. —DJUNA BARNES

The really frightening thing about middle age is the knowledge that you'll grow out of it. —DORIS DAY

The years between fifty and seventy are the hardest. You are always being asked to do things, and yet you are not decrepit enough to turn them down. —T. S. ELIOT

Being middle-aged is a nice change from being young. —DOROTHY CANFIELD FISHER

Men, like peaches and pears, grow sweet a little while before they begin to decay. —OLIVER WENDELL HOLMES, SR.

And then, not expecting it, you become middle-aged and anonymous. No one notices you. You achieve a wonderful freedom. It is a positive thing. You can move about, unnoticed and invisible. —DORIS LESSING

As we reach midlife in the middle thirties or early forties, we are not prepared for the idea that time can run out on us, or for the startling truth that if we don't hurry to pursue our own definition of a meaningful existence, life can become a repetition of trivial maintenance duties. —GAIL SHEEHY

My forties are the best time I have ever gone through. —ELIZABETH TAYLOR

THE MIDDLE CLASS

(also see concepts 118, 607, 780)

The best political community is formed by citizens of the middle class. —ARISTOTLE

The middle class is always a firm champion of equality when it concerns a class above it; but it is its inveterate foe when it concerns elevating a class below it. —ORESTES A. BROWNSON

Destroy him as you will, the bourgeois always bounces up. Execute him, expropriate him, starve him out en masse, and he reappears in your children. —CYRIL CONNOLLY

The picture of a despotic God who wants unrestricted power over men and their submission and humiliation, was the projection of the middle class's own hostility and envy. —ERICH FROMM

The bourgeoisie prefers comfort to pleasure, convenience to liberty, and a pleasant temperature to the deathly inner consuming fire. —HERMANN HESSE

The way to crush the bourgeoisie is to grind them between the millstones of taxation and inflation. —V. I. LENIN

The upper classes are...a nation's past; the middle class is its future. —AYN RAND

I have to live for others and not for myself; that's middle-class morality. —GEORGE BERNARD SHAW

THE MILITARY

(also see concepts 573, 695, 850, 857)

Military intelligence is a contradiction in terms. —GROUCHO MARX

Military men are the scourges of the world. —GUY DE MAUPASSANT

The military caste did not originate as a party of patriots, but as a party of bandits. —H. L. MENCKEN

It is the blood of the soldier that makes the general great. —ITALIAN PROVERB

The soldier's body becomes a stock of accessories that are no longer his property. —ANTOINE DE SAINT-EXUPÉRY

Soldiers are citizens of death's grey land, / Drawing no dividend from time's tomorrows. —SIEGFRIED SASSOON

An army is a nation within a nation; it is one of the vices of our age. —ALFRED DE VIGNY

THE MIND

(also see concepts 142, 151, 179, 224, 373, 381, 382, 485, 492, 501, 634, 635, 697, 758, 823)

I can do something else besides stuff a ball through a hoop. My biggest resource is my mind. —KAREEM ABDUL-JABBAR

That priceless galaxy of misinformation called the mind...
—DJUNA BARNES

We should take care not to make the intellect our god; it has, of course, powerful muscles, but no personality. —ALBERT EINSTEIN

What we think and feel and are is to a great extent determined by the state of our ductless glands and our viscera. —ALDOUS HUXLEY

The mind is a strange machine which can combine the materials offered to it in the most astonishing ways. —BERTRAND RUSSELL

The dogma of the Ghost in the Machine. —GILBERT RYLE

The human mind always makes progress, but it is a progress in spirals. —GERMAINE DE STAËL

Minds differ still more than faces. —VOLTAIRE

The mind can also be an erogenous zone. —RAQUEL WELCH

MIND AND BODY

(also see concepts 219, 350, 500)

Bodily decay is gloomy in prospect, but of all human contemplation the most abhorrent is body without mind. —THOMAS JEFFERSON

All the soarings of my mind begin in my blood.
—RAINER MARIA RILKE

Nothing can so pierce the soul as the uttermost sigh of the body.
—GEORGE SANTAYANA

The human body is the best picture of the human soul.
—LUDWIG WITTGENSTEIN

MINORITY

(also see concept 650)

I am visible–see this Indian face–yet I am invisible. I both blind them with my beak nose and am their blind spot. But I exist, we exist. They'd like to think I have melted in the pot. But I haven't, we haven't. —GLORIA ANZALDÚA

It is the curse of minorities in this power-worshipping world that either from fear or from an uncertain policy of expedience they distrust their own standards and hesitate to give voice to their deeper convictions, submitting supinely to estimates and characterizations of themselves as handed down by a not unprejudiced dominant majority. —ANNA JULIA COOPER

When great changes occur in history, when great principles are involved, as a rule the majority are wrong. The minority are right. —EUGENE VICTOR DEBS

Every effort for progress, for enlightenment, for science, for religious, political, and economic liberty, emanates from the minority, and not from the mass. —EMMA GOLDMAN

All, too, will bear in mind this sacred principle, that though the will of the majority is in all cases to prevail, that will to be rightful must be reasonable; that the minority possess their equal rights, which equal law must protect, and to violate would be oppression. —THOMAS JEFFERSON

Being a minority in both caste and class, we moved about anyway on the hem of life, struggling to consolidate our weaknesses and hang on, or to creep singly up into the major folds of the garment. —TONI MORRISON

How a minority, / Reaching majority, / Seizing authority, / Hates a minority! —LEONARD H. ROBBINS

MIRACLES
(also see concepts 251, 526, 612, 784)

God is a character, a real and consistent being, or He is nothing. If God did a miracle He would deny His own nature and the universe would simply blow up, vanish, become nothing. —JOYCE CARY

There is in every miracle a silent chiding of the world, and a tacit reprehension of them who require, or who need miracles. —JOHN DONNE

A miracle may be accurately defined, a transgression of a law of nature by a particular volition of the Deity, or by the interposition of some invisible agent. —DAVID HUME

Men talk about Bible miracles because there is no miracle in their lives. Cease to gnaw that crust. There is ripe fruit over your head. —HENRY DAVID THOREAU

MIRRORS
(also see concepts 74, 381, 383, 586, 741)

We look into mirrors but we only see the effects of our times on us –not our effects on others. —PEARL BAILEY

Almost always it is the fear of being ourselves that brings us to the mirror. —ANTONIO PORCHIA

The best mirror is an old friend. —GERMAN PROVERB

MISERS
(also see concepts 329, 487, 512, 723, 806, 856)

The prodigal robs his heir, the miser himself. —THOMAS FULLER

The miser puts his gold pieces into a coffer; but as soon as the coffer is closed, it is as if it were empty. —ANDRÉ GIDE

What greater evil could you wish a miser, than long life? —PUBLILIUS SYRUS

MISERY
(also see concepts 17, 237, 564, 779, 812)

The human mind can bear plenty of reality but not too much intermittent gloom. —MARGARET DRABBLE

It is misery, not pleasure, which contains the secret of divine wisdom. —SIMONE WEIL

MISTAKES
(also see concepts 281, 387)

Show me a person who has never made a mistake and I'll show you somebody who has never achieved much. —JOAN COLLINS

There is glory in a great mistake. —NATHALIA CRANE

Two wrongs do not make a right. —PROVERB

If we had more time for discussion we should probably have made a great many more mistakes. —LEON TROTSKY

It is very easy to forgive others their mistakes; it takes more grit and gumption to forgive them for having witnessed your own. —JESSAMYN WEST

MODERATION
(also see concepts 103, 436, 456, 490, 572, 806)

Moderation is a virtue only in those who are thought to have an alternative. —HENRY KISSINGER

Moderation in people who are contented comes from the calm that good fortune lends to their spirit. —FRANÇOIS DE LA ROCHEFOUCAULD

MODERNITY
(also see concepts 538, 562, 808)

Modernity is always striving to go beyond exchange. —ROLAND BARTHES

Modern culture is defined by this extraordinary freedom to ransack the world storehouse and to engorge any and every style it comes upon. Such freedom comes from the fact that the axial principle of modern culture is the expression and remaking of the "self" in order to achieve self-realization and self-fulfillment. —DANIEL BELL

A single sentence will suffice for modern man: he fornicated and read the papers. —ALBERT CAMUS

No idea is so antiquated that it was not once modern. No idea is so modern that it will not someday be antiquated. —ELLEN GLASGOW

People in those old times had convictions; we moderns only have opinions. And it needs more than a mere opinion to erect a Gothic cathedral. —HEINRICH HEINE

It is only the modern that ever becomes old-fashioned.
—OSCAR WILDE

MODESTY
(also see concepts 369, 547, 737)

I wasn't really naked. I simply didn't have any clothes on.
—JOSEPHINE BAKER

At least I have the modesty to admit that lack of modesty is one of my failings. —HECTOR BERLIOZ

Modesty is the only sure bait when you angle for praise.
—EARL OF CHESTERFIELD

Modesty is a vastly overrated virtue. —JOHN KENNETH GALBRAITH

Modesty: the gentle art of enhancing your charm by pretending not to be aware of it. —OLIVER HERFORD

I have often wished I had time to cultivate modesty....But I am too busy thinking about myself. —EDITH SITWELL

Modesty died when clothes were born. —MARK TWAIN

MONARCHS AND MONARCHY
(also see concepts 44, 445, 542, 767)

Royalty does good and is badly spoken of. —ANTISTHENES

The king never dies. —WILLIAM BLACKSTONE

Such grace had kings when the world begun! —ROBERT BROWNING

The monarchy is the oldest profession in the world.
—PRINCE CHARLES OF WALES

There is no middle course between the throne and the scaffold.
—KING CHARLES X

A crown is merely a hat that lets the rain in.
—KING FREDERICK THE GREAT

We're not a family; we're a firm. —KING GEORGE VI

Kings and such are just as funny as politicians.
—THEODORE ROOSEVELT

The foremost art of kings is the power to endure hatred. —SENECA

Uneasy lies the head that wears a crown. —WILLIAM SHAKESPEARE

Kings is mostly rapscallions. —MARK TWAIN

The first who was king was a fortunate soldier. —VOLTAIRE

The monarchy is a labour-intensive industry. —HAROLD WILSON

MONEY
(also see concepts 57, 78, 81, 84, 85, 187, 231, 329, 421, 487, 505, 574, 794)

If you would know what the Lord God thinks of money, you have only to look at those to whom he gives it. —MAURICE BARING

The love of money is the root of all evil. —BIBLE, 1 TIMOTHY 6:10

Money you know will hide many faults. —MIGUEL DE CERVANTES

Where large sums of money are concerned, it is advisable to trust nobody. —AGATHA CHRISTIE

If possible honestly, if not, somehow, make money. —HORACE

Some people think they are worth a lot of money just because they have it. —FANNIE HURST

Moral principle is a looser bond than pecuniary interest.
—ABRAHAM LINCOLN

I don't like money, actually, but it quiets my nerves. —JOE LOUIS

The two most beautiful words in the English language are "check enclosed." —DOROTHY PARKER

Easy come, easy go. —PROVERB

I finally know what distinguishes man from the other beasts: financial worries. —JULES RENARD

The way to make money is to buy when blood is running in the streets. —JOHN D. ROCKEFELLER

Money is always there but the pockets change; it is not in the same pocket after a change, and that is all there is to say about money.
—GERTRUDE STEIN

Keep cool and collect. —MAE WEST

You can be young without money but you can't be old without it.
—TENNESSEE WILLIAMS

MONTHS

(also see concepts 705, 807)

November is the most disagreeable month in the whole year.
—LOUISA MAY ALCOTT

Hard is the heart that loveth nought / In May. —GEOFFREY CHAUCER

Fallen leaves lying on the grass in November bring more happiness than the daffodils. —RICHARD CRASHAW

There is no season when such pleasant and sunny spots may be lighted on, and produce so pleasant an effect on the feelings, as now in October. —NATHANIEL HAWTHORNE

In May Nature holds up at us a chiding finger, bidding us remember that we are not gods, but overconceited members of her own great family. —O. HENRY

August creates as she slumbers, replete and satisfied. —JOSEPH WOOD KRUTCH

No price is set on the lavish summer, / June may be had by the poorest comer. —JAMES RUSSELL LOWELL

April / Comes like an idiot, babbling and strewing flowers. —EDNA ST. VINCENT MILLAY

November's sky is chill and drear, / November's leaf is red and sear. —WALTER SCOTT

Sweet April showers / Do spring May flowers. —THOMAS TUSSER

THE MOON
(also see concepts 342, 541, 766)

The summer moon hung full in the sky. For the time being it was the great fact of the world. —WILLA CATHER

There is something haunting in the light of the moon; it has all the dispassionateness of a disembodied soul, and something of its inconceivable mystery. —JOSEPH CONRAD

For years politicians have promised the moon. I'm the first one to be able to deliver it. —RICHARD NIXON

The moon is a friend for the lonesome to talk to. —CARL SANDBURG

MORALITY
(also see concepts 95, 150, 249, 316, 319, 321, 332, 587, 620, 696, 743, 843)

Grub first, then ethics. —BERTOLT BRECHT

Everything's got a moral, if only you can find it. —LEWIS CARROLL

Too many moralists begin with a dislike of reality. —CLARENCE DAY

Morality is largely a matter of geography. —ELBERT HUBBARD

The quality of moral behaviour varies in inverse ratio to the number of human beings involved. —ALDOUS HUXLEY

Do the right thing. —SPIKE LEE

There is nothing so bad but it can masquerade as moral.
—WALTER LIPPMANN

If your morals make you dreary, depend upon it, they are wrong.
—ROBERT LOUIS STEVENSON

Morality is simply the attitude we adopt towards people whom we personally dislike. —OSCAR WILDE

MORNING
(also see concepts 125, 541, 782)

The morning is wiser than the evening. —RUSSIAN PROVERB

Only dull people are brilliant at breakfast. —OSCAR WILDE

To what human ill does not dawn seem to be an alternative?
—THORNTON WILDER

MORTALITY
(also see concepts 368, 425, 813)

Mortality has its compensations: one is that all evils are transitory, another that better times may come. —GEORGE SANTAYANA

We are such stuff / As dreams are made on, and our little life / Is rounded with a sleep. —WILLIAM SHAKESPEARE

Old and young, we are all on our last cruise.
—ROBERT LOUIS STEVENSON

MOTHERS

(also see concepts 106, 273, 280, 566, 667)

I'm not against mothers. I am against the ideology which expects every woman to have children, and I'm against the circumstances under which mothers have to have their children.
—SIMONE DE BEAUVOIR

A mother starts out as the most important person in her child's world and if she's successful in her work, she will eventually become the stupidest. —MARY KAY BLAKELY

Life is nothing but a series of crosses for us mothers. —COLETTE

The only thing that seems eternal and natural in motherhood is ambivalence. —JANE LAZARRE

When the strongest words for what I have to offer come out of me sounding like words I remember from my mother's mouth, then I either have to reassess the meaning of everything I have to say now, or re-examine the worth of her old words. —AUDRE LORDE

If you bungle raising your children, I don't think whatever else you do well matters very much. —JACQUELINE KENNEDY ONASSIS

God could not be everywhere, and therefore he made mothers.
—JEWISH PROVERB

No matter how old a mother is, she watches her middle-aged children for signs of improvement. —FLORIDA SCOTT-MAXWELL

Most mothers are instinctive philosophers.
—HARRIET BEECHER STOWE

Motherhood is the most emotional experience of one's life. One joins a kind of women's mafia. —JANET SUZMAN

MOTIVES

(also see concepts 31, 50, 94, 198, 376)

All that we do is done with an eye to something else. —ARISTOTLE

Never ascribe to an opponent motives meaner than your own.
—J. M. BARRIE

Great men will never do great mischief but for some great end.
—EDMUND BURKE

Men are not only bad from good motives, but also often good from
bad motives. —G. K. CHESTERTON

We know nothing about motivation. All we can do is write books
about it. —PETER DRUCKER

We should often feel ashamed of our best actions if the world could
see all of the motives which produced them.
—FRANÇOIS DE LA ROCHEFOUCAULD

If the outcome is good, what's the difference between motives that
sound good and good sound motives? —LAWRENCE J. PETER

MOURNING
(also see concepts 9, 175, 302, 665, 757, 779, 827)

Let mourning stop when one's grief is fully expressed. —CONFUCIUS

The sorrow for the dead is the only sorrow from which we refuse
to be divorced. —WASHINGTON IRVING

MOVIES
(also see concepts 11, 33, 53, 351, 586)

A film is a petrified fountain of thought. —JEAN COCTEAU

Photography is truth. And cinema is truth twenty-four times a
second. —JEAN-LUC GODARD

A wide screen just makes a bad film twice as bad.
—SAMUEL GOLDWYN

It's difficult being homosexual in life, but in cinema it's almost
impossible. Heterosexuals have hogged the screen so much we've
barely got space for a kiss left. —DEREK JARMAN

Movies have just become a kind of hallucination. An excuse to go hallucinate, like drugs. Movies are a dream world. Eat popcorn and dream. —SAM SHEPARD

When you get the personality, you don't need the nudity. —MAE WEST

MULTICULTURALISM
(also see concepts 22, 49, 347, 530)

We really are 15 countries, and it's really remarkable that each of us thinks we represent the real America. The Midwesterner in Kansas, the black American in Durham—both are certain they are the real American. —MAYA ANGELOU

This world is white no longer, and it will never be white again. —JAMES BALDWIN

We become not a melting pot but a beautiful mosaic. Different people, different beliefs, different yearnings, different hopes, different dreams. —JIMMY CARTER

It isn't a matter of black is beautiful as much as it is white is not *all* that's beautiful. —BILL COSBY

History has given the Jewish people a difficult row to hoe; but so long as we remain devoted servants of truth, justice, and liberty, we shall continue not merely to survive as the oldest of living peoples, but by creative work to bring forth fruits which contribute to the ennoblement of the human race, as heretofore. —ALBERT EINSTEIN

The notion of multiculturalism can easily turn to the idea we only relate to each other because of our particular nationality and gender. —DAVID HENRY HWANG

I hear that melting pot stuff a lot, and all I can say is that we haven't melted. —JESSE JACKSON

There is nowhere you can go and only be with people who are like you. Give it up. —BERNICE JOHNSON REAGON

For the past thirty years or so, people have tended to see themselves, and have tended to be seen, as members of interest groups (racial, national, sexual) and not as individuals, making every life both political and potentially publishable; the leap between a private complaint and a public cause is semiautomatic. Multiculturalism insists that everybody is a class of being, as do other bad current ideas. —ROGER ROSENBLATT

If I had to choose my place of birth, I would have chosen a state in which everyone knew everyone else, so that neither the obscure tactics of vice nor the modesty of virtue could have escaped public scrutiny and judgement. —JEAN JACQUES ROUSSEAU

When one member of a group changes, the balance shifts for everyone, and when one group changes, it shifts the balance of society–just as a few molecules shift the whole. New pride among African Americans inspired a contagion of changed consciousness in the national family. It helped women of all races to see the parallels of racial and sexual discrimination and also led to an atmosphere in which many ethnic groups found more pride, from Jews who reconsidered changing their names in spite of continuing anti-Semitism to Italians who protested stereotyped associations with organized crime. One group's efforts often directly benefited the next: for instance, Native Americans, whose history and languages were forbidden in schools well into the 1970s, were aided by bilingual education laws that Hispanic Americans initiated. —GLORIA STEINEM

THE   MUNDANE
(also see concepts 228, 609, 657, 658, 784, 871)

Most of us swim in the ocean of the commonplace. —PIÓ BAROJA

What a day-to-day affair life is. —JULES LAFORGUE

That which one cannot experience in daily life is not true for oneself. —D. H. LAWRENCE

Commonplaces are the tramways of intellectual transportation. —JOSÉ ORTEGA Y GASSET

MUSICIANS AND MUSIC

(also see concepts 182, 429, 543, 554, 640, 655, 686, 745)

Musicians don't retire; they stop when there's no more music in them. —LOUIS ARMSTRONG

Brass bands are all very well in their place–outdoors and several miles away. —THOMAS BEECHAM

Where there's music there can be no evil. —MIGUEL DE CERVANTES

Strange how potent cheap music is. —NOËL COWARD

Music is the arithmetic of sounds as optics is the geometry of light. —CLAUDE DEBUSSY

Music was invented to confirm human loneliness. —LAWRENCE DURRELL

I've been told that nobody sings the word "hunger" like I do. —BILLIE HOLIDAY

When a piece gets difficult, make faces. —VLADIMIR HOROWITZ

The only sensual pleasure without vice. —SAMUEL JOHNSON

Music is essentially useless, as life is. —GEORGE SANTAYANA

The notes I handle no better than many pianists. But the pauses between the notes–ah, that is where the art resides. —ARTUR SCHNABEL

Music revives the recollections it would appease. —GERMAINE DE STAËL

My music is best understood by children and animals. —IGOR STRAVINSKY

MYSTICISM

(also see concepts 550, 559, 560, 706, 758, 763, 784, 833)

I've found a perfect description of mysticism–it's the attempt to get rid of mystery. —ROGER FRY

Without mysticism man can achieve nothing great. —ANDRÉ GIDE

Mystics always hope that science will some day overtake them.
——BOOTH TARKINGTON

MYTH

(also see concepts 503, 785, 811)

A myth is a fixed way of looking at the world which cannot be destroyed because, looked at through the myth, all evidence supports that myth. ——EDWARD DE BONO

The great enemy of the truth is very often not the lie–deliberate, contrived and dishonest–but the myth–persistent, persuasive and unrealistic. ——JOHN F. KENNEDY

Contemporary man has rationalized the myths, but he has not been able to destroy them. ——OCTAVIO PAZ

Science must begin with myths, and with the criticism of myths.
——KARL POPPER

There's myth in the sense of a lie. There's myth in the sense of fantasy. There's myth in all those senses. But the traditional meaning of myth is that it served a purpose in our life. The purpose had to do with being able to trace ourselves back through time and follow our emotional self....And that's been destroyed. Myth in its truest form has been demolished....All we have is fantasies about it. ——SAM SHEPARD

When myth meets myth, the collision is very real.
——KING STANISLAUS I

NAMES

(also see concept 672)

There is everything in a name. A rose by any other name would smell as sweet, but would not cost half as much during the winter months. ——GEORGE ADE

A nickname is the hardest stone that the devil can throw at a man.
——WILLIAM HAZLITT

The name of a man is a numbing blow from which he never recovers. —MARSHALL MCLUHAN

Titles are but nicknames, and every nickname is a title.
—THOMAS PAINE

What's in a name? That which we call a rose / By any other name would smell as sweet. —WILLIAM SHAKESPEARE

NATIONALISM

(also see concepts 287, 353, 573)

I love my country too much to be a nationalist. —ALBERT CAMUS

It is not easy to see how the more extreme forms of nationalism can long survive when men have seen the Earth in its true perspective as a single small globe against the stars. —ARTHUR C. CLARKE

Nationalism is an infantile disease. It is the measles of mankind.
—ALBERT EINSTEIN

Nationalism is our form of incest, is our idolatry, is our insanity. "Patriotism" is its cult. —ERICH FROMM

Altogether, national hatred is something peculiar. You will always find it strongest and most violent where there is the lowest degree of culture. —JOHANN WOLFGANG VON GOETHE

No man has a right to fix the boundary of the march of a nation; no man has a right to say to his country–thus far shalt thou go and no further. —CHARLES STEWART PARNELL

Nations whose nationalism is destroyed are subject to ruin.
—MUHAMMAR QADDAFI

Every nation ridicules other nations, and all are right.
—ARTHUR SCHOPENHAUER

National Pride is a modern form of tribalism. —ROBERT SHNAYERSON

NATIONS

(also see concepts 21, 82, 87, 114, 287, 296, 312, 328, 423, 428, 528, 573, 598, 602, 691, 703, 754, 760, 789, 851)

The nation exists as a kind of continual irritant. Today, when the term "nation" is invoked, we are much more aware of what it doesn't do and how it doesn't work than how it does.
—HOMI K. BHABBA

I have no country to fight for: my country is the earth, and I am a citizen of the world. —EUGENE V. DEBS

The spirit of a nation is what counts–the look in its eyes.
—JEAN GIRAUDOUX

A nation is a society united by a delusion about its ancestry and by a common hatred of its neighbours. —WILLIAM RALPH INGE

Nations, like men, have their infancy. —HENRY ST. JOHN

It has been proved that the land can exist without the country–and be better for it; it has not been proved that the country can live without the land. —ALICE WALKER

NATIVE AMERICANS

(also see concepts 32, 522, 650)

An odd thing occurs in the minds of Americans when Indian civilization is mentioned: little or nothing. —PAULA GUNN ALLEN

Indians think it is important to remember, while Americans think it is important to forget. —PAULA GUNN ALLEN

When asked by an anthropologist what the Indians called America before the white man came, an Indian said simply, "Ours."
—VINE DELORIA, JR.

Being Indian is an attitude, a state of mind, a way of being in harmony with all things and all beings. It is allowing the heart to be the distributor of energy on this planet: to allow feelings and sensitivities to determine where energy goes; bringing aliveness up from the Earth and down from the Sky, putting it in and giving it out from the heart. —BROOKE MEDICINE EAGLE

Our tribe unraveled like a coarse rope, frayed at either end as the old and new among us were taken. —LOUISE ERDRICH

...The dominating culture imbues the Indian past with great meaning and significance; it is valued more because it is seen as part of the past. And it is the romantic past, not the present, that holds meaning and spiritual significance for so many members of the dominating culture. It has seemed so strange to me that the larger culture, with its own absence of spirit and lack of attachment for the land, respects these things about Indian traditions, without adopting those respected ways themselves. —LINDA HOGAN

The biggest enemy the Indian ever had was lack of education.... Everybody always did our thinking for us.
—WINIFRED JOURDAIN

Maybe the people are afraid that if the Indian kids get too well-educated they might try to take this land back. We don't want it after all the damage that has been done to it. All we want is the part that's undamaged and that belongs to us. —IRENE MACK PYAWASIT

NATURE
(also see concepts 92, 100, 166, 275, 289, 306, 350, 532, 580, 657, 658, 685, 701, 704, 708, 764, 815, 839, 871)

I am at two with nature. —WOODY ALLEN

Art is nature as seen through a temperament.
—JEAN-BAPTISTE CAMILLE-COROT

Nature is the art of God. —DANTE

All Nature wears one universal grin. —HENRY FIELDING

Never does nature say one thing and wisdom another. —JUVENAL

The roaring wind is my wife and the stars through the window pane are my children. —JOHN KEATS

Nature does not proceed by leaps and bounds. —LINNAEUS

There is not so contemptible a plant or animal that does not confound the most enlarged understanding. —JOHN LOCKE

The day, water, sun, moon, night–I do not have to purchase these things with money. —PLAUTUS

Nature is usually wrong. —JAMES WHISTLER

NECESSITY
(also see concepts 196, 260, 606, 794)

Necessity hath no law. —OLIVER CROMWELL

The finest poems of the world have been expedients to get bread. —RALPH WALDO EMERSON

Necessity never made a good bargain. —BENJAMIN FRANKLIN

Necessity dispenseth with decorum. —THOMAS FULLER

Necessity is not an established fact, but an interpretation. —FRIEDRICH WILHELM NIETZSCHE

Necessity, mother of invention. —WILLIAM WYCHERLEY

NEIGHBORS
(also see concepts 87, 134)

Thou shalt love thy neighbor as thyself. —BIBLE, LEVITICUS 19:18

For it is your business, when the wall next door catches fire. —HORACE

Nothing makes you more tolerant of a neighbor's noisy party than being there. —FRANKLIN P. JONES

A neighborhood is where, when you go out of it, you get beat up. —MURRAY KEMPTON

The good neighbor looks beyond the external accidents and discerns those inner qualities that make all men human and, therefore, brothers. —MARTIN LUTHER KING, JR.

NEUROSIS

(also see concepts 146, 340, 634, 635, 693)

If you be sick, your own thoughts make you sick. —BEN JONSON

Neurosis is always a substitute for legitimate suffering.
—CARL JUNG

Modern neurosis began with the discoveries of Copernicus. Science made man feel small by showing him that the earth was not the center of the universe. —MARY MCCARTHY

Neurotic means he is not as sensible as I am, and psychotic means he's even worse than my brother-in-law. —KARL MENNINGER

Everything great in the world is done by neurotics; they alone founded our religions and created our masterpieces.
—MARCEL PROUST

Work and love–these are the basics. Without them there is neurosis.
—THEODOR REIK

NEUTRALITY

(also see concepts 392, 771, 789, 879)

People who demand neutrality in any situation are usually not neutral but in favor of the status quo. —MAX EASTMAN

Neutrality consists in having the same weights and measures for each. —NAPOLEON I

NEW ENGLAND

(see also concepts 32, 79)

The most serious charge which can be brought against New England is not Puritanism but February. —JOSEPH WOOD KRUTCH

NEW YORK

(also see concepts 32, 113)

New York makes one think of the collapse of civilization, about Sodom and Gomorrah, the end of the world. The end wouldn't come as a surprise here. Many people already bank on it. —SAUL BELLOW

New York is an exciting town where something is happening all the time, most of it unsolved. —JOHNNY CARSON

It is often said that New York is a city for only the very rich and the very poor. It is less often said that New York is also, at least for those of us who came there from somewhere else, a city for only the very young. —JOAN DIDION

New York...that unnatural city where everyone is an exile, none more so than the American. —CHARLOTTE PERKINS GILMAN

The faces in New York remind me of people who played a game and lost. —MURRAY KEMPTON

New York is a catastrophe–but a magnificent catastrophe. —LE CORBUSIER

The crime problem in New York is getting really serious. The other day the Statue of Liberty had both hands up. —JAY LENO

New York now leads the world's great cities in the number of people around whom you shouldn't make a sudden move. —DAVID LETTERMAN

New York, the nation's thyroid gland. —CHRISTOPHER MORLEY

I miss the animal buoyancy of New York, the animal vitality. I did not mind that it had no meaning and no depth. —ANAÏS NIN

New York...is not Mecca. It just smells like it. —NEIL SIMON

One belongs to New York instantly. One belongs to it as much in five minutes as in five years. —THOMAS WOLFE

NEWNESS

(also see concepts 509, 562, 671)

There is nothing new except what has been forgotten.
——MARIE ANTOINETTE

There is no new thing under the sun. ——BIBLE, ECCLESIASTES 1:9

Novelties please less than they impress. ——LORD BYRON

It is always the latest song that an audience applauds the most.
——HOMER

There are three things which the public will always clamor for, sooner or later: namely, Novelty, novelty, novelty. ——THOMAS HOOD

NEWS

(also see concepts 432, 476, 482, 540, 797)

The one function that TV news performs very well is that when there is no news we give it to you with the same emphasis as if there were.
——DAVID BRINKLEY

If it's far away, it's news, but if it's close at home, it's sociology.
——JAMES RESTON

Nobody likes the bringer of bad news. ——SOPHOCLES

In the case of news, we should always wait for the sacrament of confirmation. ——VOLTAIRE

News is what a chap who doesn't care much about anything wants to read. And it is only news until he has read it. After that it's dead.
——EVELYN WAUGH

NEWSPAPERS

(also see concepts 432, 482, 539)

If newspapers are useful in overthrowing tyrants, it is only to establish a tyranny of their own. ——JAMES FENIMORE COOPER

A newspaper is the lowest thing there is! ——RICHARD J. DALEY

They are so filthy and bestial that no honest man would admit one into his house for a water-closet doormat. —CHARLES DICKENS

Headlines twice the size of the events. —JOHN GALSWORTHY

Were it left to me to decide whether we should have a government without newspapers, or newspapers without a government, I should not hesitate a moment to prefer the latter.
—THOMAS JEFFERSON

Once a newspaper touches a story, the facts are lost forever, even to the protagonists. —NORMAN MAILER

The art of newspaper paragraphing is to stroke a platitude until it purrs like an epigram. —DON MARQUIS

A good newspaper, I suppose, is a nation talking to itself.
—ARTHUR MILLER

Four hostile newspapers are more to be feared than a thousand bayonets. —NAPOLEON I

Early in life I had noticed that no event is ever correctly reported in a newspaper. —GEORGE ORWELL

All I know is just what I read in the papers. —WILL ROGERS

The window to the world can be covered by a newspaper.
—KING STANISLAUS I

NIGHT
(also see concepts 514, 516, 748)

In a real dark night of the soul it is always three o'clock in the morning. —F. SCOTT FITZGERALD

Night is the mother of counsels. —GEORGE HERBERT

The thought of suicide is a great source of comfort: with it a calm passage is to be made across many a bad night.
—FRIEDRICH WILHELM NIETZSCHE

When man reassembles his fragmentary self and grows with the calm of a tree. —ANTOINE DE SAINT-EXUPÉRY

Night brings our troubles to the light, rather than banishes them.
—SENECA

NOBILITY
(also see concepts 44, 207, 327, 511)

Real nobility is based on scorn, courage, and profound indifference.
—ALBERT CAMUS

Virtue is the only true nobility. —THOMAS FULLER

All that is noble is in itself of a quiet nature, and appears to sleep
until it is aroused and summoned forth by contrast.
—JOHANN WOLFGANG VON GOETHE

Nobility has its own obligations. —FRANÇOIS-GASTON DE LÉVIS

Put more trust in nobility of character than in an oath. —SOLON

NOISE
(also see concepts 175, 524, 554, 655, 686, 740)

Much outcry, little outcome. —AESOP

Noise is the most impertinent of all forms of interruption.
—ARTHUR SCHOPENHAUER

NONSENSE
(also see concepts 155, 475, 775)

Good sense about trivialities is better than nonsense about things
that matter. —MAX BEERBOHM

Forgive me my nonsense as I also forgive the nonsense of those who
think they can talk sense. —ROBERT FROST

It is a far, far better thing to have a firm anchor in nonsense than to
put on the troubled seas of thought. —JOHN KENNETH GALBRAITH

Don't talk to me about a man's being able to talk sense; everyone
can talk sense–can he talk nonsense? —WILLIAM PITT THE ELDER

Nonsense is good only because common sense is so limited.
——GEORGE SANTAYANA

NONVIOLENCE
(also see concepts 27, 575, 842)

Non-violence is a flop. The only bigger flop is violence.
——JOAN BAEZ

Whosoever shall smite thee on thy right cheek, turn to him the other also. ——BIBLE, MATTHEW 5:39

Non-violence is not a garment to be put on and off at will. Its seat is in the heart, and it must be an inseparable part of our very being.
——MOHANDAS K. GANDHI

Nonviolence is fine as long as it works. ——MALCOLM X

Sometime they'll give a war and nobody will come.
——CARL SANDBURG

NUCLEAR WEAPONS
(also see concepts 126, 499, 702, 796, 850, 857)

Nuclear weapons are not in my line; unfortunately I am in their line.
——E. M. FORSTER

No country without an atom bomb could properly consider itself independent. ——CHARLES DE GAULLE

What the scientists have in their briefcases is terrifying.
——NIKITA KHRUSHCHEV

We have genuflected before the god of science only to find that it has given us the atomic bomb, producing fears and anxieties that science can never mitigate. ——MARTIN LUTHER KING, JR.

Hitherto man had to live with the idea of death as an individual; from now onward mankind will have to live with the idea of its death as a species. ——ARTHUR KOESTLER

It's just a few people in the world, powerful people, still thinking in terms of collecting medals and doing things in a macho way. But it no longer works, because no matter how macho you are, nuclear power is stronger than you. —YOKO ONO

I am become death, the destroyer of worlds. —J. ROBERT OPPENHEIMER

Building up arms is not a substitute for diplomacy. —SAMUEL PISAR

There is no evil in the atom; only in men's souls. —ADLAI STEVENSON

NUDITY
(also see concepts 124, 510, 603)

Nakedness is uncomely as well in the mind, as body.
—FRANCIS BACON

To see you naked is to recall the Earth. —FEDERICO GARCÍA LORCA

How idiotic civilization is! Why be given a body if you have to keep it shut up in a case like a rare, rare fiddle? —KATHERINE MANSFIELD

Man is the sole animal whose nudities offend his own companions, and the only one who, in his natural actions, withdraws and hides himself from his own kind. —MICHEL DE MONTAIGNE

I wouldn't do nudity in films. For me, personally...to act with my clothes on is a performance; to act with my clothes off is a documentary. —JULIA ROBERTS

OBEDIENCE
(also see concepts 54, 147, 311, 470, 583, 675)

Those who know the least obey the best. —GEORGE FARQUHAR

It is right that what is just should be obeyed; it is necessary that what is strongest should be obeyed. —BLAISE PASCAL

Every good servant does not all commands. —WILLIAM SHAKESPEARE

It is much safer to obey than to rule. —THOMAS Á KEMPIS

OBLIGATION

(also see concepts 129, 187, 227, 326, 574, 676, 794)

Just because you like my stuff doesn't mean I owe you anything.
——BOB DYLAN

There are minds so impatient of inferiority, that their gratitude is a species of revenge, and they return benefits, not because recompense is a pleasure, but because obligation is a pain. ——SAMUEL JOHNSON

It is the nature of men to be bound by the benefits they confer as much as by those they receive. ——NICCOLO MACHIAVELLI

Possession without obligation to the object possessed approaches felicity. ——GEORGE MEREDITH

OBSCURITY

(also see concepts 117, 148, 271, 622, 706, 833)

Obscurity often brings safety. ——AESOP

How can one not speak about war, poverty, and inequality when people who suffer from these afflictions don't have a voice to speak? ——ISABEL ALLENDE

Where misunderstanding serves others as an advantage, one is helpless to make oneself understood. ——LIONEL TRILLING

Obscurity and a competence–that is the life that is best worth living.
——MARK TWAIN

It is better to be looked over than overlooked. ——MAE WEST

OBSERVATION

(also see concepts 91, 261, 265, 577, 581, 739, 845)

Observation is an old man's memory. ——JONATHAN SWIFT

OLD AGE

(also see concepts 24, 454, 455, 463, 497, 678, 877)

Old folks are the nation. —TONI CADE BAMBARA

Old age is life's parody. —SIMONE DE BEAUVOIR

Perhaps one has to be very old before one learns to be amused rather than shocked. —PEARL S. BUCK

You can't help getting older but you don't have to get old. —GEORGE BURNS

Every time I think that I'm getting old, and gradually going to the grave, something else happens. —LILLIAN CARTER

The heart never grows better by age; I fear rather worse, always harder. —EARL OF CHESTERFIELD

One keeps forgetting old age up to the very brink of the grave. —COLETTE

By the time we've made it, we've had it. —MALCOLM FORBES

Old age is a shipwreck. —CHARLES DE GAULLE

Time goes by: reputation increases, ability declines. —DAG HAMMARSKJÖLD

When grace is joined with wrinkles, it is adorable. There is an unspeakable dawn in happy old age. —VICTOR HUGO

I look forward to growing old and wise and audacious. —GLENDA JACKSON

I'm like old wine. They don't bring me out very often, but I'm well preserved. —ROSE KENNEDY

Few people know how to be old. —FRANÇOIS DE LA ROCHEFOUCAULD

Old age is like a plane flying through a storm. Once you're aboard, there's nothing you can do. —GOLDA MEIR

Age imprints more wrinkles in the mind than it does on the face. —MICHEL DE MONTAIGNE

Growing old is like being increasingly penalized for a crime you haven't committed. —ANTHONY POWELL

Age seldom arrives smoothly or quickly. It's more often a succession of jerks. —JEAN RHYS

The old woman I will become will be quite different from the woman I am now. Another "I" is beginning, and so far I have not had to complain of her. —GEORGE SAND

Old age is not an illness, it is a timeless ascent. As power diminishes, we grow towards the light. —MAY SARTON

Time and trouble will tame an advanced young woman, but an advanced old woman is uncontrollable by any earthly force. —DOROTHY SAYERS

I wasted time, and now doth time waste me. —WILLIAM SHAKESPEARE

One of the most disconcerting aspects of old age is that we usually haven't the vaguest notion of when it will end, or how. —PAGE SMITH

I shall not grow conservative with age. —ELIZABETH CADY STANTON

It must become a right of every person to die of old age. And if we secure this right for ourselves we can, coincidentally, assure it for the planet. —ALICE WALKER

The older one grows, the more one likes indecency. —VIRGINIA WOOLF

OPEN-MINDEDNESS
(also see concepts 117, 123, 220, 411, 809)

You must learn day by day, year by year, to broaden your horizon. The more things you love, the more you are interested in, the more you enjoy, the more you are indignant about–the more you have left when anything happens. —ETHEL BARRYMORE

The only means of strengthening one's intellect is to make up one's mind about nothing–to let the mind be a thoroughfare for all thoughts. —JOHN KEATS

Where there is an open mind, there will always be a frontier.
——CHARLES F. KETTERING

The beautiful souls are they that are universal, open, and ready for all things. ——MICHEL DE MONTAIGNE

OPERA

(also see concepts 524, 543, 745)

Nothing is capable of being well set to music that is not nonsense.
——JOSEPH ADDISON

No good opera plot can be sensible, for people do not sing when they are feeling sensible. ——W. H. AUDEN

People are wrong when they say the opera isn't what it used to be. That's what's wrong with it. ——NÖEL COWARD

Opera in English, is, in the main, just about as sensible as baseball in Italian. ——H. L. MENCKEN

An unalterable and unquestioned law of the musical world required that the German text of French operas sung by Swedish artists should be translated into Italian for the clearer understanding of English-speaking audiences. ——EDITH WHARTON

OPINIONS

(also see concepts 67, 107, 171, 172, 189, 220, 435, 674)

Opinions differ most when there is least scientific warrant for having any. ——DAISY BATES

Men get opinions as boys learn to spell, / By reiteration chiefly.
——ELIZABETH BARRETT BROWNING

We credit scarcely any persons with good sense except those who are of our opinion. ——FRANÇOIS DE LA ROCHEFOUCAULD

Refusing to have an opinion is a way of having one, isn't it?
——LUIGI PIRANDELLO

I agree with no man's opinion. I have some of my own.
——IVAN TURGENEV

It were not best that we should all think alike; it is difference of opinion that makes the horse races. ——MARK TWAIN

It is just when opinions universally prevail and we have added lip service to their authority that we become sometimes most keenly conscious that we do not believe a word that we are saying.
——VIRGINIA WOOLF

OPPORTUNITY

(also see concepts 97, 112, 471, 808)

Why not seize the pleasure at once? How often is happiness destroyed by preparation, foolish preparation! ——JANE AUSTEN

Too often, the opportunity knocks, but by the time you push back the chain, push back the bolt, unhook the two locks and shut off the burglar alarm, it's too late. ——RITA COOLIDGE

Plough deep while sluggards sleep. ——BENJAMIN FRANKLIN

When the doors of opportunity swing open, we must make sure that we are not too drunk or too indifferent to walk through.
——JESSE JACKSON

Opportunities are usually diguised as hard work, so most people don't recognize them. ——ANN LANDERS

There is no security on this earth; there is only opportunity.
——DOUGLAS MACARTHUR

I make the most of all that comes and the least of all that goes.
——SARA TEASDALE

Never miss a chance to have sex or appear on television.
——GORE VIDAL

Arrange whatever pieces come your way. ——VIRGINIA WOOLF

OPPOSITION

(also see concepts 161, 205, 206, 414, 494, 502, 773, 821)

No government can be long secure without formidable opposition.
——BENJAMIN DISRAELI

I respect only those who resist me, but I cannot tolerate them.
——CHARLES DE GAULLE

One fifth of the people are against everything all the time.
——ROBERT F. KENNEDY

...I have spent many years of my life in opposition and I rather like the role. ——ELEANOR ROOSEVELT

OPPRESSION

(also see concepts 206, 773, 821)

The most potent weapon in the hands of the oppressor is the mind of the oppressed. ——STEVEN BIKO

A poorly extinguished fire is quickly re-ignited. ——PIERRE CORNEILLE

People can be slave-ships in shoes. ——ZORA NEALE HURSTON

Trying to help an oppressed person is like trying to put your arm around somebody with a sunburn. ——FLORYNCE KENNEDY

The history of an oppressed people is hidden in the lies and the agreed-upon myth of its conquerors. ——MERIDEL LE SUEUR

If you're going to hold someone down you're going to have to hold on by the other end of the chain. You are confined by your own repression. ——TONI MORRISON

This is a world that cages all warblers with a beautiful voice.
——NOMURA MOTONI

Among those who dislike oppression are many who like to oppress.
——NAPOLEON I

If you want a picture of the future, imagine a boot stamping on a human face–for ever. ——GEORGE ORWELL

To pardon the oppressor is to deal harshly with the oppressed.
—SA'DI

OPTIMISM

(also see concepts 237, 357, 584)

Let other pens dwell on guilt and misery. —JANE AUSTEN

My sun sets to rise again. —ROBERT BROWNING

The place where optimism most flourishes is the lunatic asylum.
—HAVELOCK ELLIS

Optimism is the content of small men in high places.
—F. SCOTT FITZGERALD

If I didn't have spiritual faith, I would be a pessimist. But I'm an
optimist. I've read the last page in the Bible. It's all going to turn
out all right. —BILLY GRAHAM

We are all in the gutter, but some of us are looking at the stars.
—OSCAR WILDE

OPTIMISM AND PESSIMISM

(also see concepts 237, 559, 584)

The pessimist is the man who believes things couldn't possibly be
worse, to which the optimist replies, "Oh yes they could."
—VLADIMIR BUKOVSKY

The optimist proclaims that we live in the best of all possible
worlds; and the pessimist fears this is true. —JAMES BRANCH CABELL

The man who is a pessimist before forty-eight knows too much; if
he is an optimist after it, he knows too little. —MARK TWAIN

ORDER

(also see concepts 120, 130, 575, 591, 596, 614, 654)

Some people like to make a little garden out of life and walk down
a path. —JEAN ANOUILH

A place for everything and everything in its place.
—ISABELLA MARY BEETON

Good order is the foundation of all things. —EDMUND BURKE

Order marches with weighty and measured strides; disorder is always in a hurry. —NAPOLEON I

Order is heaven's first law. —ALEXANDER POPE

ORIGINALITY
(also see concepts 169, 212, 420, 538, 590)

An original writer is not one who imitates nobody, but one whom nobody can imitate. —VICOMTE DE CHATEAUBRIAND

Everything has been thought of before, but the problem is to think of it again. —JOHANN WOLFGANG VON GOETHE

Originality is undetected plagiarism. —WILLIAM RALPH INGE

Originality is the one thing which unoriginal minds cannot feel the use of. —JOHN STUART MILL

Who is original? Everything that we are doing, everything that we think, exists already, and we are only intermediaries, that's all, who make use of what is in the air. —HENRY MILLER

Nothing is said now that has not been said before. —TERENCE

Another unsettling element in modern art is that common symptom of immaturity, the dread of doing what has been done before. —EDITH WHARTON

OTHERS
(also see concepts 294, 368, 576)

Just as much as we see in others we have in ourselves.
—WILLIAM HAZLITT

We are never the same with others as when we are alone; we are different, even, when we are in the dark with them.
—MAURICE MAETERLINCK

Other people are quite dreadful. The only possible society is one's self. —OSCAR WILDE

PAIN
(also see concepts 237, 481, 693, 710, 725, 757, 779)

Who, except the gods, / can live time through forever without any pain? —AESCHYLUS

The greatest evil is physical pain. —ST. AUGUSTINE OF HIPPO

There is no point in being overwhelmed by the appalling total of human suffering; such a total does not exist. Neither poverty nor pain is accumulable. —JORGE LUIS BORGES

Pain and death are a part of life. To reject them is to reject life itself. —HAVELOCK ELLIS

The most frustrating thing about unwelcome and chronic pain is its mandate to revise your life. Revision marks a measure of acceptance. —CAROLYN HARDESTY

Even pain / Pricks to livelier living. —AMY LOWELL

When there is pain, there are no words; all pain is the same. —TONI MORRISON

Pain of mind is worse than pain of body. —PUBLILIUS SYRUS

If pain could have cured us we should long ago have been saved. —GEORGE SANTAYANA

Pleasure is nothing else but the intermission of pain. —JOHN SELDEN

Remember that pain has this most excellent quality: if prolonged, it cannot be severe, and if severe it cannot be prolonged. —SENECA

PAINTERS AND PAINTING
(also see concepts 46, 48, 90, 266)

Good painters imitate nature, bad ones spew it up. —MIGUEL DE CERVANTES

The day is coming when a single carrot, freshly observed, will set off a revolution. —PAUL CÉZANNE

Each painting insists that the eye that's awake in all this sleep of attention is the artist's, making a basic definition, sweetly obvious but extraordinarily important, of what a painting is in the most archaic meaning of image, the seen. —GUY DAVENPORT

I don't much enjoy looking at paintings in general. I know too much about them. I take them apart. —GEORGIA O'KEEFFE

How vain painting is—we admire the realistic depiction of objects which in their original state we don't admire at all. —BLAISE PASCAL

I paint objects as I think them, not as I see them. —PABLO PICASSO

For me, painting is a way to forget life. It is a cry in the night, a strangled laugh. —GEORGES ROUAULT

Every time I paint a portrait I lose a friend. —JOHN SINGER SARGENT

Every portrait that is painted with feeling is a portrait of the artist, not of the sitter. —OSCAR WILDE

PARENTS AND PARENTHOOD
(also see concepts 106, 211, 273, 280, 518, 666, 667)

We are the buffoons of our children. —PIETRO ARETINO

You have to love your children unselfishly. That's hard. But it's the only way. —BARBARA BUSH

Parents are the last people on earth who ought to have children. —SAMUEL BUTLER

Parents are not quite interested in justice, they are interested in quiet. —BILL COSBY

If you have never been hated by your child, you have never been a parent. —BETTE DAVIS

To nourish children and raise them against odds is in any time, any place, more valuable than to fix bolts in cars or design nuclear weapons. —MARILYN FRENCH

Where parents do too much for their children, the children will not do much for themselves. —ELBERT HUBBARD

The most ferocious animals are disarmed by caresses to their young. —VICTOR HUGO

Before we can leave our parents, they stuff our heads like the suitcases which they jam-pack with homemade underwear. —MAXINE HONG KINGSTON

In order to influence a child, one must be careful not to be that child's parent or grandparent. —DON MARQUIS

Parents are sometimes a bit of a disappointment to their children. They don't fulfil the promise of their early years. —ANTHONY POWELL

Making the decision to have a child–it's momentous. It is to decide forever to have your heart go walking around outside your body. —ELIZABETH STONE

Parents are the bones on which children sharpen their teeth. —PETER USTINOV

PARIS
(also see concepts 113, 296)

The cafe of Europe. —FERDINANDO GALIANI

If you are lucky enough to have lived in Paris as a young man, then wherever you go for the rest of your life, it stays with you, for Paris is a moveable feast. —ERNEST HEMINGWAY

To err is human. To loaf is Parisian. —VICTOR HUGO

When Paris sneezes, Europe catches cold. —PRINCE METTERNICH

As an artist, a man has no home in Europe save in Paris. —FRIEDRICH WILHELM NIETZSCHE

PARTIES

(also see concepts 33, 598)

The sooner every party breaks up the better. —JANE AUSTEN

Nothing spoils a good party like a genius. —ELSA MAXWELL

I love such mirth as does not make friends ashamed to look upon one another next morning. —IZAAK WALTON

PARTING

(also see concepts 3, 9, 465, 678)

It is never any good dwelling on goodbyes. It is not the being together that it prolongs, it is the parting. —ELIZABETH BIBESCO

Parting is all we know of heaven, / And all we need of hell. —EMILY DICKINSON

Ever has it been that love knows not its own depth until the hour of separation. —KAHLIL GIBRAN

The return makes one love the farewell. —ALFRED DE MUSSET

Every parting gives a foretaste of death, every reunion a hint of the resurrection. —ARTHUR SCHOPENHAUER

PASSION

(also see concepts 237, 242, 472, 564, 726, 798, 878, 880)

We are minor in everything but our passions. —ELIZABETH BOWEN

Nothing great in the world has been accomplished without passion. —GEORG WILHELM FRIEDRICH HEGEL

A man who has not passed through the inferno of his passions has never overcome them. —CARL JUNG

It is with our passions as it is with fire and water–they are good servants, but bad masters. —ROGER L'ESTRANGE

A man that is ashamed of passions that are natural and reasonable, is generally proud of those that are shameful and silly.
—MARY WORTLEY MONTAGU

We must act out passion before we can feel it. —JEAN-PAUL SARTRE

The only sin passion can commit is to be joyless.
—DOROTHY SAYERS

THE PAST

(also see concepts 35, 245, 304, 348, 615, 807, 813)

Even God cannot change the past. —AGATHON

It is not I that belong to the past, but the past that belongs to me.
—MARY ANTIN

I love my past. I love my present. I'm not ashamed of what I've had, and I'm not sad because I have it no longer. —COLETTE

We have to do with the past only as we can make it useful to the present and the future. —FREDERICK DOUGLASS

Time and words can't be recalled. —THOMAS FULLER

In the carriages of the past you can't go anywhere. —MAXIM GORKY

They spend their time mostly looking forward to the past.
—JOHN OSBORNE

The next day is never so good as the day before. —PUBLILIUS SYRUS

I tell you the past is a bucket of ashes. —CARL SANDBURG

Look back, and smile at perils past. —WALTER SCOTT

We have seen better days. —WILLIAM SHAKESPEARE

The past is the only dead thing that smells sweet. —EDWARD THOMAS

The past is only the present become invisible and mute; and because it is invisible and mute, its memoried glances and its murmurs are infinitely precious. We are tomorrow's past.
—MARY WEBB

The past, at least, is secure. —DANIEL WEBSTER

The destruction of the past is perhaps the greatest of all crime.
——SIMONE WEIL

PATIENCE
(also see concepts 77, 86, 508, 709, 809)

Beware the fury of a patient man. ——JOHN DRYDEN

They also serve who only stand and wait. ——JOHN MILTON

Patience, and the mulberry leaf becomes a silk gown.
——CHINESE PROVERB

Rome was not built in a day. ——PROVERB

Though patience be a tired mare, yet she will plod.
——WILLIAM SHAKESPEARE

I'm extraordinarily patient provided I get my own way in the end.
——MARGARET THATCHER

Patience is the art of hoping. ——MARQUIS DE VAUVENARGUES

PATRIOTISM
(also see concepts 287, 353, 528)

It is a sweet and seemly thing to die for one's country. ——HORACE

I think patriotism is like charity–it begins at home. ——HENRY JAMES

Patriotism is the last refuge of a scoundrel. ——SAMUEL JOHNSON

You're not supposed to be so blind with patriotism that you can't
face reality. Wrong is wrong, no matter who does it or who says it.
——MALCOLM X

Who saves his country violates no law. ——NAPOLEON I

Patriotism is often an arbitrary veneration of real estate above
principles. ——GEORGE JEAN NATHAN

PAYMENT

(also see concepts 187, 512, 549, 676, 682, 794)

Alas! How deeply painful is all payment! —LORD BYRON

Recompense injury with justice, and recompense kindness with kindness. —CONFUCIUS

Nothing is to be had for nothing. —EPICTETUS

It doesn't pay well to fight for what we believe in.
—LILLIAN HELLMAN

It is by not paying one's bills that one can hope to live in the memory of the commercial classes. —OSCAR WILDE

PEACE

(also see concepts 86, 143, 159, 240, 248, 337, 415, 545, 561, 677, 850, 851)

He knows peace who has forgotten desire. —BHAGAVADGITA, CH. 2

Don't tell me peace has broken out. —BERTOLT BRECHT

What all men are really after is some form, or perhaps only some formula, of peace. —JOSEPH CONRAD

Mankind has grown strong in eternal struggles and it will only perish through eternal peace. —ADOLF HITLER

Please, we can get along here. —RODNEY KING

When we say "War is over if you want it," we mean that if everyone demanded peace instead of another TV set, we'd have peace. —JOHN LENNON

Peace is indivisible. —MAXIM LITVINOV

Inner peace and outer peace are synonymous in the sense that without one, the other wouldn't happen. —YOKO ONO

The peace dividend is peace. —DAN QUAYLE

Peace is when time doesn't matter as it passes by. —MARIA SCHELL

Peace is the one condition of survival in this nuclear age.
——ADLAI STEVENSON

Peace has to be created in order to be maintained. It is the product of Faith, Strength, Energy, Will, Sympathy, Justice, Imagination and the triumph of principle. It will never be achieved by passivity and quietism. Passivity and quietism are invitations to war.
——DOROTHY THOMPSON

Only a peace between equals can last. ——WOODROW WILSON

PEOPLE
(also see concepts 134, 135, 173, 364, 368, 563, 602, 650)

I've been with the best and the worst in my life, and the secret is they're all people. ——HELEN DRAZENOVICH BERKLICH

Everything's designed for us to learn about people–about ourselves –better. And we understand that we, as a human race, will always try to find out how different people act or how they look or how they feel, in order for us to realize that we are all the same. ——CHUCK D.

The people are to be taken in very small doses.
——RALPH WALDO EMERSON

Remember that you are all people and that all people are you.
——JOY HARJO

There is not a more mean, stupid, dastardly, pitiful, selfish, spiteful, envious, ungrateful animal than the public. It is the greatest of cowards, for it is afraid of itself. ——WILLIAM HAZLITT

The people long eagerly for just two things–bread and circuses.
——JUVENAL

We hold the view that the people make the best judgment in the long run. ——JOHN F. KENNEDY

The people, and the people alone, are the motive force in the making of world history. ——MAO TSE-TUNG

The mind of the people is like mud, from which arise strange and beautiful things. ——W. J. TURNER

The public is a ferocious beast: one must either chain it up or flee from it. —VOLTAIRE

PERCEPTION
(also see concepts 265, 435, 551, 739, 824)

If the doors of perception were cleansed everything would appear to man as it is, infinite. —WILLIAM BLAKE

No object is mysterious. The mystery is your eye.
—ELIZABETH BOWEN

PERFECTION
(also see concepts 253, 375, 783)

Perfection has one grave defect: it is apt to be dull.
—W. SOMERSET MAUGHAM

The essence of being human is that one does not seek perfection.
—GEORGE ORWELL

All excellent things are as difficult as they are rare.
—BENEDICT SPINOZA

So much perfection argues rottenness somewhere.
—BEATRICE WEBB

PERSEVERANCE
(also see concepts 8, 155, 202, 671, 674, 774, 787, 860)

The best way out is always through. —ROBERT FROST

They told me to fix my teeth, change my nose, even get out of the business. But I stayed, and learned and didn't give up.
—LAUREN HUTTON

Though I have no productive worth, I have a certain value as an indestructible quantity. —ALICE JAMES

Hard times ain't quit and we ain't quit. —MERIDEL LE SUEUR

Somehow life doesn't always pay off to those who are most insistent. —MAX LERNER

Many strokes overthrow the tallest oaks. —JOHN LYLY

When you put your hand to the plow, you can't put it down until you get to the end of the row. —ALICE PAUL

Never say die. —PROVERB

The darkest hour is just before the dawn. —PROVERB

An ox at the roadside, when it is dying of hunger and thirst, does not lie down; it walks up and down–up and down, seeking it knows not what–but it does not lie down. —OLIVE SCHREINER

I am a kind of burr; I shall stick. —WILLIAM SHAKESPEARE

PERSONALITY
(also see concepts 45, 100, 102, 330, 364, 377, 384, 708)

She defiled the very meaning of personality in her passion to be a person; somewhere about her was the tension of the accident that made the beast the human endeavor. —DJUNA BARNES

There are two kinds of people in the world–those who walk into a room and say, "There you are"–and those who say, "Here I am!"
—ABIGAIL VAN BUREN

PERSPECTIVE
(also see concepts 551, 577)

Distance has the same effect on the mind as on the eye.
—SAMUEL JOHNSON

Every man takes the limits of his own field of vision for the limits of the world. —ARTHUR SCHOPENHAUER

Everything must be taken seriously, nothing tragically.
—LOUIS ALDOLPHE THIERS

PERSUASION

(also see concepts 19, 43, 236, 400, 627, 637, 639)

Would you persuade, speak of interest, not of reason.
——BENJAMIN FRANKLIN

The persuasion of a friend is a strong thing. ——HOMER

There are two levers for moving men–interest and fear.
——NAPOLEON I

PERVERSITY

(also see concepts 401, 507, 693, 774)

We trifle with, make sport of, and despise those who are attached
to us, and follow those that fly from us. ——WILLIAM HAZLITT

Few people want the pleasures they are free to take. ——OVID

PESSIMISM

(also see concepts 181, 237, 559, 560)

He that hopes no good fears no ill. ——THOMAS FULLER

We all agree that pessimism is a mark of superior intellect.
——JOHN KENNETH GALBRAITH

Sleep is good, death is better; but of course, the best thing would
be never to have been born at all. ——HEINRICH HEINE

Nothing makes me more pessimistic than the obligation not to be
pessimistic. ——EUGÉNE IONESCO

No pessimist ever discovered the secrets of the stars, or sailed to an
uncharted land, or opened a new heaven to the human spirit.
——HELEN KELLER

Pessimism is as American as apple pie–frozen apple pie with a
slice of processed cheese. ——GEORGE F. WILL

PHILOSOPHERS   AND   PHILOSOPHY

(also see concepts 26, 30, 34, 52, 90, 257, 258, 366, 376, 410, 559, 560, 771, 879)

All are lunatics, but he who can analyze his delusion is called a philosopher. —AMBROSE BIERCE

There is nothing so strange and so unbelievable that it has not been said by one philosopher or another. —RENÉ DESCARTES

The philosophers have only interpreted the world in various ways; the point is to change it. —KARL MARX

Every philosophy is the philosophy of some stage of life. —FRIEDRICH WILHELM NIETZSCHE

In other words, apart from the known and the unknown, what else is there? —HAROLD PINTER

Philosophy is the product of wonder. —ALFRED NORTH WHITEHEAD

Philosophy is not a theory but an activity. —LUDWIG WITTGENSTEIN

PHOTOGRAPHY

(also see concepts 521, 603)

Photography can never grow up if it imitates some other medium. It has to walk alone; it has to be itself. —BERENICE ABBOTT

A photograph is a secret about a secret; the more it tells you the less you know. —DIANE ARBUS

It takes a lot of imagination to be a good photographer. You need less imagination to be a painter, because you can invent things. But in photography everything is so ordinary; it takes a lot of looking before you learn to see the ordinary. —DAVID BAILEY

The Photograph does not call up the past....The effect it produces upon me is not to restore what has been abolished (by time, by distance) but to attest that what I see has indeed existed. —ROLAND BARTHES

...cameras, in short, were clocks for seeing, and perhaps in me someone very old still hears in the photographic mechanism the living sound of the wood. —ROLAND BARTHES

While there is perhaps a province in which the photograph can tell us nothing more than what we see with our own eyes, there is another in which it proves to us how little our eyes permit us to see. —DOROTHEA LANGE

The camera is an instrument of detection. We photograph not only what we know, but also what we don't know. —LISETTE MODEL

Personally, I like my photography straight, unmanipulated, devoid of all tricks; a print not looking like anything but a photograph, living through its own inherent qualities and revealing its own spirit. —ALFRED STIEGLITZ

PIETY
(also see concepts 237, 374, 515, 612)

Love of God is not always the same as love of good. —HERMANN HESSE

Piety is the tinfoil of pretense. —ELBERT HUBBARD

Nothing is more repulsive than a furtively prurient spirituality; it is just as unsavoury as gross sensuality. —CARL JUNG

Experience makes us see an enormous difference between piety and goodness. —BLAISE PASCAL

PITY
(also see concepts 237, 495, 790)

A tear dries quickly, especially when it is shed for the troubles of others. —CICERO

Compassion for the friend should conceal itself under a hard shell. —FRIEDRICH WILHELM NIETZSCHE

Pity is treason. —MAXIMILIEN ROBESPIERRE

What value has compassion that does not take its object in its arms?
——ANTOINE DE SAINT-EXUPÉRY

PLACES

(also see concepts 105, 113, 536, 537, 759, 777)

One always begins to forgive a place as soon as it's left behind.
——CHARLES DICKENS

PLAGIARISM

(also see concepts 562, 769)

About the most originality that any writer can hope to achieve honestly is to steal with good judgment. ——JOSH BILLINGS

They lard their lean books with the fat of others' work.
——ROBERT BURTON

The Eighth Commandment was not made for bards.
——SAMUEL TAYLOR COLERIDGE

Nothing is new except arrangement. ——WILL DURANT

I pinch. ——LAWRENCE DURRELL

Good swiping is an art in itself. ——JULES FEIFFER

When a thing has been said and said well, have no scruple. Take it and copy it. ——ANATOLE FRANCE

Begin with another's to end with your own. ——BALTASAR GRACIÁN

For such kind of borrowing as this, if it be not bettered by the borrower, among good authors it is accounted plagiary.
——JOHN MILTON

Immature artists imitate. Mature artists steal. ——LIONEL TRILLING

PLANS

(also see concepts 130, 224, 496, 561, 647)

It is a mistake to look too far ahead. Only one link in the chain of destiny can be handled at a time. —WINSTON CHURCHILL

Do not plan for ventures before finishing what's at hand. —EURIPIDES

We must ask where we are and whither we are tending.
—ABRAHAM LINCOLN

It is a bad plan that admits of no modification. —PUBLILIUS SYRUS

Our plans miscarry because they have no aim. When a man does not know what harbor he is making for, no wind is the right wind.
—SENECA

PLAY

(also see concepts 33, 593, 764, 801)

Play is the exultation of the possible. —MARTIN BUBER

It should be noted that children's games are not merely games; one should regard them as their most serious activities.
—MICHEL DE MONTAIGNE

In our play we reveal what kind of people we are. —OVID

PLEASURE

(also see concepts 102, 104, 182, 237, 337, 433, 442, 592, 619)

One half of the world cannot understand the pleasures of the other.
—JANE AUSTEN

Draw your pleasure–paint your pleasure–express your pleasure strongly. —PIERRE BONNARD

Pleasure is none, if not diversified. —JOHN DONNE

You wear yourself out in the pursuit of wealth or love or freedom, you do everything to gain some right, and once it is gained, you take no pleasure in it. —ORIANA FALLACI

No man is a hypocrite in his pleasures. —SAMUEL JOHNSON

Waiting for one's pleasures is tiresome work. —PETRONIUS

People have many different kinds of pleasure. The real one is that for which they will forsake the others. —MARCEL PROUST

Marred pleasure's best, shadow makes the sun strong.
—STEVIE SMITH

Everyone is dragged on by their favourite pleasure. —VIRGIL

There is a pleasure in not being pleased. —VOLTAIRE

All the things I really like to do are either immoral, illegal, or fattening. —ALEXANDER WOOLLCOTT

POETRY AND POETS

(also see concepts 90, 236, 514, 595, 745, 761)

A verbal art like poetry is reflective. Music is immediate, it goes on to become. —W. H. AUDEN

Poetry makes nothing happen: it survives / In the valley of its saying. —W. H. AUDEN

The poet is like the prince of the clouds, who rides the tempest and scorns the archer. Exiled on the ground, amidst boos and insults, his giant's wings prevent his walking. —CHARLES BAUDELAIRE

Poets have to dream, and dreaming in America is no cinch.
—SAUL BELLOW

Poetry is life distilled. —GWENDOLYN BROOKS

A true poet does not bother to be poetical. Nor does a nursery gardener scent his roses. —JEAN COCTEAU

To a poet, silence is an acceptable response, even a flattering one.
—COLETTE

If I feel physically as if the top of my head were taken off, I know that is poetry. —EMILY DICKINSON

All one's inventions are true, you can be sure of that. Poetry is as exact a science as geometry. —GUSTAVE FLAUBERT

We all write poems; it is simply that poets are the ones who write in words. —JOHN FOWLES

Poets die in different ways: most of them do not die into the grave, but into business or criticism. —ROBERT FROST

There's no money in poetry, but there's no poetry in money either. —ROBERT GRAVES

In one sense the efficacy of poetry is nil—no lyric has ever stopped a tank. In another sense, it is unlimited. It is like writing in the sand in the face of which accusers and accused are left speechless. —SEAMUS HEANEY

...no verse can give pleasure for long, nor last, that is written by drinkers of water. —HORACE

A good poet's made as well as born. —BEN JONSON

A poet is not a public figure. A poet should be read and not seen. —C. DAY LEWIS

Poetry is what Milton saw when he went blind. —DON MARQUIS

The courage of the poet is to keep ajar the door that leads into madness. —CHRISTOPHER MORLEY

There is no advice to give young poets. —PABLO NERUDA

Poetry is adolescence fermented, and thus preserved. —JOSÉ ORTEGA Y GASSET

Twentieth-century poetry has become garrulous. We are drowning not in a sea but in a swamp of words. We have forgotten that poetry is not in what words say but in what is said between them, that which appears fleetingly in pauses and silences. In the poetry workshops of universities there should be a required course for young poets: learning to be silent. —OCTAVIO PAZ

The blood jet is poetry / There is no stopping it. —SYLVIA PLATH

A beautiful line of verse has twelve feet, and two wings. —JULES RENARD

It is a perfectly possible means of overcoming chaos.
——I. A. RICHARDS

Poetry is the achievement of the synthesis of hyacinths and biscuits. ——CARL SANDBURG

I've written some poetry I don't understand myself.
——CARL SANDBURG

It's a little mad, but I believe I am many people. When I am writing a poem, I feel I am the person who should have written it.
——ANNE SEXTON

Poets are the unacknowledged legislators of the world.
——PERCY BYSSHE SHELLEY

Poetry is an orphan of silence. The words never quite equal the experience behind them. ——CHARLES SIMIC

The poet speaks to all men of that other life of theirs that they have smothered and forgotten. ——EDITH SITWELL

The poet is the priest of the invisible. ——WALLACE STEVENS

Poetry. I like to think of it as statements made on the way to the grave. ——DYLAN THOMAS

Poetry is trouble dunked in tears. ——GWYN THOMAS

Poets have to learn karate, these days. ——YEVGENY YEVTUSHENKO

POETRY AND PROSE
(also see concepts 46, 594, 640, 868)

Prose—words in their best order; poetry—the best words in their best order. ——SAMUEL TAYLOR COLERIDGE

The poet gives us his essence, but prose takes the mould of the body and mind entire. ——VIRGINIA WOOLF

THE POLICE
(also see concepts 54, 170, 621)

I have never seen a situation so dismal that a policeman couldn't make it worse. —BRENDAN BEHAN

For the middle class, the police protect property, give directions, and help old ladies. For the urban poor, the police are those who arrest you. —MICHAEL HARRINGTON

Every society gets the kind of criminal it deserves. What is equally true is that every community gets the kind of law enforcement it insists on. —ROBERT F. KENNEDY

With their souls of patent leather they come down the road. Hunched and nocturnal, where they breathe they impose silence of dark rubber and fear of fine sand. —FEDERICO GARCÍA LORCA

One always has the air of someone who is lying when one speaks to a policeman. —CHARLES-LOUIS PHILIPPE

POLITENESS
(also see concepts 478, 689)

If a man be gracious and courteous to strangers, it shows he is a citizen of the world. —FRANCIS BACON

Politeness is only one half good manners and the other half good lying. —MARY WILSON LITTLE

Civility costs nothing. —PROVERB

POLITICAL PARTIES
(also see concepts 149, 568, 599)

All political parties die at last swallowing their own lies.
—JOHN ARBUTHNOT

He serves his party best who serves the country best.
—RUTHERFORD B. HAYES

Any party which takes credit for the rain must not be surprised if its opponents blame it for the drought. —DWIGHT W. MORROW

The more you read about politics, you got to admit that each party is worse than the other. —WILL ROGERS

POLITICIANS AND POLITICS

(also see concepts 90, 91, 149, 378, 450, 568, 598, 636, 638)

Politics, as a practice, whatever its professions, has always been the systematic organization of hatreds. —HENRY BROOKS ADAMS

Man is by nature a political animal. —ARISTOTLE

Politics are usually the executive expression of human immaturity. —VERA BRITTAIN

It is dangerous for a national candidate to say things that people might remember. —DAVID BRODER

U.S. politics is a beautiful fraud that has been imposed on the people for years, whose practitioners exchange gelded promises for the most valuable thing their victims own, their votes. —SHIRLEY CHISHOLM

Politics are almost as exciting as war, and quite dangerous. In war, you can only be killed once, but in politics many times. —WINSTON CHURCHILL

Women are on the outside when the door to the smoke-filled room is closed. —MILLICENT FENWICK

There are times in politics when you must be on the right side and lose. —JOHN KENNETH GALBRAITH

Politics consists of choosing between the disastrous and the unpalatable. —JOHN KENNETH GALBRAITH

...there is a greater awareness now that the countries and people of the East, the West, the North and the South–however different their social systems and levels of development, and however dissimilar their cultures, beliefs and ideologies–are part of a single world and have basic, vital interests in common. These elements of unity and

this new self-awareness form the foundation on which modern world politics should be built. And this is already happening.
—MIKHAIL GORBACHEV

It is not true that only coldhearted, cynical, arrogant, haughty or brawling persons can succeed in politics. Such people are naturally attracted by politics. In the end, however, politeness and good manners weigh more. —VÁCLAV HAVEL

The essential thing is the formation of the political will of the nation: that is the starting point for political action. —ADOLF HITLER

Politics are now nothing more than a means of rising in the world.
—SAMUEL JOHNSON

Political action is the highest responsibility of a citizen.
—JOHN F. KENNEDY

This is gastric juices churning. This is enzymes and acids, this is intestinal is what this is, bowel movement and blood-red meat–this stinks, this is politics, the game of being alive. —TONY KUSHNER

The politicians were talking themselves red, white and blue in the face. —CLARE BOOTHE LUCE

The political alternatives in America now are like putting a Band-Aid on cancer. —SHIRLEY MACLAINE

When you're abroad you're a statesman; when you're at home you're just a politician. —HAROLD MACMILLAN

Political power grows out of the barrel of a gun. —MAO TSE-TUNG

It is very unfair to expect a politician to live in private up to the statements he makes in public. —W. SOMERSET MAUGHAM

In our time, political speech and writing are largely the defense of the indefensible. —GEORGE ORWELL

If you can't stand a little sacrifice and you can't stand a trip across the desert with limited water, we're never going to straighten this country out. —ROSS PEROT

I used to say that politics was the second lowest profession and I have come to know that it bears a great similarity to the first. —RONALD REAGAN

Ninety-eight percent of the adults in this country are decent, hard-working, honest Americans. It's the other lousy two percent that get all the publicity. But then–we elected them. —LILY TOMLIN

Prosperity is necessarily the first theme of a political campaign. —WOODROW WILSON

POLLUTION
(also see concepts 120, 230)

No witchcraft, no enemy action had silenced the rebirth of new life in this stricken world. The people had done it themselves. —RACHEL CARSON

The most important pathological effects of pollution are extremely delayed and indirect. —RENÉ DUBOS

Pollution is nothing but the resources we are not harvesting. We allow them to disperse because we've been ignorant of their value. —BUCKMINSTER FULLER

Sanctions against polluters are feeble and out of date, and, in any case, are rarely invoked. —RALPH NADER

POPULARITY
(also see concept 672)

Popularity? Three-penny fame. —VICTOR HUGO

We're more popular than Jesus Christ now. I don't know which will go first, rock and roll or Christianity. —JOHN LENNON

Avoid popularity if you would have peace. —ABRAHAM LINCOLN

The more one pleases everybody, the less one pleases profoundly. —STENDHAL

POPULATION
(also see concepts 134, 576)

Babies are the enemies of the human race. —ISAAC ASIMOV

We have come to a turning point in the human habitation of the earth. —BARRY COMMONER

The command Be fruitful and multiply [was] promulgated, according to our authorities, when the population of the world consisted of two persons. —WILLIAM RALPH INGE

Instead of needing lots of children, we need high-quality children. —MARGARET MEAD

With more people, there are more voices to tune out. —SUSAN SONTAG

We have been God-like in our planned breeding of our domesticated plants and animals, but we have been rabbit-like in our unplanned breeding of ourselves. —ARNOLD JOSEPH TOYNBEE

It is obvious that the best qualities in man must atrophy in a standing-room-only environment. —STEWART L. UDALL

PORNOGRAPHY
(also see concepts 547, 586, 848)

I don't think pornography is very harmful, but it is terribly, terribly boring. —NOËL COWARD

A sodomite got very excited looking at a zoology text. Does this make it pornography? —STANISLAW LEC

The difference between pornography and erotica is lighting. —GLORIA LEONARD

I would like to see all people who read pornography or have anything to do with it put in a mental hospital for observation so we could find out what we have done to them. —LINDA LOVELACE

Pornography is sexual reality for me. If a person cannot deal with pornography, he cannot deal with the reality of sex....I am radically propornography. I draw the line nowhere. Every fantasy must be permitted. —CAMILLE PAGLIA

If I'm looking at a men's magazine and I just look at the surface, I might be able to enjoy it. But if I know that this person is really messed up and that person's messed up and they're being used by the person who set up the photo session, then it'll turn my stomach. —AXL ROSE

Pornography is one of the branches of literature–science fiction is another–aiming at disorientation, at psychic dislocation. —SUSAN SONTAG

Pornography is the instruction; rape is the practice, battered women are the practice, battered children are the practice. —GLORIA STEINEM

Pornography tells lies about women. But pornography tells the truth about men. —JOHN STOLTENBERG

The worst that can be said about pornography is that it leads not to "anti-social" acts but to the reading of more pornography. —GORE VIDAL

POSSESSION
(also see concepts 72, 85, 197, 352, 483, 628, 769)

...possession is the most extreme form of fear. When you feel yourself possessed to do something that you regard with the most profound horror or repulsion or disgust, that's the basic fear. —WILLIAM S. BURROUGHS

To keep demands as much skill as to win. —GEOFFREY CHAUCER

I did not have three thousand pairs of shoes, I had one thousand and sixty. —IMELDA MARCOS

An object in possession seldom retains the same charm that it had in pursuit. —PLINY THE YOUNGER

By touching you may kill, by keeping away you may possess. —RABINDRANATH TAGORE

No one worth possessing / Can be quite possessed. —SARA TEASDALE

POTENTIAL
(also see concepts 1, 608, 626)

There is no meaning to life except the meaning man gives his life by the unfolding of his powers. —ERICH FROMM

Treat people as if they were what they ought to be and you help them to become what they are capable of being. —JOHANN WOLFGANG VON GOETHE

Compared to what we ought to be, we are only half awake. We are making use of only a small part of our physical and mental resources. Stating the thing broadly, the human individual thus lives far within his limits. He possesses power of various sorts which he habitually fails to use. —WILLIAM JAMES

By virtue of being born to humanity, every human being has a right to the development and fulfillment of his potentialities as a human being. —ASHLEY MONTAGU

The world which credits what is done / Is cold to all that might have been. —ALFRED, LORD TENNYSON

POVERTY
(also see concepts 371, 532, 607, 661, 856)

Poverty is the parent of revolution and crime. —ARISTOTLE

Single women have a dreadful propensity to being poor. —JANE AUSTEN

The poor man's wisdom is despised and his words are not heard. —BIBLE, ECCLESIASTES 9:16

The poor you always have with you. —BIBLE, JOHN 12:8

Poverty makes you sad as well as wise. —BERTOLT BRECHT

The trouble with being poor is that it takes up all your time. —WILLEM DE KOONING

It is seldom that the miserable of the world can help regarding their misery as a wrong inflicted by those who are less miserable. —GEORGE ELIOT

You lose your manners when you're poor. —LILLIAN HELLMAN

There is something about poverty that smells like death. —ZORA NEALE HURSTON

A man who has nothing can whistle in a robber's face. —JUVENAL

If thy wealth waste, thy wit will give but small warmth. —JOHN LYLY

Look at me: I worked my way up from nothing to a state of extreme poverty. —GROUCHO MARX

Empty pockets make empty heads. —WILLIAM CARLOS WILLIAMS

POVERTY AND WEALTH
(also see concepts 118, 483, 498, 606, 856)

The conspicuously wealthy turn up urging the character-building value of privation for the poor. —JOHN KENNETH GALBRAITH

If a free society cannot help the many who are poor, it cannot save the few who are rich. —JOHN F. KENNEDY

If the rich could hire other people to die for them, the poor could make a wonderful living. —YIDDISH PROVERB

Wealth is conspicuous, but poverty hides. —JAMES RESTON

When the rich wage war it is the poor who die. —JEAN-PAUL SARTRE

The difference between rich and poor is that the poor do everything with their own hands and the rich hire hands to do things. —BETTY SMITH

America is an enormous frosted cupcake in the middle of millions of starving people. —GLORIA STEINEM

POWER

(also see concepts 15, 167, 293, 400, 605, 666, 772)

Arbitrary power is like most other things which are very hard, very liable to be broken. —ABIGAIL ADAMS

A friend in power is a friend lost. —HENRY BROOKS ADAMS

We thought, because we had power, we had wisdom.
—STEPHEN VINCENT BENÉT

Power is no longer substantially identified with an individual who possesses or exercises it by right of birth; it becomes a machinery that no one owns. —MICHEL FOUCAULT

...power is something of which I am convinced there is no innocence this side of the womb. —NADINE GORDIMER

Once, power was considered a masculine attribute. In fact, power has no sex. —KATHERINE GRAHAM

Power never takes a back step–only in the face of more power.
—MALCOLM X

There are questions of real power and then there are questions of phony authority. You have to break through the phony authority to begin to fight the real questions of power. —KAREN NUSSBAUM

The property of power is to protect. —BLAISE PASCAL

He who pays the piper calls the tune. —PROVERB

What do I care about the law? Hain't I got the power?
—CORNELIUS VANDERBILT

PRACTICALITY

(also see concepts 496, 523, 835, 837)

A mariner must have his eye upon rocks and sands, as well as upon the North Star. —THOMAS FULLER

Admire a little ship, but put your cargo in a big one. —HESIOD

PRAISE

(also see concepts 40, 41, 139)

Praise out of season, or tactlessly bestowed, can freeze the heart as much as blame. —PEARL S. BUCK

I praise loudly; I blame softly. —QUEEN CATHERINE II

He who praises everybody, praises nobody. —SAMUEL JOHNSON

There's no praise to beat the sort you can put in your pocket. —MOLIÉRE

Praise shames me, for I secretly beg for it. —RABINDRANATH TAGORE

PRAYER

(also see concepts 121, 587, 612, 673, 873)

We little know the things for which we pray. —GEOFFREY CHAUCER

Religion's in the heart, not in the knees. —DOUGLAS WILLIAM JERROLD

Pray to God but continue to row to the shore. —RUSSIAN PROVERB

Prayer, among sane people, has never superseded practical efforts to secure the desired end. —GEORGE SANTAYANA

Why is it when we talk to God, we're praying–but when God talks to us, we're schizophrenic? —LILY TOMLIN

You can't pray a lie. —MARK TWAIN

PREACHERS AND PREACHING

(also see concepts 19, 90, 121, 587, 611, 629, 668)

He preaches well that lives well. —MIGUEL DE CERVANTES

Sermons remain one of the last forms of public discourse where it is culturally forbidden to talk back. —HARVEY COX

Go into the street, and give one man a lecture on morality, and another a shilling, and see which will respect you most. —SAMUEL JOHNSON

When I hear a man preach, I like to see him act as if he were fighting bees. —ABRAHAM LINCOLN

Preaching is heady wine. It is pleasant to tell people where they get off. —ARNOLD LUNN

Few sinners are saved after the first twenty minutes of a sermon. —MARK TWAIN

PREJUDICE
(also see concepts 206, 213, 220, 403, 619, 651, 732)

Prejudice is being down on something you're not up on. —ANONYMOUS

Common sense is the collection of prejudices acquired by age eighteen. —ALBERT EINSTEIN

Dogs bark at a person whom they do not know. —HERACLITUS

Everyone is a prisoner of his own experiences. No one can eliminate prejudices–just recognize them. —EDWARD R. MURROW

PREPAREDNESS
(also see concepts 233, 633, 795)

She felt that those who prepared for all the emergencies of life beforehand may equip themselves at the expense of joy. —E. M. FORSTER

I always knew I would turn a corner and run into this day, but I ain't prepared for it nohow. —LOUISE MERIWETHER

Where observation is concerned, chance favors only the prepared mind. —LOUIS PASTEUR

It is seldom in life that one knows that a coming event is to be of crucial importance. —ANYA SETON

Shape your heart to front the hour, but dream not that the hour will last. —ALFRED, LORD TENNYSON

THE PRESENT

(also see concepts 304, 509, 571, 807, 808, 820)

Real generosity toward the future lies in giving all to the present.
—ALBERT CAMUS

There's no present. There's only the immediate future and the recent past. —GEORGE CARLIN

Seize the day. —HORACE

We live in stirring times–tea-stirring times.
—CHRISTOPHER ISHERWOOD

The word "now" is like a bomb through the window, and it ticks.
—ARTHUR MILLER

Keep in mind always the present you are constructing. It should be the future you want. —ALICE WALKER

PRESIDENTS AND THE PRESIDENCY

(also see concepts 323, 445, 636, 767, 847)

The office of President is such a bastardized thing, half royalty and half democracy, that nobody knows whether to genuflect or spit.
—JIMMY BRESLIN

Who knows? Somewhere out in this audience may even be someone who will one day follow in my footsteps and preside over the White House as the President's spouse. I wish him well!
—BARBARA BUSH

Have faith in me. I am a Christian. —JIMMY CARTER

A President's hardest task is not to do what is right, but to know what is right. —LYNDON B. JOHNSON

I know that when things don't go well they like to blame the Presidents, and that is one of the things which Presidents are paid for. —JOHN F. KENNEDY

When the President does it, that means that it is not illegal.
—RICHARD NIXON

Most of us aren't as clean as a hound's tooth. But most of us aren't running for President. —LIZ SMITH

You know how it is in an election year. They pick a president and then for four years they pick on him. —ADLAI STEVENSON

The American Presidency, it occurs to us, is merely a way station en route to the blessed condition of being an ex-President. —JOHN UPDIKE

Any American who is prepared to run for President should automatically, by definition, be disqualified from ever doing so. —GORE VIDAL

PRESS, FREEDOM OF THE
(also see concepts 115, 157)

A free press can, of course, be good or bad, but, most certainly, without freedom it will never be anything but bad. —ALBERT CAMUS

Freedom of the press is not an end in itself but a means to the end of a free society. —FELIX FRANKFURTER

The freedom of the press works in such a way that there is not much freedom from it. —PRINCESS GRACE OF MONACO

The liberty of the press is most generally approved when it takes liberties with the other fellow, and leaves us alone. —EDGAR WATSON HOWE

The freedom of the press is one of the great bulwarks of liberty, and can never be restrained but by despotic government. —GEORGE MASON

PRETENSION
(also see concepts 31, 45, 50, 72, 405, 544, 750, 838)

All human beings have gray little souls–and they all want to rouge them up. —MAXIM GORKY

The qualities we have do not make us so ridiculous as those which we affect. —FRANÇOIS DE LA ROCHEFOUCAULD

Those who wish to seem learned to fools, seem fools to the learned.
—QUINTILIAN

PRIDE
(also see concepts 45, 72, 237, 715, 838)

Pride, perceiving humility honourable, often borrows her cloak.
—THOMAS FULLER

There is false modesty, but there is no false pride. —JULES RENARD

Pride is over-estimation of oneself by reason of self-love.
—BENEDICT SPINOZA

PRINCIPLE
(also see concepts 94, 150, 317, 375, 690)

If one sticks too rigidly to one's principles one would hardly see
anybody. —AGATHA CHRISTIE

Amid the pressure of great events, a general principle gives no
help. —GEORG WILHELM FRIEDRICH HEGEL

Everywhere the basis of principle is tradition.
—OLIVER WENDELL HOLMES, JR.

Prosperity is the best protector of principle. —MARK TWAIN

PRISONS
(also see concepts 89, 170, 434, 436, 596, 642, 747)

Prisons don't rehabilitate, they don't punish, they don't protect, so
what the hell do they do? —JERRY BROWN

In prison, those things withheld from and denied to the prisoner
become precisely what he wants most of all. —ELDRIDGE CLEAVER

Wherever anyone is against his will, that is to him a prison.
—EPICTETUS

Penology...has become torture and foolishness, a waste of money and a cause of crime...a blotting out of sight and heightening of social anxiety. —PAUL GOODMAN

PRIVACY
(also see concepts 204, 417, 678, 706)

The boom mike has done what twelve years of the Reagan-Bush Supreme Court couldn't do to abolish the right to privacy. —BILL CLINTON

I never said, "I want to be alone." I only said, "I want to be left alone." There is all the difference. —GRETA GARBO

Let there be spaces in your togetherness. —KAHLIL GIBRAN

In a crowd, on a journey, at a banquet even, a line of thought can itself provide its own seclusion. —QUINTILIAN

PROBLEMS
(also see concepts 194, 206, 648)

What concerns everyone can only be resolved by everyone. —FRIEDRICH DÜRRENMATT

It is a commonplace of modern technology that problems have solutions before there is knowledge of how they are to be solved. —JOHN KENNETH GALBRAITH

Problems are messages. —SHAKTI GAWAIN

We don't get offered crises, they arrive. —ELIZABETH JANEWAY

Problems are only opportunities in work clothes. —HENRY J. KAISER

It's a good thing to have all the props pulled out from under us occasionally. It gives us some sense of what is rock under our feet, and what is sand. —MADELEINE L'ENGLE

PROCRASTINATION

(also see concepts 194, 391, 749)

Procrastination is the art of keeping up with yesterday.
——DON MARQUIS

In delay there lies no plenty. ——WILLIAM SHAKESPEARE

Procrastination is the thief of time. ——EDWARD YOUNG

PROGRESS

(also see concepts 116, 194, 304, 330, 389, 663, 682, 778)

As enunciated today, "progress" is simply a comparative of which
we have not settled the superlative. ——G. K. CHESTERTON

I was taught that the way of progress is neither swift nor easy.
——MARIE CURIE

Restlessness and discontent are the necessities of progress.
——THOMAS EDISON

All that is human must retrograde if it does not advance.
——EDWARD GIBBON

All progress is precarious, and the solution of one problem brings
us face to face with another problem. ——MARTIN LUTHER KING, JR.

Man's 'progress' is but a gradual discovery that his questions have
no meaning. ——ANTOINE DE SAINT-EXUPÉRY

All progress means war with Society. ——GEORGE BERNARD SHAW

In all things that are purely social we can be as separate as the
fingers, yet one as the hand in all things essential to mutual
progress. ——BOOKER T. WASHINGTON

PROMISES

(also see concepts 129, 605, 788)

The best way to keep one's word is not to give it. ——NAPOLEON I

Everyone's a millionaire where promises are concerned. ——OVID

Vows made in storms are forgot in calms. —ENGLISH PROVERB

Promises and pie-crust are made to be broken. —JONATHAN SWIFT

PROPAGANDA
(also see concepts 18, 251, 637, 639)

The greater the lie, the greater the chance that it will be believed.
—ADOLF HITLER

The propagandist's purpose is to make one set of people forget that certain other sets of people are human. —ALDOUS HUXLEY

I wonder if we could contrive...some magnificent myth that would in itself carry conviction to our whole community. —PLATO

Why is propaganda so much more successful when it stirs up hatred than when it tries to stir up friendly feeling?
—BERTRAND RUSSELL

PROPERTY
(also see concepts 88, 362, 421, 630)

Where your treasure is, there will your heart be also.
—BIBLE, MATTHEW 6:21

By abolishing private property one takes away the human love of aggression. —SIGMUND FREUD

Property is intended to serve life, and no matter how much we surround it with rights and respect, it has no personal being. It is part of the earth man walks on; it is not man.
—MARTIN LUTHER KING, JR.

Private property was the original source of freedom. It still is its main bulwark. —WALTER LIPPMANN

Where there is no property there is no injustice. —JOHN LOCKE

Landlords, like all other men, love to reap where they never sowed.
—KARL MARX

Property is organised robbery. —GEORGE BERNARD SHAW

PROPHECY
(also see concepts 66, 224, 304)

Prophecy is the most gratuitous form of error. —GEORGE ELIOT

Beware the ides of March. —WILLIAM SHAKESPEARE

PROSPERITY
(also see concepts 778, 856)

A full cup must be carried steadily. —ENGLISH PROVERB

When you ascend the hill of prosperity, may you not meet a friend.
—MARK TWAIN

PROTEST
(also see concepts 138, 664)

While there is a lower class, I am in it; while there is a criminal
element, I am of it; and while there is a soul in prison, I am not free.
—EUGENE V. DEBS

Sometimes a scream is better than a thesis. —RALPH WALDO EMERSON

America I'm putting my queer shoulder to the wheel.
—ALLEN GINSBERG

Lean, hungry, savage, anti-everythings.
—OLIVER WENDELL HOLMES, SR.

If I cannot air this pain and alter it, I will surely die of it. That's the
beginning of social protest. —AUDRE LORDE

It's the kind of gathering where one feels a need to apologize for
never having been to prison. —VERA LAUGHTON MATHEWS

PROVERBS
(also see concepts 66, 649, 818)

They are like the clue in the labyrinth, or the compass in the night.
—JOSEPH JOUBERT

A proverb is the child of experience. —ENGLISH PROVERB

The proverb is something musty. —WILLIAM SHAKESPEARE

The proverbist knows nothing of the two sides of a question. He knows only the roundness of answers. —KARL SHAPIRO

A short saying oft contains much wisdom. —SOPHOCLES

PRUDENCE
(also see concepts 91, 386, 697)

Judgment is not upon all occasions required, but discretion always is. —EARL OF CHESTERFIELD

When you have nothing to say, or to hide, there is no need to be prudent. —ANDRÉ GIDE

Sincerity is glass, discretion is diamond. —ANDRÉ MAUROIS

Be nice to people on your way up because you'll meet 'em on your way down. —WILSON MIZNER

An ounce of discretion is worth a pound of learning. —PROVERB

We schoolmasters must temper discretion with deceit.
—EVELYN WAUGH

PSYCHIATRY
(also see concepts 146, 224, 364, 373, 475, 489, 500, 534, 635, 693, 697, 823)

Psychiatry's chief contribution to philosophy is the discovery that the toilet is the seat of the soul. —ALEXANDER CHASE

Psychoanalysis is confession without absolution. —G. K. CHESTERTON

The greatest happiness is to know the source of unhappiness.
—FYODOR DOSTOYEVSKY

It might be said of psychoanalysis that if you give it your little finger it will soon have your whole hand. —SIGMUND FREUD

The examined life has always been pretty well confined to a privileged class. —EDGAR Z. FRIEDENBERG

Anybody who goes to see a psychiatrist ought to have his head examined. —SAMUEL GOLDWYN

Freud is the father of psychoanalysis. It has no mother.
—GERMAINE GREER

If the nineteenth century was the age of the editorial chair, ours is the century of the psychiatrist's couch. —MARSHALL MCLUHAN

Every life is, more or less, a ruin among whose debris we have to discover what the person ought to have been.
—JOSÉ ORTEGA Y GASSET

The unexamined life is not worth living. —SOCRATES

One should only see a psychiatrist out of boredom. —MURIEL SPARK

PSYCHOLOGY

(also see concepts 146, 224, 364, 373, 475, 500, 534, 634, 697, 702)

Psychology has a long past, but only a short history.
—HERMANN EBBINGHAUS

Idleness is the parent of psychology. —FRIEDRICH WILHELM NIETZSCHE

A large part of the popularity and persuasiveness of psychology comes from its being a sublimated spiritualism: a secular, ostensibly scientific way of affirming the primacy of "spirit" over matter.
—SUSAN SONTAG

The object of psychology is to give us a totally different idea of the things we know best. —PAUL VALÉRY

PUBLIC OFFICE

(also see concepts 599, 616)

It is not easy for a person to do any great harm when his tenure of office is short, whereas long possession begets tyranny. —ARISTOTLE

A man ain't got no right to be a public man, unless he meets the public views. —CHARLES DICKENS

When a man assumes a public trust, he should consider himself as public property. —THOMAS JEFFERSON

It's no accident many accuse me of conducting public affairs with my heart instead of my head. Well, what if I do?...Those who don't know how to weep with their whole heart don't know how to laugh either. —GOLDA MEIR

PUBLIC OPINION
(also see concepts 114, 400, 582, 627, 639)

What we call public opinion is generally public sentiment.
—BENJAMIN DISRAELI

A straw vote only shows which way the hot air blows. —O. HENRY

A universal feeling, whether well or ill founded, cannot be safely disregarded. —ABRAHAM LINCOLN

Public opinion is the thermometer a monarch should constantly consult. —NAPOLEON I

PUBLIC SPEAKING
(also see concepts 236, 599)

All epoch-making revolutionary events have been produced not by the written but the spoken word. —ADOLF HITLER

If you haven't struck oil in your first three minutes, stop boring!
—GEORGE JESSEL

What orators lack in depth they make up to you in length.
—BARON DE MONTESQUIEU

I never failed to convince an audience that the best thing they could do was to go away. —THOMAS LOVE PEACOCK

It is terrible to speak well and be wrong. —SOPHOCLES

I sometimes marvel at the extraordinary docility with which Americans submit to speeches. —ADLAI STEVENSON

PUBLICITY
(also see concepts 18, 144, 627, 637, 819)

I don't care what you say about me, as long as you say *something* about me, and as long as you spell my name right.
—GEORGE M. COHAN

The most amazing feature of American life is its boundless publicity. Everybody has to meet everybody, and they seem to enjoy this enormity. —CARL JUNG

Even though we never like it, and even though we wish they didn't write it, and even though we disapprove, there isn't any doubt at all that we could not do the job at all in a free society without a very, very active press. —JOHN F. KENNEDY

In order to fuel the engines of publicity the media suck so much love and adulation out of the atmosphere that unknown men must gasp for breath. —LEWIS H. LAPHAM

PUBLISHING
(also see concepts 132, 232, 459, 639)

The printing press is either the greatest blessing or the greatest curse of modern times, one sometimes forgets which. —J. M. BARRIE

You write a book, you invest your imagination in it, and then you hand it over to a bunch of people who have no imagination and no understanding of their own enterprise. —SAUL BELLOW

I wonder whether what we are publishing now is worth cutting down trees to make paper for the stuff. —RICHARD BRAUTIGAN

As repressed sadists are supposed to become policemen or butchers so those with irrational fear of life become publishers.
—CYRIL CONNOLLY

Publication is the auction of the Mind of Man. —EMILY DICKINSON

No author is a man of genius to his publisher. —HEINRICH HEINE

Publishers don't nurse you; they buy and sell you. —P. D. JAMES

Publishers are demons, there's no doubt about it. —WILLIAM JAMES

Publication is a self-invasion of privacy. —MARSHALL MCLUHAN

Since the discovery of printing, knowledge has been called to power, and power has been used to make knowledge a slave. —NAPOLEON I

Publishing is a literary mafia. —PETER OWEN

Publishing is a very mysterious business. It is hard to predict what kind of sale or reception a book will have, and advertising seems to do very little good. —THOMAS WOLFE

PUNCTUALITY

(also see concepts 762, 808)

We are not saints, but we have kept our appointment. How many people can boast as much? —SAMUEL BECKETT

The trouble with being punctual is that nobody's there to appreciate it. —FRANKLIN P. JONES

Punctuality is the politeness of the kings. —KING LOUIS XVIII OF FRANCE

I've been on a calendar, but never on time. —MARILYN MONROE

Better three hours too soon than a minute too late. —WILLIAM SHAKESPEARE

Better never than late. —GEORGE BERNARD SHAW

If you're there before it's over, you're on time. —JAMES J. WALKER

Punctuality is the virtue of the bored. —EVELYN WAUGH

PUNISHMENT

(also see concepts 170, 211, 343, 436, 437, 643, 679, 680, 875)

All punishment is mischief. All punishment in itself is evil.
——JEREMY BENTHAM

The refined punishments of the spiritual mode are usually much more indecent and dangerous than a good smack. ——D. H. LAWRENCE

The broad effects which can be obtained by punishment in man and beast are the increase of fear, the sharpening of the sense of cunning, the mastery of the desires; so it is that punishment tames man, but it does not make him "better."
——FRIEDRICH WILHELM NIETZCHE

Whipping and abuse are like laudanum: You have to double the dose as the sensibilities decline. ——HARRIET BEECHER STOWE

PUNISHMENT, CAPITAL

(also see concepts 437, 642)

Let us call it by the name which, for lack of any other nobility, will at least give the nobility of truth, and let us recognize it for what it essentially is: a revenge. ——ALBERT CAMUS

The death penalty will seem to the next generation, as it seems to many even now, an anachronism too discordant to be suffered, mocking with grim reproach all our clamorous professions of the sanctity of life. ——BENJAMIN N. CARDOZO

It is fairly obvious that those who are in favor of the death penalty have more affinity with assassins than those who are not.
——REMY DE GOURMONT

The compensation for a death sentence is knowledge of the exact hour when one is to die. A great luxury, but one that is well earned.
——VLADIMIR NABOKOV

Capital punishment in my view achieved nothing except revenge.
——ALBERT PIERREPOINT

Men are not hanged for stealing horses, but that horses may not be stolen. —GEORGE SAVILLE

PUNS
(also see concepts 80, 128, 370, 442, 649, 699, 866)

Who makes a pun will pick a pocket. —ENGLISH PROVERB

PURITANS AND PURITANISM
(also see concepts 79, 536, 646, 721)

To the Puritan all things are impure, as somebody says.
—D. H. LAWRENCE

Puritanism—The haunting fear that someone, somewhere, may be happy. —H. L. MENCKEN

There are no more thorough prudes than those who have some little secret to hide. —GEORGE SAND

Intolerance is the besetting sin of moral fervour.
—ALFRED NORTH WHITEHEAD

PURITY
(also see concepts 356, 843)

I'm as pure as the driven slush. —TALLULAH BANKHEAD

Unto the pure all things are pure. —BIBLE, TITUS 1:15

My strength is as the strength of ten, / Because my heart is pure.
—ALFRED, LORD TENNYSON

It is one of the superstitions of the human mind to have imagined that virginity could be a virtue. —VOLTAIRE

I used to be Snow White...but I drifted. —MAE WEST

PURPOSE

(also see concepts 94, 189, 486, 488, 519, 591, 860)

Everything's got a moral, if only you can find it. —LEWIS CARROLL

The idea of life having a purpose stands and falls with the religious system. —SIGMUND FREUD

A useless life is an early death. —JOHANN WOLFGANG VON GOETHE

That's our function in life. To make a declarative statement.
—CORINNE JACKER

Fortunately, in her kindness and patience, Nature has never put the fatal question as to the meaning of their lives into the mouths of most people. And where no one asks, no one needs to answer.
—CARL JUNG

Many persons have a wrong idea of what constitutes true happiness. It is not attained through self-gratification but through fidelity to a worthy purpose. —HELEN KELLER

The soul that has no established aim loses itself.
—MICHEL DE MONTAIGNE

QUESTIONS

(also see concepts 179, 206, 550, 623, 673)

Answer a fool according to his folly, lest he be wise in his own conceit. —BIBLE, PROVERBS 26:5

An answer is always a form of death. —JOHN FOWLES

'Tis not every question that deserves an answer. —THOMAS FULLER

There is really nothing more to say—except why. But since why is difficult to handle, one must take refuge in how. —TONI MORRISON

The only interesting answers are those which destroy the questions.
—SUSAN SONTAG

There ain't no answer. There ain't going to be any answer. There never has been an answer. That's the answer. —GERTRUDE STEIN

How do you like what you have? This is a question that anybody can ask anybody. Ask it. —GERTRUDE STEIN

QUOTATIONS
(also see concepts 122, 644)

The surest way to make a monkey of a man is to quote him. —ROBERT BENCHLEY

It is a good thing for the uneducated man to read books of quotations. —WINSTON CHURCHILL

That's the point of quotations, you know: one can use another's words to be insulting. —AMANDA CROSS

I hate quotations. Tell me what you know. —RALPH WALDO EMERSON

I often quote myself. It adds spice to my conversation. —GEORGE BERNARD SHAW

It's better to be quotable than to be honest. —TOM STOPPARD

One has to secrete a jelly in which to slip quotations down people's throats and one always secretes too much jelly. —VIRGINIA WOOLF

RACE
(also see concepts 21, 22, 49, 347, 502, 522, 530)

Whites must be made to realize that they are only human, not superior. Same with blacks. They must be made to realize that they are also human, not inferior. —STEVEN BIKO

Purity of race does not exist. Europe is a continent of energetic mongrels. —H. A. L. FISHER

Is the notion of "race" real–or is it mythology? We make certain assumptions about people based on skin color. Is this some mass delusion we're all participating in? —DAVID HENRY HWANG

I realize that I'm black, but I like to be viewed as a person, and that's everybody's wish. —MICHAEL JORDAN

After all there is but one race–humanity. —GEORGE MOORE

Small use it will be to save democracy for the race if we cannot save the race for democracy. —JEANNETTE RANKIN

The truth is that Mozart, Pascal, Boolean algebra, Shakespeare, parliamentary government, baroque churches, Newton, the emancipation of women, Kant, Marx, and Ballanchine ballets don't redeem what this particular civilization has wrought upon the world. The white race is the cancer of human history. —SUSAN SONTAG

RACISM

(also see concepts 396, 403, 502, 563, 650)

Sometimes, it's like a hair across your cheek. You can't see it, you can't find it with your fingers, but you keep brushing at it because the feel of it is irritating. —MARIAN ANDERSON

Race prejudice decreases values both real estate and human; crime, ignorance and filth decrease values. —W. E. B. DU BOIS

Sometimes I feel discriminated against, but it does not make me angry. It merely astonishes me. How can any deny themselves the pleasure of my company? It's beyond me. —ZORA NEALE HURSTON

Racism is a bacterium, potentially curable but presently deadly; anti-Semitism is a virus, potentially deadly but presently contained. —LETTY COTTIN POGREBIN

Racism does affect us all, but it doesn't affect us all equally. Some have more defenses against racism. It's like bad weather. All of us are affected by it, but some have boots and rain gear and some are naked to the elements. —WILLIAM RASPBERRY

Here the melting pot stands open–if you're willing to get bleached first. —BUFFY SAINTE-MARIE

I don't believe racism is as powerful a force today as what it's left in its wake–the cycle of cultural poverty that gets perpetuated. —SHELBY STEELE

RADICALISM

(also see concepts 154, 659, 681, 752, 753)

What this country needs is radicals who will stay that way regardless of the creeping years. —JOHN FISCHER

Radical: A person whose left hand does know what his other left hand is doing. —BERNARD ROSENBERG

The radical of one century is the conservative of the next. —MARK TWAIN

RAIN

(also see concepts 705, 854, 858, 862)

Nature, like man, sometimes weeps for gladness. —BENJAMIN DISRAELI

The good rain, like a bad preacher, does not know when to leave off. —RALPH WALDO EMERSON

RAINBOWS

(also see concepts 653, 854)

The way I see it, if you want the rainbow, you gotta put up with the rain. —DOLLY PARTON

One can enjoy a rainbow without necessarily forgetting the forces that made it. —MARK TWAIN

RANK

(also see concepts 118, 561)

Detestation of the high is the involuntary homage of the low. —CHARLES DICKENS

A throne is only a bench covered with velvet. —NAPOLEON I

The sparrow is sorry for the peacock at the burden of its tail. —RABINDRANATH TAGORE

It is an interesting question how far men would retain their relative rank if they were divested of their clothes. —HENRY DAVID THOREAU

RAP MUSIC
(also see concepts 524, 543)

A lot of serious rap talks about the end of things–illusions, lives, neighborhoods, rock 'n' roll, the World itself. If it is a true genre, it's one conspicuous for the darkness of its vision: a kind of dystopian present from which no imaginative future can even emerge. —MARK COSTELLO AND DAVID FOSTER WALLACE

Rap is Black America's TV station....Black life doesn't get the total spectrum of information through anything else. —CHUCK D.

There's not a lot of it that's reverie, there's not a lot of it that's happy talk. A lot of it is didactic, a lot of it is protest, a lot of it is fear, and a lot of it is anger. In every society, there was this angry poetry, angry songs, angry music. I am not surprised that this generation should have its angry sounds. There's more anger because there's more failure, and there's more perceived failure. —MARIO CUOMO

It wasn't a cop or social worker who got me here. It was my boys, like the ones now on death row, who are the reason I'm doing it. That's why there's a real allegiance to the street in my music. —ICE-T

Blues is rap, just singing it. —QUEEN LATIFAH

I have often thought that if there had been a good rap group around in those days, I might have chosen a career in music instead of politics. —RICHARD NIXON

You know, rap is the only type of music that I know that expresses all of the human feelings and encourages people to make something of themselves. —SINEAD O'CONNOR

RAPE

(also see concept 170, 707)

Rape is nothing more or less than a conscious process of intimidation by which all men keep all women in a state of fear.
—SUSAN BROWNMILLER

Perhaps rape itself is a gesture, a violent repudiation of the female, in the assertion of maleness that would seem to require nothing beyond physical gratification of the crudest kind. The supreme macho gesture–like knocking out an opponent and standing over his fallen body, gloves raised in triumph. —JOYCE CAROL OATES

I see the sexual impulse as egotistical and dominating, and therefore I have no problem understanding rape. —CAMILLE PAGLIA

REALISM

(also see concept 47, 267, 523, 609, 658)

Realists do not fear the results of their study. —FYODOR DOSTOYEVSKY

We must find our duties in what comes to us, not in what might have been. —GEORGE ELIOT

It is only by knowing how little life has in store for us that we are able to look on the bright side and avoid disappointment.
—ELLEN GLASGOW

We must rediscover the distinction between hope and expectation.
—IVAN ILLICH

If someone tells you he is going to make a "realistic decision," you immediately understand that he has resolved to do something bad.
—MARY MCCARTHY

Reality is something you rise above. —LIZA MINNELLI

REALITY

(also see concepts 5, 47, 96, 191, 267, 284, 523, 609, 657)

I like reality. It tastes of bread. —JEAN ANOUILH

He who confronts the paradoxical exposes himself to reality.
—FRIEDRICH DÜRRENMATT

Human kind / Cannot bear very much reality. —T. S. ELIOT

The supreme reality of our time is...the vulnerability of this planet.
—JOHN F. KENNEDY

To mention a loved object, a person, or a place to someone else is
to invest that object with reality. —ANNE MORROW LINDBERGH

Reality is a staircase going neither up nor down, we don't move,
today is today, always is today. —OCTAVIO PAZ

Prejudices, hierarchies, ideas allow us to cut up reality, order it, that
is, deprive it of light, of a thousand shades of meaning, its majestic
splendor. —ADAM ZAGAJEWSKI

REBELLION
(also see concepts 583, 652, 681)

A populace never rebels from passion for attack, but from impatience
of suffering. —EDMUND BURKE

Every act of rebelling expresses a nostalgia for innocence.
—ALBERT CAMUS

No one can go on being a rebel too long without turning into an
autocrat. —LAWRENCE DURRELL

A riot is at bottom the language of the unheard.
—MARTIN LUTHER KING, JR.

The path that leads from moral standards to political activity is
strewn with our dead selves. —ANDRÉ MALRAUX

RECEIVING
(also see concepts 9, 314, 662, 861)

Nothing costs so much as what is given us. —THOMAS FULLER

Should not the giver be thankful that the receiver received? Is not giving a need? Is not receiving mercy?
——FRIEDRICH WILHELM NIETZSCHE

RECESSION
(also see concepts 84, 231)

We're enjoying sluggish times–and not enjoying them very much.
——GEORGE BUSH

The American economic system is far from perfect...Its greatest defect is its striking instability; its proclivity to booms and depressions. ——EVANS CLARK

We've had trickle down economics in the country for ten years now, and most of us aren't even damp yet. ——MOLLY IVINS

Recession is when a neighbor loses his job; depression is when you lose yours. ——RONALD REAGAN

RECIPROCITY
(also see concepts 140, 679, 735)

The sort of thing you say is the thing that will be said to you.
——HOMER

Men seldom give pleasure when they are not pleased themselves.
——SAMUEL JOHNSON

REFORMERS AND REFORM
(also see concepts 450, 652, 681, 752)

Let my name stand among those who are willing to bear ridicule and reproach for the truth's sake, and so earn some right to rejoice when the victory is won. ——LOUISA MAY ALCOTT

Cautious, careful people, always casting about to preserve their reputation and social standing, never can bring about a reform. Those who are really in earnest must be willing to be anything or nothing in the world's estimation, and publicly and privately in

season and out, avow their sympathies with despised and persecuted ideas and their advocates, and bear the consequences.
—SUSAN B. ANTHONY

There is little place in the political scheme of things for an independent, creative personality, for a fighter. Anyone who takes that role must pay a price. —SHIRLEY CHISHOLM

Experience has two things to teach: the first is that we must correct a great deal; the second, that we must not correct too much.
—EUGÉNE DELACROIX

Reformers must expect to be disowned by those who are only too happy to enjoy what has been won for them. —DORIS LESSING

The urge to save humanity is almost always only a false-face for the urge to rule it. —H. L. MENCKEN

You have to make more noise than anybody else, you have to make yourself more obtrusive than anybody else, you have to fill all the papers more than anybody else, in fact you have to be there all the time and see that they do not snow you under, if you are really going to get your reform realized. —EMMELINE PANKHURST

Nothing so needs reforming as other people's habits.
—MARK TWAIN

Every abuse ought to be reformed, unless the reform is more dangerous than the abuse itself. —VOLTAIRE

When history moves backward, the most maligned are the extroverts, the people of action. —ADAM ZAGAJEWSKI

REFUSAL
(also see concepts 190, 631)

Better a friendly denial than unwilling compliance.
—GERMAN PROVERB

The prompter the refusal, the less the disappointment.
—PUBLILIUS SYRUS

REGRET
(also see concepts 38, 255, 520, 670, 718, 757)

I have no regrets. I wouldn't have lived my life the way I did if I was going to worry about what people were going to say.
——INGRID BERGMAN

One doesn't recognize in one's life the really important moments–not until it's too late. ——AGATHA CHRISTIE

Regrets are the natural property of grey hairs. ——CHARLES DICKENS

Let us not burden our remembrance with / A heaviness that's gone.
——WILLIAM SHAKESPEARE

The bitterest tears shed over graves are for words left unsaid and deeds left undone. ——HARRIET BEECHER STOWE

RELATIONSHIPS
(also see concepts 51, 422, 466, 469, 494)

The intense happiness of our union is derived in a high degree from the perfect freedom with which we each follow and declare our own impressions. ——GEORGE ELIOT

I present myself to you in a form suitable to the relationship I wish to achieve with you. ——LUIGI PIRANDELLO

The bonds that unite another person to ourself exist only in our mind. ——MARCEL PROUST

There is no hope of joy except in human relations.
——ANTOINE DE SAINT-EXUPÉRY

Relationships. That's all there really is. There's your relationship with the dust that just blew in your face, or with the person who just kicked you end over end....You have to come to terms, to some kind of equilibrium, with those people around you, those people who care for you, your environment. ——LESLIE MARMON SILKO

Relationship is a pervading and changing mystery...brutal or lovely, the mystery waits for people wherever they go, whatever extreme they run to. ——EUDORA WELTY

RELATIVES

(also see concept 273)

When our relatives are at home, we have to think of all their good points or it would be impossible to endure them.
——GEORGE BERNARD SHAW

RELIGION

(also see 26, 52, 66, 67, 108, 110, 111, 121, 176, 269, 270, 274, 316, 317, 319, 427, 431, 587, 611, 612, 645, 696, 701, 802, 873, 879)

I'm a Communist by day and a Catholic as soon as it gets dark.
——BRENDAN BEHAN

It may be that religion is dead, and if it is, we had better know it and set ourselves to try to discover other sources of moral strength before it is too late. ——PEARL S. BUCK

Nothing is so fatal to religion as indifference. ——EDMUND BURKE

I neglect God and his angels for the noise of a fly, for the rattling of a coach, for the whining of a door. ——JOHN DONNE

The cosmic religious experience is the strongest and the noblest driving force behind scientific research. ——ALBERT EINSTEIN

God enters by a private door into every individual.
——RALPH WALDO EMERSON

Religion is an illusion and it derives its strength from the fact that it falls in with our instinctual desires. ——SIGMUND FREUD

There exists no politician in India daring enough to attempt to explain to the masses that cows can be eaten. ——INDIRA GANDHI

The best religion is the most tolerant. ——DELPHINE DE GIRARDIN

Nobody can have the consolations of religion or philosophy unless he has first experienced their desolations. ——ALDOUS HUXLEY

I often ask myself uneasily: is religion indeed a blessing to mankind? Religion, which is meant to save us from our sins, how many sins are committed in thy name? ——RADEN ADJENG KARTINI

I count religion but a childish toy, / And hold there is no sin but ignorance. ——CHRISTOPHER MARLOWE

Religion is the sign of the oppressed creature, the sentiment of a heartless world, and the soul of soulless conditions. It is the opium of the people. ——KARL MARX

Man is certainly stark mad; he cannot make a flea, and yet he will be making gods by dozens. ——MICHEL DE MONTAIGNE

There is a very good saying that if triangles invented a god, they would make him three-sided. ——BARON DE MONTESQUIEU

Knowledge and history are the enemies of religion. ——NAPOLEON I

In some ways, religion is to spirituality as ideology is to thought. ——ARNOLD RAMPERSAD

Life doesn't lend itself to this Christian bureaucracy, where the Father, Son, and Holy Ghost are like the FBI, and the Virgin Mary interceded for you like the executive secretary in the office. ——CAROLYN SEE

Religion has nothing more to fear than not being sufficiently understood. ——KING STANISLAUS I

The Bible and the Church have been the greatest stumbling blocks in the way of women's emancipation. ——ELIZABETH CADY STANTON

Religion without humanity is a poor human stuff. ——SOJOURNER TRUTH

Religions are such stuff as dreams are made of. ——H. G. WELLS

REMEDIES
(also see concepts 344, 684)

Well, now, there's a remedy for everything except death. ——MIGUEL DE CERVANTES

When a lot of remedies are suggested for a disease, that means it can't be cured. ——ANTON CHEKHOV

The cure for anything is salt water–sweat, tears, or the sea.
——ISAK DINESEN

Most men die of their remedies, not of their diseases. ——MOLIÉRE

There are some remedies worse than the disease. ——PUBLILIUS SYRUS

It is part of the cure to wish to be cured. ——SENECA

REPENTANCE

(also see concepts 332, 665)

But mind you, when I did go to confession, I never told the priest what I thought I'd really done wrong. I'd make up other, smaller crimes. I thought, look, if I think I've done something wrong, I have a private line to God, and I'll just tell him in my bedroom.
——MADONNA

Remorse is impotence; it will sin again. Only repentance is strong; it can end everything. ——HENRY MILLER

Remorse sleeps during prosperity but awakes bitter consciousness during adversity. ——JEAN JACQUES ROUSSEAU

Life is a slate where all our sins are written; from time to time we rub the sponge of repentance over it so we can begin sinning again.
——GEORGE SAND

But with the morning cool repentance came. ——WALTER SCOTT

REPETITION

(also see concepts 180, 335)

There are only two or three human stories and they go on repeating themselves as fiercely as if they never happened before.
——WILLA CATHER

There is repetition everywhere, and nothing is found only once in the world. ——JOHANN WOLFGANG VON GOETHE

What so tedious as a twice-told tale? ——HOMER

Repetition is the only form of permanence that nature can achieve. ——GEORGE SANTAYANA

REPUTATION

(also see concepts 315, 527, 601, 604, 654, 746)

Until you've lost your reputation, you never realize what a burden it was or what freedom really is. ——MARGARET MITCHELL

It is generally much more shameful to lose a good reputation than never to have acquired it. ——PLINY THE YOUNGER

My reputation grew with every failure. ——GEORGE BERNARD SHAW

One can survive everything nowadays, except death, and live down anything except a good reputation. ——OSCAR WILDE

REQUESTS

(also see concept 648)

A fair request should be followed by the deed in silence. ——DANTE

Not to ask is not to be denied. ——JOHN DRYDEN

RESOLUTION

(also see concepts 64, 202)

Resolve to perform what you ought. Perform without fail what you resolve. ——BENJAMIN FRANKLIN

We have more ability than will power, and it is often an excuse to ourselves that we imagine that things are impossible. ——FRANÇOIS DE LA ROCHEFOUCAULD

RESPECT

(also see concepts 14, 139, 188, 356, 548, 672)

Without feelings of respect, what is there to distinguish men from beasts? ——CONFUCIUS

The respect that is only bought by gold is not worth much.
——FRANCES ELLEN WATKINS HARPER

When I was young there was no respect for the young, and now that I am old there is no respect for the old. I missed out coming and going. ——J. B. PRIESTLY

I hate victims who respect their executioners. ——JEAN-PAUL SARTRE

We owe respect to the living; to the dead we owe only truth.
——VOLTAIRE

Now that I'm over sixty I'm veering toward respectability.
——SHELLEY WINTERS

RESPONSIBILITY
(also see concepts 129, 227, 549)

Unto whomsoever much is given, of him shall much be required.
——BIBLE, LUKE 12:48

To be a man is precisely, to be responsible.
——ANTOINE DE SAINT-EXUPÉRY

The salvation of mankind lies only in making everything the concern of all. ——ALEXANDER SOLZHENITSYN

The buck stops here. ——HARRY S TRUMAN

In dreams begin responsibility. ——WILLIAM BUTLER YEATS

REST
(also see concepts 125, 349, 379, 678, 748)

A vacation is over when you begin to yearn for your work.
——MORRIS FISHBEIN

If you rest, you rust. ——HELEN HAYES

Too much rest itself becomes a pain. ——HOMER

Nothing gives rest but the sincere search for truth. ——BLAISE PASCAL

It is well to lie fallow for a while. ——MARTIN FARQUHAR TUPPER

RETIREMENT

(also see concepts 447, 462, 571, 622, 756)

Retirement...may be looked upon either as a prolonged holiday or as a rejection, a being thrown on to the scrap-heap.
——SIMONE DE BEAUVOIR

Retirement at sixty-five is ridiculous. When I was sixty-five I still had pimples. ——GEORGE BURNS

Cessation of work is not accompanied by cessation of expenses.
——CATO THE ELDER

Retirement is the ugliest word in the language. ——ERNEST HEMINGWAY

Few men of action have been able to make a graceful exit at the appropriate time. ——MALCOLM MUGGERIDGE

RETRIBUTION

(also see concepts 436, 642, 680)

There's no need to hang about waiting for the Last Judgment—it takes place every day. ——ALBERT CAMUS

But men never violate the laws of God without suffering the consequences, sooner or later. ——LYDIA M. CHILD

Justice divine / Mends not her slowest pace for prayers or cries.
——JOHN MILTON

REVENGE

(also see concepts 436, 679)

A man that studieth revenge keeps his own wounds green.
——FRANCIS BACON

Just vengeance does not call for punishment. ——PIERRE CORNEILLE

Revenge is a luscious fruit which you must leave to ripen.
——ÉMILE GABORIAU

Don't get mad, get even. ——JOSEPH P. KENNEDY

The best manner of avenging ourselves is by not resembling him who has injured us. —JANE PORTER

Heat not a furnace for your foe so hot / That it do singe yourself. —WILLIAM SHAKESPEARE

REVOLUTIONARIES AND REVOLUTION

(also see concepts 34, 631, 652, 659, 663, 691, 752)

Revolutionaries do not make revolutions. The revolutionaries are those who know when power is lying in the street and then they can pick it up. —HANNAH ARENDT

In revolutions the occasions may be trifling but great interests are at stake. —ARISTOTLE

Revolution begins with the self, in the self. —TONI CADE BAMBARA

Every revolutionary ends up by becoming either an oppressor or a heretic. —ALBERT CAMUS

A revolution is not a bed of roses. A revolution is a struggle between the future and the past. —FIDEL CASTRO

Plots, true or false, are necessary things, / To raise up commonwealths, and ruin kings. —JOHN DRYDEN

To be a revolutionary you have to be a human being. You have to care about people who have no power. —JANE FONDA

The successful revolutionary is a statesman, the unsuccessful one a criminal. —ERICH FROMM

A great revolution is never the fault of the people, but of the government. —JOHANN WOLFGANG VON GOETHE

I was probably the only revolutionary referred to as "cute." —ABBIE HOFFMAN

The tree of liberty must be refreshed from time to time, with the blood of patriots and tyrants. It is its natural manure. —THOMAS JEFFERSON

The more there are riots, the more repressive action will take place, and the more we face the danger of a right-wing takeover and eventually a fascist society. —MARTIN LUTHER KING, JR.

We are dead men on furlough. —V. I. LENIN

Revolution is a trivial shift in the emphasis of suffering.
—TOM STOPPARD

You can build a throne out of bayonets, but you can't sit on them long. —BORIS YELTSIN

REWARD
(also see concepts 574, 684)

Vice is its own reward. —QUENTIN CRISP

The reward of a thing well done, is to have done it.
—RALPH WALDO EMERSON

RIDICULE
(also see concepts 158, 181, 408, 698, 699)

Mockery is often the result of a poverty of wit.
—JEAN DE LA BRUYÉRE

Ridicule dishonours more than dishonour.
—FRANÇOIS DE LA ROCHEFOUCAULD

Ridicule often checks what is absurd, and fully as often smothers that which is noble. —WALTER SCOTT

RIGHT
(also see concepts 669, 682)

Right is its own defense. —BERTOLT BRECHT

Be always sure you are right–then go ahead. —DAVY CROCKETT

Few sometimes may know, when thousands err. —JOHN MILTON

A child becomes an adult when he realizes that he has a right not only to be right but also to be wrong. —THOMAS SZASZ

RIVERS
(also see concepts 286, 531, 704, 854)

Rivers are roads which move, and which carry us whither we desire to go. —BLAISE PASCAL

ROCK 'N' ROLL
(also see concepts 524, 543)

Rock 'n' roll has always been as black as a mine–but you could find a jewel down there that made it all worthwhile. —BONO

That is, rock 'n' roll is only rock 'n' roll if it's not safe...the real thing is always brash. Violence and energy–that's really what rock 'n' roll is all about. —MICK JAGGER

People keep writing songs about how rock 'n' roll will never die. Well, rock 'n' roll died a long time ago. It never even made it into the '60s. A certain joy went out of rock 'n' roll, and what was left was militancy–which I guess makes sense because of the times. —JONI MITCHELL

I don't know anything about music. In my line you don't have to. —ELVIS PRESLEY

I was in love with rock 'n' roll because rock does this thing to you. You get directly to somebody, unfiltered. —LOU REED

There is no new fuel in rock music. People are archivists, basically. They dig out old records from the fifties and '60s, even the '70s, and they regurgitate them. That's why pop is stagnating. It's eating its own babies. The only hope is to look outside of it. —STING

My advice is don't spend your money on therapy. Spend it in a record store. —WIM WENDERS

ROMANCE

(also see concepts 466, 526, 727)

You need someone to love you while you're looking for someone to love. —SHELAGH DELANEY

Romance, like the rabbit at the dog track, is the elusive, fake, and never attained reward which, for the benefit and amusement of our masters, keeps us running and thinking in safe circles. —BEVERLY JONES

Romance is a love affair in other than domestic surroundings. —WALTER RALEIGH

ROMANTICISM

(also see concepts 459, 727)

Men may be allowed romanticism; women, who can create life in their own bodies, dare not indulge in it. —PHYLLIS MCGINLEY

Is not this the true romantic feeling–not to desire to escape life, but to prevent life from escaping you? —THOMAS WOLFE

RUDENESS

(also see concepts 401, 408, 424, 597, 848)

Rudeness is the weak man's imitation of strength. —ERIC HOFFER

The right people are rude. They can afford to be. —W. SOMERSET MAUGHAM

RULES

(also see concepts 54, 94, 130, 180, 443, 620)

No rule is so general, which admits not some exception. —ROBERT BURTON

Rules and models destroy genius and art. —WILLIAM HAZLITT

If you obey all the rules you miss all the fun. —KATHARINE HEPBURN

You cannot put the same shoe on every foot. —PUBLILIUS SYRUS

The golden rule is that there are no golden rules.
—GEORGE BERNARD SHAW

RUSSIA AND THE RUSSIANS
(also see concepts 126, 133, 247, 681, 753)

Moscow seethes and bubbles and gasps for air. It's always thirsting for something new, the newest events, the latest sensation. Everyone wants to be the first to know. —SVETLANA ALLILUYEVA

You know, our country is on such a low socioeconomic level that at the moment we cannot afford to divide ourselves into "us women" and "us men." We share a common struggle for democracy, a struggle to feed the country. —ELENA BONNER

Our achievements leave class enemies breathless.
—LEONID BREZHNEV

Don't you forget what's divine in the Russian soul–and that's resignation. —JOSEPH CONRAD

It's easier for a Russian to become an atheist than for anyone else in the world. —FYODOR DOSTOYEVSKY

[Are not] you too, Russia, speeding along like a spirited *troika* that nothing can overtake?...Everything on earth is flying past, and looking askance, other nations and states draw aside and make way. —NIKOLAI GOGOL

The Soviet people want full-blooded and unconditional democracy.
—MIKHAIL GORBACHEV

Perestroika has already awakened our people. They've changed. We have a different society now. We will never slip backward. There's still a question of whether the process will go slower or faster, whether it will be more or less painful. But we will certainly keep moving ahead. —MIKHAIL GORBACHEV

Gaiety is the most outstanding feature of the Soviet Union.
—JOSEPH STALIN

From being a patriotic myth, the Russian people have become an awful reality. —LEON TROTSKY

SACRIFICE
(also see concepts 201, 480, 696, 712)

Sacrificers are not the ones to pity. The ones to pity are those they sacrifice. —ELIZABETH BOWEN

Nothing so much enhances a good as to make sacrifices for it. —GEORGE SANTAYANA

SADISM
(also see concepts 174, 481, 534, 564)

Pleasure is sweetest when 'tis paid for by another's pain. —OVID

SAFETY
(also see concepts 96, 183, 334)

Only in growth, reform, and change, paradoxically enough, is true security to be found. —ANNE MORROW LINDBERGH

Most people want security in this world, not liberty. —H. L. MENCKEN

Better to be safe than sorry. —AMERICAN PROVERB

To keep oneself safe does not mean to bury oneself. —SENECA

SAILORS AND SAILING
(also see concepts 704, 736, 854)

Don't talk to me about naval tradition. It's nothing but rum, sodomy and the lash. —WINSTON CHURCHILL

There is nothing more enticing, disenchanting, and enslaving than the life at sea. —JOSEPH CONRAD

The wonder is always new that any sane man can be a sailor.
—RALPH WALDO EMERSON

Being in a ship is being in a jail, with the chance of being drowned.
—SAMUEL JOHNSON

The sailor is frankness, the landsman is finesse. —HERMAN MELVILLE

We sailors get money like horses, and spend it like asses.
—TOBIAS SMOLLETT

SAINTS AND SAINTHOOD
(also see concepts 108, 480, 503)

Being a saint, which I'm not, is a pain, to be honest. —BOB GELDOF

Many of the insights of the saint stem from his experience as a
sinner. —ERIC HOFFER

It is easier to make a saint out of a libertine than out of a prig.
—GEORGE SANTAYANA

Saints are usually killed by their own people. —ERIC SEVAREID

The saints are the sinners who keep on going.
—ROBERT LOUIS STEVENSON

I don't believe in God, but I do believe in His saints.
—EDITH WHARTON

The only difference between the saint and the sinner is that every
saint has a past, and every sinner has a future. —OSCAR WILDE

SANITY
(also see concepts 475, 534, 633, 634, 635, 863)

Who, then, is sane? —HORACE

Who in the rainbow can draw the line where the violet tint ends and
the orange tint begins? Distinctly we see the difference of the
colors, but where exactly does the first one blendingly enter into the
other? So with sanity and insanity. —HERMAN MELVILLE

Every man has a sane spot somewhere. —ROBERT LOUIS STEVENSON

SARCASM
(also see concepts 181, 683)

Sarcasm I now see to be, in general, the language of the devil. —THOMAS CARLYLE

SATIRE
(also see concepts 683, 698)

Satirists gain the applause of others through fear, not through love. —WILLIAM HAZLITT

It's hard not to write satire. —JUVENAL

Satire is moral outrage transformed into comic art. —PHILIP ROTH

Satire is a sort of glass, wherein beholders do generally discover everybody's face but their own. —JONATHAN SWIFT

Satire is always as sterile as it is shameful and as impotent as it is insolent. —OSCAR WILDE

SCHOLARS AND SCHOLARSHIP
(also see concepts 233, 348, 410, 440, 446, 451, 484, 702, 795, 803, 804)

When nature exceeds culture, we have the rustic. When culture exceeds nature, we have the pedant. —CONFUCIUS

A scholar is like a book written in a dead language: it is not every one that can read in it. —WILLIAM HAZLITT

Difficulty is a coin the learned make use of like jugglers, to conceal the inanity of their art. —MICHEL DE MONTAIGNE

This is the great vice of academicism, that it is concerned with ideas rather than with thinking. —LIONEL TRILLING

SCIENCE AND RELIGION

(also see concept 702)

Science knows only one commandment: contribute to science.
—BERTOLT BRECHT

Science without religion is lame, religion without science is blind.
—ALBERT EINSTEIN

The religion that is afraid of science dishonors God and commits suicide. —RALPH WALDO EMERSON

It is a mistake to believe that a science consists in nothing but conclusively proved propositions, and it is unjust to demand that it should. It is a demand only made by those who feel a craving for authority in some form and a need to replace the religious catechism by something else, even if it be a scientific one. —SIGMUND FREUD

The radical novelty of modern science lies precisely in the rejection of the belief, which is at the heart of all popular religion, that the forces which move the stars and atoms are contingent upon the preferences of the human heart. —WALTER LIPPMANN

SCIENTISTS AND SCIENCE

(also see concepts 90, 484, 546, 701, 796)

Science has nothing to be ashamed of, even in the ruins of Nagasaki. —JACOB BRONOWSKI

The whole of science is nothing more than a refinement of everyday thinking. —ALBERT EINSTEIN

The great tragedy of Science–the slaying of a beautiful hypothesis by an ugly fact. —THOMAS HUXLEY

The progress of science is strewn, like an ancient desert trail, with the bleached skeleton of discarded theories which once seemed to possess eternal life. —ARTHUR KOESTLER

In science, all facts, no matter how trivial or banal, enjoy democratic equality. —MARY MCCARTHY

The physicists have known sin; and this is a knowledge which they cannot lose. —J. ROBERT OPPENHEIMER

There are no such things as applied sciences, only applications of science. —LOUIS PASTEUR

Traditional scientific method has always been at the very best, 20-20 hindsight. It's good for seeing where you've been. —ROBERT M. PIRSIG

SCOTLAND AND THE SCOTTISH
(also see concepts 82, 247)

There are few more impressive sights in the world than a Scotsman on the make. —J. M. BARRIE

A land of meanness, sophistry and lust. —LORD BYRON

Seeing Scotland, Madam, is only seeing a worse England. —SAMUEL JOHNSON

I have been trying all my life to like Scotchmen, and am obliged to desist from the experiment in despair. —CHARLES LAMB

That garret of the earth–that knuckle-end of England–that land of Calvin, oat-cakes, and sulphur. —SYDNEY SMITH

SCRATCHING
(also see concepts 9, 426, 724)

Scratching is one of nature's sweetest gratifications, and nearest at hand. —MICHEL DE MONTAIGNE

THE SEA
(also see concepts 230, 286, 531, 600, 685, 695, 736, 854)

For all at last return to the sea–to Oceanus, the ocean river, like the ever-flowing stream of time, the beginning of the end. —RACHEL CARSON

The voice of the sea speaks to the soul. The touch of the sea is sensuous, enfolding the body in its soft, close embrace.
——KATE CHOPIN

How inappropriate to call this planet Earth when clearly it is Ocean. ——ARTHUR CLARKE

The sea has never been friendly to man. At most it has been the accomplice of human restlessness. ——JOSEPH CONRAD

The snotgreen sea. The scrotumtightening sea. ——JAMES JOYCE

Whenever I find myself growing grim about the mouth; whenever it is a damp, drizzly November in my soul—then I account it high time to get to sea as soon as I can. ——HERMAN MELVILLE

The sea speaks a language polite people never repeat. It is a colossal scavenger slang and has no respect. ——CARL SANDBURG

SEASONS
(also see concepts 513, 653, 858)

Autumn wins you best by this, its mute / Appeal to sympathy for its decay. ——ROBERT BROWNING

Spring never is Spring unless it comes too soon. ——G. K. CHESTERTON

Do what we can, summer will have its flies.
——RALPH WALDO EMERSON

Is there anything more soothing than the quiet whir of a lawnmower on a summer afternoon? ——F. SCOTT FITZGERALD

Summer afternoon—summer afternoon; to me those have always been the two most beautiful words in the English language.
——HENRY JAMES

Four seasons fill the measure of the year; / There are four seasons in the mind of men. ——JOHN KEATS

Every year, back spring comes, with nasty little birds yapping their fool heads off, and the ground all mucked up with arbutus.
——DOROTHY PARKER

Spring has returned. The earth is like a child that knows poems.
—RAINER MARIA RILKE

If Winter comes, can Spring be far behind? —PERCY BYSSHE SHELLEY

How sad would be November if we had no knowledge of the spring! —EDWIN WAY TEALE

SECRETS AND SECRECY
(also see concepts 622, 740, 833)

To know that one has a secret is to know half the secret itself.
—HENRY WARD BEECHER

Stolen waters are sweet, and bread eaten in secret is pleasant.
—BIBLE, PROVERBS 9:17

O fie miss, you must not kiss and tell. —WILLIAM CONGREVE

In the mind and nature of a man a secret is an ugly thing, like a hidden physical defect. —ISAK DINESEN

Three may keep a secret if two of them are dead.
—BENJAMIN FRANKLIN

No one ever keeps a secret so well as a child. —VICTOR HUGO

SEDUCTION
(also see concepts 582, 656, 799)

Venus yields to caresses, not to compulsion. —PUBLILIUS SYRUS

It is not enough to conquer; one must know how to seduce.
—VOLTAIRE

THE SELF
(also see concepts 55, 74, 235, 377, 394, 580)

I am playing with my Self, I am playing with the world's soul, I am the dialogue between my Self and *el espiritu del mundo*. I change myself, I change the world. —GLORIA ANZALDÚA

Inside myself is a place where I live all alone and that's where you renew your springs that never dry up. —PEARL S. BUCK

The ideal is in thyself, the impediment too is in thyself.
—THOMAS CARLYLE

How many cares one loses when one decides not to be something, but to be someone. —COCO CHANEL

One may understand the cosmos, but never the ego; the self is more distant than any star. —G. K. CHESTERTON

We are all serving a life-sentence in the dungeon of the self.
—CYRIL CONNOLLY

We are well advised to keep on nodding terms with the people we used to be, whether we find them attractive company or not....We forget all too soon the things we thought we could never forget.
—JOAN DIDION

Perhaps the rare and simple pleasure of being seen for what one is compensates for the misery of being it. —MARGARET DRABBLE

What we must decide is perhaps how we are valuable, rather than how valuable we are. —F. SCOTT FITZGERALD

Some of the reasons that I am the way I am is precisely because of a negative history. Why would I erase that? If I was a black man, wouldn't I want to have the history of what that has meant? Not that you have to act on it every day, but it's so much a part of your decision-making. —JODIE FOSTER

One should examine oneself for a very long time before thinking of condemning others. —MOLIÉRE

You need only claim the events of your life to make yourself yours. When you truly possess all you have been and done, which may take some time, you are fierce with reality.
—FLORIDA SCOTT-MAXWELL

SELF-CONTROL

(also see concepts 86, 572, 604, 712, 720, 737)

What it lies in our power to do, it lies in our power not to do.
—ARISTOTLE

The highest possible stage in moral culture is when we recognize that we ought to control our thoughts. —CHARLES DARWIN

Remember that there is always a limit to self-indulgence, but none to self-restraint. —MOHANDAS K. GANDHI

When things are steep, remember to stay level-headed. —HORACE

Self-restraint may be alien to the human temperament, but humanity without restraint will dig its own grave. —MARYA MANNES

SELF-CRITICISM

(also see concepts 481, 665, 670, 714, 716, 734)

I have always disliked myself at any given moment; the total of such moments is my life. —CYRIL CONNOLLY

I am always with myself, and it is I who am my tormentor.
—LEO TOLSTOY

SELF-DECEPTION

(also see concepts 214, 452)

Monkeys are superior to men in this: when a monkey looks into a mirror, he sees a monkey. —MALCOLM DE CHAZAL

Most of our platitudes notwithstanding, self-deception remains the most difficult deception. The tricks that work on others count for nothing in that very well-lit back alley where one keeps assignations with oneself: no winning smiles will do here, no prettily drawn lists of good intentions. —JOAN DIDION

Lying to ourselves is more deeply ingrained than lying to others.
—FYODOR DOSTOYEVSKY

We are never deceived; we deceive ourselves.
—JOHANN WOLFGANG VON GOETHE

Life is the art of being well deceived. —WILLIAM HAZLITT

"Isn't it pretty to think so?" —ERNEST HEMINGWAY

We lie loudest when we lie to ourselves. —ERIC HOFFER

What's terrible is to pretend that the second-rate is first-rate. To pretend that you don't need love when you do; or you like your work when you know quite well you're capable of better.
—DORIS LESSING

The most common sort of lie is the one uttered to one's self.
—FRIEDRICH WILHELM NIETZSCHE

We like to be deceived. —BLAISE PASCAL

The art of living is the art of knowing how to believe lies.
—CESARE PAVESE

The ablest man I ever met is the man you think you are.
—FRANKLIN D. ROOSEVELT

Our society allows people to be absolutely neurotic and totally out of touch with their feelings and everyone else's feelings, and yet be very respectable. —NTOZAKE SHANGE

SELF-DENIAL

(also see concepts 395, 510, 664, 692, 709, 737, 834)

The abstinent run away from what they desire / But carry their desires with them. —BHAGAVADGITA, CH. 2

The same people who can deny others everything are famous for refusing themselves nothing. —LEIGH HUNT

Self-denial is not a virtue; it is only the effect of prudence on rascality. —GEORGE BERNARD SHAW

SELF-DESTRUCTION
(also see concepts 481, 716, 781)

We often give our enemies the means for our own destruction.
——AESOP

Our greatest foes, and whom we must chiefly combat, are within.
——MIGUEL DE CERVANTES

But I do nothing upon myself, and yet I am my own Executioner.
——JOHN DONNE

SELF-DOUBT
(also see concepts 146, 148, 710)

The fearful Unbelief is unbelief in yourself. ——THOMAS CARLYLE

If I have accomplished anything good, then it's mainly because
I've been driven by the need to know whether I can accomplish
things I'm not sure I have the capacity for. ——VÁCLAV HAVEL

SELF-ESTEEM
(also see concepts 74, 235, 510, 618, 619, 838)

Love yourself first and everything else falls into line. You really
have to love yourself to get anything done in this world.
——LUCILLE BALL

It is easy to live for others; everybody does. I call on you to live for
yourselves. ——RALPH WALDO EMERSON

Respect yourself if you would have others respect you.
——BALTASAR GRACIÁN

The recognition of self as valuable for being what it is can be a
strong basis for solidarity among the oppressed whether black in a
white society, female in a male-dominated society or Muslim in a
Hindu society. ——DVAKI JAIN

Don't compromise yourself. You are all you've got. ——JANIS JOPLIN

I respect my work for the reason that no one else does.
—YURI KAGEYAMA

It is hard to fight an enemy who has outposts in your own head.
—SALLY KEMPTON

We've been taught to respect our fears, but we must learn to respect ourselves and our needs. —AUDRE LORDE

Self-respect–the secure feeling that no one, as yet, is suspicious.
—H. L. MENCKEN

Self-love seems so often unrequited. —ANTHONY POWELL

No one can make you feel inferior without your consent.
—ELEANOR ROOSEVELT

SELF-HATRED
(also see concepts 235, 481, 781)

How shall we expect charity towards others, when we are uncharitable to ourselves? —THOMAS BROWNE

Innocence ends when one is stripped of the notion that one likes oneself. —JOAN DIDION

The dupe of friendship, and the fool of love; have I not reason to hate and to despise myself? Indeed I do; and chiefly for not having hated and despised the world enough. —WILLIAM HAZLITT

SELF-KNOWLEDGE
(also see concepts 377, 719)

I'm not afraid of storms, for I'm learning how to sail my ship.
—LOUISA MAY ALCOTT

There's a period of life when we swallow a knowledge of ourselves and it becomes either good or sour inside. —PEARL BAILEY

The questions which one asks oneself begin, at last, to illuminate the world, and become one's key to the experience of others.
—JAMES BALDWIN

"I know myself," he cried, "but that is all." —F. SCOTT FITZGERALD

Know thyself? If I knew myself, I'd run away.
—JOHANN WOLFGANG VON GOETHE

I have the true feeling of myself only when I am unbearably unhappy. —FRANZ KAFKA

When one is a stranger to oneself then one is estranged from others too. —ANNE MORROW LINDBERGH

You can live a lifetime and, at the end of it, know more about other people than you know about yourself. —BERYL MARKHAM

I used to consider myself as great as a pyramid, and now I realize that I am only a shadow that passes. —RACHEL

Who's not sat tense before his own heart's curtain?
—RAINER MARIA RILKE

We know what we are, but know not what we may be.
—WILLIAM SHAKESPEARE

Explore thyself. Herein are demanded the eye and the nerve.
—HENRY DAVID THOREAU

SELF-PITY

(also see concepts 491, 665)

Self-pity in its early stages is as snug as a feather mattress. Only when it hardens does it become uncomfortable. —MAYA ANGELOU

God put self-pity by the side of despair like the cure by the side of the disease. —ALBERT CAMUS

Self-pity comes so naturally to all of us, that the most solid happiness can be shaken by the compassion of a fool.
—ANDRÉ MAUROIS

SELF-REALIZATION

(also see concepts 16, 717)

Is there not a terrible hollowness, mockery, want, craving, in that existence which is given away to others, for want of something of your own to bestow it on? —CHARLOTTE BRONTË

A woman who is willing to be herself and pursue her own potential runs not so much the risk of loneliness as the challenge of exposure to more interesting men–and people in general. —LORRAINE HANSBERRY

One can never consent to creep when one feels an impulse to soar. —HELEN KELLER

I want, by understanding myself, to understand others. I want to be all that I am capable of becoming. —KATHERINE MANSFIELD

We have to dare to be ourselves, however frightening or strange that self may prove to be. —MAY SARTON

SELF-RELIANCE

(also see concepts 1, 75, 145, 167, 722)

The greatest thing in the world is to know how to be self-sufficient. —MICHEL DE MONTAIGNE

Our remedies oft in ourselves do lie, / Which we ascribe to heaven. —WILLIAM SHAKESPEARE

Let me listen to me and not to them. —GERTRUDE STEIN

SELF-RIGHTEOUSNESS

(also see concepts 393, 587, 645)

The righteous one has no sense of humor. —BERTOLT BRECHT

Self-righteousness is a loud din raised to drown the voice of guilt within us. —ERIC HOFFER

SELF-SUFFICIENCY

(also see concepts 145, 709, 720)

We carry our homes within us which enables us to fly. —JOHN CAGE

Be thine own palace, or the world's thy jail. —JOHN DONNE

I don't need a man to rectify my existence. The most profound relationship we'll ever have is the one with ourselves. —SHIRLEY MACLAINE

If you want a thing done well, do it yourself. —NAPOLEON I

How wrong it is for woman to expect the man to build the world she wants, rather than set out to create it herself. —ANAÏS NIN

The proverb warns that, "You should not bite the hand that feeds you." But maybe you should, if it prevents you from feeding yourself. —THOMAS SZASZ

SELFISHNESS

(also see concepts 235, 237, 260, 264, 395, 692, 834)

I have been a selfish being all my life, in practice, though not in principle. —JANE AUSTEN

Human history is the sad result of each one looking out for himself. —JULIO CORTÁZAR

The least pain in our little finger gives us more concern and uneasiness than the destruction of millions of our fellow-beings. —WILLIAM HAZLITT

Next to the very young, I suppose the very old are the most selfish. —WILLIAM MAKEPEACE THACKERAY

THE SENSES

(also see concepts 151, 739, 793)

Nothing awakens a reminiscence like an odour. —VICTOR HUGO

We are astonished at thought, but sensation is equally wonderful. —VOLTAIRE

SENSITIVITY

(also see concept 790)

If we had keen vision and feeling of all ordinary human life, it would be like hearing the grass grow and the squirrel's heart beat, and we should die of that roar which lies on the other side of silence.
—GEORGE ELIOT

SENSUALITY

(also see concepts 570, 731)

How good is man's life, the mere living! how fit to employ / All the heart and the soul and the senses forever in joy! —ROBERT BROWNING

Intellectual passion drives out sensuality. —LEONARDO DA VINCI

I had a feeling that Pandora's box contained the mysteries of women's sensuality, so different from man's, and for which man's language was inadequate. The language of sex had yet to be invented. The language of the senses was yet to be explored. Although women's attitude to sex was quite different from that of men, we had not yet learned to write about it. —ANAÏS NIN

They never taste who always drink. —MATTHEW PRIOR

SENTIMENTALITY

(also see concepts 688, 816)

Sentimentality is a superstructure covering brutality. —CARL JUNG

One may not regard the world as a sort of metaphysical brothel for emotions. —ARTHUR KOESTLER

Sentimentality is only sentiment that rubs you up the wrong way.
—W. SOMERSET MAUGHAM

Sentimentality is a failure of feeling. —WALLACE STEVENS

SERIOUSNESS
(also see concepts 388, 730, 744)

Solemnity is the shield of idiots. —BARON DE MONTESQUIEU

Almost everything serious is difficult, and everything is serious.
—RAINER MARIA RILKE

SERVICE
(also see concepts 344, 873)

To serve is beautiful, but only if it is done with joy and a whole heart
and a free mind. —PEARL S. BUCK

To oblige persons often costs little and helps much.
—BALTASAR GRACIÁN

The pleasure we derive from doing favors is partly in the feeling it
gives us that we are not altogether worthless. —ERIC HOFFER

The charity that is a trifle to us can be precious to others. —HOMER

Human service is the highest form of self-interest for the person
who serves. —ELBERT HUBBARD

Small service is true service, while it lasts. —WILLIAM WORDSWORTH

SEVERITY
(also see concept 174, 728)

Excessive severity misses its own aim. —PUBLILIUS SYRUS

I must be cruel, only to be kind. —WILLIAM SHAKESPEARE

SEX
(also see concepts 4, 24, 28, 95, 160, 283, 354, 417, 448, 472, 494, 656, 707, 867)

It was the most fun I ever had without laughing. —WOODY ALLEN

It's pitch, sex. Once you touch it, it clings to you.
—MARGERY ALLINGHAM

Money, it turned out, was exactly like sex, you thought of nothing else if you didn't have it and thought of other things if you did. —JAMES BALDWIN

I tend to agree that celibacy for a time is worth considering, for sex is dirty if all it means is winning a man, conquering a woman, beating someone out of something, abusing each other's dignity in order to prove that I am a man, I am a woman. —TONI CADE BAMBARA

I wish I had invented sex. Sex is No. 1. —BRIGITTE BARDOT

Sexuality is the lyricism of the masses. —CHARLES BAUDELAIRE

Neither history nor literature has left us any worthwhile evidence on the sexuality of old women. It is an even more strictly forbidden subject than the sexuality of old men. —SIMONE DE BEAUVOIR

In America sex is an obsession, in other parts of the world it is a fact. —MARLENE DIETRICH

The sexual embrace can only be compared with music and with prayer. —HAVELOCK ELLIS

The human need for love and sex is made to bear the burden of all our bodily starvation for contact and sensation, all our creative starvation, all our need for social contact, and even our need to find some meaning in our lives. —DEIRDRE ENGLISH

When modern woman discovered the orgasm it was (combined with modern birth control) perhaps the biggest single nail in the coffin of male dominance. —EVA FIGES

What is peculiar to modern societies is not that they consigned sex to a shadow of existence, but that they dedicated themselves to speaking of it ad infinitum, while exploiting it as the secret. —MICHEL FOUCAULT

Personally I know nothing about sex because I've always been married. —ZSA ZSA GABOR

I'd rather hit than have sex. —REGGIE JACKSON

Sex is good, but not as good as fresh sweet corn. —GARRISON KEILLOR

The only unnatural sex act is that which you cannot perform.
——ALFRED KINSEY

Sex is hardly ever just about sex. ——SHIRLEY MACLAINE

You mustn't force sex to do the work of love or love to do the work of sex. ——MARY MCCARTHY

If sex is such a natural phenomenon, how come there are so many books on how to? ——BETTE MIDLER

The orgasm has replaced the Cross as the focus of longing and the image of fulfillment. ——MALCOLM MUGGERIDGE

Sex is much bigger than genitals. It's a matter of sensory awareness, living in the physical world and reacting to it in a sensory way.
——CAMILLE PAGLIA

It is not sex that gives the pleasure, but the lover. ——MARGE PIERCY

Civilized people cannot fully satisfy their sexual instinct without love. ——BERTRAND RUSSELL

Never miss a chance to have sex or appear on television.
——GORE VIDAL

Sex is the biggest nothing of all time. ——ANDY WARHOL

American teens have the worst of all worlds....Our children are bombarded and confronted with sexual messages, sexual exploitation, and all manner of sexual criticism. But our society is by and large sexually illiterate. ——FAYE WATTLETON

When I'm good I'm very good, but when I'm bad I'm better.
——MAE WEST

An orgasm is just a reflex like a sneeze. ——RUTH WESTHEIMER

SEXISM

(also see concepts 396, 867)

If all men are born free, how is it that all women are born slaves?
——MARY ASTELL

The dogma of women's complete historical subjection to men must be rated as one of the most fantastic myths ever created by the human mind. —MARY RITTER BEARD

Dear sirs, man to man, manpower, craftsman, working men, the thinking man, the man in the street, fellow countrymen, the history of mankind, one-man show, man in his wisdom, statesman, forefathers, masterful, masterpiece, old masters, the brotherhood of man, Liberty, Equality, Fraternity, sons of free men, faith of our fathers, god the father, god the son, yours fraternally, amen. Words fail me. —STEPHANIE DOWRICK

In spite of her supposed segregation to maternal duties, the human female, the world over, works at extra-maternal duties for hours enough to provide her with an independent living, and then is denied independence on the ground that motherhood prevents her working! —CHARLOTTE PERKINS GILMAN

Many women do not recognize themselves as discriminated against; no better proof could be found of the totality of their conditioning. —KATE MILLETT

The world has never yet seen a truly great and virtuous nation, because in the degradation of woman the very fountains of life are poisoned at their source. —LUCRETIA MOTT

I consider that women who are authors, lawyers, and politicians are monsters. —PIERRE AUGUSTE RENOIR

I've always had the feeling I could do anything; my daddy told me I could and I was in college before I found out he might be wrong. —ANN RICHARDS

SEXUAL HARASSMENT

(also see concepts 115, 867)

You know, it would probably be easier for me not to speak out, not to ever say anything about the issues of sexual harassment or the role of women in the workplace and politics, not talk about those things ever again in my life. But I think it would be irresponsible for me not to say what I really believe in my heart to be true–that there are some serious inequities that we face as women and that we can work to address these inequities. —ANITA HILL

Men don't understand that caged feeling. But women know what sexual harassment is. It's when your neck hairs stand up, when you feel like you're being stalked. —SUSAN MARSHALL

Today, on an Ivy League campus, if a guy tells a girl she's got great tits, she can charge him with sexual harassment. Chickenshit stuff. Is this what strong women do? —CAMILLE PAGLIA

SHAME
(also see concepts 71, 158, 237, 683)

Blushing is the color of virtue. —DIOGENES THE CYNIC

We never forgive those who make us blush.
—JEAN-FRANÇOIS DE LA HARPE

Man is the only animal that blushes. Or needs to. —MARK TWAIN

The man that blushes is not quite a brute. —EDWARD YOUNG

SHARING
(also see concepts 101, 309, 662)

Sharing is sometimes more demanding than giving.
—MARY CATHERINE BATESON

Blessed are those who can give without remembering, and take without forgetting. —ELIZABETH BIBESCO

I think that, as life is action and passion, it is required of a man that he should share the passion and action of his time at peril of being judged not to have lived. —OLIVER WENDELL HOLMES, JR.

There's no delight in owning anything unshared. —SENECA

We are rich only through what we give, and poor only through what we refuse. —ANNE-SOPHIE SWETCHINE

SHIPS AND BOATS

(also see concepts 695, 814)

The anchor heaves, the ship swings free, The sails swell full. To sea, to sea! —THOMAS LOVELL BEDDOES

As idle as a painted ship / Upon a painted ocean.
—SAMUEL TAYLOR COLERIDGE

The ship, a fragment detached from the earth, went on lonely and swift like a small planet. —JOSEPH CONRAD

SHYNESS

(also see concepts 71, 91, 168, 369, 510, 740)

I'm really a timid person–I was beaten up by Quakers.
—WOODY ALLEN

Do not be too timid and squeamish about your actions. All life is an experiment. —RALPH WALDO EMERSON

I used to hang out by the food table at parties because you don't really have to talk to anybody, and if you do, you can talk about the food. —JENNIFER JASON LEIGH

Happiness hates the timid! So does Science! —EUGENE O'NEILL

SICKNESS

(also see concepts 28, 209, 340, 373, 402, 489)

To be too conscious is an illness–a real thorough-going illness.
—FYODOR DOSTOYEVSKY

Disease is an experience of so-called mortal mind. It is fear made manifest on the body. —MARY BAKER EDDY

All diseases run into one, old age. —RALPH WALDO EMERSON

The most important thing in illness is never to lose heart.
—V. I. LENIN

Diseases are the tax on pleasures. —JOHN RAY

The diseases which destroy a man are no less natural than the instincts which preserve him. —GEORGE SANTAYANA

Disease is not of the body but of the place. —SENECA

We are so fond of one another, because our ailments are the same. —JONATHAN SWIFT

SIGHT
(also see concepts 70, 265, 504, 551, 577, 581, 724, 797)

Eyes are more accurate witnesses than ears. —HERACLITUS

Make the most of every sense: glory in all facets of pleasure and beauty which the world reveals to you through the several means of contact which nature provides. But of all the senses, sight must be the most delightful. —HELEN KELLER

SILENCE
(also see concepts 543, 677, 678, 706, 737, 756)

Silences have a climax, when you have got to speak. —ELIZABETH BOWEN

Speech is of time, silence is of eternity. —THOMAS CARLYLE

Do not the most moving moments of our lives find us all without words? —MARCEL MARCEAU

Let a fool hold his tongue and he will pass for a sage. —PUBLILIUS SYRUS

An absolute silence leads to sadness: it is the image of death. —JEAN JACQUES ROUSSEAU

Silence is the most perfect expression of scorn. —GEORGE BERNARD SHAW

My personal hobbies are reading, listening to music, and silence. —EDITH SITWELL

Whereof one cannot speak, thereon one must remain silent. —LUDWIG WITTGENSTEIN

SIMILARITY
(also see concepts 136, 147, 244, 490, 831)

The fact that we are human beings is infinitely more important than all the peculiarities that distinguish human beings from one another. ——SIMONE DE BEAUVOIR

Not at all similar are the race of the immortal gods and the race of men who walk upon the earth. ——HOMER

But it is not really difference the oppressor fears so much as similarity. ——CHERRIE MORAGA

Birds of a feather flock together. ——PROVERB

SIMPLICITY
(also see concepts 117, 380, 775)

Less is more. ——ROBERT BROWNING

Simplicity is the peak of civilization. ——JESSIE SAMPTER

Our life is frittered away by detail....Simplify, simplify. ——HENRY DAVID THOREAU

The art of art, the glory of expression and the sunshine of the light of letters, is simplicity. ——WALT WHITMAN

SIN
(also see concepts 4, 144, 150, 164, 186, 203, 249, 332, 437, 515, 643, 670, 840)

All sins tend to be addictive, and the terminal point of addiction is what is called damnation. ——W. H. AUDEN

Sin brought death, and death will disappear with the disappearance of sin. ——MARY BAKER EDDY

Really to sin you have to be serious about it. ——HENRIK IBSEN

Adam ate the apple, and our teeth still ache. ——HUNGARIAN PROVERB

Sins cannot be undone, only forgiven. ——IGOR STRAVINSKY

There is not sin except stupidity. —OSCAR WILDE

SINCERITY
(also see concepts 297, 355, 728)

Best be yourself, imperial, plain and true! —ROBERT BROWNING

Sincerity is not a spontaneous flower nor is modesty either.
—COLETTE

I'm afraid of losing my obscurity. Genuineness only thrives in the dark. Like celery. —ALDOUS HUXLEY

The way I see it, it doesn't matter what you believe just so you're sincere. —CHARLES M. SCHULTZ

A little sincerity is a dangerous thing, and a great deal of it is absolutely fatal. —OSCAR WILDE

SINGING
(also see concepts 9, 524, 543, 554, 761)

These days, what isn't worth saying is sung.
—PIERRE DE BEAUMARCHAIS

It is the best of all trades, to make songs, and the second best to sing them. —HILAIRE BELLOC

I can't stand to sing the same song the same way two nights in succession. If you can, then it ain't music, it's close-order drill, or exercise or yodeling or something, not music. —BILLIE HOLIDAY

I can hold a note as long as the Chase National Bank.
—ETHEL MERMAN

SLANDER
(also see concepts 322, 408, 527)

Every one in a crowd has the power to throw dirt: nine out of ten have the inclination. —WILLIAM HAZLITT

Calumnies are answered best with silence. —BEN JONSON

Be thou as chaste as ice, as pure as snow, thou shalt not escape calumny. —WILLIAM SHAKESPEARE

SLAVERY
(also see concepts 89, 196)

Men would rather be starving and free than fed in bonds.
—PEARL S. BUCK

The future is the only kind of property that the masters willingly concede to slaves. —ALBERT CAMUS

The whole commerce between master and slave is a perpetual exercise of the most boisterous passions, the most unremitting despotism on the one part, and degrading submissions on the other.
—THOMAS JEFFERSON

Slaves lose everything in their chains, even the desire of escaping from them. —JEAN JACQUES ROUSSEAU

All spirits are enslaved which serve things evil.
—PERCY BYSSHE SHELLEY

Servitude debases men to the point where they end up liking it.
—MARQUIS DE VAUVENARGUES

SLEEP
(also see concepts 60, 77, 224, 541, 677)

Laugh and the world laughs with you; snore and you sleep alone.
—ANTHONY BURGESS

Fatigue is the best pillow. —BENJAMIN FRANKLIN

Sleep is when all the unsorted stuff comes flying out as from a dustbin upset in a high wind. —WILLIAM GOLDING

O soft embalmer of the still midnight. —JOHN KEATS

Sleeping is no mean art: for its sake one must stay awake all day.
—FRIEDRICH WILHELM NIETZSCHE

No day is so bad it can't be fixed with a nap. —CARRIE SNOW

SLOWNESS
(also see concepts 338, 641, 762)

Slow and steady wins the race. —AESOP

There is a slowness in affairs which ripens them, and a slowness which rots them. —JOSEPH ROUX

The haste of a fool is the slowest thing in the world.
—THOMAS SHADWELL

SMOKING
(also see concepts 9, 12, 226, 840)

Smokers, male and female, inject and excuse idleness in their lives every time they light a cigarette. —COLETTE

The believing we do something when we do nothing is the first illusion of tobacco. —RALPH WALDO EMERSON

Tobacco surely was designed / To poison, and destroy mankind.
—PHILIP FRENEAU

Smoking is, as far as I'm concerned, the entire point of being an adult. —FRAN LEBOWITZ

A cigarette is the perfect type of a perfect pleasure. It is exquisite, and it leaves one unsatisfied. What more can one want?
—OSCAR WILDE

SNOBBERY
(also see concepts 44, 45, 618, 619)

Snobs talk as if they had begotten their own ancestors.
—HERBERT AGAR

Philistine–a term of contempt applied by prigs to the rest of their species. —LESLIE STEPHEN

Laughter would be bereaved if snobbery died. —PETER USTINOV

SNOW

(also see concepts 127, 789, 858, 862)

Only in the snow can both sexagenarian and child squat on the same small sledges and abandon themselves to the slopes. They feel alike and exchange smiles....Oh simple, precarious, eternal realm of snow! —COLETTE

The first fall of snow is not only an event, it is a magical event. You go to bed in one kind of world and wake up in another quite different, and if this is not without enchantment then where is it to be found? —J. B. PRIESTLEY

SOCIAL   CHANGE

(also see concepts 663, 681)

Everybody wants to do something to help, but nobody wants to be first. —PEARL BAILEY

Most Americans have never seen the ignorance, degradation, hunger, sickness, and futility in which many other Americans live....They won't become involved in economic or political change until something brings the seriousness of the situation home to them. —SHIRLEY CHISHOLM

We criticize and separate ourselves from the process. We've got to jump right in there with both feet. —DOLORES HUERTA

There have been times in American history when privileged children were profoundly subject to pangs of conscience and willing to take action....And thousands of decent kids took a role in changing history. But nowadays they are anesthetized. They are either unwilling to take action or they're persuaded that it won't make any difference. —JONATHAN KOZOL

Art school in 1968 was about...suggesting to you in a certain way that you might be out to change things, but not by going through the committees and the socialist cult movements that existed in art

school at the time. You could change things by–dare I say–sloganing a wall, throwing a brick through a hamburger bar. It seems trite now, but at the time we were delighting in it.
—MALCOLM MCLAREN

Anytime you have change that challenges the traditional acceptance of a certain situation, you will have people who are worried that this is going to take us down the path to destruction. It's amazing to me how long that has been with us–probably since we evolved.
—FAYE WATTLETON

The '80s are wilder than the '60s...in the mid-'60s the idea of a coed dorm, putting those nubile young things and these young men in the season of the rising sap in the same dormitories, on the same floors! Now the coed dorm is like I-95. It's there. It hums. And you don't notice it. —TOM WOLFE

SOCIALISM
(also see concepts 133, 231)

There is nothing in Socialism that a little age or a little money will not cure. —WILL DURANT

Under socialism *all* will govern in turn and will soon become accustomed to no one governing. —V. I. LENIN

As with the Christian religion, the worst advertisement for Socialism is its adherents. —GEORGE ORWELL

Socialism must come down from the brain and reach the heart.
—JULES RENARD

SOCIETY
(also see concepts 135, 177, 561)

...society is a complex and mysterious creation and...it's extremely imprudent to believe in the face it presents you with at a given moment, let alone to consider it the one and only true face.
—VÁCLAV HAVEL

Society is always trying in some way or other to grind us down to a single flat surface. —OLIVER WENDELL HOLMES, SR.

The spirit of truth and the spirit of freedom–they are the pillars of society. —HENRIK IBSEN

The great society is a place where men are more concerned with the quality of their goods than with the quantity of their goods. —LYNDON B. JOHNSON

Society is no comfort / To one not sociable. —WILLIAM SHAKESPEARE

Man is a social animal. —BENEDICT SPINOZA

SOLIDARITY
(also see concepts 143, 831)

We're all spokes in the wheel, going to the point, getting the ball rolling. Have you ever seen a wheel with one spoke? It's not a wheel. You got to come from different directions to get to the same point. And roll. —ICE CUBE

Solidarity still exists inside us, even in those who deny it. —LECH WALESA

SOLITUDE
(also see concepts 30, 462, 622, 678, 706)

Whosoever is delighted in solitude is either a beast or a god. —FRANCIS BACON

Solitary trees, if they grow at all, grow strong. —WINSTON CHURCHILL

Hell is oneself; Hell is alone, the other figures in it merely projections. There is nothing to escape from and nothing to escape to. One is always alone. —GEORGE ELIOT

We never touch but at points. —RALPH WALDO EMERSON

I want to be left alone. —GRETA GARBO

Solitude is un-American. —ERICA JONG

What a commentary on our civilization when being alone is considered suspect; when one has to apologize for it, make excuses, hide the fact that one practices it–like a secret vice! —ANNE MORROW LINDBERGH

The nurse of full-grown souls is solitude. —JAMES RUSSELL LOWELL

There is a confinement and a discipline and a preparation for leadership that you develop through being alone, which women are fearful of. —JEWELL JACKSON MCCABE

Solitude is the playfield of Satan. —VLADIMIR NABOKOV

Life is for each man a solitary cell whose walls are mirrors. —EUGENE O'NEILL

One would not be alone even in Paradise. —ITALIAN PROVERB

One can acquire everything in solitude except character. —STENDHAL

I never found the companion that was so companionable as solitude. —HENRY DAVID THOREAU

SORROW

(also see concepts 175, 199, 237, 491, 665, 670, 718, 790, 827)

Joys impregnate. Sorrows bring forth. —WILLIAM BLAKE

It is better to learn early of the inevitable depths, for then sorrow and death take their proper place in life, and one is not afraid. —PEARL S. BUCK

There is something pleasurable in calm remembrance of a past sorrow. —CICERO

One often calms one's grief by recounting it. —PIERRE CORNEILLE

Grief is the agony of an instant; the indulgence of grief the blunder of a life. —BENJAMIN DISRAELI

Grief can't be shared. Everyone carries it alone, his own burden, his own way. —ANNE MORROW LINDBERGH

There is not grief that does not speak. —HENRY WADSWORTH LONGFELLOW

Rapture's self is three parts sorrow. —AMY LOWELL

He truly sorrows unseen. —MARTIAL

Sorrow is so easy to express and yet so hard to tell. —JONI MITCHELL

Sorrow is tranquillity remembered in emotion. —DOROTHY PARKER

It is such a secret place, the land of tears.
—ANTOINE DE SAINT-EXUPÉRY

When sorrows come, they come not single spies, / But in battalions!
—WILLIAM SHAKESPEARE

Where there is sorrow there is holy ground. —OSCAR WILDE

THE SOUL
(also see concepts 23, 763)

Why do you hasten to remove anything which hurts your eye, while if something affects your soul you postpone the cure until next year? —HORACE

It is the still small voice that the soul heeds; not the deafening blasts of doom. —WILLIAM DEAN HOWELLS

Every soul is a melody which needs renewing. —STÉPHANE MALLARME

A beautiful soul has no other merit than its existence.
—JOHANN FRIEDRICH VON SCHILLER

SPACE, OUTER
(also see concepts 342, 766, 832)

The sky hides the night behind it, and shelters the person beneath from the horror that lies above. —PAUL BOWLES

Don't tell me that man doesn't belong there. Man belongs wherever he wants to go; and he'll do plenty when he gets there.
—WERNHER VON BRAUN

Walking in space, man has never looked more puny or more significant. —ALEXANDER CHASE

Today we can no more predict what use mankind may make of the Moon than could Columbus have imagined the future of the continent he had discovered. —ARTHUR C. CLARKE

In curved Einsteinian space we are at all times, technically, looking at the back of our own head. —GUY DAVENPORT

Space flights are merely an escape, a fleeing away from oneself, because it is easier to go to Mars or to the moon than it is to penetrate one's own being. —CARL JUNG

The eternal silence of these infinite spaces frightens me.
—BLAISE PASCAL

I would be very ashamed of my civilization if we did not try to find out if there is life in outer space. —CARL SAGAN

I see nothing in space as promising as the view from a Ferris wheel.
—E. B. WHITE

SPAIN AND THE SPANISH
(also see concepts 212, 247)

In Spain, the dead are more alive than the dead of any other country in the world. —FEDERICO GARCIÁ LORCA

SPEAKING
(also see concepts 132, 144, 162, 236, 322, 441, 457, 631, 638, 868)

Little said is soon amended. —MIGUEL DE CERVANTES

No glass renders a man's form or likeness so true as his speech.
—BEN JONSON

What is uttered is finished and done with. —THOMAS MANN

They always talk who never think. —MATTHEW PRIOR

Speak when you are spoken to. —PROVERB

In speech with a man a woman is at a disadvantage—because they speak different languages. She may understand his. Hers he will never speak nor understand. In pity, or from other motives, she must therefore, stammeringly, speak his. He listens and is flattered and thinks he has her mental measure when he has not touched even the fringe of her consciousness. —DOROTHY RICHARDSON

When I think over what I have said, I envy dumb people. —SENECA

Speech is the mirror of action. —SOLON

When women are supposed to be quiet, a talkative woman is a woman who talks at all. —DALE SPENDER

Talk low, talk slow, and don't say too much. —JOHN WAYNE

SPEED
(also see concepts 10, 194, 241, 338, 641)

In skating over thin ice our safety is in our speed.
—RALPH WALDO EMERSON

Celerity is never more admired / Than by the negligent.
—WILLIAM SHAKESPEARE

SPIRITUALITY
(also see concepts 313, 324, 483, 525, 696, 758, 784)

Invest in the human soul. Who knows, it might be a diamond in the rough. —MARY MCLEOD BETHUNE

There is one spectacle grander than the sea, that is the sky; there is one spectacle grander than the sky, that is the interior of the soul.
—VICTOR HUGO

Science can point out dangers, but science cannot turn the direction of minds and hearts. That is the province of spiritual powers within and without our very beings–powers that are the mysteries of life itself. —OREN LYONS

If you surrendered to the air, you could ride it. —TONI MORRISON

Physical strength can never permanently withstand the impact of spiritual force. —FRANKLIN D. ROOSEVELT

SPONTANEITY
(also see concepts 338, 419, 592)

Spontaneity is only a term for man's ignorance of the gods.
—SAMUEL BUTLER

The most decisive actions of our life–I mean those that are most likely to decide the whole course of our future–are, more often than not, unconsidered. —ANDRÉ GIDE

The essence of pleasure is spontaneity. —GERMAINE GREER

SPORTS AND GAMES
(also see concepts 10, 58, 137, 256, 286, 292, 305, 318, 359, 372)

In America, it is sport that is the opiate of the masses.
—RUSSELL BAKER

If they cut my bald head open, they will find one big boxing glove. That's all I am. I live it. —MARVIN HAGLER

When I step onto the court, I don't have to think about anything. If I have a problem off the court, I find that after I play, my mind is clearer and I can come up with a better solution. It's like therapy. It relaxes me and allows me to solve problems. —MICHAEL JORDAN

Champions take responsibility. When the ball is coming over the net, you can be sure I want the ball. —BILLIE JEAN KING

Serious sport has nothing to do with fair play. It is bound up with hatred, jealousy, boastfulness, disregard of all rules and sadistic pleasure in witnessing violence: in other words it is war minus the shooting. —GEORGE ORWELL

Games are for people who can neither read nor think.
—GEORGE BERNARD SHAW

STARS

(also see concepts 342, 514, 759, 782, 832)

When it is dark enough you can see the stars.
—RALPH WALDO EMERSON

If we could count the stars, we should not weep before them.
—GEORGE SANTAYANA

THE STATE

(also see conepts 83, 111, 596, 616, 636, 794)

The state exists for the sake of a good life, and not for the sake of life only. —ARISTOTLE

A state worthy of the name has no friends–only interests.
—CHARLES DE GAULLE

States, like men, have their growth, their manhood, their decrepitude, their decay. —WALTER SAVAGE LANDOR

While the state exists there is no freedom; when there is freedom there will be no state. —V. I. LENIN

Our object in the construction of the state is the greatest happiness of the whole, and not that of any one class. —PLATO

The fundamental fact of political and social life today is that all states are impure hybrids. It is this tension between the idea of the hybrid and homogeneous state that is the great social and political problem to be resolved. —EDWARD SAID

The responsibility of great states is to serve and not to dominate the world. —HARRY S TRUMAN

STATISTICS

(also see concepts 267, 484)

I could prove God statistically. —GEORGE GALLUP

Statistics are like alienists–they will testify for either side. —FIORELLO LA GUARDIA

Statistics are like a bikini. What they reveal is suggestive, but what they conceal is vital. —AARON LEVENSTEIN

I am one of the unpraised, unrewarded millions without whom Statistics would be a bankrupt science. It is we who are born, who marry, who die, in constant ratio. —LOGAN PEARSALL SMITH

There are three kinds of lies–lies, damned lies and statistics. —MARK TWAIN

STEALING
(also see concepts 9, 214, 590)

All stealing is comparative. If you come to absolutes, pray who does not steal? —RALPH WALDO EMERSON

Opportunity makes the thief. —ENGLISH PROVERB

The faults of the burglar are the qualities of the financier. —GEORGE BERNARD SHAW

STEREOTYPES
(also see concepts 147, 180, 252, 335, 727, 830)

In the great blooming, buzzing confusion of the outer world we pick out what our culture has already defined for us, and we tend to perceive that which we have picked out in the form stereotyped for us by our culture. —WALTER LIPPMANN

Instead of being presented with stereotypes by age, sex, color, class, or religion, children must have the opportunity to learn that within each range, some people are loathsome and some are delightful. —MARGARET MEAD

Every society has a tendency to reduce its opponents to caricatures. —FRIEDRICH WILHELM NIETZSCHE

What is repugnant to every human being is to be reckoned always as a member of a class and not as an individual person. —DOROTHY L. SAYERS

We all know we are unique individuals, but we tend to see others as representatives of groups. —DEBORAH TANNEN

STOICISM

(also see concepts 86, 127, 392, 535, 879)

Let a man accept his destiny, / No pity and no tears. —EURIPIDES

Be content with what you are, and wish not change; nor dread your last day, nor long for it. —MARTIAL

The stoical scheme of supplying our wants by lopping off our desires, is like cutting off our feet, when we want shoes. —JONATHAN SWIFT

STRENGTH

(also see concepts 167, 239, 293, 608)

Let women be provided with living strength of their own. Let them have the means to attack the world and wrest from it their own subsistence, and their dependence will be abolished–that of man also. —SIMONE DE BEAUVOIR

The awareness of our own strength makes us modest. —PAUL CÉZANNE

Like strength is felt from hope, and from despair. —HOMER

What is strength without a double share / Of wisdom? —JOHN MILTON

True strength is delicate. —LOUISE NEVELSON

O! it is excellent to have a giant's strength; but it is tyrannous to use it like a giant. —WILLIAM SHAKESPEARE

There are two ways of exerting one's strength: one is pushing down, the other is pulling up. —BOOKER T. WASHINGTON

STRESS

(also see concepts 239, 426, 532, 558)

One of my problems is that I internalize everything. I can't express anger; I grow a tumor instead. —WOODY ALLEN

You don't get ulcers from what you eat. You get them from what's eating you. —VICKI BAUM

It has long been my belief that in times of great stress, such as a four-day vacation, the thin veneer of family wears off almost at once, and we are revealed in our true personalities.... —SHIRLEY JACKSON

For fast-acting relief try slowing down. —LILY TOMLIN

STUBBORNNESS

(also see concepts 202, 579, 583, 623)

For every why he had a wherefore. —SAMUEL BUTLER

Obstinacy is the sister of constancy, at least in vigor and stability. —MICHEL DE MONTAIGNE

Time has a way of demonstrating / the most stubborn are the most intelligent. —YEVGENY YEVTUSHENKO

STUPIDITY

(also see concepts 5, 123, 291, 544, 689, 749)

A learned blockhead is a greater blockhead than an ignorant one. —BENJAMIN FRANKLIN

It is so pleasant to come across people more stupid than ourselves. We love them at once for being so. —JEROME K. JEROME

STYLE

(also see concepts 124, 277, 324, 509, 793, 808)

Style is primarily a matter of instinct. —BILL BLASS

Style is the perfection of a point of view. —RICHARD EBERHART

Everybody wants to know about my style and how it came about. It's no big secret. It's the way I feel. —ELLA FITZGERALD

Style is the mind skating circles round itself as it moves forward. —ROBERT FROST

Style is character. A good style cannot come from a bad, undisciplined character. —NORMAN MAILER

A good style should show no sign of effort. What is written should seem a happy accident. —W. SOMERSET MAUGHAM

Style is the hallmark of a temperament stamped upon the material at hand. —ANDRÉ MAUROIS

Style is the physiognomy of the mind, and a safer index to character than the face. —ARTHUR SCHOPENHAUER

Style, like the human body, is specially beautiful when the veins are not prominent and the bones cannot be counted. —TACITUS

In matters of grave importance, style, not sincerity, is the vital thing. —OSCAR WILDE

THE SUBURBS
(also see concepts 113, 166, 589)

Slums may well be breeding-grounds of crime, but middle-class suburbs are incubators of apathy and delirium. —CYRIL CONNOLLY

Conformity may not always reign in the prosperous bourgeois suburb, but it ultimately always governs. —LOUIS KRONENBERGER

Suburbs are things to come into the city from. —ART LINKLETTER

SUCCESS
(also see concepts 31, 50, 268, 630, 841)

Success is as ice cold and lonely as the North Pole. —VICKI BAUM

The toughest thing about success is that you've got to keep on being a success. —IRVING BERLIN

Never lose sight of the fact that the most important yardstick of your success will be how you treat other people–your family, friends, and coworkers, and even strangers you meet along the way. —BARBARA BUSH

Success is counted sweetest / By those who ne'er succeed.
—EMILY DICKINSON

Success is relative: It is what we can make of the mess we have made of things. —T. S. ELIOT

I've got two reasons for success and I'm standing on both of them.
—BETTY GRABLE

Apparent failure may hold in its rough shell the germs of a success that will blossom in time, and bear fruit throughout eternity.
—FRANCES ELLEN WATKINS HARPER

Success and failure are both difficult to endure. Along with success come drugs, divorce, fornication, bullying, travel, meditation, medication, depression, neurosis and suicide. With failure comes failure. —JOSEPH HELLER

I'm always making a comeback but nobody ever tells me where I've been. —BILLIE HOLIDAY

The way to rise is to obey and please. —BEN JONSON

Success didn't spoil me; I've always been insufferable.
—FRAN LEBOWITZ

There is only one success–to be able to spend your life in your own way. —CHRISTOPHER MORLEY

The ultimate of being successful is the luxury of giving yourself the time to do what you want to do. —LEONTYNE PRICE

Success is not greedy, as people think, but insignificant. That's why it satisfies nobody. —SENECA

The trouble with being in the rat race is that even if you win, you're still a rat. —LILY TOMLIN

Success can make you go one of two ways. It can make you a prima donna, or it can smooth the edges, take away the insecurities, let the nice things come out. —BARBARA WALTERS

Success and failure are equally disastrous. —TENNESSEE WILLIAMS

SUFFERING
(also see concepts 239, 506, 564, 872)

Suffering is the sole origin of consciousness. —FYODOR DOSTOYEVSKY

God will not look you over for medals, degrees or diplomas, but for scars! —ELBERT HUBBARD

Pleasure is oft a visitant; but pain / Clings cruelly to us.
—JOHN KEATS

Although the world is full of suffering, it is full also of the overcoming of it. —HELEN KELLER

What really raises one's indignation against suffering is not suffering intrinsically, but the senselessness of suffering.
—FRIEDRICH WILHELM NIETZSCHE

We are healed of a suffering only by experiencing it to the full.
—MARCEL PROUST

SUFFICIENCY
(also see concepts 329, 856)

You never know what is enough unless you know what is more than enough. —WILLIAM BLAKE

SUICIDE
(also see concepts 185, 710, 713)

If I had the use of my body, I would throw it out the window.
—SAMUEL BECKETT

As soon as one does not kill oneself, one must keep silent about life.
—ALBERT CAMUS

When even despair ceases to serve any creative purpose, then surely we are justified in suicide. —CYRIL CONNOLLY

...I don't like the fact that death, which is a pretty important moment in my life, I don't like this to have no meaning: The only way you can do anything about that is to control the moment and the means of your death. And that means suicide, basically.
—DAVID CRONENBERG

I take it that no man is educated who has never dallied with the thought of suicide. —WILLIAM JAMES

If you are of the opinion that the contemplation of suicide is sufficient evidence of a poetic nature, do not forget that actions speak louder than words. —FRAN LEBOWITZ

No one ever lacks a good reason for suicide. —CESARE PAVESE

When you're between any sort of devil and the deep blue sea, the deep blue sea sometimes looks very inviting. —TERENCE RATTIGAN

How many people have wanted to kill themselves, and have been content with tearing up their photograph! —JULES RENARD

We cannot tear out a single page from our life, but we can throw the whole book into the fire. —GEORGE SAND

Just as I shall select my ship when I am about to go on a voyage, or my house when I propose to take a residence, so I shall choose my death when I am about to depart from life. —SENECA

THE SUN
(also see concepts 342, 514, 516, 766, 832)

I have a horror of sunsets, they're so romantic, so operatic.
—MARCEL PROUST

Thank heavens, the sun has gone in, and I don't have to go out and enjoy it. —LOGAN PEARSALL SMITH

Goodness comes out of people who bask in the sun, as it does out of a sweet apple roasted before the fire. —CHARLES DUDLEY WARNER

SUPERIORITY

(also see concepts 244, 310, 398, 578, 608)

Never look down on anybody unless you're helping them up.
——JESSE JACKSON

It is brought home to you...that it is only because miners sweat their guts out that superior persons can remain superior.
——GEORGE ORWELL

Class supremacy, male supremacy, white supremacy–it's all the same game. If you're on top of someone, the society tells you you are better. ——COLETTA REID AND CHARLOTTE BUNCH

THE   SUPERNATURAL

(also see concepts 503, 523, 525)

A belief in a supernatural source of evil is not necessary; men alone are quite capable of every wickedness. ——JOSEPH CONRAD

The supernatural is the natural not yet understood.
——ELBERT HUBBARD

Faith in the supernatural is a desperate wager made by man at the lowest ebb of his fortunes. ——GEORGE SANTAYANA

SUPERSTITION

(also see concepts 503, 526)

Superstition is the religion of feeble minds. ——EDMUND BURKE

Superstition is the poetry of life. ——JOHANN WOLFGANG VON GOETHE

Men become superstitious, not because they have too much imagination, but because they are not aware that they have any.
——GEORGE SANTAYANA

They say there is divinity in odd numbers, either in nativity, chance, or death. ——WILLIAM SHAKESPEARE

No one is so thoroughly superstitious as the godless man.
——HARRIET BEECHER STOWE

Superstition sets the whole world in flames; philosophy quenches them. —VOLTAIRE

SURPRISE
(also see conceps 212, 259)

Surprise is the greatest gift which life can grant us.
—BORIS PASTERNAK

Life is very singularly made to surprise us (where it does not utterly appall us). —RAINER MARIA RILKE

SURVIVAL
(also see concepts 239, 250)

People are inexterminable–like flies and bed-bugs. There will always be some that survive in cracks and crevices–that's us.
—ROBERT FROST

Self-preservation is the first principle of our nature.
—ALEXANDER HAMILTON

Surviving means being born over and over. —ERICA JONG

If you live among wolves you have to act like a wolf.
—NIKITA KHRUSHCHEV

To survive it is often necessary to fight, and to fight you have to dirty yourself. —GEORGE ORWELL

When you get to the end of your rope, tie a knot and hang on.
—FRANKLIN D. ROOSEVELT

Nature is indifferent to the survival of the human species, including Americans. —ADLAI STEVENSON

The more we exploit nature, the more our options are reduced, until we have only one: to fight for survival. —MORRIS K. UDALL

SWEARING

(also see concepts 9, 798, 848)

'Twas but my tongue, 'twas not my soul that swore. —EURIPIDES

Grant me some wild expression, Heavens, or I shall burst.
—GEORGE FARQUHAR

Let us swear while we may, for in heaven it will not be allowed.
—MARK TWAIN

Profanity furnishes a relief denied even to prayer. —MARK TWAIN

SWITZERLAND AND THE SWISS

(also see concepts 247, 529)

The Swiss...are not a people so much as a neat clean quite solvent business. —WILLIAM FAULKNER

I look upon Switzerland as an inferior sort of Scotland.
—SYDNEY SMITH

SYMPATHY

(also see concepts 438, 588, 725, 809, 824)

Sympathy is a supporting atmosphere, and in it we unfold easily and well. —RALPH WALDO EMERSON

To be sympathetic without discrimination is so very debilitating.
—RONALD FIRBANK

She was a machine-gun riddling her hostess with sympathy.
—ALDOUS HUXLEY

Pathos is the sense of distance. —ANTOINE DE SAINT-EXUPÉRY

There is nothing sweeter than to be sympathized with.
—GEORGE SANTAYANA

TACT

(also see concepts 91, 208, 863)

One shouldn't talk of halters in the hanged man's house.
——MIGUEL DE CERVANTES

Tact consists in knowing how far we may go too far.
——JEAN COCTEAU

Tact is after all a kind of mind reading. ——SARAH ORNE JEWETT

TALENT

(also see concepts 1, 178, 253, 605, 608)

I believe talent is like electricity. We do not understand electricity.
We use it. Electricity makes no judgement. You can plug into it,
and light up a lamp, keep a heart pump going, light a cathedral, or
you can electrocute a person with it....I think talent is like that. I
believe every person is born with talent. ——MAYA ANGELOU

It takes little talent to see clearly what lies under one's nose, a good
deal of it to know in what direction to point that organ.
——W. H. AUDEN

Tremendous amounts of talent are being lost to our society just
because that talent wears a skirt. ——SHIRLEY CHISHOLM

Whom the gods wish to destroy they first call promising.
——CYRIL CONNOLLY

The most gifted natures are perhaps also the most trembling.
——ANDRÉ GIDE

Talent develops in quiet places, character in the full current of
human life. ——JOHANN WOLFGANG VON GOETHE

There is no substitute for talent. Industry and all the virtues are of
no avail. ——ALDOUS HUXLEY

Everyone has talent. What is rare is the courage to follow the talent
to the dark place where it leads. ——ERICA JONG

Talent is a question of quantity. Talent does not write one page: it writes three hundred. —JULES RENARD

Be equal to your talent, not your age. / At times let the gap between them be embarrassing. —YEVGENY YEVTUSHENKO

TASTE
(also see concepts 290, 724, 776)

Between friends differences in taste or opinion are irritating in direct proportion to their triviality. —W. H. AUDEN

What is food to one man is bitter poison to others. —LUCRETIUS

In literature as in love, we are astonished at what is chosen by others. —ANDRÉ MAUROIS

All of life is a dispute over taste and tasting.
—FRIEDRICH WILHELM NIETZSCHE

The kind of people who always go on about whether a thing is in good taste invariably have very bad taste. —JOE ORTON

Taste is the enemy of creativeness. —PABLO PICASSO

Good taste is the worst vice ever invented. —EDITH SITWELL

Taste has no system and no proofs. —SUSAN SONTAG

TAXES
(also see concepts 114, 227, 323, 574)

Read my lips: no new taxes. —GEORGE BUSH

The hardest thing in the world to understand is income tax.
—ALBERT EINSTEIN

Only little people pay taxes. —LEONA HELMSLEY

The avoidance of taxes is the only pursuit that still carries any reward. —JOHN MAYNARD KEYNES

The power to tax involves the power to destroy. —JOHN MARSHALL

Taxes, after all, are the dues that we pay for the privileges of membership in an organized society. —FRANKLIN D. ROOSEVELT

Income taxes are the most imaginative fiction written today. —HERMAN WOUK

TEACHERS AND TEACHING
(also see concepts 19, 90, 233, 446, 458, 614)

A professor is one who talks in someone else's sleep. —W. H. AUDEN

A university is what a college becomes when the faculty loses interest in students. —JOHN CIARDI

One good schoolmaster is worth a thousand priests. —ROBERT G. INGERSOLL

To teach is to learn twice over. —JOSEPH JOUBERT

It is easier for a tutor to command than to teach. —JOHN LOCKE

He who can, does. He who cannot, teaches. —GEORGE BERNARD SHAW

Children should be led into the right paths, not by severity, but by persuasion. —TERENCE

TECHNOLOGY
(also see concepts 29, 56, 141, 474, 546, 797, 820)

Technology is the science of arranging life so that one need not experience it. —ANONYMOUS

Any sufficiently advanced technology is indistinguishable from magic. —ARTHUR C. CLARKE

Where there is the necessary technical skill to move mountains, there is no need for the faith that moves mountains. —ERIC HOFFER

Technology made large populations possible; large populations now make technology indispensable. —JOSEPH WOOD KRUTCH

The new electronic interdependence recreates the world in the image of a global village. —MARSHALL MCLUHAN

It is critical vision alone which can mitigate the unimpeded operation of the automatic. —MARSHALL MCLUHAN

TELEVISION
(also see concepts 33, 132, 482, 539, 796, 820)

Television is the first truly democratic culture–the first culture available to everybody and entirely governed by what the people want. The most terrifying thing is what the people do want.
—CLIVE BARNES

Some television programs are so much chewing gum for the eyes.
—JOHN MASON BROWN

Art is moral passion married to entertainment. Moral passion without entertainment is propaganda, and entertainment without moral passion is television. —RITA MAE BROWN

Television is democracy at its ugliest. —PADDY CHAYEFSKY

Television is for appearing on, not looking at. —NOËL COWARD

It is a medium of entertainment which permits millions of people to listen to the same joke at the same time, and yet remain lonesome. —T. S. ELIOT

Television is an invention that permits you to be entertained in your living room by people you wouldn't have in your home.
—DAVID FROST

Why should people go out and pay to see bad films when they can stay at home and see bad television for nothing? —SAMUEL GOLDWYN

It is just four weeks into the new television season, and already you can't tell the pregnancies, the false alarms, and the in-vitro fertilizations without a score card. —CARYN JAMES

A medium, so called because it is neither rare nor well done.
—ERNIE KOVACS

Television has proved that people will look at anything rather than at each other. —ANN LANDERS

It is television's primary damage that it provides ten million children with the same fantasy, ready-made and on a platter. —MARYA MANNES

I find television very educational. Every time someone switches it on I go into another room and read a good book. —GROUCHO MARX

Television was not intended to make human beings vacuous, but it is an emanation of their vacuity. —MALCOLM MUGGERIDGE

Literature has taken a back seat to the television, don't you think? It really has. We don't have a culture anymore that favors the creation of writers, or supports them very well. —TENNESSEE WILLIAMS

TEMPER
(also see concepts 386, 426, 580, 788)

All music jars when the soul's out of tune. —MIGUEL DE CERVANTES

We boil at different degrees. —RALPH WALDO EMERSON

A tart temper never mellows with age, and a sharp tongue is the only edged tool that grows keener with constant use. —WASHINGTON IRVING

Certainly there are good and bad times, but our mood changes more often than our fortune. —JULES RENARD

TEMPTATION
(also see concepts 102, 198, 707)

Don't worry about avoiding temptation. As you grow older it will avoid you. —JOEY ADAMS

No temptation can ever be measured by the value of its object. —COLETTE

I have a simple principle for the conduct of life—never to resist an adequate temptation. —MAX LERNER

If you can't be good, be careful. —PROVERB

Is this her fault or mine? / The tempter or the tempted, who sins most? —WILLIAM SHAKESPEARE

It is easier to stay out than get out. —MARK TWAIN

I generally avoid temptation unless I can't resist it. —MAE WEST

TERRORISM
(also see concepts 183, 282, 358, 805, 821)

The terrorist and the policeman both come from the same basket. —JOSEPH CONRAD

Men who use terrorism as a means to power, rule by terror once they are in power. —HELEN MACINNES

THEATER
(also see concepts 11, 53, 223, 592)

In the theatre the audience want to be surprised—but by things that they expect. —TRISTAN BERNARD

The drama is make-believe. It does not deal with truth but with effect. —W. SOMERSET MAUGHAM

The structure of a play is always the story of how the birds came home to roost. —ARTHUR MILLER

I never deliberately set out to shock, but when people don't walk out of my plays I think there is something wrong. —JOHN OSBORNE

A novelist may lose his readers for a few pages; a playwright never dares lose his audience for a minute. —TERENCE RATTIGAN

The play was a great success, but the audience was a disaster. —OSCAR WILDE

THEOLOGY

(also see concepts 66, 108, 316, 317, 319, 427, 431, 515, 668)

I have only a small flickering light to guide me in the darkness of a thick forest. Up comes a theologian and blows it out.
——DENIS DIDEROT

The most tedious of all discourses are on the subject of the Supreme Being. ——RALPH WALDO EMERSON

One man's theology is another man's belly laugh.
——ROBERT HEINLEIN

My theology, briefly, is that the universe was dictated but not signed. ——CHRISTOPHER MORLEY

Theology in religion is what poisons are in food. ——NAPOLEON I

THEORY

(also see concepts 307, 376, 555, 620, 700, 804)

No theory is good except on condition that one use it to go beyond.
——ANDRÉ GIDE

Dear friend, theory is all grey, / And the golden tree of life is green.
——JOHANN WOLFGANG VON GOETHE

A theory is no more like a fact than a photograph is like a person.
——EDGAR WATSON HOWE

Those who are enamoured of practice without science are like a pilot who goes into a ship without rudder or compass and never has any certainty where he is going. Practice should always be based upon a sound knowledge of theory. ——LEONARDO DA VINCI

It is only theory that makes men completely incautious.
——BERTRAND RUSSELL

THINKING AND THOUGHT

(also see concepts 376, 410, 411, 460, 591, 803)

One thought fills immensity. ——WILLIAM BLAKE

I think, therefore I am. —RENÉ DESCARTES

What was once thought can never be unthought.
—FRIEDRICH DÜRRENMATT

To think great thoughts you must be heroes as well as idealists.
—OLIVER WENDELL HOLMES, JR.

Our life is what our thoughts make it. —MARCUS AURELIUS

The thinkers of the world should by rights be guardians of the world's mirth. —AGNES REPPLIER

Many people would sooner die than think. In fact they do.
—BERTRAND RUSSELL

Thoughts are energy. And you can make your world or break your world by thinking. —SUSAN TAYLOR

I have no riches but my thoughts, / Yet these are wealth enough for me. —SARA TEASDALE

Great thoughts come from the heart. —MARQUIS DE VAUVENARGUES

In order to draw a limit to thinking, we should have to be able to think both sides of this limit. —LUDWIG WITTGENSTEIN

THREAT
(also see concepts 183, 282, 358, 800, 842)

Threatened folks live long. —THOMAS FULLER

THRIFT
(also see concept 505)

A penny saved is a penny to squander. —AMBROSE BIERCE

Economy is a distributive virtue, and consists not in saving but in selection. —EDMUND BURKE

Everybody is always in favour of general economy and particular expenditure. —ANTHONY EDEN

TIME

(also see concepts 304, 308, 513, 516, 541, 615, 705, 808, 813)

Time is a dressmaker specializing in alterations. —FAITH BALDWIN

Time is a great teacher, but unfortunately it kills all its pupils. —HECTOR BERLIOZ

Killing time is the chief end of our society. —UGO BETTI

There is a time for work. And a time for love. That leaves no other time. —COCO CHANEL

Time is born in the eyes, everybody knows that. —JULIO CORTÁZAR

Time is the rider that breaks youth. —GEORGE HERBERT

The now, the here, through which all future plunges into the past. —JAMES JOYCE

I must govern the clock, not be governed by it. —GOLDA MEIR

Wait for that wisest of all counselors, Time. —PERICLES

Time and I against any two. —SPANISH PROVERB

Time is that in which all things pass away. —ARTHUR SCHOPENHAUER

Our costliest expenditure is time. —THEOPHRASTUS

Time is but the stream I go a-fishing in. —HENRY DAVID THOREAU

TIMELINESS

(also see concepts 509, 538, 615, 641, 807)

To every thing there is a season, and a time to every purpose under the heaven. —BIBLE, ECCLESIASTES 3:1

In season, all is good. —SOPHOCLES

TOLERANCE

(also see concepts 495, 508, 553)

There is, however, a limit at which forbearance ceases to be a virtue. —EDMUND BURKE

It does no injury for my neighbor to say there are twenty gods, or no God. —THOMAS JEFFERSON

The highest result of education is tolerance. —HELEN KELLER

By being civilized we mean that there is a certain list of things about which we permit a man to have an opinion different from ours. Usually they are things which we have ceased to care about: for instance, the worship of God. —AUBREY MENEN

TOTALITARIANISM
(also see concepts 276, 445, 747, 821)

I suspect that in our loathing of totalitarianism, there is infused a good deal of admiration for its efficiency. —T. S. ELIOT

You have not converted a man because you have silenced him. —JOHN MORLEY

TRADITION
(also see concepts 119, 147, 154, 180, 335)

The dead govern the living. —AUGUSTE COMTE

A precedent embalms a principle. —BENJAMIN DISRAELI

A tradition without intelligence is not worth having. —T. S. ELIOT

Tradition is a guide and not a jailer. —W. SOMERSET MAUGHAM

TRAGEDY
(also see concepts 17, 491)

Only a great mind overthrown yields tragedy. —JACQUES BARZUN

What would be left of our tragedies if a literate insect were to present us his? —E. M. CIORAN

In tragedy every moment is eternity; in comedy, eternity is a moment. —CHRISTOPHER FRY

We participate in a tragedy; at a comedy we only look.
—ALDOUS HUXLEY

There are two tragedies in life: one is to lose your heart's desire, the other is to gain it. —GEORGE BERNARD SHAW

The bad end unhappily, the good unluckily. That is what tragedy means. —TOM STOPPARD

I always thought it mattered, to know what is the worst possible thing that can happen to you, to know how you can avoid it, to not be drawn by the magic of the unspeakable. —AMY TAN

TRANSIENCE
(also see concepts 807, 816)

The entire most beautiful order of things that are very good, when their measures have been accomplished, is to pass away.
—ST. AUGUSTINE OF HIPPO

Faith, Sir, we are here today, and gone tomorrow. —APHRA BEHN

They are not long, the days of wine and roses. —ERNEST DOWSON

A permanent state of transition is man's most noble condition.
—JUAN RAMÓN JIMÉNEZ

Everything is only for a day, both that which remembers and that which is remembered. —MARCUS AURELIUS

Fame is a vapor, popularity is accident; the only earthly certainty is oblivion. —MARK TWAIN

TRAVEL
(also see concepts 10, 29, 56, 331, 361, 625, 849)

My favorite thing is to go where I've never been. —DIANE ARBUS

I have recently been all round the world and have formed a very poor opinion of it. —THOMAS BEECHAM

Traveling is the ruin of all happiness! There's no looking at a building here after seeing Italy. —FANNY BURNEY

Travellers, like poets, are mostly an angry race. —RICHARD BURTON

Travelling is almost like talking with men of other centuries. —RENÉ DESCARTES

Too often travel, instead of broadening the mind, merely lengthens the conversation. —ELIZABETH DREW

I read, much of the night, and go south in the winter. —T. S. ELIOT

He gave the impression that very many cities had rubbed him smooth. —GRAHAM GREENE

They change their climate, not their soul, who rush across the sea. —HORACE

He who would travel happily must travel light. —ANTOINE DE SAINT-EXUPÉRY

For my part, I travel not to go anywhere, but to go. I travel for travel's sake. The great affair is to move. —ROBERT LOUIS STEVENSON

Travel is glamorous only in retrospect. —PAUL THEROUX

I never travel without my diary. One should always have something sensational to read in the train. —OSCAR WILDE

TREES
(also see concepts 228, 230)

Groves were God's first temples. —WILLIAM CULLEN BRYANT

I like trees because they seem more resigned to the way they have to live than other things do. —WILLA CATHER

He who plants a tree plants hope. —LUCY LARCOM

The pine is the mother of legends. —JAMES RUSSELL LOWELL

The difference between a gun and a tree is a difference of tempo. The tree explodes every spring. —EZRA POUND

The forest is the poor man's overcoat. —NEW ENGLAND PROVERB

If you've seen one redwood tree, you've seen 'em all. —RONALD REAGAN

Except during the nine months before he draws his first breath, no man manages his affairs as well as a tree does.
——GEORGE BERNARD SHAW

Trees are the earth's endless effort to speak to the listening heaven.
——RABINDRANATH TAGORE

Why are there trees I never walk under but large and melodious thoughts descend upon me? ——WALT WHITMAN

TRIVIALITY
(also see concepts 303, 487, 727, 813, 828)

You should treat all disasters as if they were trivialities but never treat a triviality as if it were a disaster. ——QUENTIN CRISP

Little things affect little minds. ——BENJAMIN DISRAELI

It has long been an axiom of mine that the little things are infinitely the most important. ——ARTHUR CONAN DOYLE

To great evils we submit; we resent little provocations.
——WILLIAM HAZLITT

A toothache will cost a battle, a drizzle cancel an insurrection.
——VLADIMIR NABOKOV

To suckle fools and chronicle small beer. ——WILLIAM SHAKESPEARE

Trifles make up the happiness or the misery of human life.
——ALEXANDER SMITH

TRUST
(also see concepts 65, 145, 196, 237, 259, 300, 333, 470, 694)

We are inclined to believe those whom we do not know because they have never deceived us. ——SAMUEL JOHNSON

Confidence is the only bond of friendship. ——PUBLILIUS SYRUS

Love all, trust a few. ——WILLIAM SHAKESPEARE

TRUTH

(also see concepts 297, 307, 355, 452, 585, 620, 632, 657, 658, 717, 818, 819)

Truth sits upon the lips of dying men. —MATTHEW ARNOLD

You never find yourself until you face the truth. —PEARL BAILEY

The truth shall make you free. —BIBLE, JOHN 8:32

We call first truths those we discover after all the others.
—ALBERT CAMUS

Truth is so rare it's delightful to tell it. —EMILY DICKINSON

Truth, like time, is an idea arising from, and dependent upon, human intercourse. —ISAK DINESEN

Truth disappears with the telling of it. —LAWRENCE DURRELL

We are subjected to the production of truth through power and we cannot exercise power except through the production of truth.
—MICHEL FOUCAULT

To be modest in speaking truth is hypocrisy. —KAHLIL GIBRAN

Truth, like a torch, the more it's shook it shines.
—WILLIAM HAMILTON

What the imagination seizes as beauty must be truth. —JOHN KEATS

Duration is not a test of true or false. —ANNE MORROW LINDBERGH

There are no new truths, but only truths that have been recognized by those who have perceived them without noticing.
—MARY MCCARTHY

To me the truth is something which cannot be told in a few words, and those who simplify the universe only reduce the expansion of its meaning. —ANAÏS NIN

A Hair perhaps divides the False and True. —OMAR KHAYYÁM

They deem him their worst enemy who tells them the truth. —PLATO

The greater amount of truth is impulsively uttered; thus the greater amount is spoken, not written. —EDGAR ALLAN POE

When a woman tells the truth she is creating the possibility for more truth around her. —ADRIENNE RICH

Truth lives on in the midst of deception.
—JOHANN FRIEDRICH VON SCHILLER

Truth has no special time of its own. Its hour is now–always.
—ALBERT SCHWEITZER

Truth hath a quiet breast. —WILLIAM SHAKESPEARE

My way of joking is to tell the truth. It's the funniest joke in the world. —GEORGE BERNARD SHAW

Deep truth is imageless. —PERCY BYSSHE SHELLEY

When truth is discovered by someone else, it loses something of its attractiveness. —ALEXANDER SOLZHENITSYN

The truth is balance, but the opposite of truth, which is unbalance, may not be a lie. —SUSAN SONTAG

I have a theory that the truth is never told during the nine-to-five hours. —HUNTER S. THOMPSON

Rather than love, than money, than fame, give me truth.
—HENRY DAVID THOREAU

If truth is beauty, how come no one has their hair done in a library?
—LILY TOMLIN

Truth is more of a stranger than fiction. —MARK TWAIN

Whatever satisfies the soul is truth. —WALT WHITMAN

If you're going to tell people the truth, be funny or they'll kill you.
—BILLY WILDER

TRUTH AND FALSEHOOD

(also see concepts 214, 440, 452, 460, 590, 627, 711, 746, 818)

Fraud and falsehood only dread examination. Truth invites it.
—THOMAS COOPER

Tell the truth / But tell it slant. —EMILY DICKINSON

Though truth and falsehood be / Near twins, yet truth a little elder is. —JOHN DONNE

Telling the truth to people who misunderstand you is generally promoting falsehood. —ANTHONY HOPE HAWKINS

It is error alone which needs the support of government. Truth can stand by itself. —THOMAS JEFFERSON

I've done more harm by the falseness of trying to please than by the honesty of trying to hurt. —JESSAMYN WEST

THE TWENTIETH CENTURY
(also see concepts 29, 56, 141, 276, 796, 797, 807)

In the nineteenth century the problem was that God is dead; in the twentieth century the problem is that man is dead. —ERICH FROMM

But the fact remains that this change, perestroika, is a fitting conclusion to the 20th century. It is an event that has engaged not only the Soviet people but people throughout the world, including those from societies quite different from ours. —MIKHAIL GORBACHEV

Today we are seeing remarkable things around us. I would particularly enjoy mapping the basic existential ground—not just for fear of the future, or fear of freedom, but we're starting to see fear of our own past. —VÁCLAV HAVEL

The trouble with our age is that it is all signpost and no destination. —LOUIS KRONENBERGER

The horror of the Twentieth Century is the size of each event and the paucity of its reverberation. —NORMAN MAILER

In these times you have to be an optimist to open your eyes when you awake in the morning. —CARL SANDBURG

The second half of the twentieth century is a complete flop. —ISAAC BASHEVIS SINGER

TYRANNY
(also see concepts 54, 89, 276, 299, 558, 608, 747, 800, 810)

Death is a softer thing by far than tyranny. —AESCHYLUS

You cannot run faster than a bullet. —IDI AMIN

So long as men worship the Caesars and Napoleons, Caesars and Napoleons will arise to make them miserable. —ALDOUS HUXLEY

Resistance to tyrants is obedience to God. —THOMAS JEFFERSON

A police state finds it cannot command the grain to grow. —JOHN F. KENNEDY

It is better that a man should tyrannize over his bank balance than over his fellow citizens. —JOHN MAYNARD KEYNES

The most insupportable of tyrannies is that of inferiors. —NAPOLEON I

Big Brother is watching you. —GEORGE ORWELL

Shall we go on conferring our Civilization upon the peoples that sit in darkness, or shall we give those poor things a rest? —MARK TWAIN

UGLINESS
(also see concepts 39, 165, 387)

The secret of ugliness consists not in irregularity, but in being uninteresting. —RALPH WALDO EMERSON

The epithet beautiful is used by surgeons to describe operations which their patients describe as ghastly, by physicists to describe methods of measurement which leave sentimentalists cold, by lawyers to describe cases which ruin all the parties to them, and by lovers to describe the objects of their infatuation, however unattractive they may appear to the unaffected spectators. —GEORGE BERNARD SHAW

THE   UNCONSCIOUS
(also see concept 492)

To die is to go into the Collective Unconscious, to lose oneself in order to be transformed into form, into pure form. —HERMANN HESSE

We call the unconscious "nothing," and yet it is a reality *in potentia*. The thought we shall think, the deed we shall do, even the fate we shall lament tomorrow, all lie in our unconscious today. —CARL JUNG

UNDERSTANDING
(also see concepts 13, 27, 272, 486, 577, 588, 790, 809)

Nothing in life is to be feared. It is only to be understood. —MARIE CURIE

The motto should not be: Forgive one another; rather, understand one another. —EMMA GOLDMAN

Perfect understanding will sometimes almost extinguish pleasure. —A. E. HOUSMAN

Nothing can be loved or hated unless it is first known. —LEONARDO DA VINCI

I have striven not to laugh at human actions, not to weep at them, nor to hate them, but to understand them. —BENEDICT SPINOZA

All, everything that I understand, I understand only because I love. —LEO TOLSTOY

UNEMPLOYMENT
(also see concepts 836, 869, 870)

A man willing to work, and unable to find work, is perhaps the saddest sight that fortune's inequality exhibits under this sun. —THOMAS CARLYLE

We believe that if men have the talent to invent new machines that put men out of work, they have the talent to put those men back to work. —JOHN F. KENNEDY

Better wear out shoes than sheets. —ENGLISH PROVERB

O that we now had here / But one ten thousand of those men in England / That do no work today! —WILLIAM SHAKESPEARE

UNFAITHFULNESS
(also see concepts 65, 156, 216, 374)

The world wants to be cheated. So cheat. —XAVIERA HOLLANDER

You know, of course, that the Tasmanians, who never committed adultery, are now extinct. —W. SOMERSET MAUGHAM

Adultery is the application of democracy to love. —H. L. MENCKEN

Husbands are chiefly good lovers when they are betraying their wives. —MARILYN MONROE

A man can have two, maybe three love affairs while he's married. After that, it's cheating. —YVES MONTAND

I don't think there are any men who are faithful to their wives. —JACQUELINE KENNEDY ONASSIS

Those who are faithful know only the trivial side of love; it is the faithless who know love's tragedies. —OSCAR WILDE

UNHAPPINESS
(also see concepts 199, 237, 491)

Resolve to be thyself: and know, that he / Who finds himself, loses his misery. —MATTHEW ARNOLD

Nothing is miserable unless you think it so. —BOETHIUS

Unhappiness does make people look stupid. —ANATOLE FRANCE

Sadness is almost never anything but a form of fatigue. —ANDRÉ GIDE

How quick the old woe follows a little bliss! ——PETRARCH

Misery acquaints a man with strange bedfellows.
——WILLIAM SHAKESPEARE

While not exactly disgruntled, he was far from feeling gruntled.
——P. G. WODEHOUSE

UNIMPORTANCE
(also see concept 816)

Our insignificance is often the cause of our safety. ——AESOP

There are some people who leave impressions not so lasting as the imprint of an oar upon the water. ——KATE CHOPIN

I don't know, I don't care, and it doesn't make any difference.
——JACK KEROUAC

UNIONS
(also see concepts 825, 869, 870)

There is no right to strike against the public safety by anybody, anywhere, any time. ——CALVIN COOLIDGE

Unionism, seldom, if ever, uses such power as it has to insure better work; almost always it devotes a large part of that power to safeguarding bad work. ——H. L. MENCKEN

It is one of the characteristics of a free and democratic modern nation that it have free and independent labor unions.
——FRANKLIN D. ROOSEVELT

Trade Unionism is not Socialism: it is the Capitalism of the Proletariat. ——GEORGE BERNARD SHAW

UNIQUENESS
(also see concepts 179, 205, 310, 346, 377, 394, 490, 538, 831)

Nothing is repeated, and everything is unparalleled.
——EDMOND AND JULES DE GONCOURT ·

UNITY

(also see concepts 142, 155, 217, 561, 575, 742, 755, 830)

All for one, one for all, that is our device.
—ALEXANDRE DUMAS THE ELDER

We must all hang together or assuredly we shall all hang separately.
—BENJAMIN FRANKLIN

Not vain the weakest, if their force unite. —HOMER

There are no problems we cannot solve together, and very few that we can solve by ourselves. —LYNDON B. JOHNSON

We must learn to live together as brothers or perish together as fools. —MARTIN LUTHER KING, JR.

A house divided against itself cannot stand. —ABRAHAM LINCOLN

There are only two forces that unite men—fear and interest.
—NAPOLEON I

Horror causes men to clench their fists, and in horror men join together. —ANTOINE DE SAINT-EXUPÉRY

On this shrunken globe, men can no longer live as strangers.
—ADLAI STEVENSON

UNIVERSE

(also see concepts 228, 531, 701, 759, 766, 782, 871)

Listen; there's a hell of a good universe next door: let's go.
—E. E. CUMMINGS

The universe does not jest with us, but is in earnest.
—RALPH WALDO EMERSON

The universe begins to look more like a great thought than like a great machine. —JAMES JEANS

Nothing puzzles me more than time and space; and yet nothing troubles me less. —CHARLES LAMB

The whole visible world is only an imperceptible atom in the ample bosom of nature. No idea approaches it. —BLAISE PASCAL

THE UNKNOWN
(also see concepts 316, 525)

The mind loves the unknown. It loves images whose meaning is unknown, since the meaning of the mind itself is unknown.
——RENÉ MAGRITTE

Would there be this eternal seeking if the found existed?
——ANTONIO PORCHIA

Did you ever get somethin' stuck in your teeth and you didn't know what the heck it was? ——GILDA RADNER

The unknown always passes for the marvellous. ——TACITUS

However much you knock at nature's door, she will never answer you in comprehensible words. ——IVAN TURGENEV

UNSELFISHNESS
(also see concepts 309, 438, 692, 712)

To reach perfection, we must all pass, one by one, through the death of self-effacement. ——DAG HAMMARSKJÖLD

USEFULNESS
(also see concepts 388, 609, 728, 837, 869)

Success can corrupt; usefulness can only exalt.
——DIMITRI MITROPOULOS

Utility is the great idol of the age, to which all powers must do service and all talents swear allegiance.
——JOHANN FRIEDRICH VON SCHILLER

USELESSNESS
(also see concepts 303, 825, 853)

To be employed in useless things is half to be idle.
——THOMAS FULLER

A useless life is early death. ——JOHANN WOLFGANG VON GOETHE

VALUE

(also see concepts 40, 41, 207, 388, 486, 675, 835)

To live is, in itself, a value judgment. To breathe is to judge.
—ALBERT CAMUS

That which cost little is less valued. —MIGUEL DE CERVANTES

We are valued either too highly or not high enough; we are never
taken at our real worth. —MARIE VON EBNER-ESCHENBACH

Nothing can have value without being an object of utility.
—KARL MARX

Those things are dearest to us that have cost us most.
—MICHEL DE MONTAIGNE

What we obtain too cheap, we esteem too lightly; 'tis dearness only
that gives everything its value. —THOMAS PAINE

Everything is worth what its purchaser will pay for it.
—PUBLILIUS SYRUS

We can tell our values by looking at out checkbook stubs.
—GLORIA STEINEM

VANITY

(also see concepts 45, 72, 235, 715, 750, 783)

It seems to be a law of nature that no man ever is loth to sit for his
portrait. —MAX BEERBOHM

Nobody can be kinder than the narcissist while you react to life in
his own terms. —ELIZABETH BOWEN

Vanity plays lurid tricks with our memory. —JOSEPH CONRAD

Vanity, like murder, will out. —HANNAH COWLEY

We are so vain that we even care for the opinion of those we don't
care for. —MARIE VON EBNER-ESCHENBACH

There are no grades of vanity, there are only grades of ability in
concealing it. —MARK TWAIN

VEGETARIANISM

(also see concepts 290, 340)

A vegetarian is a person who won't eat anything that can have children. —DAVID BRENNER

If you knew how meat was made, you'd probably lose your lunch. I know–I'm from cattle country. That's why I became a vegetarian. —K. D. LANG

A man of my spiritual density does not eat corpses. —GEORGE BERNARD SHAW

Becoming a vegetarian is not merely a symbolic gesture. Nor is it an attempt to isolate oneself from the ugly realities of the world....Becoming a vegetarian is a highly practical and effective step one can take toward ending both the killing of nonhuman animals and the infliction of suffering upon them. —PETER SINGER

I have no doubt that it is a part of the destiny of the human race, in its gradual improvement, to leave off eating animals, as surely as the savage tribes have left off eating each other when they came in contact with the more civilized. —HENRY DAVID THOREAU

VICE

(also see concepts 164, 186, 249)

Half the vices which the world condemns most loudly have seeds of good in them and require moderate use rather than total abstinence. —SAMUEL BUTLER

Let them show me a cottage where there are not the same vices of which they accuse courts. —EARL OF CHESTERFIELD

Vice knows she's ugly, so puts on her mask. —BENJAMIN FRANKLIN

For lawless joys a bitter ending waits. —PINDAR

Every vice has its excuse ready. —PUBLILIUS SYRUS

Whenever I'm caught between two evils, I take the one I've never tried. —MAE WEST

VICTORY

(also see concepts 192, 630, 778)

I came, I saw, I conquered. —JULIUS CAESAR

Winning isn't everything, but wanting to win is. —VINCE LOMBARDI

VIOLENCE

(also see concepts 25, 285, 545)

You know I hate fighting. If I knew how to make a living some other way, I would. —MUHAMMAD ALI

A bit of shooting takes your mind off your troubles–it makes you forget the cost of living. —BRENDAN BEHAN

I write about violence as naturally as Jane Austen wrote about manners. Violence shapes and obsesses our society, and if we do not stop being violent we have no future. —EDWARD BOND

The proliferation of guns must be stopped....We must also stop glorifying the materialism that drives people to violence. —MARIAN WRIGHT EDELMAN

It is better to be violent, if there is violence in our hearts, than to put on the cloak of non-violence to cover impotence. —MOHANDAS K. GANDHI

In violence we forget who we are. —MARY MCCARTHY

Today violence is the rhetoric of the period. —JOSÉ ORTEGA Y GASSET

VIRTUE

(also see concepts 103, 188, 321, 355, 409, 646)

Virtue is like a rich stone, best plain set. —FRANCIS BACON

Make not the consequences of virtue the ends thereof. —THOMAS BROWNE

If we've learned anything in the past quarter century, it is that we cannot federalize virtue. —GEORGE BUSH

Virtue consisted in avoiding scandal and venereal disease.
——ROBERT CECIL

The existence of virtue depends entirely upon its use. ——CICERO

Virtue, though in rags, will keep me warm. ——JOHN DRYDEN

There may be guilt when there is too much virtue. ——JEAN RACINE

Virtue must shape itself in deed. ——ALFRED, LORD TENNYSON

If virtue were its own reward, it would no longer be a human
quality, but supernatural. ——MARQUIS DE VAUVENARGUES

I have seen men incapable of the sciences, but never any incapable
of virtue. ——VOLTAIRE

It is queer how it's always one's virtues and not one's vices that
precipitate one into disaster. ——REBECCA WEST

VIRTUE AND VICE
(also see concepts 150, 467, 646)

Search others for their virtues, thy self for thy vices.
——BENJAMIN FRANKLIN

Our virtues are most frequently but vices disguised.
——FRANÇOIS DE LA ROCHEFOUCAULD

Some rise by sin, and some by virtue fall. ——WILLIAM SHAKESPEARE

Virtue consists, not in abstaining from vice, but in not desiring it.
——GEORGE BERNARD SHAW

VISION
(also see concepts 169, 581, 758, 797)

No man sees far, the most see no farther than their noses.
——THOMAS CARLYLE

Things don't change. You change your way of looking, that's all.
——CARLOS CASTANEDA

Rosiness is not a worse windowpane than gloomy grey when viewing the world. —GRACE PALEY

Vision is the art of seeing things invisible. —JONATHAN SWIFT

VOCATIONS
(also see concepts 90, 869)

Vocations which we wanted to pursue, but didn't, bleed, like colors, on the whole of our existence. —HONORÉ DE BALZAC

Each honest calling, each walk of life, has its own elite, its own aristocracy based upon excellence of performance.
—JAMES BRYANT CONANT

The player envies only the player, the poet envies only the poet.
—WILLIAM HAZLITT

Every calling is great when greatly pursued.
—OLIVER WENDELL HOLMES, JR.

The test of a vocation is the love of the drudgery it involves.
—LOGAN PEARSALL SMITH

VOTING
(also see concepts 9, 107, 114)

Disfranchisement is the deliberate theft and robbery of the only protection of poor against rich and black against white.
—W. E. B. DU BOIS

The ignorance of one voter in a democracy impairs the security of all. —JOHN F. KENNEDY

The ballot is stronger than the bullet. —ABRAHAM LINCOLN

If you don't vote, you're going to get a spankie. —MADONNA

Voting is simply a way of determining which side is the stronger without putting it to the test of fighting. —H. L. MENCKEN

Bad officials are elected by good citizens who do not vote.
—GEORGE JEAN NATHAN

VULGARITY

(also see concepts 603, 689, 788)

You gotta have a swine to show you where the truffles are.
——EDWARD ALBEE

The vulgar man is always the most distinguished, for the very desire to be distinguished is vulgar. ——G. K. CHESTERTON

Vulgarity is the garlic in the salad of taste. ——CYRIL CONNOLLY

It is disgusting to pick your teeth. What is vulgar is to use a gold toothpick. ——LOUIS KRONENBERGER

Think with the wise, but talk with the vulgar. ——GREEK PROVERB

WALKING

(also see concepts 9, 814)

I like long walks, especially when they are taken by people who annoy me. ——FRED ALLEN

People seem to think there is something inherently noble and virtuous in the desire to go for a walk. ——MAX BEERBOHM

WAR

(also see concepts 25, 240, 248, 285, 293, 415, 499, 545, 546, 573, 575, 842, 851, 857)

Women will always fear war more than men because they are mothers. A woman will always have a baby, her own or her children's, in her arms. She will always be tormented by fear for her children, the fear that one day she might be a witness to their own deaths. ——NATALYA BARANSKAYA

War is like love, it always finds a way. ——BERTOLT BRECHT

War's a brain-spattering, windpipe-splitting art. ——LORD BYRON

All the gods are dead except the god of war. ——ELDRIDGE CLEAVER

To lead an uninstructed people to war is to throw them away.
——CONFUCIUS

As peace is of all goodness, so war is an emblem, a hieroglyphic, of all misery. —JOHN DONNE

Men love war because it allows them to look serious. Because it is the one thing that stops women laughing at them. —JOHN FOWLES

Morality is contraband in war. —MOHANDAS K. GANDHI

I'd like to see the government get out of war altogether and leave the whole feud to private industry. —JOSEPH HELLER

War? War is an organized bore. —OLIVER WENDELL HOLMES, JR.

Mankind must put an end to war or war will put an end to mankind. —JOHN F. KENNEDY

It is well that war is so terrible; else we would grow too fond of it. —ROBERT E. LEE

All wars are boyish, and are fought by boys. —HERMAN MELVILLE

War will never cease until babies begin to come into the world with larger cerebrums and smaller adrenal glands. —H. L. MENCKEN

How different the new order would be if we could consult the veteran instead of the politician. —HENRY MILLER

War alone brings up to its highest tension all human energy and puts the stamp of nobility upon the peoples who have the courage to face it. —BENITO MUSSOLINI

The quickest way of ending a war is to lose it. —GEORGE ORWELL

I could not give my name to aid the slaughter in this war, fought on both sides for grossly material ends, which did not justify the sacrifice of a single mother's son. Clearly, I must continue to oppose it, and expose it, to all whom I could reach with voice or pen. —SYLVIA PANKHURST

Don't fire until you see the whites of their eyes. —WILLIAM PRESCOTT

You can no more win a war than you can win an earthquake. —JEANNETTE RANKIN

War is not an adventure. It is a disease. It is like typhus. —ANTOINE DE SAINT-EXUPÉRY

I am tired and sick of war. Its glory is all moonshine....War is hell.
——WILLIAM T. SHERMAN

If women ruled the world and we all got massages, there would be no war. ——CARRIE SNOW

War is capitalism with the gloves off. ——TOM STOPPARD

They make a desert and call it peace. ——TACITUS

War is the unfolding of miscalculations. ——BARBARA TUCHMAN

WAR AND PEACE
(also see concepts 208, 415, 575, 850)

In war, resolution; in defeat, defiance; in victory, magnanimity; in peace, goodwill. ——WINSTON CHURCHILL

There never was a good war or a bad peace. ——BENJAMIN FRANKLIN

Peace is not only better than war, but infinitely more arduous.
——GEORGE BERNARD SHAW

WASHINGTON, D.C.
(also see concepts 113, 149, 616)

Washington is an endless series of mock palaces clearly built for clerks. ——ADA LOUISE HUXTABLE

Washington is a city of Southern efficiency and Northern charm.
——JOHN F. KENNEDY

New York has total depth in every area. Washington has only politics; after that, the second biggest thing is white marble.
——JOHN V. LINDSAY

WASTE
(also see concepts 197, 201, 254, 338, 806, 825, 836)

Waste is not grandeur. ——WILLIAM MASON

Waste not, want not. ——PROVERB

WATER

(also see concepts 225, 653, 685, 695, 704, 736, 751)

Water, water, everywhere... / Nor any drop to drink.
——SAMUEL TAYLOR COLERIDGE

Human beings were invented by water as a device for transporting itself from one place to another. ——TOM ROBBINS

WEAKNESS

(also see concepts 168, 190, 281, 391, 749, 775)

The spirit indeed is willing, but the flesh is weak.
——BIBLE, MATTHEW 26:41

We cannot win the weak by sharing our wealth with them. They feel our generosity as oppression. ——ERIC HOFFER

To be weak is miserable, / Doing or suffering. ——JOHN MILTON

WEALTH

(also see concepts 15, 44, 395, 473, 483, 606, 607, 628, 630, 776, 780)

Wealth unused might as well not exist. ——AESOP

A man who has a million dollars is as well off as if he were rich.
——JOHN JACOB ASTOR

The only thing I like about rich people is their money.
——NANCY ASTOR

Wealth maketh many friends. ——BIBLE, PROVERBS 19:4

The meek shall inherit the earth but not the mineral rights.
——J. PAUL GETTY

It is better to live rich than to die rich. ——SAMUEL JOHNSON

Wealth is well known to be a great comforter. ——PLATO

You can't take it with you when you go. ——PROVERB

As long as there are rich people in the world, they will be desirous of distinguishing themselves from the poor. —JEAN JACQUES ROUSSEAU

One can never be too thin or too rich. —DUCHESS OF WINDSOR

WEAPONS
(also see concepts 25, 499, 850)

You may be obliged to wage war, but not to use poisoned arrows. —BALTASAR GRACIÁN

We may find in the long run that tinned food is a deadlier weapon than the machine-gun. —GEORGE ORWELL

A weapon is an enemy even to its owner. —TURKISH PROVERB

...bombs are unbelievable until they actually fall. —PATRICK WHITE

WEATHER
(also see concepts 705, 751, 862)

What dreadful hot weather we have! It keeps me in a continual state of inelegance. —JANE AUSTEN

We shall never be content until man makes his own weather and keeps it to himself. —JEROME K. JEROME

So foul and fair a day I have not seen. —WILLIAM SHAKESPEARE

Everybody talks about the weather, but nobody does anything about it. —CHARLES DUDLEY WARNER

WEDDINGS
(also see concepts 479, 494)

If it were not for the presents, an elopement would be preferable. —GEORGE ADE

Next to hot chicken soup, a tattoo of an anchor on your chest, and penicillin, I consider a honeymoon one of the most overrated events in the world. —ERMA BOMBECK

The wedding march always reminds me of the music played when soldiers go into battle. —HEINRICH HEINE

Blest is the bride the sun shines on. —OLD ENGLISH PROVERB

WILL

(also see concept 579)

Will cannot be quenched against its will. —DANTE

Will springs from the two elements of moral sense and self-interest. —ABRAHAM LINCOLN

Great souls have wills; feeble ones have only wishes.
—CHINESE PROVERB

WILLS AND INHERITANCE

(also see concepts 35, 44, 345, 628, 856)

The art of will-making chiefly consists in baffling the importunity of expectation. —WILLIAM HAZLITT

It's going to be fun to watch and see how long the meek can keep the earth after they inherit it. —KIN HUBBARD

The weeping of an heir is laughter in disguise.
—MICHEL DE MONTAIGNE

Die, and endow a college, or a cat. —ALEXANDER POPE

WIND

(also see concept 858)

I came like Water, and like Wind I go. —EDWARD FITZGERALD

It's an ill wind that blows nobody any good. —PROVERB

Who has seen the wind? / Neither you nor I: / But when the trees bow down their heads / The wind is passing by.
—CHRISTINA ROSSETTI

The wind in the grain is the caress to the spouse, it is the hand of peace stroking her hair. —ANTOINE DE SAINT-EXUPÉRY

In my garden goes a fiend / Dark and wild, Whose name is Wind. —GEOFFREY SCOTT

WISDOM
(also see concepts 19, 260, 262, 291, 585, 632, 633, 811)

Life is a festival only to the wise. —RALPH WALDO EMERSON

Knowledge can be communicated, but not wisdom. —HERMANN HESSE

The art of being wise is the art of knowing what to overlook. —WILLIAM JAMES

By the time your life is finished, you will have learned just enough to begin it well. —ELEANOR MARX

There is more wisdom in your body than in your deepest philosophy. —FRIEDRICH WILHELM NIETZSCHE

Nine-tenths of wisdom is being wise in time. —THEODORE ROOSEVELT

WISDOM AND FOOLISHNESS
(also see concept 291)

For ye suffer fools gladly, seeing ye yourselves are wise. —BIBLE, II CORINTHIANS 11:19

A fool sees not the same tree that a wise man sees. —WILLIAM BLAKE

It is very foolish to wish to be exclusively wise. —FRANÇOIS DE LA ROCHEFOUCAULD

WISHES
(also see concepts 198, 860)

Ships at a distance have every man's wish on board. —ZORA NEALE HURSTON

The poor wish to be rich, the rich wish to be happy, the single wish to be married, and the married wish to be dead. —ANN LANDERS

WIT

(also see concepts 80, 122, 128, 370, 442, 644, 649, 698, 699)

In the midst of the fountain of wit there arises something bitter, which stings in the very flowers. —LUCRETIUS

Wit is the epitaph of an emotion. —FRIEDRICH WILHELM NIETZSCHE

Wit has truth in it; wisecracking is simply calisthenics with words. —DOROTHY PARKER

Brevity is the soul of wit. —WILLIAM SHAKESPEARE

Wit is the sudden marriage of ideas which before their union were not perceived to have any relation. —MARK TWAIN

WOMEN

(also see concepts 2, 160, 283, 448, 656, 732, 733)

I like to help women help themselves, as that is, in my opinion, the best way to settle the woman question. Whatever we can do and do well we have a right to, and I don't think any one will deny us. —LOUISA MAY ALCOTT

One is not born a woman, one becomes one. —SIMONE DE BEAUVOIR

Women have a way of treating people more softly. We treat souls with kid gloves. —SHIRLEY CAESAR

I don't wish not to be a woman, but I'd certainly like to be a woman whose sense of purpose comes from within. —UNO CHIYO

Women share with men the need for personal success, even the taste for power, and no longer are we willing to satisfy those needs through the achievements of surrogates, whether husbands, children, or merely role models. —ELIZABETH DOLE

The great question...which I have not been able to answer, despite my thirty years of research into the feminine soul, is "What does a woman want?" —SIGMUND FREUD

The especial genius of women I believe to be electrical in movement, intuitive in function, spiritual in tendency. —MARGARET FULLER

The choices that women make to survive, or to appear good to others, are often at the expense of [other] women....I would like to see older women ally themselves with young girls to help them resist a world that devalues them. —CAROL GILLIGAN

Women must learn not to be subservient to the wishes of their fathers, husbands and partners, because then they do not fulfill their own ambitions. —PETRA KELLY

I believe that what a woman resents most is not so much giving herself in pieces as giving herself purposelessly.
—ANNE MORROW LINDBERGH

I may be dressing like a traditional bimbo, whatever, but I'm in charge....And isn't that what feminism is all about, you know, equality for men and women? And aren't I in charge of my life, doing the things I want to do? —MADONNA

Women are not inherently passive or peaceful. We're not inherently anything but human. —ROBIN MORGAN

Woman was God's second mistake. —FRIEDRICH WILHELM NIETZSCHE

There are two kinds of women: those who want power in the world, and those who want power in bed. —JACQUELINE KENNEDY ONASSIS

There will never be a new world order until women are part of it.
—ALICE PAUL

A strong woman is a woman at work, cleaning out the cesspool of the ages, and while she shovels, she talks about how she doesn't mind crying, it opens the ducts of the eyes, and throwing up develops the stomach muscles, and she goes on shoveling with tears in her nose. —MARGE PIERCY

A woman is like a tea bag. It's only when she's in hot water that you realize how strong she is. —NANCY REAGAN

Women have been the truly active people in all cultures, without whom human society would long ago have perished, though our activity has most often been on the behalf of men and children.
——ADRIENNE RICH

Woman: the peg on which the wit hangs his jest, the preacher his text, the cynic his grouch and the sinner his justification.
——HELEN ROWLAND

We bear the world and we make it....There was never a great man who had not a great mother. ——OLIVE SCHREINER

I have a brain and a uterus, and I use both. ——PATRICIA SCHROEDER

Any woman who has a great deal to offer the world is in trouble. And if she's a black woman, she's in deep trouble. ——HAZEL SCOTT

Some of us are becoming the men we wanted to marry.
——GLORIA STEINEM

Women have served all these centuries as looking-glasses possessing the magic and delicious power of reflecting the figure of man at twice its natural size. ——VIRGINIA WOOLF

WORDS

(also see concepts 66, 68, 76, 132, 441, 451, 457, 594, 745, 761)

A word after a word after a word is power. ——MARGARET ATWOOD

Words are all we have. ——SAMUEL BECKETT

All words are pegs to hang ideas on. ——HENRY WARD BEECHER

...words are a form of action, capable of influencing change. Their articulation represents a complete, lived experience.
——INGRID BENGIS

Words make love with one another. ——ANDRÉ BRETON

Who has words at the right moment? ——CHARLOTTE BRONTË

Words are...awkward instruments and they will be laid aside eventually, probably sooner than we think. ——WILLIAM S. BURROUGHS

Words, as is well known, are the great foes of reality.
—JOSEPH CONRAD

If the word has the potency to revive and make us free, it has also the power to blind, imprison, and destroy. —RALPH ELLISON

You can stroke people with words. —F. SCOTT FITZGERALD

For just when ideas fail, a word comes in to save the situation.
—JOHANN WOLFGANG VON GOETHE

This is a confusing and uncertain period, when a thousand wise words can go completely unnoticed, and one thoughtless word can provoke an utterly nonsensical furor. —VÁCLAV HAVEL

Words form the thread on which we string our experiences.
—ALDOUS HUXLEY

Words are, of course, the most powerful drug used by mankind.
—RUDYARD KIPLING

Words are like water–the assumption being that it moves in any direction. —BERNARD MALAMUD

All our life is crushed by the weight of words: the weight of the dead. —LUIGI PIRANDELLO

Words are the small change of thought. —JULES RENARD

The more articulate one is, the more dangerous words become.
—MAY SARTON

Words are loaded pistols. —JEAN-PAUL SARTRE

The difference between the right word and the almost right word is the difference between lightning and the lightning bug.
—MARK TWAIN

Our words must seem to be inevitable. —WILLIAM BUTLER YEATS

WORK
(also see concepts 10, 90, 825, 829, 846)

Don't condescend to unskilled labor. Try it for a half a day first.
—BROOKS ATKINSON

To work is to pray. —ST. BENEDICT OF NURSIA

It is better to wear out than to rust out. —RICHARD CUMBERLAND

Diligence is the mother of good luck. —BENJAMIN FRANKLIN

By working faithfully eight hours a day you may eventually get to be a boss and work twelve hours a day. —ROBERT FROST

Work is love made visible. —KAHLIL GIBRAN

Like the bee, we should make our industry our amusement. —OLIVER GOLDSMITH

When work is a pleasure, life is a joy! When work is a duty, life is slavery. —MAXIM GORKY

The world is sown with good; but unless I turn my glad thoughts into practical living and till my own field, I cannot reap a kernel of the good. —HELEN KELLER

There are very few jobs which require a penis or vagina. All other jobs should be open to everybody. —FLORYNCE KENNEDY

Thou, O God, dost sell us all good things at the price of labor. —LEONARDO DA VINCI

Occupation is the scythe of time. —NAPOLEON I

How Sunday into Monday melts! —OGDEN NASH

We need love and creative imagination to do constructive work. —PAULA OLLENDORF

Work is the province of cattle. —DOROTHY PARKER

Work is necessary for man. Man invented the alarm clock. —PABLO PICASSO

The only place where success comes before work is a dictionary. —VIDAL SASSOON

Every woman is a human being—one cannot repeat that too often —and a human being must have occupation if he or she is not to become a nuisance to the world. —DOROTHY SAYERS

The fruit derived from labor is the sweetest of all pleasures.
——MARQUIS DE VAUVENARGUES

Work spares us from three great evils: boredom, vice, and need.
——VOLTAIRE

WORKERS
(also see concepts 90, 825, 829, 846)

If you want creative workers, give them enough time to play.
——JOHN CLEESE

The employer generally gets the employees he deserves.
——WALTER GILBEY

Give the labourer his wage before his perspiration be dry.
——MUHAMMAD

There is perhaps one human being in a thousand who is passionately
interested in job for job's sake. The difference is that if one person
in a thousand is a man, we say, simply, that he is passionately keen
on his job; if she is a woman, we say she is a freak.
——DOROTHY SAYERS

Work is the curse of the drinking classes. ——OSCAR WILDE

THE WORLD
(also see concepts 228, 523, 531, 658, 832)

For the world, I count it not an inn, but an hospital; and a place not
to live, but to die in. ——THOMAS BROWNE

You do not reform a world by ignoring it. ——GEORGE BUSH

Traditional nationalism cannot survive the fissioning of the atom.
One world or none. ——STUART CHASE

The world is a fine place and worth the fighting for and I hate very
much to leave it. ——ERNEST HEMINGWAY

Set the foot down with distrust on the crust of the world–it is thin.
——EDNA ST. VINCENT MILLAY

The world is not to be put in order, the world is order. It is for us to put ourselves in unison with this order. ——HENRY MILLER

I have made my world and it's a much better world than I ever saw outside. ——LOUISE NEVELSON

It takes all sorts to make a world. ——ENGLISH PROVERB

We read the world wrong and say that it deceives us.
——RABINDRANATH TAGORE

When will the world know that peace and propagation are the two most delightful things in it? ——HORACE WALPOLE

We are citizens of the world; and the tragedy of our times is that we do not know this. ——WOODROW WILSON

WORRY

(also see concept 199)

Never trouble trouble till trouble troubles you. ——ANONYMOUS

When you're an orthodox worrier, some days are worse than others. ——ERMA BOMBECK

The misfortunes hardest to bear are these which never came.
——JAMES RUSSELL LOWELL

Worry affects circulation, the heart and the glands, the whole nervous system and profoundly affects the heart. I have never known a man who died from overwork, but many who died from doubt. ——CHARLES H. MAYO

WORSHIP

(also see concepts 316, 692, 729)

Where it is a duty to worship the sun, it is pretty sure to be a crime to examine the laws of heat. ——JOHN MORLEY

We adore, we invoke, we seek to appease, only that which we fear.
——VOLTAIRE

WRITERS AND WRITING

(also see concepts 48, 55, 68, 76, 90, 204, 223, 232, 325, 432, 449, 459, 590, 594, 595, 640)

I always wanted to write a book that ended with the word *mayonnaise*. —RICHARD BRAUTIGAN

I think a little menace is fine to have in a story. For one thing, it's good for the circulation. —RAYMOND CARVER

I love being a writer. What I can't stand is the paperwork.
—PETER DE VRIES

Writers are always selling somebody out. —JOAN DIDION

Whenever citizens are seen routinely as enemies of their own government, writers are routinely seen to be the most dangerous enemies. —E. L. DOCTOROW

All you need is a room without any particular interruptions.
—JOHN DOS PASSOS

Writers should be read, but neither seen nor heard.
—DAPHNE DU MAURIER

You don't write because you want to say something; you write because you've got something to say. —F. SCOTT FITZGERALD

I suppose I am a born novelist, for the things that I imagine are more vital and vivid to me than the things I remember. —ELLEN GLASGOW

He who does not expect a million readers should not write a line.
—JOHANN WOLFGANG VON GOETHE

A novel is an impression, not an argument. —THOMAS HARDY

They're fancy talkers about themselves, writers. If I had to give young writers advice, I would say don't listen to writers talking about writing or themselves. —LILLIAN HELLMAN

The secret of all good writing is sound judgment. —HORACE

I like to write when I feel spiteful: it's like having a good sneeze.
—D. H. LAWRENCE

The multitude of books is a great evil. There is no limit to this fever for writing. —MARTIN LUTHER

The writer is more concerned to know than to judge.
—W. SOMERSET MAUGHAM

Sin is the writer's element. —FRANÇOIS MAURIAC

I always do the first line well, but I have trouble doing the others.
—MOLIÉRE

All the world knows me in my book, and my book in me.
—MICHEL DE MONTAIGNE

A writer is unfair to himself when he is unable to be hard on himself. —MARIANNE MOORE

The role of the writer is not to say what we can all say, but what we are unable to say. —ANAÏS NIN

Why has the South produced so many good writers? Because we got beat. —WALKER PERCY

Good writing excites me, and makes life worth living.
—HAROLD PINTER

Nothing stinks like a pile of unpublished writing. —SYLVIA PLATH

Most people won't realize that writing is a craft. You have to take your apprenticeship in it like anything else.
—KATHERINE ANNE PORTER

Among the many problems which beset the novelist, not the least weighty is the choice of the moment at which to begin his novel.
—VITA SACKVILLE-WEST

The trade of authorship is a violent and indestructible obsession.
—GEORGE SAND

It's like striking a match. Sometimes it lights. —NEIL SIMON

A writer is someone who always sells. An author is one who writes a book that makes a big splash. —MICKEY SPILLANE

The profession of book writing makes horse racing seem like a solid, stable business. —JOHN STEINBECK

Writing is the only thing that, when I do it, I don't feel I should be doing something else. —GLORIA STEINEM

Writing is a form of self-flagellation. —WILLIAM STYRON

Writing is pretty crummy on the nerves. —PAUL THEROUX

Whatever sentence will bear to be read twice, we may be sure was thought twice. —HENRY DAVID THOREAU

I'm not sure a bad person can write a good book. If art doesn't make us better, then what on earth is it for? —ALICE WALKER

I put the words down and push them a bit. —EVELYN WAUGH

There is no royal path to good writing; and such paths as exist do not lead through neat critical gardens, various as they are, but through the jungles of self, the world, and of craft. —JESSAMYN WEST

Literature is strewn with the wreckage of men who have minded beyond reason the opinion of others. —VIRGINIA WOOLF

It's not a writer's business to hold opinions.
—WILLIAM BUTLER YEATS

WRONG AND WRONGDOING
(also see concepts 7, 144, 437, 642, 734, 743, 769)

A small demerit extinguishes a long service. —THOMAS FULLER

Those who are once found to be bad are presumed so forever.
—LATIN PROVERB

YOUTH
(also see concepts 24, 384, 404, 455, 877)

The young are permanently in a state resembling intoxication; for youth is sweet and they are growing. —ARISTOTLE

Americans began by loving youth, and now, out of adult self-pity, they worship it. —JACQUES BARZUN

Very young people are true but not resounding instruments.
—ELIZABETH BOWEN

The young always have the same problem—how to rebel and conform at the same time. They have now solved this by defying their parents and copying one another. —QUENTIN CRISP

While we are young the idea of death or failure is intolerable to us; even the possibility of ridicule we cannot bear. —ISAK DINESEN

Youth will come here and beat on my door, and force its way in.
—HENRIK IBSEN

Remember that as a teenager you are at the last stage in your life when you will be happy to hear that the phone is for you.
—FRAN LEBOWITZ

It is an illusion that youth is happy, an illusion of those who have lost it. —W. SOMERSET MAUGHAM

The American ideal is youth—handsome, empty youth.
—HENRY MILLER

Youth does not require reasons for living, it only needs pretexts.
—JOSE ORTEGÁ Y GASSET

Far too good to waste on children. —GEORGE BERNARD SHAW

Youth smiles without any reason. It is one of its chiefest charms.
—OSCAR WILDE

YOUTH AND AGE
(also see concepts 24, 308, 463, 876)

The dead might as well try to speak to the living as the old to the young. —WILLA CATHER

In youth we learn; in age we understand.
—MARIE VON EBNER-ESCHENBACH

The passions of the young are vices in the old. —JOSEPH JOUBERT

Paradoxical as it may seem, to believe in youth is to look backward; to look forward we must believe in age. —DOROTHY PARKER

The young have aspirations that never come to pass, the old have reminiscences of what never happened. —SAKI

The young man who has not wept is a savage, and the old man who will not laugh is a fool. —GEORGE SANTAYANA

It's all that the young can do for the old, to shock them and keep them up to date. —GEORGE BERNARD SHAW

All sorts of allowances are made for the illusions of youth; and none, or almost none, for the disenchantments of age. —ROBERT LOUIS STEVENSON

The old believe everything, the middle-aged suspect everything, the young know everything. —OSCAR WILDE

ZEAL

(also see concepts 237, 242, 274, 880)

Through zeal, knowledge is gotten, through lack of zeal, knowledge is lost; let a man who knows this double path of gain and loss thus place himself that knowledge may grow. —BUDDHA

Zeal without knowledge is fire without light. —THOMAS FULLER

I do not love a man who is zealous for nothing. —OLIVER GOLDSMITH

Not too much zeal. —CHARLES MAURICE DE TALLEYRAND-PÉRIGORD

ZEN

(also see concepts 585, 771)

The only Zen you find on the top of mountains is the Zen you bring up there. —ROBERT M. PIRSIG

Zen makes a religion of tranquility. Zen is not a religion which arouses emotions, causing tears to race down from our eyes or stirring us to shout aloud the name of God. —SOKEI-AN

What Zen does is to delineate itself on the infinite canvas of time and space the way the flying wild geese cast their shadow on the water below without any idea of doing so, while the water reflects the geese just as naturally and unintentionally. —D. T. SUZUKI

Zen is a way of liberation, concerned not with discovering what is good or bad or advantageous, but what is. —ALAN WATTS

ZEST

(also see concepts 242, 274, 878)

Zest is the secret of all beauty. There is no beauty that is attractive without zest. —CHRISTIAN DIOR

What hunger is in relation to food, zest is in relation to life. —BERTRAND RUSSELL

CONCEPT INDEX

1. ABILITY confidence, cunning, genius, intelligence, potential, self-reliance, talent

2. ABORTION birth, civil rights, contraception, feminism, women

3. ABSENCE death, loss, love, love, loss of, parting

4. ABSTINENCE clergy, drinks and drinking, drugs, sex, sin

5. ABSURDITY fools and foolishness, reality, stupidity

6. ACCIDENTS adversity, fate, injury, luck

7. ACCUSATION communication, confession, conscience, wrong and wrongdoing

8. ACHIEVEMENT ambition, aspiration, concentration, effort, enterprise, perseverance

9. ACTION(S) achievement, activity, blushing, boasting, borrowing and lending, business, buying and selling, crying, dancing, deeds, enterprise, gambling, hunting, killing, kissing, learning, listening, mourning, parting, receiving, scratching, singing, smoking, stealing, swearing, voting, walking

10. ACTIVITY banks and banking, baseball, books and reading, deeds, discovery, enterprise, fish and fishing, gardens and gardening, golf, gossip, housework, human nature, hunting, idleness, learning, leisure, letters and letter writing, speed, sports and games, travel, work

11. ACTORS AND ACTING art, artists, careers, dramatists and drama, Hollywood, movies, theater

12. ADDICTIONS abstinence, coffee, drinks and drinking, drugs, smoking

13. ADJUSTMENT agreement, compromise, conformity, understanding

14. ADMIRATION approval, emotions, respect

15. ADVANTAGE competition, help, interest, power, wealth

16. ADVENTURE events, experience, human nature, life, self-realization

17. ADVERSITY accidents, difficulty, misery, tragedy

18. ADVERTISING exploitation, propaganda, publicity

19. ADVICE persuasion, preachers and preaching, teachers and teaching, wisdom

20. AFFECTION commitment, emotions, friends and friendship, love

21. AFRICA AND THE AFRICANS nations, race

22. AFRICAN AMERICANS   America and the Americans, multiculturalism, race

23. AFTERLIFE death, eternity, ghosts, heaven, hell, immortality, the soul

24. AGE children, life stages, middle age, old age, sex, youth, youth and age

25. AGGRESSION   action, deeds, fights and fighting, violence, war, weapons

26. AGNOSTICISM belief, doubt, God, philosophers and philosophy, religion

27. AGREEMENT adjustment, communication, compromise, conciliation, nonviolence, understanding

28. AIDS health, medicine, sex, sickness

29. AIRPLANES machines, technology, travel, the twentieth century

30. ALIENATION community, existentialism, loneliness, philosophers and philosophy, solitude

31. AMBITION aspiration, motives, pretension, success

32. AMERICA AND THE AMERICANS   African Americans, Asian Americans, Boston, Canada and the Canadians, Chicago, Hispanic Americans, jazz, Native Americans, New England, New York

33. AMUSEMENT interest, joy, leisure, movies, parties, play, television

34. ANARCHY   chaos, diversity, philosophers and philosophy, revolutionaries and revolution

35. ANCESTRY aristocracy, family, good breeding, heredity, the past, wills and inheritance

36. ANGER aggression, emotions, enemies, fights and fighting, hate, indignation, irritation

37. ANIMALS   cats, dogs, fish and fishing, horses and horse racing, hunting

38. APOLOGY communication, excuses, explanation, regret

83. BUREAUCRACY   church and state, committees, government, institutions, the state

84. BUSINESS banks and banking, borrowing and lending, bureaucracy, buying and selling, money, recession

85. BUYING AND SELLING   banks and banking, bribery, business, corruption, investment, money, possession

86. CALMNESS gentleness, patience, peace, self-control, stoicism

87. CANADA AND THE CANADIANS   America and the Americans, nations, neighbors

88. CAPITALISM   banks and banking, business, buying and selling, economics, ideology, property

89. CAPTIVITY dependence, freedom, prisons, slavery, tyranny

90. CAREERS   actors and acting, cooks and cooking, diplomats and diplomacy, dramatists and drama, editors and editing, farms and farming, journalists and journalism, lawyers and law, painters and painting, philosophers and philosophy, poetry and poets, politicians and politics, preachers and preaching, scientists and science, teachers and teaching, vocations, work, workers, writers and writing

91. CAREFULNESS haste, observation, politicians and politics, prudence, shyness, tact

92. CATS animals, dogs, nature

93. CAUSE AND EFFECT beginning, beginning and end, consequences, ending, means and ends

94. CAUSES circumstance, explanation, inspiration, motives, principle, purpose, rules

95. CENSORSHIP authority, cleanliness, judges, judgment, limitations, morality, sex

96. CERTAINTY   belief, confidence, faith, faithfulness, inevitability, reality, safety

97. CHANCE cause and effect, destiny, fate, gambling, luck, opportunity

98. CHANGE evolution, growth and development, life stages

99. CHAOS anarchy, civilization, confusion

100. CHARACTER honor, individualism, integrity, nature, personality

101. CHARITY Christianity, forgiveness, sharing

102. CHARM grace, personality, pleasure, temptation

103. CHASTITY coldness, decency, honor, innocence, moderation, virtue

104. CHEERFULNESS happiness, joy, pleasure

105. CHICAGO America and the Americans, cities, jazz, places

106. CHILDREN birth, family, fathers, mothers, parents and parenthood

107. CHOICE decision, determination, opinions, voting

108. CHRISTIANITY Christmas, church, clergy, God, martyrs and martyrdom, religion, saints and sainthood, theology

109. CHRISTMAS Christianity, generosity, gifts and giving, holidays

110. CHURCH Christianity, clergy, Jews and Judaism, religion

111. CHURCH AND STATE bureaucracy, institutions, religion, the state

112. CIRCUMSTANCE causes, destiny, events, facts, opportunity

113. CITIES Boston, Chicago, London, New York, Paris, places, the suburbs, Washington, D.C.

114. CITIZENSHIP democracy, government, nations, public opinion, taxes, voting

115. CIVIL RIGHTS abortion, free speech, human rights, press, freedom of the, sexual harrassment

116. CIVILIZATION cities, culture, education, ignorance, internationalism, knowledge, progress

117. CLARITY brevity, innocence, obscurity, open-mindedness, simplicity

118. CLASS aristocracy, the middle class, poverty and wealth, rank

119. THE CLASSICS knowledge, tradition

120. CLEANLINESS decency, innocence, order, pollution

121. CLERGY Christianity, church, prayer, preachers and preaching, religion

122. CLEVERNESS common sense, cunning, intelligence, quotations, wit

123. CLOSED-MINDEDNESS bigotry, dogmatism, open-mindedness, stupidity

167. COURAGE adventure, boldness, enterprise, heroes and heroism, power, self-reliance, strength

168. COWARDICE fear, shyness, weakness

169. CREATION AND CREATIVITY art, originality, vision

170. CRIMINALS AND CRIME bribery, corruption, the police, prisons, punishment, rape

171. CRITICISM censorship, critics, judgment, opinions

172. CRITICS authority, criticism, experts, judges, judgment, opinions

173. CROWDS company, force, people

174. CRUELTY coldness, indifference, malice, masochism, sadism, severity

175. CRYING funerals, mourning, noise, sorrow

176. CULTS admiration, church, fanaticism, religion

177. CULTURE civilization, custom, education, growth and development, internationalism, knowledge, society

178. CUNNING ability, cleverness, intelligence, talent

179. CURIOSITY interest, the mind, questions, uniqueness

180. CUSTOM culture, habit, method, repetition, rules, stereotypes, tradition

181. CYNICISM distrust, pessimism, ridicule, sarcasm

182. DANCING exercise, joy, musicians and music, pleasure

183. DANGER aggression, injury, safety, terrorism, threat

184. DEAFNESS blindness, disability, injury

185. DEATH absence, afterlife, immortality, irrevocability, killing, life and death, suicide

186. DEBAUCHERY corruption, evil, sin, vice

187. DEBT money, obligation, payment

188. DECENCY chastity, honesty, respect, virtue

189. DECISION choice, determination, judgment, opinions, purpose

190. DECLINE civilization, defeat, ending, loss, refusal, weakness

191. DEEDS achievement, action, activity, reality

192. DEFEAT competition, decline, destruction, frustration, loss, victory

193. DEFENSE aggression, apology, excuses, explanation, fights and fighting

194. DELAY problems, procrastination, progress, speed

195. DEMOCRACY citizenship, Congress, freedom, government

196. DEPENDENCE confidence, necessity, slavery, trust

197. DEPRIVATION loss, possession, waste

198. DESIRES aspiration, motives, temptation, wishes

199. DESPAIR frustration, sorrow, unhappiness, worry

200. DESTINY choice, circumstance, fate, freedom, inevitability

201. DESTRUCTION defeat, injury, killing, sacrifice, waste

202. DETERMINATION boldness, certainty, decision, perseverance, resolution, stubbornness

203. THE DEVIL afterlife, evil, God, heaven, hell, sin

204. DIARIES autobiography, biography, letters and letter writing, life, privacy, writers and writing

205. DIFFERENCE contrast, diversity, individualism, inequality, opposition, uniqueness

206. DIFFICULTY adversity, frustration, opposition, oppression, prejudice, problems, questions

207. DIGNITY character, greatness, importance, nobility, value

208. DIPLOMATS AND DIPLOMACY conciliation, foreigners and foreignness, government, international relations, tact, war and peace

209. DISABILITY blindness, deafness, injury, sickness

210. DISAPPOINTMENT disillusionment, emotions, expectation, frustration

211. DISCIPLINE authority, parents and parenthood, punishment

212. DISCOVERY inspiration, invention, originality, Spain and the Spanish, surprise

213. DISCRIMINATION bigotry, humanism, inequality, prejudice

214. DISHONESTY decency, honesty, lies and lying, self-deception, stealing, truth and falsehood

215. DISILLUSIONMENT defeat, disappointment, idealism, illusion

216. DISTRUST betrayal, cynicism, doubt, gullibility, unfaithfulness

217. DIVERSITY chaos, conformity, difference, interests, divided, unity

218. DIVORCE alienation, lawyers and law, love, loss of, marriage

219. DOCTORS the body, health, the heart, holistic medicine, medicine, mind and body

220. DOGMATISM closed-mindedness, ideology, intolerance, open-mindedness, opinions, prejudice

221. DOGS animals, cats, friends and friendship, loyalty

222. DOUBT agnosticism, belief, certainty, distrust, faith, indecision

223. DRAMATISTS AND DRAMA actors and acting, art, artists, theater, writers and writing

224. DREAMS the mind, plans, prophecy, psychology, psychiatry, sleep

225. DRINKS AND DRINKING abstinence, coffee, intemperance, water

226. DRUGS abstinence, coffee, consciousness, medicine, smoking

227. DUTY obligation, responsibility, taxes

228. EARTH ecology, flowers and plants, the mundane, trees, universe, the world

229. EATING DISORDERS exercise, health, food and eating

230. ECOLOGY animals, conservation, earth, pollution, the sea, trees

231. ECONOMICS business, capitalism, communism, inflation, money, recession, socialism

232. EDITORS AND EDITING books and reading, careers, grammar, publishing, writers and writing

233. EDUCATION books and reading, learning, literacy, preparedness, scholars and scholarship, teachers and teaching

234. EFFORT achievement, aspiration, deeds, discipline, enterprise

235. EGOTISM the self, self-esteem, self-hatred, selfishness, vanity

236. ELOQUENCE influence, persuasion, poetry and poets, public speaking, speaking

237. EMOTIONS admiration, affection, aggression, ambition, amusement, anger, approval, arrogance, boldness, cheerfulness, closed-mindedness, coldness, confidence, confusion, contempt, contentment, courage, cowardice, cruelty, curiosity, cynicism, despair, determination, disillusionment, doubt, envy, faith, fear, forgiveness, greed, hate, honor, hope, humility, impatience, indignation, jealousy, joy, loneliness, love, love and hate, loyalty, lust, malice, melancholy, misery, optimism, optimism and pessimism, pain, passion, pessimism, piety, pity, pleasure, pride, selfishness, shame, sorrow, trust, unhappiness, zeal

238. ENDING death, decline, destruction, the future

239. ENDURANCE discipline, experience, strength, stress, suffering, survival

240. ENEMIES hate, interests, divided, peace, war

241. ENTERPRISE achievement, action, activity, business, effort, speed

242. ENTHUSIASM interest, involvement, passion, zeal, zest

243. ENVY desires, greed, jealousy

244. EQUALITY comparison, human rights, justice, similarity, superiority

245. ERAS age, generations, the past

246. ETERNITY afterlife, death, God, heaven, hell, immortality

247. EUROPE Britain and the British, France and the French, Germany and the Germans, Greece and the Greeks, Ireland and the Irish, Italy and the Italians, Russia and the Russians, Scotland and the Scottish, Spain and the Spanish, Switzerland and the Swiss

248. EVENTS adventure, birth, circumstance, experience, fights and fighting, peace, war

249. EVIL hell, morality, sin, vice

250. EVOLUTION animals, the Bible, change, growth and development, survival

251. EXAGGERATION boasting, excess, miracles, propaganda

252. EXAMPLE imitation, learning, stereotypes

253. EXCELLENCE achievement, genius, greatness, perfection, talent

254. EXCESS exaggeration, inflation, intemperance, luxury, waste

255. EXCUSES apology, defense, explanation, regret

303. FUTILITY frustration, triviality, uselessness

304. THE FUTURE the past, the present, progress, prophecy, time

305. GAMBLING baseball, horses and horse racing, sports and games

306. GARDENS AND GARDENING flowers and plants, leisure, nature

307. GENERALIZATION ideas, theory, truth

308. GENERATIONS age, eras, time, youth and age

309. GENEROSITY charity, Christmas, gifts and giving, kindness, sharing, unselfishness

310. GENIUS ability, artists, excellence, superiority, uniqueness

311. GENTLENESS carefulness, humility, kindness, obedience

312. GERMANY AND THE GERMANS Europe, fascism, nations

313. GHOSTS death, materialism, memory, spirituality

314. GIFTS AND GIVING charity, Christmas, generosity, receiving

315. GLORY fame, heroes and heroism, honor, reputation

316. GOD atheism, Christianity, evolution, heaven, morality, religion, theology, the unknown, worship

317. THE GOLDEN RULE Christianity, principle, religion, theology

318. GOLF exercise, leisure, sports and games

319. GOOD AND EVIL morality, religion, theology

320. GOOD BREEDING ancestry, aristocracy, heredity, manners

321. GOODNESS evil, God, morality, virtue

322. GOSSIP conversation, malice, slander, speaking

323. GOVERNMENT authority, bureaucracy, citizenship, Congress, constitutions, democracy, presidents and the presidency, taxes

324. GRACE charm, spirituality, style

325. GRAMMAR editors and editing, education, learning, literature, writers and writing

326. GRATITUDE appreciation, grace, honor, obligation

327. GREATNESS ability, excellence, genius, nobility

328. GREECE AND THE GREEKS the Classics, democracy, Europe, nations

499. THE MILITARY aggression, enemies, fights and fighting, nuclear weapons, war, weapons

500. THE MIND concentration, hypochondria, illusion, memory, mind and body, psychiatry, psychology

501. MIND AND BODY the body, holistic medicine, medicine, the mind

502. MINORITY losers, opposition, race, racism

503. MIRACLES myth, saints and sainthood, the supernatural, superstition

504. MIRRORS appearance, eyes, sight

505. MISERS greed, meanness, money, thrift

506. MISERY adversity, despair, suffering

507. MISTAKES confusion, failure, faults, illusion, perversity

508. MODERATION justice, limitations, mediocrity, patience, tolerance

509. MODERNITY internationalism, newness, the present, style, timeliness

510. MODESTY conservatism, humility, nudity, self-denial, self-esteem, shyness

511. MONARCHS AND MONARCHY ancestry, aristocracy, government, heredity, leaders and leadership, nobility

512. MONEY banks and banking, borrowing and lending, debt, economics, misers, payment

513. MONTHS eras, seasons, time

514. THE MOON heaven, night, poetry and poets, stars, the sun

515. MORALITY cleanliness, good and evil, goodness, piety, sin, theology

516. MORNING coffee, night, the sun, time

517. MORTALITY animals, death, humankind, irrevocability, life, life and death

518. MOTHERS children, fathers, parents and parenthood

519. MOTIVES ambition, aspiration, causes, ideas, purpose

520. MOURNING complaints, crying, death, funerals, loss, love, loss of, regret

521. MOVIES actors and acting, audiences, Hollywood, photography

522. MULTICULTURALISM African Americans, America and the Americans, Asian Americans, Hispanic Americans, Native Americans, race

523. THE MUNDANE practicality, realism, reality, the supernatural, the world

524. MUSICIANS AND MUSIC dancing, jazz, noise, opera, rap music, rock 'n' roll, singing

525. MYSTICISM enthusiasm, idealism, spirituality, the supernatural, the unknown

526. MYTH fiction, literature, miracles, romance, superstition

527. NAMES identity, reputation, slander

528. NATIONALISM the flag, homeland, loyalty, nations, patriotism

529. NATIONS Africa and the Africans, America and the Americans, Britain and the British, Canada and the Canadians, France and the French, Germany and the Germans, Greece and the Greeks, Ireland and the Irish, Italy and the Italians, Switzerland and the Swiss

530. NATIVE AMERICANS America and the Americans, multiculturalism, race

531. NATURE character, civilization, the country and the countryside, insects, rivers, the sea, universe, the world

532. NECESSITY expediency, nature, poverty, stress

533. NEIGHBORS community, friends and friendship

534. NEUROSIS emotions, madness, masochism, psychiatry, psychology, sadism, sanity

535. NEUTRALITY indifference, involvement, stoicism

536. NEW ENGLAND America and the Americans, Boston, places, puritans and puritanism

537. NEW YORK America and the Americans, cities, jazz, places

538. NEWNESS modernity, originality, timeliness, uniqueness

539. NEWS events, journalists and journalism, magazines, mass media, newspapers, television

540. NEWSPAPERS editors and editing, journalists and journalism, mass media, news

541. NIGHT bed, the moon, morning, sleep, time

542. NOBILITY aristocracy, dignity, glory, greatness, monarchs and monarchy

543. NOISE musicians and music, opera, rap music, rock 'n' roll, silence, singing

544. NONSENSE consistency and inconsistency, fools and foolishness, madness, pretension, stupidity

545. NONVIOLENCE agreement, compromise, peace, violence, war

546. NUCLEAR WEAPONS the Cold War, scientists and science, technology, war

547. NUDITY appearance, the body, clothes and clothing, modesty, pornography

548. OBEDIENCE authority, conformity, faithfulness, irreverence, loyalty, respect

549. OBLIGATION commitment, conscience, debt, duty, gratitude, payment, responsibility

550. OBSCURITY indecision, mysticism, questions

551. OBSERVATION eyes, indifference, perception, perspective, sight

552. OLD AGE age, death, eras, generations, longevity

553. OPEN-MINDEDNESS clarity, intelligence, liberalism, tolerance

554. OPERA musicians and music, noise, singing

555. OPINIONS bigotry, choice, criticism, critics, ideas, judges, judgment, theory

556. OPPORTUNITY chance, circumstance, events, excuses, luck

557. OPPOSITION anger, competition, conflict, inner, contrast, defense, fights and fighting, interests, divided

558. OPPRESSION cruelty, fascism, force, stress, tyranny

559. OPTIMISM cynicism, hope, idealism, mysticism, optimism and pessimism, pessimism, philosophers and philosophy

560. OPTIMISM AND PESSIMISM cynicism, hope, idealism, mysticism, pessimism, philosophers and philosophy

561. ORDER chaos, confusion, method, peace, plans, rank, society, unity

584. PESSIMISM despair, melancholy, optimism, optimism and pessimism

585. PHILOSOPHERS AND PHILOSOPHY agnosticism, atheism, belief, existence, existentialism, truth, wisdom, Zen

586. PHOTOGRAPHY art, mirrors, movies, pornography

587. PIETY decency, morality, prayer, preachers and preaching, religion, self-righteousness

588. PITY charity, kindness, mercy, sympathy, understanding

589. PLACES cities, community, the country and the countryside, home, houses, the suburbs

590. PLAGIARISM originality, stealing, truth and falsehood, writers and writing

591. PLANS dreams, order, purpose, thinking and thought

592. PLAY amusement, dramatists and drama, happiness, leisure, pleasure, spontaneity, theater

593. PLEASURE contentment, joy, play

594. POETRY AND POETS artists, eloquence, literature, poetry and prose, words, writers and writing

595. POETRY AND PROSE art, literature, poetry and poets, writers and writing

596. THE POLICE authority, criminals and crime, order, prisons, the state

597. POLITENESS civilization, culture, gentleness, manners, rudeness

598. POLITICAL PARTIES government, nations, parties, politicians and politics

599. POLITICIANS AND POLITICS government, lawyers and law, political parties, public office, public speaking

600. POLLUTION cleanliness, corruption, ecology, the sea

601. POPULARITY admiration, approval, fame, familiarity, reputation

602. POPULATION citizenship, community, nations, people

603. PORNOGRAPHY nudity, photography, vulgarity

604. POSSESSION calmness, home, houses, materialism, reputation, self-control

650. RACE African Americans, Asian Americans, Hispanic Americans, minority, Native Americans, people, racism

651. RACISM inequality, injustice, prejudice

652. RADICALISM conservatism, intemperance, liberalism, rebellion, reformers and reform, revolutionaries and revolution

653. RAIN farms and farming, rainbows, seasons, water

654. RANK ancestry, authority, circumstance, class, excess, order, reputation

655. RAP MUSIC jazz, musicians and music, noise

656. RAPE criminals and crime, seduction, sex, women

657. REALISM literature, the mundane, nature, reality, truth

658. REALITY absurdity, the mundane, nature, realism, truth, the world

659. REBELLION anarchy, radicalism, revolutionaries and revolution

660. RECEIVING charity, Christmas, generosity, gifts and giving

661. RECESSION business, economics, poverty

662. RECIPROCITY agreement, communication, compromise, receiving, sharing

663. REFORMERS AND REFORM improvement, liberalism, progress, revolutionaries and revolution, social change

664. REFUSAL decline, excuses, protest, self-denial

665. REGRET conscience, mourning, repentance, self-criticism, self-pity, sorrow

666. RELATIONSHIPS association, authority, friends and friendship, marriage, men and women, parents and parenthood, power

667. RELATIVES family, fathers, mothers, parents and parenthood

668. RELIGION atheism, the Bible, Christianity, church, clergy, God, Islam, Jews and Judaism, preachers and preaching, theology

669. REMEDIES change, drugs, help, right

670. REPENTANCE apology, conscience, guilt, regret, self-criticism, sin, sorrow

671. REPETITION bores and boredom, custom, habit, newness, perseverance

672. REPUTATION   fame, heroes and heroism, names, popularity, respect

673. REQUESTS desires, prayer, questions

674. RESOLUTION belief, determination, ideas, opinions, perseverance

675. RESPECT admiration, appreciation, honor, obedience, value

676. RESPONSIBILITY   commitment, duty, faithfulness, loyalty, obligation, payment

677. REST coffee, holidays, leisure, peace, silence, sleep

678. RETIREMENT loneliness, old age, parting, privacy, rest, silence, solitude

679. RETRIBUTION punishment, reciprocity, revenge

680. REVENGE cruelty, justice, punishment, retribution

681. REVOLUTIONARIES AND REVOLUTION radicalism, rebellion, reformers and reform, Russia and the Russians, social change

682. REWARD honor, payment, progress, right

683. RIDICULE sarcasm, satire, shame

684. RIGHT advantage, freedom, justice, remedies, reward

685. RIVERS nature, the sea, water

686. ROCK 'N' ROLL art, musicians and music, noise

687. ROMANCE affection, kissing, love, lovers

688. ROMANTICISM idealism, literature, sentimentality

689. RUDENESS contempt, ignorance, ingratitude, insults, manners, politeness, stupidity, vulgarity

690. RULES custom, habit, principle

691. RUSSIA AND THE RUSSIANS the Cold War, Europe, nations, revolutionaries and revolution

692. SACRIFICE loss, martyrs and martyrdom, self-denial, selfishness, unselfishness, worship

693. SADISM aggression, cruelty, masochism, neurosis, pain, perversity, psychiatry

694. SAFETY carefulness, certainty, danger, trust

695. SAILORS AND SAILING the military, the sea, ships and boats, water

696. SAINTS AND SAINTHOOD Christianity, martyrs and martyrdom, morality, religion, sacrifice, spirituality

697. SANITY health, madness, the mind, prudence, psychiatry, psychology

698. SARCASM contempt, ridicule, satire, wit

699. SATIRE comedy, puns, ridicule, wit

700. SCHOLARS AND SCHOLARSHIP education, historians and history, ideas, knowledge, learning, libraries, theory

701. SCIENCE AND RELIGION faith, God, knowledge, nature, religion, scientists and science, universe

702. SCIENTISTS AND SCIENCE knowledge, mathematics, medicine, nuclear weapons, psychology, scholars and scholarship, science and religion

703. SCOTLAND AND THE SCOTTISH Britain and the British, Europe, nations

704. THE SEA fish and fishing, nature, rivers, sailors and sailing, water

705. SEASONS months, rain, time, weather

706. SECRETS AND SECRECY alienation, censorship, mysticism, obscurity, privacy, silence, solitude

707. SEDUCTION corruption, debauchery, men and women, rape, sex, temptation

708. THE SELF character, egotism, identity, nature, personality

709. SELF-CONTROL calmness, discipline, patience, self-denial, self-sufficiency

710. SELF-CRITICISM masochism, pain, suicide, self-doubt

711. SELF-DECEPTION dishonesty, exaggeration, hypocrisy, lies and lying, truth and falsehood

712. SELF-DENIAL generosity, martyrs and martyrdom, sacrifice, self-control, unselfishness

713. SELF-DESTRUCTION death, masochism, suicide

714. SELF-DOUBT conflict, inner, confusion, self-criticism

715. SELF-ESTEEM egotism, pride, vanity

716. SELF-HATRED masochism, self-criticism, self-destruction

717. SELF-KNOWLEDGE conscience, consciousness, knowledge, self-realization, truth

718. SELF-PITY conflict, inner, crying, melancholy, regret, sorrow

719. SELF-REALIZATION consciousness, knowledge, self-knowledge

720. SELF-RELIANCE ability, confidence, determination, enterprise, self-control, self-sufficiency

721. SELF-RIGHTEOUSNESS boasting, egotism, hypocrisy, puritans and puritanism

722. SELF-SUFFICIENCY confidence, determination, self-reliance

723. SELFISHNESS egotism, greed, indulgence, meanness, misers

724. THE SENSES appreciation, consciousness, eyes, scratching, sight, taste

725. SENSITIVITY emotions, pain, sympathy

726. SENSUALITY desires, emotions, love, passion

727. SENTIMENTALITY fiction, the heart, romance, romanticism, stereotypes, triviality

728. SERIOUSNESS calmness, importance, influence, interest, severity, sincerity, usefulness

729. SERVICE duty, help, worship

730. SEVERITY criticism, cruelty, seriousness

731. SEX bed, chastity, debauchery, homosexuality, lesbianism, men and women, sensuality

732. SEXISM bigotry, men, prejudice, women

733. SEXUAL HARRASSMENT men, men and women, women

734. SHAME blushing, contempt, disappointment, guilt, self-criticism, wrong and wrongdoing

735. SHARING charity, experience, kindness, reciprocity

736. SHIPS AND BOATS fish and fishing, sailors and sailing, the sea, water

803. THEORY generalization, ideas, knowledge, scholars and scholarship, thinking and thought

804. THINKING AND THOUGHT ideas, intellectuals and intellectualism, intelligence, logic, scholars and scholarship, theory

805. THREAT danger, fear, terrorism

806. THRIFT economics, excess, greed, misers, moderation, waste

807. TIME eras, the future, months, the past, the present, timeliness, transience, the twentieth century

808. TIMELINESS chance, fashion, modernity, opportunity, the present, punctuality, style, time

809. TOLERANCE charity, grace, open-mindedness, patience, sympathy, understanding

810. TOTALITARIANISM captivity, communism, fascism, government, tyranny

811. TRADITION the Classics, conservatism, culture, custom, myth, wisdom

812. TRAGEDY adversity, dramatists and drama, failure, misery

813. TRANSIENCE death, mortality, the past, time, triviality

814. TRAVEL airplanes, automobiles, hotels, ships and boats, walking

815. TREES earth, ecology, flowers and plants, nature

816. TRIVIALITY meanness, sentimentality, transience, unimportance

817. TRUST confidence, dependence, faith, gullibility, loyalty

818. TRUTH absurdity, advertising, frankness, proverbs, truth, truth and falsehood

819. TRUTH AND FALSEHOOD advertising, dishonesty, lies and lying, publicity, truth

820. THE TWENTIETH CENTURY airplanes, automobiles, computers, the present, technology, television

821. TYRANNY cruelty, fascism, freedom, opposition, oppression, terrorism, totalitarianism

822. UGLINESS appearance, beauty, imperfection, meanness

823. THE UNCONSCIOUS emotions, the mind, psychiatry

824. UNDERSTANDING conciliation, familiarity, intuition, knowledge, meaning, perception, sympathy

825. UNEMPLOYMENT leisure, unions, uselessness, waste, work, workers

826. UNFAITHFULNESS betrayal, dishonesty, distrust, faithfulness, intemperance

827. UNHAPPINESS crying, melancholy, mourning, sorrow

828. UNIMPORTANCE indifference, meanness, triviality

829. UNIONS careers, work, workers

830. UNIQUENESS conformity, difference, excellence, individualism, stereotypes, unity

831. UNITY concentration, divorce, identity, similarity, solidarity, uniqueness

832. UNIVERSE creation and creativity, God, space, outer, stars, the sun, the world

833. THE UNKNOWN afterlife, alienation, God, mysticism, obscurity, secrets and secrecy

834. UNSELFISHNESS generosity, humanism, kindness, self-denial, selfishness

835. USEFULNESS excellence, help, importance, practicality, value

836. USELESSNESS futility, illusion, imperfection, unemployment, waste

837. VALUE appreciation, approval, importance, meaning, practicality, usefulness

838. VANITY arrogance, boasting, egotism, pretension, pride, self-esteem

839. VEGETARIANISM earth, flowers and plants, food and eating, nature

840. VICE bribery, debauchery, evil, sin, smoking

841. VICTORY achievement, boasting, defeat, success

842. VIOLENCE aggression, danger, destruction, guns and gun control, nonviolence, threat, war

843. VIRTUE character, chastity, cleanliness, common sense, goodness,

865. WISHES ambition, aspiration, desires

866. WIT cleverness, cunning, humor, laughter, puns

867. WOMEN feminism, men and women, sex, sexism, sexual harassment

868. WORDS the Bible, language, literature, poetry and prose, speaking

869. WORK careers, unemployment, unions, usefulness, vocations

870. WORKERS careers, unemployment, unions

871. THE WORLD earth, the mundane, nature, universe

872. WORRY despair, suffering

873. WORSHIP church, God, prayer, religion, service

874. WRITERS AND WRITING autobiography, biography, books and reading, diaries, dramatists and drama, grammar, journalists and journalism

875. WRONG AND WRONGDOING accusation, confession, criminals and crime, punishment

876. YOUTH age, children, immaturity, innocence, youth and age

877. YOUTH AND AGE age, beginning and ending, generations, immaturity, longevity, maturity, old age, youth

878. ZEAL enthusiasm, passion, zest

879. ZEN neutrality, philosophers and philosophy, religion, stoicism

880. ZEST enthusiasm, passion, zeal

AUTHOR INDEX

AIDOO, AMA ATA (1940—   ). African poet, short-story writer, playwright. *Africa and Africans*

ALAIN (1868—1951). French philosopher, essayist, teacher. (Pseudonym of Émile-Auguste Chartier) *Doubt*

ALBEE, EDWARD (1928—   ). American playwright. *Humor, Vulgarity*

ALBERTI, LEON BATTISTA (1404—1472). Italian mathematician, architect, painter, writer. *Beauty*

ALCOTT, LOUISA MAY (1832—1888). American novelist. *Education, Experience, Genius, Housework, Love, Months, Reformers and Reform, Self-knowledge, Women*

ALDRICH, THOMAS BAILEY (1836—1907). American poet, editor, short-story writer, novelist, playwright. *Books and Reading, Bores and Boredom*

ALI, MUHAMMAD (1942—   ). American boxer, world heavyweight champion. (Original name, Cassius Marcellus Clay, Jr.) *Violence*

ALLEN, FRED (1894—1956). American comedian. (Original name, John F. Sullivan) *Ancestry, Fame, Hollywood, Walking*

ALLEN, GRACIE (1906—1964). American comedian. *Birth*

ALLEN, PAULA GUNN (1939—   ). Laguna/Lakota/Lebanese scholar, writer, activist. *Native Americans*

ALLEN, WOODY (1935—   ). American actor, writer, film director. *Afterlife, Agnosticism, Contraception, Death, Distrust, Love, Nature, Sex, Shyness, Stress*

ALLENDE, ISABEL (1942—   ). Chilean journalist, novelist. *Obscurity*

ALLILUYEVA, SVETLANA (1925—   ). Russian-born author. *Russia and the Russians*

ALLINGHAM, MARGERY (1904—1966). English writer of detective novels. *Sex*

ALT, CAROL (1960—   ). American model. *Body Image*

ALTMAN, ROBERT (1925—   ). American film director. *Cults*

AMERICAN LIBRARY ASSOCIATION. Founded in 1876. *Computers*

AMIEL, HENRI FRÉDÉRIC (1821—1881). Swiss philosopher, poet. *Charm, Doubt, Duty*

AMIN, IDI (1925—   ). Ugandan soldier, politician, dictator. (Full name, Ida Amin Dada Oumee) *Tyranny*

AMIS, KINGSLEY (1922—   ). English novelist. *Children*

ANDERSON, MARIAN (1902—   ). American contralto. *Racism*

ANDREWS, JULIE (1935—   ) British actor. *Discipline*

ANGELOU, MAYA (1928—   ). American writer, activist, teacher. *African Americans, Anger, Dreams, Life, Multiculturalism, Self-pity, Talent*

ANONYMOUS, *Accusation, Advertising, Atheism, Death, Excess, Prejudices, Technology, Worry*

ANOUILH, JEAN (1910—1987). French playwright. *Action, Art, Beauty, Courage, Death, Despair, Involvement, Order, Reality*

ANTHONY, SUSAN B. (1820—1906). American reformer, suffragist. *Feminism, Reformers and Reform*

ANTIN, MARY (1881—1949). Russian-born American writer. *Past*

ANTISTHENES (c. 445—c. 365 B.C.). Greek philosopher, founder of the Cynic school. *Enemies, Envy, Monarchs and Monarchy*

ANTONIONI, MICHELANGELO (1912—   ). Italian film director. *Hollywood*

ANZALDUA, GLORIA (NA). Contemporary Tejana Chicana poet. *Family, Minority, Self*

APOCRYPHA. A part of the sacred literature of the Alexandrian Jews. *Destruction*

APOLLINAIRE, GUILLAUME (1880—1918). Italian-born French poet. (Original name, Wilhelm Apollinaris de Kostrowitzki) *Memory*

APOSTOLIUS, MICHAEL (1422—1480). Greek scholar. *Comparison*

ARBUS, DIANE (1923—1971). American photographer. *Love, Photography, Travel*

ARBUTHNOT, JOHN (1667—1735). Scottish writer, physician. *Political Parties*

ARENDT, HANNAH (1906—1975). German-born American political scientist. *Revolutionaries and Revolution*

ARETINO, PIETRO (1492—1556). Italian satirist. *Parents and Parenthood*

ARIOSTO, LUDOVICO (1474—1553). Italian poet. *Cruelty*

ARISTOTLE (384—322 B.C.). Greek philosopher. *Affection, Cities, Citizenship, Critics, Democracy, Education, Equality, Evil, Family, Frustration, Goodness, Happiness, Hope, Humankind, Judges, Means and Ends, The Middle Class, Motives, Politicians and Politics, Poverty, Public Office, Revolutionaries and Revolution, Self-control, State, Youth*

ARMATRADING, JOAN (1947—   ). West Indian-born British singer and composer. *America and Americans*

AMORY, CLEVELAND (1917—   ). American animal-rights activist, columnist. *Hunters and Hunting*

ARMSTRONG, LOUIS (1900—1971). American jazz musician. *Music and Musicians*

ARNALL, ELLIS (1907—   ). American politician, governor of Georgia. *Boston*

ARNOLD, GEORGE (1834—1865). American poet. *Charity*

ARNOLD, MATTHEW (1822—1888). English critic, essayist, poet. *Desires, Truth, Unhappiness*

ARNOLD, ROSEANNE BARR (1952—   ). American comedian and actor. *Fat and Fatness*

ASHE, ARTHUR (1943—1993). African-American tennis player, activist. *Alienation*

ASHBERY, JOHN (1927—). American poet, art critic. *Architecture, Dreams*

ASHTON-WARNER, SYLVIA (1905—1984). New Zealand teacher, novelist. *Love*

ASIMOV, ISAAC (1920—1992). Russian-born American science-fiction writer. *Conservation, Population*

ASKEW, REUBIN O'DONOVAN (1928—). American politician, governor of Florida. *America and Americans*

ASTAIRE, FRED (1899—1987). American dancer, actor. *Dancing, Manners*

ASTELL, MARY (1668—1731). English feminist, author. *Family, Sexism*

ASTOR, JOHN JACOB (1763—1848). German-born American financier. *Wealth*

ASTOR, NANCY (1879—1964). American-born English politician. *Wealth*

ATKINSON, BROOKS (1894—1984). American drama critic, essayist. *Bureaucracy, Church, Work*

ATWOOD, MARGARET (1939—). Canadian writer. *Words*

AUDEN, W.H. (1907—1973). English-born American poet, playwright. *Books and Reading, Critics, Disability, Faces, Genius, Mass Media, Opera, Poets and Poetry, Sin, Talent, Taste, Teachers and Teaching*

AUGUSTINE, NORMAN (1935—). American businessperson. *Computers*

AUGUSTINE OF HIPPO, ST. (354—430). Early Christian church leader and philosopher. *Aspiration, Chastity, Pain, Transience*

AUSTEN, JANE (1775—1817). English novelist. *Agreement, Complaints, Country and Countryside, Historians and History, London, Love, Marriage, Opportunity, Optimism, Parties, Pleasure, Poverty, Selfishness, Weather*

BABEL, ISAAC (1894—1941). Russian writer. *Grammar*

BACALL, LAUREN (1924—). American actor. (Original name, Betty Joan Perske) *Hollywood, Imagination*

BACON, FRANCIS (1561—1626). English philosopher, politician, essayist. *Adversity, Age, Anger, Atheism, Books and Reading, Business, Charity, Children, Courage, Crowds, Death, Discovery, Education, Excess, Fear, Nudity, Politeness, Revenge, Solitude, Virtue*

BAEZ, JOAN (1941—). American folk singer, activist. *Action, Despair, Nonviolence*

BAILEY, DAVID (1938—). British photographer. *Photography*

BAILEY, PEARL (1918—1990). American singer, actor, author, special adviser in the UN. *Mirrors, Self-knowledge, Social Change, Truth*

BAKER, JOSEPHINE (1906—1975). American singer, dancer. (Original name, Freda Josephine McDonald) *Modesty*

BAKER, RUSSELL (1925—). American columnist, humorist. *Men, Sports and Games*

BALANCHINE, GEORGE (1904—1983). Russian-born American choreographer. (Original name, Georgy Melitonovich Ballanchivadze), *Dancing*

BALDWIN, FAITH (1893—1978). American novelist. *Character, Time*

BALDWIN, JAMES (1924—1987). American novelist, essayist. *African Americans, Artists, Careers, Children, Cities, Dependence, Education, Europe, Experience, Future, Historians and History, Multiculturalism, Self-knowledge, Sex*

BALL, LUCILLE (1910—1989). American actor. *Divorce, Self-esteem*

BALZAC, HONORÉ DE (1799—1850). French novelist. *Bureaucracy, Equality, Manners, Vocations*

BAMBARA, TONI CADE (1939—   ). Writer, editor, teacher. *Old Age, Revolutionaries and Revolution, Sex*

BANCROFT, GEORGE (1800—1891). American historian. *Greed*

BANKHEAD, TALLULAH (1903—1968). American actor. *Debauchery, Drugs, Intellectuals and Intellectualism, Purity*

BARANSKAIA, NATALYA (1908—   ). Russian writer. *War*

BARDOT, BRIGITTE (1934—   ). French actor. *Faithfulness, Feminism, Maturity, Sex*

BARING, MAURICE (1874—1945). English journalist, writer. *Money*

BARKER, MYRTLE (1910—   ). American columnist. *Gossip*

BARKIN, ELLEN (1955—   ). American actor. *Actors and Acting*

BARNES, CLIVE (1927—   ). British-born America drama critic. *Television*

BARNES, DJUNA (1892—1982). American novelist, short-story writer, playwright. *Emotions, Europe, Life, Love, Middle Age, Mind, Personality*

BARNES, JULIAN (1946—   ). English novelist. *Love*

BARNUM, P.T. (1810—1891). American sideshow and circus owner. *Audience, Gullibility*

BAROJA, PÍO (1872—1956). Spanish author. (Full surname, Baroja y Nessi) *The Mundane*

BARRIE, J.M. (1860—1937). Scottish dramatist, novelist. *Adventure, Courage, Flowers and Plants, Motives, Publishing, Scotland and the Scottish*

BARROWS, SYDNEY BIDDLE (1952—   ). American owner and operator of house of prostitution. *Integrity*

BARRYMORE, ETHEL (1879—1959). American actor. *Actors and Acting, Hollywood, Open-mindedness*

BARRYMORE, JOHN (1882—1942). American actor. *America and Americans, Divorce*

BARTH, ALLAN (NA). Contemporary American political writer. *Criticism*

BARTHES, ROLAND (1915—1980). French critic, author. *Automobiles, Literature, Modernity, Photography*

BARTÓK, BÉLA (1881—1945). Hungarian composer, pianist, collector of folk songs. *Competition*

BARUCH, BERNARD M. (1870—1965). American business leader, diplomat, adviser to presidents. *Cold War, Government*

BARZUN, JACQUES (1907—   ). French-born American critic, educator. *Art, Intellectuals and Intellectualism, Tragedy, Youth*

BATES, DAISY (1863—1951). Irish-born Australian anthropologist. *Dignity, Idealism, Opinions*

BATESON, MARY CATHERINE (1939—   ). American anthropologist and writer. *Sharing*

BAUDELAIRE, CHARLES (1821—1867). French poet. *Debauchery, Poets and Poetry, Sex*

BAUM, VICKI (1888—1960). Austrian-born American novelist. *Stress, Success*

BEARD, MARY RITTER (1876—1958). American social historian, feminist. *Sexism*

BEAUMARCHAIS, PIERRE DE (1732—1799). French playwright, courtier, watchmaker to Louis XV. (Full name, Pierre-Augustin Caron de Beaumarchais) *Humankind, Singing*

BEAUMONT, FRANCIS (1584—1616). English playwright. *Indifference, Melancholy*

BEAUVOIR, SIMONE DE (1908—1986). French existentialist novelist, essayist, political activist, feminist. (Full name, Simone de Bertrand de Beauvoir) *Art, Change, Difficulty, Disillusionment, Equality, Feminism, Individualism, Love, Marriage, Mothers, Old Age, Retirement, Sex, Similarity, Strength, Women*

BECKETT, SAMUEL (1906—1989). Irish-born French novelist, playwright. *Habit, Madness, Punctuality, Suicide, Words*

BECQUE, HENRY (1837—1899). French playwright. *Decision, Equality*

BEDDOES, THOMAS LOVELL (1803—1849). English poet and playwright. *Ships and Boats*

BEEBE, SPENCER (NA). American president of Ecotrust. *Conservation*

BEECHAM, THOMAS (1879—1961). English conductor. *Musicians and Music, Travel*

BEECHER, HENRY WARD (1813—1887). American cleric, editor, writer. *Anger, Business, Cheerfulness, Conservatism, Defeat, Dogs, Enthusiasm, Flowers and Plants, Libraries, Secrets and Secrecy, Words*

BEERBOHM, MAX (1872—1956). English essayist, caricaturist. *Failure, Hospitality, Insects, Mediocrity, Nonsense, Vanity, Walking*

BEETON, ISABELLA MARY (1836—1865). English food writer. *Order*

BEHAN, BRENDAN (1923—1964). Irish playwright, wit, writer. *Critics, Ireland and the Irish, Police, Religion, Violence*

BEHN, APHRA (1640—1689). English playwright, poet, novelist. *Love, Transience*

BELL, DANIEL (1919—   ). American sociologist. *Modernity*

BELLOC, HILAIRE (1870—1953). English writer. (Full name, Joseph Hilaire Pierre René Belloc) *Aristocracy, Autobiography, Critics, Singing*

BELLOW, SAUL (1915—   ). American novelist, playwright. *New York, Poets and Poetry, Publishing*

BENCHLEY, ROBERT (1889—1945). American humorist. *Quotations*

ST. BENEDICT OF NURSIA (c. 480—c. 547). Italian monk, founder of the Benedictine order. *Work*

BENÉT, STEPHEN VINCENT (1898—1943). American poet, short-story writer. *Dreams, Power*

BENGIS, INGRID (1944—   ). American writer. *Words*

BENJAMIN, WALTER (1892—1940). German-Jewish scholar, critic. *Art*

BENTHAM, JEREMY (1748—1832). English philosopher, jurist. *Lawyers and Law, Punishment*

BERGALIS, KIMBERLY (c. 1969—1992). American activist. *AIDS*

BERGEN, CANDICE (1946—   ). American actor. *Dreams*

BERGER, JOHN (1926—   ). British critic, essayist. *Advertising, Animals*

BERGMAN, INGRID (1915—1982). Swedish actor. *Happiness, Regret*

BERKLICH, HELEN DRAZENOVICH (1914—   ). American born of Yugoslavian immigrants, seen in *Dignity* (1985). *People*

BERLE, MILTON (1908—   ). American actor, comedian. (Original name, Milton Berlinger) *Committees*

BERLIN, IRVING (1888—1989). Russian-born American composer. (Original name, Israel Baline) *Success*

BERLIOZ, HECTOR (1803—1869). French composer. *Modesty, Time*

BERMAN, MORRIS (1944—   ). American professor, writer, lecturer. *Ecology*

BERNARD, TRISTAN (1866—1947). French playwright, novelist. (Original name, Paul Bernard) *Theater*

BERNE, ERIC (1910—   ). American psychiatrist, writer. *Civilization*

BERRA, YOGI (1925—   ). American baseball player. *Baseball*

BERRY, JOHN (1915—   ). American poet, fiction writer. *Happiness*

BERTON, PIERRE (1727—1780). French musician. *Canada and the Canadians*

BETHUNE, MARY MCLEOD (1875—1955). American educator, writer. *Spirituality*

BETTI, UGO (1892—1953). Italian playwright. *Family, Funerals, Time*

BHABBA, HOMI K. (NA). Contemporary lecturer, author. *Nations*

BHAGAVADGITA (250 B.C.—A.D. 250). Sanskrit, *The Song of God. Action, Hell, Peace, Self-denial*

BIBESCO, ELIZABETH (1897—1945). English-born Rumanian poet. *Parting, Sharing*

and Heroism, Historians and History, Identity, Involvement, Morality, Peace, Poverty, Right, Science and Religion, Self-righteousness, War

BRENAN, GERALD (1894—1987). English travel writer, novelist. *Leisure*

BRENNAN, JR., WILLIAM J. (1906—   ). American lawyer, associate justice on the U.S. Supreme Court. *The Flag*

BRENNER, DAVID (1945—   ). American comedian. *Vegetarianism*

BRESLIN, JIMMY (1930—   ). American journalist, novelist, writer. *Presidents and Presidency*

BRETON, ANDRÉ (1896—1966). French poet, essayist, critic. *Words*

BREZHNEV, LEONID (1906—1982). Soviet leader. *Russia and the Russians*

BRIGHT, JOHN (1811—1889). English politician, orator. *Force*

BRILLAT-SAVARIN, ANTHELME (1755—1826). French politician, gourmet. *Food and Eating*

BRINKLEY, DAVID (1920—   ) American newscaster. *News*

BRITTAIN, VERA (c. 1896—1970). English writer. *Politicians and Politics*

BRODER, DAVID (1929—   ). American writer. *Politicians and Politics*

BROMFIELD, LOUIS (1896—1956). American writer. *Ecology*

BRONOWSKI, JACOB (1908—1974). English scientist, mathematician, lecturer. *Scientists and Science*

BRONSON, CHARLES (1922—   ). American actor. (Original name, Charles Buchinsky) *Faces*

BRONTÈ, CHARLOTTE (1816—1855). English novelist. *Carefulness, Expectation, Eyes, Flowers and Plants, Ideology, Self-realization, Words*

BROOKE, CHARLOTTE (1740—1793). Irish poet. *Ireland and the Irish*

BROOKS, GWENDOLYN (1917—   ). American poet, novelist. *Poetry and Poets*

BROOKS, LOUISE (1906—1985). American actor. *Actors and Acting*

BROSSARD, NICOLE (1943—   ). Canadian poet, writer. *Language*

BROTHERS, JOYCE (1925—   ). American psychologist. *Listening*

BROWN, JERRY (1938—   ). American politician, governor of California. *Action, Change, Government, Prisons*

BROWN, JOHN MASON (1900—1969). American literary critic. *Television*

BROWN, RITA MAE (1944—   ). American novelist. *Birth, Divorce, Homosexuality, Intuition, Love, Television*

BROWN, THOMAS EDWARD (1830—1897). English poet. *Gardens and Gardening*

BROWNE, THOMAS (1605—1682). English writer, scholar, physician. *Appearance, Blindness, Death, Envy, Faith, Flattery, Gardens and Gardening, Humankind, Self-hatred, Virtue, The World*

BROWNING, ELIZABETH BARRETT (1806—1861). English poet, spouse of Robert Browning. *Books and Reading, Genius, Heaven, Opinions*

BROWNING, ROBERT (1812—1889). English poet, spouse of Elizabeth Barrett Browning. *Ambition, Christianity, Conflict, Inner, Earth, Emotions, Ignorance, Italy and the Italians, Monarchs and Monarchy, Optimism, Seasons, Sensuality, Simplicity, Sincerity*

BROWNMILLER, SUSAN (1935—   ). Journalist, author, feminist. *Rape*

BROWNSON, ORESTES A. (1803—1876). American clergy, writer. *The Middle Class*

BRUCE, LENNY (1923—1966). American comedian. *Communism, Drugs, Liberalism*

BRYANT, ANITA (1940—   ). American singer, activist. *Homosexuality*

BRYANT, WILLIAM CULLEN (1794—1878). American poet, critic, editor. *Trees*

BUBER, MARTIN (1878—1965). German-Jewish theologian, philosopher, writer. *Play*

BUHAN, JOHN (1875—1940). Scottish author, administrator. *Atheism*

BUCK, PEARL S. (1892—1973). American novelist, humanitarian. (Full name, Pearl Comfort Buck, née Sydenstricker) *Children, Civilization, Debt, Despair, Dogmatism, Faith, Old Age, Praise, Religion, The Self, Service, Slavery, Sorrow*

BUCKLEY, WILLIAM F. (1925—   ). American journalist, writer. *AIDS, Idealism, France and the French*

BUDDHA (c. 563—c. 483 B.C.). Founder of Buddhism. (Real name, Siddhartha Gautama) *Eternity, Zeal*

BUKOVSKY, VLADIMIR (1942—   ). Russian political activist. *Optimism and Pessimism*

BUKOWSKI, CHARLES (1920—   ). American author. *Censorship, Friends and Friendship, Knowledge*

BULWER-LYTTON, EDWARD (1803—1873). English novelist, politician. *Italy and the Italians*

BUNCH, CHARLOTTE (1944—   ). Feminist theorist, lecturer, writer, consultant. *America and Americans, Superiority*

BURBANK, LUTHER (1849—1926). American horticulturist. *Ancestry*

BURGESS, ANTHONY (1917—   ). English novelist. *Books and Reading, Britain and the British, Inspiration, Sleep*

BURKE, EDMUND (1729—1797). British diplomat, orator, writer. *Arrogance, Corruption, Custom, Example, Historians and History, Malice, Motives, Order, Rebellion, Religion, Superstition, Thrift, Tolerance*

BURNETT, CAROL (1933—   ). American comedian, actor. *Comedy*

BURNETT, FRANCES HODGSON (1849—1924) English-born author. *Discovery*

BURNEY, FANNY (1752—1840). English novelist. *Travel*

BURNS, GEORGE (1896—   ). American comedian. (Real name, Nathan Birnbaum) *Family, Government, Old Age, Retirement*

BURROUGHS, JOHN (1837—1921). American naturalist, essayist, poet. *Belief*

BURROUGHS, WILLIAM S. (1914—   ). American author. *Possession, Words*

BURTON, RICHARD (1821—1890). British explorer. *Travel*

BURTON, ROBERT (1577—1640). English cleric, writer. *Corruption, Humility, Melancholy, Plagiarism, Rules*

BUSH, BARBARA (1925—   ). American First Lady. *Parents and Parenthood, Presidents and Presidency, Success*

BUSH, GEORGE (1924—   ). Forty-first president of the United States. *Food and Eating, Homosexuality, Recession, Taxes, Virtue, World*

BUTLER, JOSEPHINE (1828—1906). English reformer. *Ireland and the Irish*

BUTLER, SAMUEL (1612—1680). English poet, satirist. *Action, Certainty, Clergy, Conscience, Dogs, Excess, Food and Eating, Historians and History, Parents and Parenthood, Spontaneity, Stubbornness, Vice*

LORD BYRON (1788—1824). English Romantic poet. (Full name, George Gordon Byron) *Adversity, Chastity, Drinks and Drinking, Historians and History, Laughter, Longevity, Newness, Payment, Scotland and the Scottish, War*

CABELL, JAMES BRANCH (1879—1958). American novelist, essayist. *Optimism and Pessimism*

CADMAN, SAMUEL PARKS (1864—1936). *Earth*

CAESAR, JULIUS (100—44 B.C.). Roman general, statesperson. *Lawyers and Law, Victory*

CAESAR, SHIRLEY (1938—   ). American gospel singer. *Women*

CAGE, JOHN (1912—1992). American composer. *Self-sufficiency*

CALDERONE, MARY (1904—   ). Physician, author, lecturer, former medical director of Planned Parenthood World Population. *Love*

CAMPBELL, JOSEPH (1904—1987). American author, scholar. *Experience, Happiness*

CAMPBELL, THOMAS (1777—1844). Scottish poet. *Endurance, Immortality*

CAMUS, ALBERT (1913—1960). French philosopher, novelist, playwright, journalist. *Alienation, Arrogance, Beauty, Commitment, Death, Experience, Greatness, Guilt, Happiness, Humankind, Intellectuals and Intellectualism, Life, Martyrs and Martyrdom, Modernity, Nationalism, Nobility, The Present, Press, Freedom of the, Punishment, Capital, Rebellion, Retribution, Revolutionaries and Revolution, Self-pity, Slavery, Suicide, Truth, Value*

CAMUS, RENAUD (1946—   ). French writer. *Homosexuality*

CANETTI, ELIAS (1905—   ). Bulgarian author. *Animals*

CAPONE, AL (1899—1947). Italian-born American gangster. (Nickname, Scarface) *Canada and the Canadians, Chicago*

CAPOTE, TRUMAN (1924—1984). American novelist, short-story writer. *Gardens and Gardening, Italy and the Italians, Literature*

CARDOZO, BENJAMIN N. (1870—1938). American jurist, associate justice on the U.S. Supreme Court. *Punishment, Capital*

CARLIN, GEORGE (1937—   ). American comedian, talk-show host. *The Present*

CARLYLE, JANE (1801—1866). Scottish writer. *Injustice*

CARLYLE, THOMAS (1795—1881). Scottish-born English essayist, historian. *Action, Biography, Bribery, Careers, Christianity, Civilization, Debt, Facts, Intuition, Meanness, Sarcasm, The Self, Self-doubt, Silence, Unemployment, Vision*

CARNEGIE, ANDREW (1835—1919). British-born American industrialist. *Determination*

CARROLL, LEWIS (1832—1919). English writer and mathematician. (Pseudonym of Charles Lutwidge Dodgson) *Belief, Meaning, Morality, Purpose*

CARSON, JOHNNY (1925—   ). American talk-show host, comedian. *Guns and Gun Control, Life, New York*

CARSON, RACHEL (1907—1964). American writer, biologist. *Pollution, The Sea*

CARTER, JIMMY (1924—   ). Thirty-eighth president of the United States. *Multiculturalism, Presidents and Presidency*

CARTER, LILLIAN (1898—1983). Georgia community leader, mother of Jimmy Carter. *Old Age*

CARTLAND, BARBARA (1901—   ). English romantic novelist. *Cosmetics*

CARVER, RAYMOND (1939—1988). American poet, short-story writer. *Writers and Writing*

CARY, JOYCE (1888—1957). British novelist. *Miracles*

CASSON, HUGH (1910—   ). English architect, professor, president of the Royal Academy. *Britain and the British*

CASTANEDA, CARLOS (1931—   ). Brazilian-born American anthropologist, writer. *Vision*

CASTRO, FIDEL (1926—   ). Premier of Cuba. *Revolutionaries and Revolution*

CATHER, WILLA (1873—1947). American journalist, novelist. *Dependence, Editors and Editing, Historians and History, Kindness, Memory, The Moon, Repetition, Trees, Youth and Age*

CATHERINE II (1729—1796). Empress of Russia, known as Catherine the Great. (Original name, Sophie Friederike Auguste von Anhalt-Zerbst) *Praise*

CATO THE ELDER (234—149 B.C.). Roman politician. (Full name, Marcus Porcius Cato) *Farms and Farming, Retirement*

CATULLUS (c. 84—c. 54 B.C.). Roman poet. (Full name, Gaius Valerius Catullus) *Love and Hate*

CHEEVER, JOHN (1912—1982). American author. *Editors and Editing*

CHEKHOV, ANTON (1860—1904). Russian playwright, author. *Doctors, Remedies*

CHER (1946—   ). American singer, actor. (Real name, Cherylynn La Piere) *Exercise, Intimacy*

CHERNIN, KIM (1940—   ). American author, psychologist. *Body Image, Eating Disorders*

CHESLEY, ROBERT (1943—1990). American playwright. *Homosexuality*

CHESTERFIELD, EARL OF (1694—1773). English politician, scholar. (Full name, Philip Dormer Stanhope) *Argument, Conformity, Crowds, Divorce, Egotism, Good Breeding, Human Nature, Modesty, Old Age, Prudence, Vice*

CHESTERTON, G.K. (1874—1936). English journalist, author. *Apology, Artists, Bores and Boredom, Bureaucracy, Civilization, Cleanliness, Courage, Emotions, Experience, Good and Evil, Haste, Hypocrisy, Indignation, Interests, Divided, Justice, Motives, Progress, Psychiatry, Seasons, The Self, Vulgarity*

CHEVALIER, MAURICE (1888—1972). French singer, actor. *Artists*

CHILD, JULIA (1912—   ). American gourmet, food writer. *Life*

CHILD, LYDIA M. (1802—1880). American reformer, author. *Retribution*

CHISHOLM, SHIRLEY (1924—   ). African-American politician. *Contraception, Discrimination, Politics and Politicians, Reformers and Reform, Social Change, Talent*

CHIYO, UNO (1897—   ). Japanese author. *Women*

CHOPIN, KATE (1851—1904). American writer. *The Sea, Unimportance*

CHOU EN-LAI (1898—1976). Chinese revolutionary, Communist politician. *Diplomats and Diplomacy*

CHRISTIE, AGATHA (1890—1976). English detective-story writer, playwright. *Friends and Friendship, Habit, Money, Principle, Regret*

CHRISTINA (1626—1689). Queen of Sweden. *Growth and Development*

CHRYSOSTOM, JOHN (c.347—407). Syrian monk, preacher. *Hell*

CHUANG-TZU (c. 369—c. 286 B.C.). Chinese philosopher, teacher. *Fools and Foolishness*

CHUCK D. (1960—   ). African-American musician, social activist. (Real name, Carlton Ridenhour) *People, Rap Music*

CHURCHILL, WINSTON (1874—1965). British statesperson, author, prime minister of Great Britain. *Architecture, Art, Betrayal, Britain and the British, Children, The Cold War, Democracy, Destiny, Diplomats and Diplomacy, Doubt, Fanaticism, Golf, Investment, Plans, Politicians and Politics, Quotations, Sailors and Sailing, Solitude, War and Peace*

CIARDI, JOHN (1916—1986). American poet, teacher, critic. *Constitutions, Teachers and Teaching*

CICERO (106—43 B.C.). Roman orator, statesperson, writer, philosopher. (Full name, Marcus Tullius Cicero) *Hope, Life Stages, Pity, Sorrow, Virtue*

CIORAN, E.M., (1911—   ). Philosopher, author. *Tragedy*

CLARK, EVANS (1888—1970). Economic research director of the Twentieth Century Fund. *Recession*

CLARK, FRANCINE JULIAN (NA). American actor, writer. *Future*

CLARK, KENNETH (1903—1983). British art historian. *Cynicism*

CLARKE, ARTHUR C. (1917—   ). English science-fiction writer. *Nationalism, The Sea, Space, Outer, Technology*

CLAY, HENRY (1777—1852). American politician. *Church and State*

CLEAVER, ELDRIDGE (1935—   ). African-American writer, a leader of the Black Panther movement. *America and the Americans, Conversation, Hate, Prisons, War*

CLEESE, JOHN (1939—   ). English comic actor, writer. *Workers*

CLEMENCEAU, GEORGES (1841—1929). French politician. *America and Americans*

CLINTON, BILL (1946—   ). Forty-second president of the United States. *America and Americans, Privacy*

COCHRAN, JACQUELINE (c. 1910—1980). American aviator. *Aspiration*

COCTEAU, JEAN (1889—1963). French author, producer, artist. *Art, Literature, Movies, Poets, Tact*

COHAN, GEORGE M. (1878—1942). American actor, playwright, producer. *Publicity*

COLBY, FRANK MOORE (1865—1925). American teacher, editor, essayist, humorist. *Anger*

COLE, KENNETH (1954—   ). American shoe designer, businessperson. *Contraception*

COLEMAN, ORNETTE (1930—   ). Jazz musician. *Jazz*

COLERIDGE, SAMUEL TAYLOR (1772—1834). English poet, essayist, critic. *Calmness, Greatness, The Heart, Plagiarism, Poetry and Prose, Ships and Boats, Water*

COLETTE (1873—1954). French novelist. (Full name, Sidonie-Gabrielle Colette) *Books and Reading, Friends and Friendship, Gardens and Gardening, Jealousy, Life, Mothers, Old Age, Past, Poets and Poetry, Sincerity, Smoking, Snow, Temptation*

COLLINS, JACKIE (1941—   ). English-born American novelist. *Fashion*

COLLINS, JOAN (1933—   ). English-born American actor. *Mistakes*

COLTON, CHARLES CALEB (1780—1832). English writer, clergyman. *Adversity, Advice, Agreement, Bed, Books and Reading, Brevity, Charity, Cities, Contentment, Creation and Creativity, Criticism, Doctors, Friends and Friendship, Killing*

DOUGLAS, JAMES (1803—1877). Canadian entrepreneur, politician. *Gardens and Gardening*

DOUGLASS, FREDERICK (1817—1895). African-American abolitionist, writer. (Original name, Frederick Augustus Washington Bailey) *The Past*

DOWRICK, STEPHANIE (NA). Contemporary American author, editor. *Sexism*

DOWSON, ERNEST (1867—1900). English lyric poet. *Transience*

DOYLE, ARTHUR CONAN (1859—1930). British physician, detective-story writer. *Triviality*

DRABBLE, MARGARET (1939—). English writer, editor. *Misery, The Self*

DREW, ELIZABETH (1887—1965). English-born American author, critic. *Travel*

DRUCKER, PETER (1909—). Austrian-born American management consultant, writer, professor. *Motives*

DRYDEN, JOHN (1631—1700). English poet, dramatist, critic. *Anger, Courage, Death, Democracy, Patience, Requests, Revolutionaries and Revolution, Virtue*

DU BOIS, W.E.B. (1868—1963). African-American writer, editor, teacher, lecturer. *Racism, Voting*

DUBOS, RENÉ (1901—1982). French-born American bacteriologist. *Pollution*

DUFFY, MAUREEN (1933—). English playwright, writer. *Love*

DUKE, PATTY (1946—). American actor. *Children*

DUMAS, ALEXANDRE, THE ELDER (1802—1870). French playwright, novelist. *Unity*

DU MAURIER, DAPHNE (1907—1989). English novelist. *Writers and Writing*

DUNCAN, ISADORA (1878—1927). American dancer. *Dancing, Life, Marriage*

DURANT, WILL (1885—1981). American teacher, philosopher, historian. *Plagiarism, Socialism*

DURRELL, LAWRENCE (1912—1990). Anglo-Irish novelist, poet, playwright. *Creation and Creativity, Love, Musicians and Music, Plagiarism, Rebellion, Truth*

DÜRRENMATT, FRIEDRICH (1921—). Swiss novelist, playwright, short-story writer. *Humanism, Justice, Problems, Reality, Thinking and Thought*

DYLAN, BOB (1941—). American musician. (Original name, Robert Zimmerman) *Obligation*

EARHART, AMELIA (1897—1937). American aviator. *Courage*

EASTMAN, MAX (1883—1969). American editor, writer. *Neutrality*

EBBINGHAUS, HERMANN (1850—1909). German experimental psychologist. *Psychology*

EBERHART, RICHARD (1904—). American poet, teacher. *Style*

EBNER-ESCHENBACH, MARIE VON (1830—1916). Austrian novelist, poet. *Kindness, Love, Value, Vanity, Youth and Age*

Sense, Communication, Conformity, Conservatism, Consistency and Inconsistency, Conversation, Criminals and Crime, Critics, Culture, Curiosity, Destiny, Destruction, Drinks and Drinking, Duty, Education, Enthusiasm, Envy, Eras, Europe, Events, Expectation, Expediency, Eyes, Facts, Familiarity, Farms and Farming, Fate, Flowers and Plants, Freedom, Friends and Friendship, Funerals, Genius, Gifts and Giving, Good and Evil, Good Breeding, Goodness, Greatness, Guests, Gullibility, Health, Heroes and Heroism, Home, Idealism, Individualism, Institutions, Language, Libraries, Love, Manners, Means and Ends, Men and Women, Method, Necessity, People, Protest, Quotations, Rain, Religion, Reward, Sailors and Sailing, Science and Religion, Seasons, Self-esteem, Shyness, Sickness, Smoking, Solitude, Speed, Stars, Stealing, Sympathy, Temper, Theology, Ugliness, Universe, Wisdom

ENGLISH, DEIRDRE (1948—   ). American writer, journalist. *Sex*

ENNIUS (239—169 B.C.). Roman poet. (Full name, Quintus Ennius) *Evolution*

EPHRON, NORA (1941—   ). American writer. *Cities*

EPICTETUS (c. 55—c. 135). Greek Stoic philosopher. *Choice, Clothes and Clothing, Education, Egotism, Greatness, Payment, Prisons*

EPICURUS (341—270 B.C.). Greek philosopher. *Character, Death*

ERDRICH, LOUISE (1954—   ). Chippewa-American author, poet. *Ideology, Native Americans*

ERSKINE, JOHN (1879—1951). American educator, writer. *Gardens and Gardening*

ERTZ, SUSAN (1884—1985). American writer. *Bores and Boredom*

EURIPIDES (c. 484—406 B.C.). Greek tragic playwright. *Aspiration, Authority, Change, Cleverness, Common Sense, Consequences, Constancy and Inconstancy, Crying, Discipline, Doubt, Effort, Food and Eating, Funerals, Homeland, Hypocrisy, Logic, Plans, Stoicism, Swearing*

EVANS, AUGUSTA (1835—1909). American novelist. *Duty*

EVERETT, CAROL (NA). Abortion clinic director. *Abortion*

FADIMAN, CLIFTON (1904—   ). American critic, lecturer, radio entertainer, editor. *Food and Eating*

FALLACI, ORIANA (1930—   ). Italian writer, journalist. *Imagination, Islam, Pleasure*

FALUDI, SUSAN (1959—   ). American author, journalist, feminist. *Body Image, Feminism*

FARQUHAR, GEORGE (1678—1707). Irish-born English playwright. *Obedience, Swearing*

FARRAKHAN, LOUIS (1933—   ). African-American Muslim leader. *African Americans*

FARRAR, JOHN (1896—1974). American publisher, writer. *Editors and Editing*

FOCH, FERDINAND (1851—1929). French soldier, marshal of France. *Cowardice*

FONDA, JANE (1937—   ). American actor, activist. *Revolutionaries and Revolution*

FORBES, MALCOLM (1919—1990). American billionaire, publisher, sportsman. *Achievement, Children, Old Age*

FORD, FORD MADOX (1873—1939). English writer, editor, critic. (Original name, Ford Hermann Hueffer) *Literature*

FORD, HENRY (1863—1947). American automobile manufacturer. *Business, Exercise, Historians and History*

FORSTER, E. M. (1879—1970). English novelist, short-story writer, essayist. *Betrayal, Boldness, Death, Fiction, Ideas, Life and Death, Nuclear Weapons, Preparedness*

FOSTER, JODIE (1962—   ). American actor and director. *The Self*

FOUCAULT, MICHEL (1926—1984). French philosopher, historian, writer. *Power, Sex, Truth*

FOURIER, CHARLES (1772—1837). French social theorist. *Feminism*

FOWLES, JOHN (1926—   ). English-born American novelist. *Poets and Poetry, Questions, War*

FRANCE, ANATOLE (1844—1924). French novelist, poet, critic. (Pseudonym of Jacques-Anatole-François Thibault) *Art, Change, Christianity, Lies and Lying, Plagiarism, Unhappiness*

FRANK, ANNE (1929—1945). German-Jewish diarist. *Beauty, Character, Happiness, Jews and Judaism*

FRANKFURTER, FELIX (1882—1965). American jurist, teacher, associate justice on the U.S. Supreme Court. *Character, Press, Freedom of the*

FRANKLIN, BENJAMIN (1706—1790). American statesperson, writer, inventor, printer, scientist. *Advice, Bed, Business, Christmas, Competition, Constitutions, Courage, Desires, Disappointment, Doctors, Haste, Hunger, Insincerity, Knowledge, Laziness, Life Stages, Necessity, Opportunity, Persuasion, Resolution, Secrets and Secrecy, Sleep, Stupidity, Unity, Vice, Virtue and Vice, War and Peace, Work*

FREDERICK II (1712—1786). King of Prussia. (Known as Frederick the Great) *Monarchs and Monarchy*

FRENCH, MARILYN (1929—   ). American writer. *Parents and Parenthood*

FRENEAU, PHILIP (1752—1832). American poet. *Smoking*

FREUD, ANNA (1835—1982). Austrian psychoanalyst, daughter of Sigmund Freud. *Creation and Creativity*

FREUD, SIGMUND (1856—1939). Austrian neurologist, founder of psychoanalysis. *America and the Americans, Children, Comparison, Conscience, Contrast, Destiny, Flowers and Plants, God, Homosexuality,*

Maturity, Property, Psychiatry, Purpose, Religion, Science and Religion, Women

FRIDAY, NANCY (1937—). American writer. *Housework*

FRIEDAN, BETTY (1921—). American writer, feminist. *Dependence, Men*

FRIEDENBERG, EDGAR Z. (1921—). American sociologist. *Psychiatry*

FRIEDMAN, MILTON (1912—). American economist. *Business, Capitalism*

FROMM, ERICH (1900—1980). German-born American psychoanalyst, philosopher. *Bores and Boredom, Coldness, Constancy and Inconstancy, Creation and Creativity, Death, Existence, Materialism, The Middle Class, Nationalism, Potential, Revolutionaries and Revolution, The Twentieth Century*

FROST, DAVID (1939—). English television entertainer. *Television*

FROST, ROBERT (1874—1963). American poet. *Company, Confusion, Education, Grammar, Happiness, Home, Nonsense, Perseverance, Poets and Poetry, Style, Survival, Work*

FROUDE, J. A. (1818—1894). English historian. *Cruelty*

FRY, CHRISTOPHER (1907—). English playwright. *Equality, Indulgence, Tragedy*

FRY, ROGER (1866—1934). English painter, critic. *Mysticism*

FULLER, R. BUCKMINSTER (1895—1983). American engineer, inventor. *Pollution, Discovery*

FULLER, MARGARET (1810—1850). American editor, essayist, poet, teacher, social reformer. *Women, Church, Love*

FULLER, THOMAS (1608—1661). English cleric. *Absence, Accusation, Action, Activity, Advantage, Anger, Argument, Belief, Birth, Bribery, Causes, Charity, Church, Clergy, Clothes and Clothing, Commitment, Comparison, Confession, Confidence, Conscience, Contentment, Cowardice, Cruelty, Cunning, Curiosity, Debauchery, Debt, Delay, Difficulty, Distrust, Drinks and Drinking, Endurance, Envy, Example, Excuses, Expectation, Flattery, Generosity, Gossip, Greed, Haste, Humanitarianism, Imperfection, Inequality, Ingratitude, Interests, Divided, Intimacy, Investment, Irrevocability, Law and Lawyers, Losers, Memory, Misers, Necessity, Nobility, The Past, Pessimism, Practicality, Pride, Questions, Receiving, Threat, Uselessness, Wrong and Wrongdoing, Zeal*

FUMIKO, HAYASHI (1903—1951). Japanese writer. *Men and Women*

GABOR, ZSA ZSA (1919—). Hungarian-born American actor. *Divorce, Sex*

GABORIAU, ÉMILE (1832—1873). French writer of detective novels. *Revenge*

GALBRAITH, JOHN KENNETH (1908—). Canadian-born American economist, diplomat, writer. *Banks and Banking, Business, Buying and Selling, Economics, Events, Fat and Fatness, Greed, Modesty, Nonsense, Pessimism, Politics and Politicians, Poverty and Wealth, Problems*

GALIANI, FERDINANDO (1728—1787). Italian economist. *Paris*

GALLOWAY, TERRY (NA). German-born American writer, activist. *Deafness*

GALLUP, GEORGE (1901—1984). American pollster. *Statistics*

GALSWORTHY, JOHN (1867—1933). English novelist, playwright. *Aspiration, Newspapers*

GANDHI, INDIRA (1917—1984). Indian politican. *Martyrs and Martyrdom, Religion*

GANDHI, MOHANDAS K. (1869—1948). Indian nationalist and spiritual leader. *Business, Causes, Forgiveness, Good and Evil, Human Rights, Materialism, Nonviolence, Self-control, Violence, War*

GANS, OLIVIA (NA). American activist. *Abortion*

GARBO, GRETA (1905—1990). Swedish-born American actor. *Privacy, Solitude*

GARCÌA LORCA, FREDERICO (1898—1936). Spanish poet, playwright. *Nudity, The Police, Spain and the Spanish*

GARDNER, JOHN W. (1912—   ). American foundation executive, public official. *Government*

GARRISON, WILLIAM LLOYD (1805—1879). American abolitionist, journalist. *Intemperance*

GASS, WILLIAM (1924—   ). American novelist, philosopher, literary critic. *Editors and Editing, Fiction*

GATES, JR., HENRY LOUIS (1950—   ). African-American writer, critic, educator. *African Americans*

GAULLE, CHARLES DE (1890—1970). French soldier, statesperson. *France and the French, Nuclear Weapons, Old Age, Opposition, The State*

GAWAIN, SHAKTI (1948—   ). American author, teacher of Eastern psychology. *Problems*

GAY, JOHN (1685—1732). English poet, playwright. *Coldness, Dishonesty, Envy*

GELDOF, BOB (1954—   ). British musician, social reformer. *Fame, Saints and Sainthood*

GEORGE V (1865—1936). King of England, emperor of India. (Full name, George Frederick Ernest Albert) *Fathers*

GEORGE VI (1895—1952). King of England, emperor of India. (Full name, Albert Frederick Arthur George) *Monarchs and Monarchy*

GETTY, J. PAUL (1892—1976). American businessman. *Wealth*

GIBBON, EDWARD (1737—1794). English historian. *Ability, Gratitude, Progress*

GIBRAN, KAHLIL (1883—1931). Syrian poet, novelist, essayist, painter. *Children, Conscience, Love, Luxury, Parting, Privacy, Truth, Work*

GIDE, ANDRÉ (1869—1951). French novelist, critic, essayist, editor, translator. *Adventure, Argument, Art, Coldness, Compliments, Compromise, Concentration, Desires, Discovery, Effort, Emotions, Eras, Faithfulness,*

GOLDMAN, EMMA (1869—1940). Russian-born American Jewish lecturer, editor, activist, anarchist. *Anarchy, Children, Defense, Dreams, Idealism, Means and Ends, Men and Women, Minority, Understanding*

GOLDSMITH, OLIVER (1730—1774). Irish-born British poet, playwright, novelist. *Business, Expectation, Law and Lawyers, Work, Zeal*

GOLDWYN, SAMUEL (1882—1974). Polish-born American motion-picture producer. (Original name, Samuel Goldfish) *Movies, Psychiatry, Television*

GONCOURT, EDMOND (1822—1896) and JULES DE (1830—1870). French writers. *Atheism, Uniqueness*

GONNE, MAUD (1866—1953). Irish actor, patriot. *Ireland and the Irish, Marriage*

GOODMAN, PAUL (1911—1972). American writer and educator, psychoanalyst. *Prisons*

GORBACHEV, MIKHAIL (1931—). Soviet politician. *The Future, Politics and Politicians, Russia and the Russians, The Twentieth Century*

GORDIMER, NADINE (1923—). South African novelist, short-story writer. *Censorship, Power*

GORE, AL (1948—). American politician, writer. *Conservation, Ecology*

GORKY, MAXIM (1868—1936). Russian novelist, short-story writer, playwright. (Pseudonym of Aleksei Maximovich Peshkov) *Country and Countryside, Hunger, Law and Lawyers, Past, Pretension, Work*

GOURMONT, RÉMY DE (1858—1915). French literary critic, novelist. *Punishment, Capital*

GRABLE, BETTY (1916—1973). American actor. *Success*

GRACIÁN, BALTASAR (1601—1658). Spanish writer, Jesuit priest. (Full name, Baltasar Gracián y Morales) *Conversation, Culture, Dishonesty, Distrust, Dependence, Desires, Enemies, Envy, Excellence, Fights and Fighting, Leisure, Madness, Memory, Plagiarism, Self-esteem, Service, Weapons*

GRAFTON, SUE (1940—). American detective novelist. *Criminals and Crime*

GRAHAM, BILLY (1918—) American Southern Baptist television evangelist. *Optimism and Pessimism*

GRAHAM, KATHERINE (1917—). American newspaper publisher. *Power*

GRAHAM, MARTHA (1893—1992). American dancer, choreographer. *The Body, Individuality*

GRANT, CARY (1904—1986). English-born American actor. (Original name, Archibald Alexander Leach) *Actors and Acting, Divorce*

GRASS, GÜNTER (1927—). Polish-born German novelist. *Citizenship*

GRAVES, ROBERT (1895—1985). English poet, novelist, critic. *Poets and Poetry*

GRAY, FRANCINE DU PLESSIX (1930—). Polish-born American writer. *Friends and Friendship*

GRAY, THOMAS (1716—1771). English poet. *Glory*

GRAYSON, DAVID (1870—1946). American journalist, biographer, essayist. (Pseudonym of Ray Stannard Baker) *Books and Reading, Goodness*

GREELEY, HORACE (1811—1872). American journalist, political leader. *Common sense, Journalism and Journalists*

GREENE, GRAHAM (1904—1991). English novelist, short-story writer, playwright. *Communism, Corruption, Despair, Eternity, Fame, Mass media, Travel*

GREER, GERMAINE (1939—). Australian writer, feminist. *Chastity, Contraception, Feminism, Freedom, Psychiatry, Spontaneity*

GREGORY, DICK (1932—). American comedian, civil rights activist. *Liberalism*

GROENING, MATT (1954—). American cartoonist. *Family*

GROPIUS, WALTER (1883—1969). German-born American architect. *Architecture*

GUINNESS, ALEC (1914—). English actor. *Actors and Acting*

HAGGADAH, PALESTINIAN TALMUD Traditional Jewish text. *Contentment*

HAGLER, MARVIN (1952—). American boxer. *Sports and Games*

HAIG, ALEXANDER (1924—). American statesperson, general. *Lies and Lying*

HALDEMAN, H.R. (1929—). Presidential assistant to Richard Nixon. *Irrevocability*

HALEY, ALEX (1921—1992). African-American author. *Family*

HALL, ARSENIO (1958—). African-American actor, TV talk show host. *Drugs*

HAMILTON, ALEXANDER (1755—1804). American stateperson, politician. *Government, Survival*

HAMILTON, WILLIAM (1939—). American author, cartoonist. *Truth*

HAMMARSKJÖLD, DAG (1905—1961). Swedish statesperson, United Nations Secretary-General. *Death, Destiny, Dignity, Immaturity, Loneliness, Old Age, Unselfishness*

HANSBERRY, LORRAINE (1930—1965). African-American playwright. *Feminism, Self-realization*

HARDESTY, CAROLYN (NA). Contemporary American writer. *Pain*

HARDIN, GARRETT (1915—). American ecologist, educator, author. *Decline*

HARDY, THOMAS (1840—1928). English novelist, poet. *Class, Cruelty, Improvement, Writers and Writing*

HARJO, JOY (1951—). American writer, poet, teacher, artist. *People*

HELPS, ARTHUR (1813—1875). British author. *Books and Reading*

HELVÉTIUS, CLAUDE-ADRIEN (1715—1771). French encyclopedist, philosopher. *Censorship*

HEMINGWAY, ERNEST (1899—1961). American novelist, short-story writer. *Conscience, Cowardice, Defeat, Fascism, Fathers, Paris, Retirement, Self-deception, The World*

HENDERSON, LEON NESBIT (1906—1960). American educator. *Inflation*

HENRY, O. (1862—1910). American short-story writer. (Pseudonym of William Sydney Porter) *Conversation, Hunger, Months, Public Opinion*

HENRY, PATRICK (1736—1799). American statesperson, orator. *Experience*

HEPBURN, KATHARINE (1909—   ). American actor. *Actors and Acting, Age, Enemies, Love, Loss of, Men and Women, Rules*

HERACLITUS (c. 540—480 B.C.). Greek philosopher. *Bigotry, Change, Dreams, Drinks and Drinking, Education, Prejudices, Sight*

HERBERT, FRANK (1920—1986). American science-fiction writer. *Journalism and Journalists*

HERBERT, GEORGE (1593—1633). English clergyman, metaphysical poet. *Compromise, Defense, Drinks and Drinking, Eyes, Gardens and Gardening, Germany and the Germans, Night, Time*

HERFORD, OLIVER (1863—1935). American writer, illustrator. *Hair, Modesty*

HERODOTUS (c. 484—c. 425 B.C.). Greek historian. *Envy*

HEROLD, DON (1889—   ). American humorous writer, artist. *Intelligence*

HESIOD (c. 800 B.C.). Greek poet. *Experience, Materialism, Practicality*

HESSE, HERMANN (1877—1962). German novelist. *Courage, Death, Hate, Middle Class, Piety, Unconscious, Wisdom*

HEYWOOD, JOHN (c. 1497—c. 1580). English poet, playwright. *Agreement, Beginning and Ending*

HIAASEN, CARL (NA). Contemporary American novelist. *Ecology*

HILL, ANITA (1956—   ). American lawyer. *Sexual Harassment*

HIPPOCRATES (c. 460—377 B.C.). Greek physician. *Exercise*

HITCHCOCK, ALFRED (1899—1980). English film director. *Actors and Acting, Dramatists and Drama*

HITLER, ADOLF (1889—1945). German Nazi politician. *Force, Germany and the Germans, Historians and History, Peace, Politics and Politicians, Propaganda, Public Speaking*

HOBBES, THOMAS (1588—1679). English philosopher. *Absurdity, Christianity, The Classics*

HOFFER, ERIC (1902—1983). American author, philosopher. *Bigotry, Corruption, Death, Dreams, Enterprise, Evil, Glory, Identity, Individualism, Kindness, Rudeness, Saints and Sainthood, Self-deception, Self-righteousness, Service, Technology, Weakness*

JANEWAY, ELIZABETH (1913—   ). American author, journalist, critic, lecturer. *Feminism, Lesbianism, Problems*

JARDINE, ALICE (NA). Contemporary feminist, critic, scholar. *Difference*

JARMAN, DEREK (1942—   ). English painter, film director, director of pop videos, writer. *Movies*

JARRELL, RANDALL (1914—1965). American poet, novelist, critic. *Children*

JEANS, JAMES (1877—1946). English physicist, astronomer, author. *Universe*

JEFFERSON, THOMAS (1743—1826). American statesperson, third president of the United States. *Agnosticism, America and Americans, Aristocracy, Censorship, Constitutions, Delay, Earth, Equality, Flowers and Plants, Gardens and Gardening, Intelligence, Malice, Mind and Body, Minority, Newspapers, Public Office, Revolutionaries and Revolution, Slavery, Tolerance, Truth and Falsehood, Tyranny*

JEROME, JEROME K. (1859—1927). English novelist, playwright, humorist. *Drinks and Drinking, Houses, Idleness, Stupidity, Weather*

JERROLD, DOUGLAS WILLIAM (1803—1857). English playwright, humorist. *Prayer*

JESSEL, GEORGE (1898—1981). American entertainer. *Public Speaking*

JEWETT, SARAH ORNE (1849—1909). American short-story writer. *Tact*

JIMÉNEZ, JUAN RAMÓN (1881—1958). Spanish poet. *Haste, Transience*

JOHN PAUL II (1920—   ). Pope. (Original name, Karol Wojtyla) *Homosexuality, Jews and Judaism*

JOHNSON, EARVIN "MAGIC" (1959—   ). American basketball player. *AIDS*

JOHNSON, LYNDON B. (1908—1973). Thirty-sixth president of the United States. *Presidents and Presidency, Society, Unity*

JOHNSON, SAMUEL (1709—1784). English lexicographer, critic, writer, conversationalist. *Absurdity, Advertising, Amusement, Britain and the British, Clergy, Clothes and Clothing, Company, Concentration, Confidence, Curiosity, Desires, Difficulty, Effort, Enterprise, Enthusiasm, Equality, Food and Eating, Friends and Friendship, Gullibility, Hunting, Idleness, Integrity, Ireland and the Irish, Italy and the Italians, Language, Libraries, London, Marriage, Melancholy, Music and Musicians, Obligation, Patriotism, Perspective, Pleasure, Politics and Politicians, Praise, Preaching and Preachers, Reciprocity, Sailors and Sailing, Scotland and the Scottish, Trust, Wealth*

JOHNSTON, JILL (1929—   ). British-born American journalist, critic. *Identity*

JONES, BEVERLY (1927—   ). American writer, feminist. *Romance*

JONES, FRANKLIN P. (1906—   ). American author. *Neighbors, Punctuality*

JONES, JOHN PAUL (1747—1792). Scottish-born American naval officer. (Original name, John Paul) *Fights and Fighting*

JONES, LE ROI (1934—   ). African-American playwright, civil rights activist. *African Americans, Culture, God*

KEATS, JOHN (1795—1821). English poet. *Afterlife, Beauty, Chaos, Conversation, Drinks and Drinking, Failure, Human Nature, Nature, Open-mindedness, Seasons, Sleep, Suffering, Truth*

KEILLOR, GARRISON (1942—). American humorous writer, radio performer. *Cats, Sex*

KELLER, HELEN (1880—1968). American memoirist, essayist, lecturer. *Adventure, Carefulness, Courage, Duty, Effort, Happiness, Intolerance, Pessimism, Purpose, Self-realization, Sight, Suffering, Tolerance, Work*

KELLEY, GRACE (1928—1982). American actor, princess of Monaco. *Press, Freedom of the*

KELLY, PETRA (1947—). German politician. *Women*

KEMPTON, MURRAY (1917—). American journalist. *Government, Neighbors, New York*

KEMPTON, SALLY (1943—). American writer. *Egotism, Self-esteem*

YOSHIDA, KENKO (1283—1350). Japanese poet, essayist, Buddhist monk. *Beginning and Ending*

KENNEDY, EDWARD (1932—). American politician. *Guns and Gun Control*

KENNEDY, FLORYNCE (1916—). African-American attorney, writer, feminist. *Abortion, Laziness, Oppression, Work*

KENNEDY, JOHN F. (1917—1963). Thirty-fifth president of the United States. *America and Americans, Art, Beginning, Canada, Captivity, Citizens, Computers, Conformity, Conservation, Defense, Democracy, Difference, Economics, Exercise, Farms and Farming, Government, Hope, International Relations, Myth, People, Politics and Politicians, Poverty and Wealth, Presidents and Presidency, Publicity, Reality, Tyranny, Unemployment, Voting, War, Washington, D.C.*

KENNEDY, JOSEPH P. (1888—1969). American entrepreneur, diplomat. *Revenge*

KENNEDY, ROBERT F. (1925—1968). American politician. *Achievement, Guns and Gun Control, Justice, Opposition, Police*

KENNEDY, ROSE (1890—). Mother of President John F. Kennedy. *Old Age*

KENT, DEBRA (1948—). American writer. *Disability*

KEROUAC, JACK (1922—1969). American novelist. *Confusion, Unimportance*

KERR, JEAN (1923—). American essayist, playwright. *Airplanes, Hope*

KESEY, KEN (1935—). American novelist. *Earth*

KETTERING, CHARLES F. (1876—1958). American engineer, inventor. *Future, Ideas, Invention, Open-mindedness*

KEYNES, JOHN MAYNARD (1883—1946). English economist. *Banks and Banking, Inflation, Taxes, Tyranny*

KHRUSHCHEV, NIKITA (1894—1971). Russian politician, premier of the Soviet Union. *Communism, Nuclear Weapons, Survival*

KING, B. B. (1925—). American blues guitarist. *Jazz*

Love, Moderation, Motives, Old Age, Opinions, Pretension, Resolution, Ridicule, Virtue and Vice, Wisdom and Foolishness

QUEEN LATIFAH (1970—   ). African-American musician. (Real name, Dana Owens) *Rap Music*

LAUGHTON, CHARLES (1899—1962). English-born American actor. *Censorship*

LAVATER, JOHANN KASPAR (1741—1801). Swiss theologian, poet, mystic. *Wills and Inheritance*

LAWRENCE, D.H. (1885—1930). English novelist, short-story writer, poet, essayist. *Britain and the British, Flowers and Plants, Generations, Horses and Horse Racing, Idealism, The Mundane, Punishment, Puritans and Puritanism, Writers and Writing*

LAWRENCE, T. E. (1888—1935). British archaeologist, soldier, writer. *Fate*

LAZARRE, JANE (1943—   ). American writer. *Mothers*

LAZARUS, EMMA (1849—1887) American poet, playwright, essayist. *Jews and Judaism*

LEACH, EDMUND (1910—   ). English anthropologist, educator, writer. *Cooks and Cooking*

LEAHY, FRANK (1908—   ). American football coach. *Egotism*

LEARY, TIMOTHY (1920—   ). American psychologist, educator, drug cult leader. *Drugs, Education, Feminism*

LEBOWITZ, FRAN (1951—   ). American writer, critic, humorist. *America and Americans, Beauty, Character, Children, Communication, Life, Magazines, Mathematics, Smoking, Success, Suicide, Youth*

LEC, STANISLAW (1909—   ). Polish poet, aphorist. *Heaven, Pornography*

LE CORBUSIER (1887—1965). Swiss architect, city planner. (Original name, Charles-Édouard Jeanneret) *Houses, New York*

LEE, GYPSY ROSE (1914—1970). American stripteaser. (Real name, Rose Louise Hovick) *Age*

LEE, HARPER (1926—   ). American novelist. *Conscience*

LEE, ROBERT E. (1807—1870). American general. *Abstinence, War*

LEE, SPIKE (1957—   ). African-American film director. (Real, name, Shelton Jackson Lee) *Civil Rights, Cults, Drugs, Morality*

LE GUIN, URSULA (1929—   ). American feminist, science fiction writer. *Action, Love*

LEIGH, JENNIFER JASON (1958—   ). American actor. *Shyness*

L'ENGLE, MADELLEINE (1918—   ). American author. (Full name, Madeleine Camp L'Engle Franklin) *Problems*

LENIN, V. I. (1870—1924). Russian Communist. (Original name, Vladimir Ilich Ulyanov) *Capitalism, Communism, Freedom, Government, The Middle Class, Revolutionaries and Revolution, Sickness, Socialism, State*

LINDNER, ROBERT (1914—1956). American psychoanalyst, writer. *Authority, Causes, Conformity*

LINDSAY, JOHN V. (1921—   ). American politician. *Washington, D.C.*

LINKLETTER, ART (1912—   ). Canadian-born American radio and television personality. *Life, Suburbs*

LINNAEUS, CAROLUS (1707—1778). Swedish botanist. (Original name, Carl von Linnè) *Conservation, Nature*

LIPPMANN, WALTER (1889—1974). American writer, editor, journalist. *Conformity, Government, Machines, Morality, Property, Science and Religion, Stereotypes*

LITTLE, MARY WILSON (1912—   ). American writer, illustrator. *Politeness*

LITVINOV, MAXIM (1876—1951). Russian Communist, diplomat. (Original name, Meir Wallach) *Peace*

LIVY (59 B.C.—A.D. 17). Roman historian. (Full name, Titus, Livius) *Crowds, Dignity, Law and Lawyers*

LLOYD, MARIE (1870—1922). English music-hall comedian. (Original name, Matilda Alice Victoria Wood) *Desires*

LOCKE, BOBBY (1917—   ). South African golfer. (Original name, Arthur D'Arcy) *Golf*

LOCKE, JOHN (1632—1704). English philosopher. *Nature, Property, Teachers and Teaching*

LOMBARDI, VINCE (1913—1970). American football coach. *Victory*

LONDON, JACK (1876—1916). American novelist. (Full name, John Griffith London) *Inspiration*

LONGEAUX Y VASQUEZ, ENRIQUETA, Contemporary Chicana journalist. *Materialism*

LONGFELLOW, HENRY WADSWORTH (1807—1882). American poet, translator. *Affection, Ambition, Beginning and Ending, Children, Endurance, Hope, Sorrow*

LONGWORTH, ALICE ROOSEVELT (1884—1980). American hostess, daughter of Theodore Roosevelt. *Life*

LOOS, ANITA (1893—1981). American novelist, screenwriter. *Fate, Hollywood, Memory*

LORDE, AUDRE (1934—1992). African-American poet, teacher, feminist. *African americans, Lesbianism, Mothers, Protest, Self-esteem*

LOREN, SOPHIA (1934—   ). Italian actor. *Food and Eating*

LOUIS XVII (1755—1824). King of France. (Full name, Louis-Xavier-Stanislas) *Punctuality*

LOUIS, JOE (1914—1981). American boxer. (Original name, Joseph Louis Barrow) *Money*

LOVEJOY, THOMAS (1941—   ). Tropical and conservation biologist. *Ecology*

LOVELACE, LINDA (1952—   ). American model, actor. *Pornography*

LOVELOCK, JAMES (1919—   ).. English biologist, environmentalist. *Ecology*

LOWELL, AMY (1874—1925). American poet, critic, biographer. *Books and Reading, Pain, Sorrow*

LOWELL, JAMES RUSSELL (1819—1891). American poet, critic, editor, diplomat. *Adversity, Aspiration, Censorship, The Classics, Deeds, Desires, Doubt, Human Rights, Interest, Manners, Months, Solitude, Trees, Worry*

LOWRY, MALCOLM (1909—1957). English novelist. *Love*

LUCAN (39—65). Roman poet, prose writer. (Full name, Marcus Annaeus Lucanus) *Losers*

LUCE, CLARE BOOTHE (1903—1987). American diplomat, writer, playwright. *Feminism, Politics and Politicians*

LUCIANO, RON (   ). Contemporary baseball umpire. *Baseball*

LUCRETIUS (c. 98—c. 55 B.C.). Roman poet, philosopher. (Full name, Titus Lucretius Carus) *Cause and Effect, Irritation, Taste, Wit*

LUNN, ARNOLD (1888—1974). British skier, writer, editor. *Preaching and Preachers*

LUTHER, MARTIN (1483—1546). German theologian, religious, reformer. *Faith, Writing and Writers*

LUXEMBURG, ROSA (1870—1919). Polish-born German Socialist activist. *Freedom*

LYLY, JOHN (c. 1554—1606). English prose writer, poet, playwright. *Perseverance, Poverty*

LYONS, OREN (NA). Faithkeeper of the Turtle Clan of the Onondaga Iroquois. *Spirituality*

MACARTHUR, DOUGLAS (1880—1964). American general. *Opportunity*

MACAULAY, ROSE (1881—1958). English novelist. *Love*

MACHADO Y RUIZ, ANTONIO (1875—1939). Spanish poet. *Irreverence*

MACHIAVELLI, NICCOLÒ (1469—1527). Florentine statesperson, political philosopher. *Obligation*

MACINNES, HELEN (1907—1985). American novelist. *Civilization, Terrorism*

MACLAINE, SHIRLEY (1934—   ). American actor, writer. *Politics and Politicians, Self-sufficiency, Sex*

MACMILLAN, H.R. (1885—1976). Canadian entrepreneur. *Canada*

MACMILLAN, HAROLD (1894—1986). British statesperson. *Criticism, Danger, Politics and Politicians*

MADONNA (1959—   ). American singer, actor. (Full name, Madonna Louise Ciccone) *Egotism, Repentance, Voting, Women*

MAETERLINCK, MAURICE (1862—1949). Belgian poet, dramatist, essayist. *Flowers and Plants, Happiness, Others*

MAGRITTE, RENÉ (1898—1967). Belgian painter. *The Unknown*

MAILER, NORMAN (1923—   ). American novelist, essayist. *Drinks and Drinking, Liberalism, Mass Media, Newspapers, Style, The Twentieth Century*

MAIMONIDES (1135—1204). Spanish-born Jewish philosopher. (Original name, Moses ben Maimon) *Knowledge*

MAINTENON, MADAME (1635—1719). Wife of Louis XIV of France. (Original name, Françoise d' Aubigné) *Hope*

MALAMUD, BERNARD (1914—1986). American Jewish novelist, short-story writer. *Comedy, Language, words*

MALCOLM X (1925—1965). African-American civil-rights activist, orator. (Original name, Malcolm Little) *America and Americans, Capitalism, Libraries, Nonviolence, Patriotism, Power*

MALLARMÉ, STÉPHANE (1842—1898). French poet. *The Soul*

MALRAUX, ANDRÉ (1901—1976). French novelist, critic. *Rebellion*

MANDELA, WINNIE (1934—   ). South African apartheid activist. *Africa and Africans*

MANN, THOMAS (1875—1955). German novelist, essayist. *Artists, Conscience, Creation and Creativity, Love, Medicine, Speaking*

MANNES, MARYA (1904—   ). American essayist, journalist. *Intelligence, Judgment, Self-control, Television*

MANSFIELD, KATHERINE (1888—1923). New Zealand-born British writer. (Original name, Kathleen Beauchamp) *Flowers and Plants, Letters and Letter-writing, Life and Death, Love, Nudity, Self-realization*

MAO TSE-TUNG (1893—1976). Chinese soldier, statesman, chairman of the Central Committee of the Chinese Communist Party. *Books and Reading, Class, Conservatism, Contentment, Diversity, People, Politics and Politicians*

MARCEAU, MARCEL (1923—   ). French actor, pantomimist. *Silence*

MARCOS, IMELDA (1931—   ). Philippine politician, wife of Philippine President Ferdinand Marcos. *Possession*

MARCUS AURELIUS (121—180). Roman emperor, Stoic philosopher. (Full name, Marcus Aurelius Antoninus) *Advice, Beauty, Community, Endurance, Goodness, Historians and History, Imitation, Injury, Insects, Integrity, Life, Loss, Thinking and Thought, Transience*

MARIE-ANTOINETTE (1755—1793). Queen of France, spouse of Louis XVI. (Full name, Josèphe-Jeanne-Marie-Antoinette) *Newness*

MARÍN, LUIS MUÑOZ (1898—1980). Puerto Rican politican, poet. *Hispanic Americans*

MARITAIN, JACQUES (1882—1973). French philosopher, writer. *Gratitude, Ideas*

MARKHAM, BERYL (1902—1986). English aviator. *Self-knowledge*

MARLOWE, CHRISTOPHER (1564—1593). English playwright, poet. *Religion*

MÁRQUEZ, GABRIEL GARCÍA (1928—   ). Colombian author. *Disappointment, Love*

MARQUIS, DON (1878—1937). American journalist, humorist. *Fish and Fishing, Ideas, Newspapers, Parents and Parenthood, Poets and Poetry, Procrastination*

MARSHALL, JOHN (1755—1835). American jurist, chief justice on the U.S. Supreme Court. *Taxes*

MARSHALL, SUSAN (1950—   ). American lawyer. *Sexual Harassment*

MARSHALL, THURGOOD (1908—1993). African-American lawyer, associate justice on the U.S. Supreme Court. *African Americans, America and the Americans*

MARTÍ, JOSÉ (1853—1895). Cuban patriot, poet, essayist. (Full name, José Julián Martí y Pérez) *Charm*

MARTIAL (c. 40—103). Spanish-born Roman poet. (Full name, Marcus Valerius Martialis) *Glory, Sorrow, Stoicism*

MARTIN, DEAN (1917—   ). American musician, actor. *Drinks and Drinking*

MARTIN, JUDITH (193—   ). American columnist, author on etiquette and society. *Civilization, Honesty*

MARTIN, STEVE (1945—   ). American comedian, actor. *Chaos, Comedy, France and the French*

MARTINEAU, HARRIET (1802—1876). English writer. *Marriage*

MARVELL, ANDREW (1621—1678). English poet, politician. *Age, Death*

MARX, GROUCHO (1890—1977). American comedian, actor. (Original name, Julius Henry Marx) *Bed, Critics, Memory, Military, Poverty, Television*

MARX, KARL (1818—1883). German political philosopher, economist, socialist. *Class, Medicine, Philosophers and Philosophy, Property, Religion, Value*

MARX, LEO (1919—   ). American educator, author. *Cities*

MASON, GEORGE (1725—1792). American statesman, author of the Virginia Constitution and Bill of Rights. *Press, Freedom of the*

MASON, WILLIAM (1725—1797). English poet, playwright, clergyman. *Waste*

MATHEWS, VERA LAUGHTON (1888—1959). British suffragist. *Protest*

MATURE, VICTOR (1916—   ). American actor. *Actors and Acting*

MAUGHAM, W. SOMERSET (1874—1965). English novelist, playwright. *Action, Adversity, Beauty, Bed, Books and Reading, Civilization, Coldness, Consequences, Criticism, Death, Evil, Excess, Expediency, Friends and Friendship, The Future, Laughter, Love, Loss of, Perfection, Politics and Politicians, Rudeness, Sentimentality, Style, Theater, Tradition, Unfaithfulness, Writers and Writing, Youth*

MAUPASSANT, GUY DE (1850—1893). French short-story writer, novelist. *Military*

MAURIAC, FRANÇOIS (1885—1970). French novelist, essayist, playwright. *Deprivation, Writers and Writing*

MAUROIS, ANDRÉ (1885—1967). French biographer, novelist, essayist. (Pseudonym of Émile Herzog) *Affection, Britain and the British, Prudence, Self-pity, Style, Taste*

MAXWELL, ELSA (1883—1963). American columnist, broadcaster, hostess. *Parties*

MAYAKOVSKY, VLADIMIR (1893—1930). Russian poet, Communist. *Art*

MAYO, CHARLES H. (1865—1939). American surgeon, brother of William J. Mayo. *Worry*

MAYO, WILLIAM J. (1861—1939). American surgeon, brother of Charles H. Mayo. *Experts*

MCCABE, JEWELL JACKSON (1945—   ). American business leader, activist. *Solitude*

MCCAFFREY, ANNE (1926—   ). American writer. *Judgment*

MCCARTHY, MARY (1912—1989). American novelist, short-story writer, critic. *Business, Heroes and Heroism, Injustice, Neurosis, Realism, Science and Scientists, Sex, Truth, Violence*

MCDONAGH, EDWARD (1915—   ). Canadian-born sociologist, educator. *Automobiles*

MCENROE, JOHN (1959—   ). American tennis player. *Defeat*

MCFEE, WILLIAM (1881—1966). English-born American novelist. *Enthusiasm*

MCGINLEY, PHYLLIS (1905—1978). American essayist, writer. *Advice, Compromise, Gardens and Gardening, Gossip, Leisure, Romanticism*

MCGOVERN, GEORGE (1922—   ). American politician. *Bureaucracy*

MCLAREN, MALCOLM (NA). Contemporary British musician. *Social Change*

MCLAUGHLIN, MIGNON (1915—   ). American writer, editor, humorist. *Courage, Incompetence*

MCLUHAN, MARSHALL (1911—1980). Canadian educator, author, communications theorist. *America and Americans, Automobiles, Names, Psychiatry, Publishing, Technology*

MCQUEEN, STEVE (1930—1980). American actor. (Real name, Terence Stephen McQueen) *Cities*

MEAD, MARGARET (1901—1978). American anthropologist, psychologist. *Behavior, Diversity, Ecology, Feminism, Mass Media, Population, Stereotypes*

MEDICINE EAGLE, BROOKE (1943—   ). Sioux/Nez Percé poet, writer. *Native Americans*

MEIR, GOLDA (1898—1978). Israeli politician. *Equality, Humility, Killing, Jews and Judaism, Leaders and Leadership, Old Age, Public Office, Time*

MELLON, ANDREW WILLIAM (1855—1937). American financier. *Economics*

MELVILLE, HERMAN (1819—1891). American novelist, short-story writer, poet. *Drinks and Drinking, Sailors and Sailing, Sanity, The Sea, War*

MENCKEN, H. L. (1880—1956). American journalist, editor, writer. *Christianity, Cleanliness, Conscience, Contraception, Criticism, Faith, Humanitarianism, Justice, Lies and Lying, Military, Opera, Puritans and Puritanism, Reformers and Reform, Safety, Self-esteem, Unfaithfulness, Unions, Voting, War*

MENNINGER, KARL (1893—   ). American psychiatrist. *Neurosis*

KRISHNA MENON, V. K. (1897—1974). Indian statesperson, lawyer. *International Relations*

MEREDITH, GEORGE (1828—1909). English novelist, poet, critic. *Cooks and Cooking, Culture, Obligation*

MERIWETHER, LOUISE (1923—   ). American author. *Preparedness*

MERMAN, ETHEL (c.1908—1984). American singer, actor. (Full name, Ethel Zimmerman) *Singing*

METTERNICH, KLEMENS VON (1773—1859). Austrian statesperson, and diplomat. *Paris*

MICHELANGELO (1475—1564). Italian sculptor, painter, architect, poet. (Full name, Michelangelo di Lodovico Buonarroti Simoni) *Desire*

MIDLER, BETTE (1945—   ). American singer, actor. *Curiosity, Sex*

MIES VAN DER ROHE, Ludwig (1886—1969). German-born American architect. *Architecture*

MILL, JOHN STUART (1806—1873). English philosopher, economist. *Closed-mindedness, Custom, Feminism, Happiness, Mediocrity, Originality*

MILLAY, EDNA ST. VINCENT (1892—1950). American poet. *Evil, Faith, Heredity, Life, Loneliness, Love, Months, World*

MILLER, ARTHUR (1915—   ). American playwright, novelist. *Europe, Newspapers, Present, Theater*

MILLER, HENRY (1891—1980). American novelist, essayist. *Actors and Acting, Art, The Classics, Confusion, Criminals and Crime, Delay, Democracy, Enemies, Equality, Food and Eating, Force, Growth and Development, Historians and History, Humankind, Leaders and Leadership, Literacy, Originality, Repentance, War, World, Youth*

MILLETT, KATE (1934—   ). American writer, feminist, educator. *Lesbianism, Sexism*

MILLIGAN, SPIKE (1918—   ). British comedian, humorous writer. *Contraception*

MILNE, A.A. (1882—1956). English poet, playwright. *Diaries*

MILOSZ, CZESLAW (1911—   ). Polish poet, diplomat. *Danger, Fear*

MONTHERLANT, HENRY DE (1896—1972). French playwright, novelist, poet, essayist. *Affection, Art*

MOORE, GEORGE (1852—1933). Irish novelist, playwright, poet, critic. *Choice, Race*

MOORE, MARIANNE (1887—1972). American poet. *Beauty, Guests, Impatience, Indecision, Writers and Writing*

MOORE, THOMAS (1779—1852). Irish poet. *Crying, Heaven*

MORAGA, CHERRIE (1952—   ). Chicana writer, editor, feminist, activist. *Lesbianism, Similarity*

MORAVIA, ALBERTO (1907—   ). Italian novelist, short-story writer, essayist. *Literacy*

MORGAN, ROBIN (1941—   ). American editor, feminist. *Freedom, Women*

MORLEY, CHRISTOPHER (1890—1957). American novelist, journalist, essayist. *Critics, Hotels, New York, Poets and Poetry, Success, Theology*

MORLEY, JOHN (1838—1923). English statesperson, scholar, writer. *Evolution, Totalitarianism, Worship*

MORRIS, DESMOND (1928—   ). English zoologist, writer. *Cities*

MORRISON, TONI (1931—   ). African-American novelist, writer. *African Americans, Children, Creation and Creativity, Freedom, Love, Oppression, Minority, Pain, Questions, Spirituality*

MORROW, DWIGHT W. (1873—1931). American lawyer, banker, diplomat. *Political Parties*

MORTON, STERLING (1832—1902). American agriculturist. *Holidays*

MOTONI, NOMURA (1806—1867). Japanese poet, activist. *Oppression*

MOTT, LUCRETIA (1793—1880). American reformer, Feminist. *Sexism*

MUGGERIDGE, MALCOLM (1903—1990). English editor, writer. *America and Americans, Britain and the British, Debauchery, Retirement, Sex, Television*

MUHAMMAD (c. 570—632). Founder of Islam. *Workers*

MUKHERJEE, BHARATI (1940—   ). Indian-born novelist. *Farms and Farming*

MUMFORD, ETHEL WATTS (1878—1940). American writer. *Gossip, Knowledge*

MUMFORD, LEWIS (1895—1990). American cultural historian, city planner. *Automobiles, Generations*

MUNRO, ALICE (1931—   ). Canadian short-story writer, novelist. *Lovers*

MURDOCH, IRIS (1919—   ). Irish novelist. *Forgiveness, Life, Literature, Love*

MURPHY, ARTHUR (1727—1805). Irish actor, playwright. *Cheerfulness*

MURROW, EDWARD R. (1908—1965). American news commentator, journalist. *Prejudice*

MUSSET, ALFRED DE (1810—1857). French poet, novelist, playwright. *Parting*

MUSSOLINI, BENITO (1883—1945). Italian dictator. *Fascism, Internationalism, War*

NABOKOV, VLADIMIR (1899—1977). Russian-born American novelist, poet, critic. *Art, Fame, Literature, Punishment, Capital, Solitude, Triviality*

NADER, RALPH (1934—   ). American consumer advocate. *Ecology, Pollution*

NAPOLÉON I (1769—1821). Emperor of France. (Full name, Napoléon Bonaparte) *Ability, Absurdity, Anarchy, Aristocracy, Boldness, Carefulness, Circumstance, Complaints, Congress, Constitutions, Courage, Decision, Diplomats and Diplomacy, Fanaticism, France and the French, Free Speech, Greatness, Hell, Interest, International Relations, Leaders and Leadership, Madness, Medicine, Mediocrity, Method, Neutrality, Newspapers, Oppression, Order, Patriotism, Persuasion, Promises, Public Opinion, Publishing, Rank, Religion, Self-sufficiency, Theology, Tyranny, Unity, Work*

NASH, OGDEN (1902—1971). American humorous poet. *Advertising, Animals, Cleverness, Drinks and Drinking, Insects, Lust, Work*

NATHAN, GEORGE JEAN (1882—1958). American drama and social critic, editor, memoirist. *Dramatists and Drama, Friends and Friendship, Patriotism, Voting*

NEHRU, JAWAHARLAL (1889—1964). Indian politician. *Democracy*

NERUDA, PABLO (1904—1973). Chilean poet, diplomat. (Original name, Neftalí Ricardo Reyes Basoalto) *Poets and Poetry*

NEVELSON, LOUISE (1899—1988). American sculptor. *Strength*

NEWMAN, JOHN HENRY (1801—1890). English prelate, theologian, writer. *Growth and Development*

NEWMAN, PAUL (1925—   ). American actor. *Losers*

NICHOLSON, JACK (1937—   ). American actor. *Drugs*

NIETZSCHE, FRIEDRICH WILHELM (1844—1900). German philosopher, poet. *Adversity, Art, Belief, Body, Bores and Boredom, Clarity, Cleanliness, Consequences, Contempt, Cooks and Cooking, Courage, Danger, Death, Debauchery, Deeds, Destiny, Egotism, Emotions, Enemies, Equality, Eternity, Events, Germany and the Germans, Hope, Humility, Hypocrisy, Indignation, Indulgence, Integrity, Laughter, Liberalism, Life, Meanness, Necessity, Night, Paris, Philosophers and Philosophy, Pity, Psychology, Punishment, Receiving, Self-deception, Sleep, Stereotypes, Suffering, Taste, Wisdom, Wit, Women*

NIN, ANAÏS (1903—1977). French-born American short-story writer, critic, diarist. *Death, Fiction, Friends and Friendship, Involvement, Life, Meaning, New York, Self-sufficiency, Sensuality, Truth, Writers and Writing*

NIXON, RICHARD (1913—   ). Thirty-seventh president of the United States. *The Moon, Presidents and the Presidency, Rap Music*

NIZER, LOUIS (1902—   ). English lawyer, author. *Insults*

NORMAN, MARSHA (1948—   ). American playwright. *Adversity*

ORWELL, GEORGE (1903—1950). English novelist, essayist, critic. (Original name, Eric Arthur Blair) *Advertising, Capitalism, Christianity, Equality, Faces, Fiction, Freedom, Generations, Human Nature, Humanitarianism, Inequality, Liberalism, Newspapers, Oppression, Perfection, Politicians and Politics, Socialism, Sports and Games, Superiority, Survival, Tyranny, War, Weapons*

OSBORNE, JOHN (1929—   ). English playwright. *Past, Theater*

OUIDA (1839—1908). English novelist. (original name, Marie Louise de la Ramée) *Christianity, Indifference*

OVID (43 B.C.—A.D. 17). Roman poet. (Full name, Publius Ovidius Naso) *Beauty, Competition, Defense, Destiny, Drinks and Drinking, Marriage, Perversity, Play, Promises, Sadism*

OWEN, PETER (1927—   ). English publisher. *Publishing*

OZICK, CYNTHIA (1931—   ). American short-story writer, novelist. *Faces*

PAGLIA, CAMILLE (1947—   ). American essayist. *Architecture, Food and Eating, Homosexuality, Pornography, Rape, Sex, Sexual Harassment*

PAINE, THOMAS (1737—1809). English-born American pamphleteer, political philosopher. *Character, Church, Hypocrisy, Internationalism, Names, Value*

PALEY, GRACE (1922—   ). American short-story writer. *Vision*

PALEY, WILLIAM (1743—1805). English theologian, philosopher. *Contempt*

PALLADIUS (c.363—431). Greek prelate, writer. *Chance*

PANKHURST, CHRISTABEL (1880—1958). English suffragist, daughter of Emmeline Pankhurst. *Ability*

PANKHURST, EMMELINE (1858—1928). English suffragist, mother of Christabel and Sylvia Pankhurst. *Reformers and Reform*

PANKHURST, SYLVIA (1882—1960). English biographer, suffragist, daughter of Emmeline Pankhurst. *War*

PARKER, DOROTHY (1893—1967). American short-story writer, critic, screenwriter. *Adventure, Art, Dogmatism, Drinks and Drinking, Love, Lovers, Money, Seasons, Sorrow, Wit, Work, Youth and Age*

PARNELL, CHARLES STEWART (1846—1891). Irish nationalist. *Nationalism*

PARTON, DOLLY (1946—   ). American singer, actor. *Limitations, Rainbows*

PASCAL, BLAISE (1623—1662). French philosopher, scientist, mathematician, writer. *Activity, Artificiality, Books and Reading, Criticism, Deeds, Effort, Eloquence, Faith, Fame, God, The Heart, Life, Listening, Obedience, Painters and Painting, Piety, Power, Rest, Rivers, Self-deception, Space, Outer, Universe*

PASTERNAK, BORIS (1890—1960). Russian poet, novelist. *Creation and Creativity, Emotions, Fear, Surprise*

PASTEUR, LOUIS (1822—1895). French chemist, microbiologist. *Preparedness, Scientists and Science*

PIAF, EDITH (1915—1963). French chanteuse. (Original name, Edith Grovanna Gassion) *Friends and Friendship*

PICASSO, PABLO (1881—1973). Spanish painter, sculptor. *Art, Artists, Computers, Painters and Painting, Taste, Work*

PIERCY, MARGE (1936—   ). Writer, feminist. *Sex, Women*

PIERREPOINT, ALBERT (1905—1992). British chief executioner. *Punishment, Capital*

PINDAR (c.522—c.438 B.C.). Greek lyric poet. *Greatness, Limitations, Vice*

PINDAR, PETER (1738—1819). English satirist, poet. (Pseudonym of John Wolcot) *Eloquence, Envy*

PINERO, ARTHUR WING (1855—1934). English playwright, actor, essayist. *Business*

PINOCHET, AUGUSTO (1915—   ). Chilean general, politician. *Faces*

PINTER, HAROLD (1930—   ). English playwright. *Philosophers and Philosophy, Writers and Writing*

PIRANDELLO, LUIGI (1867—1936). Italian playwright, novelist. *Dramatists and Drama, Human Nature, Opinions, Relationships, Words*

PIRSIG, ROBERT M. (1928—   ). American novelist. *Scientists and Science, Zen*

PISAR, SAMUEL (1929—   ). Polish-born American lawyer, author. *Nuclear Weapons*

PITT, WILLIAM (1708—1778). English statesperson. (Called the Elder Pitt) *Nonsense*

PLATH, SYLVIA (1932—1963). American poet. *Marriage, Poets and Poetry, Writers and Writing*

PLATO (c.428—c.347 B.C.). Greek philosopher, prose writer. (Original name, Aristocles) *Conversation, Courage, Democracy, Education, Health, Honesty, Immortality, Mathematics, Propaganda, The State, Truth, Wealth*

PLAUTUS (c.254—184 B.C.). Roman playwright. (Full name, Titus Maccius Plautus) *Nature*

PLINY (23—79). Roman writer, scientist. (Full name, Gaius Plinius Secundus. Known as the Elder) *Africa and Africans, Drinks and Drinking*

PLINY (c.61—c.114). Roman statesperson, letter writer. (Full name, Gaius Plinius Caecilius Secundus. Known as the Younger) *Possession, Reputation*

PLUTARCH (c.46—c.120). Greek biographer, essayist. *Ancestry, Character*

POE, EDGAR ALLAN (1809—1849). American poet, critic, short-story writer. *Books and Reading, Truth*

POGREBIN, LETTY COTTIN (1939—   ). American journalist, writer. *Racism*

POMPADOUR, MADAME DE (1721—1764). Mistress of Louis XV of France. (Original name, Jeanne-Antoinette Poisson) *Canada*

POPCORN, FAITH (1947—   ). American marketer, trend forecaster. *Buying and Selling*

Malice, Method, Misers, Pain, Past, Plans, Refusal, Remedies, Rules, Seduction, Severity, Silence, Trust, Value, Vice

PUZO, MARIO (1920—   ). American novelist. *Lawyers and Law*

PYAWASIT, IRENE MACK (   ). Menominee (Native American), interviewed in <u>Dignity</u> magazine (1985). *Native Americans*

QADDAFI, MUHAMMAR (1938—   ). Libyan politician. *Feminism, Nationalism*

QUAYLE, DAN (1947—   ). American politician. *Peace*

QUINDLEN, ANNA (NA). American writer. *American and the Americans*

QUINTILIAN (c.35—c.99). Roman rhetorician. *Pretension, Privacy*

RABELAIS, FRANÇOIS (c. 1483—1553). French scholar, humanist, physician, writer. *Desires*

RACHEL (1820—1858). French-Jewish actor. (Original name, Élisa Félix) *Self-knowledge*

RACINE, JEAN (1639—1699). French playwright. *Criminals and Crime, Honor, Innocence, Love and Hate, Love, Loss of, Virtue*

RADNER, GILDA (1947—1989). American comedian, actor. *Fashion, The Unknown*

RAKOVE, MILTON (1918—   ). American educator, political, adviser. *Citizenship*

RALEIGH, WALTER (1554—1618). English courtier, navigator, historian, poet. *Romance*

RAMOS, JUANITA (NA). African-American and Puerto Rican feminist, socialist, teacher. *Lesbianism*

RAMPERSAD, ARNOLD (1941—   ). American educator, writer, literary critic. *Religion*

RAND, AYN (1905—1982). Russian-born American novelist. *Class, Consciousness*

RANKIN, JEANNETTE (1880—1973). American reformer, suffragist, politician. *Race, War*

RASPBERRY, WILLIAM (1935—   ). American journalist. *Racism*

RATTIGAN, TERENCE (1911—1977). English playwright. *Dramatists and Drama, Suicide, Theater*

RAY, JOHN (1627—1705). English naturalist. *Sickness*

RAY, MAN (1890—1976). American painter, photographer, film maker. (Real name, Emmanuel Rudnitsky) *Machines*

REA, STEPHEN (1942—   ). Irish actor. *Ireland and the Irish*

REAGAN, NANCY (1923—   ). American First Lady, spouse of President Ronald Reagan. *Drugs, Women*

REAGAN, RONALD (1911—   ). Thirty-ninth president of the United States. *Government, Guns and Gun Control, Politicians and Politics, Recession, Trees*

REAGON, BERNICE JOHNSON (1942—). African-American scholar, musician. *Multiculturalism*

REDDY, HELEN (1941—). Australian-born American singer. *Determination*

REDFORD, ROBERT (1937—). American actor. *Actors and Acting, Ecology*

REDGRAVE, LYNN (1943—). English actor. *God*

REDGRAVE, VANESSA (1937—). English actor. *America and Americans, Integrity*

REED, LOU (1944—). American singer, guitarist, songwriter. (Real name, Louis Firbank) *Rock 'n' Roll*

REID, COLETTA (1943—). American feminist, writer. *Superiority*

REIK, THEODOR (1888—1969). Austrian-born American psychologist, writer. *Neurosis*

REINER, CARL (1922—). American actor. *Humor*

RENAN, ERNEST (1823—1892). French philosopher, philologist, historian. *Agnosticism*

RENARD, JULES (1864—1910). French novelist, playwright. *Existence, Fame, Happiness, Money, Poets and Poetry, Pride, Socialism, Suicide, Talent, Temper, Words*

RENOIR, PIERRE AUGUSTE (1841—1919). French painter. *Sexism*

REPPLIER, AGNES (1855—1950). American essayist, biographer, historian, poet. *Absurdity, Thinking and Thought*

RESTON, JAMES (1909—). Scottish-born American journalist, editor. *News, Poverty and Wealth*

REVSON, CHARLES (1906—1975). American entrepreneur, founder of Revlon Cosmetics. *Cosmetics*

REYNOLDS, JOSHUA (1723—1792). English portrait painter. *Amusement, Imitation*

RHODES, CECIL (1853—1902). British colonial administrator, financier. *Britain and the British*

RHYS, JEAN (1894—1979). British novelist, short-story writer. *Men and Women, Old Age*

RICH, ADRIENNE (1929—). American poet. *Authority, Change, Feminism, Housework, Language, Lesbianism, Truth, Women*

RICHARDS, ANN (1933—). American politician. *Sexism*

RICHARDS, BEAH (1926—). American actor. *Life*

RICHARDS, I. A. (1893—1979). English author, literary critic, scholar. (Full name, Ivor Armstrong Richards) *Poets and Poetry*

RICHARDSON, DOROTHY (1872—1957). English novelist. *Speaking*

RICHTER, JEAN PAUL (1763—1825). German novelist, aesthetician. *Contrast, Laughter*

RILKE, RAINER MARIA (1875—1926). German poet. *Machines, Mind and Body, Seasons, Self-knowledge, Seriousness, Surprise*

Relationships, Responsibility, Sorrow, Sympathy, Travel, Unity, War, Wind

St. John, Henry (1678—1751). English politician, writer. *Nations*

St. Johns, Adela Rogers (1894—1988). American author, journalist. *Joy*

Sainte-Marie, Buffy (1941—   ). Canadian Native American songwriter, activist. *Racism*

Saki (1870—1916). Scottish novelist, short-story writer. (Pseudonym of Hector Hugh Munro) *Beauty, Youth and Age*

Salinger, J.D. (1919—   ). American novelist. *Automobiles, Children, Literacy*

Sampter, Jessie (1883—1938). American-Israeli poet, writer. *Simplicity*

Samuel, Herbert (1870—1963). English politician. *Libraries*

Sand, George (1804—1876). French novelist. (Pseudonym of Amandine, Aurore Lucile Dudevant) *Beauty, Indignation, Men and Women, Old Age, Puritans and Puritanism, Repentance, Suicide, Writers and Writing*

Sandburg, Carl (1878—1967). American poet. *Cunning, Grammar, Language, Moon, Nonviolence, The Past, Poetry and Poets, The Sea, The Twentieth Century*

Sanger, Margaret H. (1879—1966). American social activist. *Contraception*

Santayana, George (1863—1952). Spanish-born American philosopher, poet, novelist, critic. *Aggression, Art, Beauty, The Bible, The Body, Boston, Britain and the British, Children, Closed-mindedness, Competition, Dignity, Disillusionment, Education, Emotions, Evolution, Fame, Fanaticism, Food and Eating, Greatness, Heaven, Homeland, Influence, Institutions, Intelligence, Internationalism, Knowledge, Life, Limitations, Madness, Mind and Body, Mortality, Musicians and Music, Nonsense, Pain, Prayer, Repetition, Sacrifice, Saints and Sainthood, Sickness, Stars, The Supernatural, Superstition, Sympathy, Youth and Age*

Sappho (c. 610—c. 580 B.C.). Greek lyric poet. *Goodness*

Sargent, John Singer (1856—1925). American painter. *Painters and Painting*

Sarraute, Nathalie (1900—   ). French writer. *Faith*

Sarton, May (1912—1985). Belgian-born American writer. *Argument, Old Age, Self-realization, Words*

Sartre, Jean-Paul (1905—1980). French existentialist philosopher, playwright, novelist, teacher. *Communication, Existentialism, Freedom, God, Hell, Loneliness, Passion, Poverty and Wealth, Respect, Words*

Sassoon, Siegfried (1886—1967). English writer, poet. *Diaries, The Military*

Sassoon, Vidal (1928—   ). English hairdresser, entrepreneur. *Work*

Saunders, Margaret Baillie (1873—1949). English writer. *Debt*

TERTULLIAN (c. 160—c. 230). Latin ecclesiastical writer, one of the Fathers of the Church. (Full name, Quintua Septimius Florens Tertullianus) *Belief*

THACKERAY, WILLIAM MAKEPEACE (1811—1863). English novelist. *Selfishness*

THARP, TWYLA (c. 1941—   ). American dancer, choreographer. *Art*

THATCHER, MARGARET (1923—   ). English politician. *Generosity, Patience*

THEOPHRASTUS (c. 372—c. 287 B.C.). Greek philosopher. *Time*

THEROUX, PAUL (1941—   ). American writer. *Travel, Writers and Writing*

THIERS, LOUIS ADOLPHE (1797—1877). French politician, historian. *Perspective*

THOMAS, DYLAN (1914—1953). Welsh poet, prose writer. *Drinks and Drinking, Life, Lovers, Poets and Poetry*

THOMAS, EDWARD (1878—1917). English poet, critic. *The Past*

THOMAS, GWYN (1913—1981). Welsh author. *Poetry*

THOMAS, MARLO (1943—   ). American actor. *Feminism*

THOMAS À KEMPIS (c. 1380—1471). German ecclesiastic, writer. (Full name, Thomas Hammerken) *Longevity, Obedience*

THOMAS AQUINAS, ST. (1225—1274). Italian theologian, philosopher. (Original name, Tommaso d'Aguino) *Closed-mindedness*

THOMPSON, DOROTHY (1894—1961). American journalist. *Peace*

THOMPSON, HUNTER S. (1939—   ). American journalist, author. *America and the Americans, Truth*

THOMSON, JAMES (1700—1748). Scottish-born English poet. *Happiness*

THOREAU, HENRY DAVID (1817—1862). American essayist, naturalist, poet. *Books and Reading, Buying and Selling, Change, Cities, Clothes and Clothing, Coldness, Company, Criticism, Crowds, Despair, Distrust, Education, Emotions, Existence, Experience, Fashion, Goodness, Government, Health, Houses, Humanism, Miracles, Rank, Self-knowledge, Simplicity, Solitude, Time, Truth, Vegetarianism, Writers and Writing*

THUCYDIDES (c.460—c.400 B.C.). Greek historian. *Democracy*

THURBER, JAMES (1894—1961). American essayist, short-story writer, humorist. *Ambition, Comedy, Conformity, Futility, Humor, Idleness, Indecision, Literature*

TOCQUEVILLE, ALEXIS DE (1805—1859). French politician, historian, writer. *Democracy, Equality, Generations*

TOLKIEN, J. R. R. (1892—1973). South African-born British writer. *Curiosity, Ending*

TOLSTOY, LEO (1828—1910). Russian novelist, moral philosopher. *Adjustment, Afterlife, Bores and Boredom, Family, Happiness, Self-criticism, Understanding*

TOMLIN, LILY (1939—   ). American actor, comedian. *Politicians and Politics, Prayer, Stress, Success, Truth*